LECTURES ON THE HISTORY
OF THE NINETEENTH CENTURY

T0382305

LECTURES ON THE
HISTORY
OF THE NINETEENTH CENTURY

Delivered at the Cambridge University
Extension Summer Meeting
August 1902

Edited by

F. A. Kirkpatrick, M.A.

Trinity College, Cambridge

Cambridge
at the University Press
1902

CAMBRIDGE UNIVERSITY PRESS
Cambridge, New York, Melbourne, Madrid, Cape Town,
Singapore, São Paulo, Delhi, Mexico City

Cambridge University Press
The Edinburgh Building, Cambridge CB2 8RU, UK

Published in the United States of America by Cambridge University Press, New York

www.cambridge.org
Information on this title: www.cambridge.org/9781107678316

© Cambridge University Press 1902

This publication is in copyright. Subject to statutory exception
and to the provisions of relevant collective licensing agreements,
no reproduction of any part may take place without the written
permission of Cambridge University Press.

First published 1902
First paperback edition 2013

A catalogue record for this publication is available from the British Library

ISBN 978-1-107-67831-6 Paperback

Cambridge University Press has no responsibility for the persistence or
accuracy of URLs for external or third-party internet websites referred to in
this publication, and does not guarantee that any content on such websites is,
or will remain, accurate or appropriate.

PREFACE.

THE lectures contained in this volume were delivered at the Summer Meeting of University Extension Students and others held at Cambridge in August, 1902.

The central design of this series of historical lectures was the treatment of recent developments in the principal countries of Europe by natives of those countries, in order that the most intimate and essential points of view might be presented. Some aspects of recent international history were also handled by lecturers who had given special study to those topics.

In order to give these essays a wider and more permanent value, the Syndics of the University Press decided to publish them, with the kind permission of the writers.

All concerned in the work of the Summer Meeting and in the production of this volume feel themselves deeply indebted to the generosity of those who delivered the lectures and consented to their publication.

F. A. K.

CAMBRIDGE.
November 1, 1902.

CONTENTS.

SOME AIMS AND ASPIRATIONS OF EUROPEAN POLITICS IN THE NINETEENTH CENTURY.

By A. W. WARD, LITT.D.

WE are apt to talk glibly of the ideas, beliefs and aspirations of a 'century'—just as if that term, or what that term conveys to us, not only had hands and feet, but were defined by limits corresponding more or less closely to the literal significance of the word, and as if it thus conveniently covered one of those broader groups or divisions in which for the ordinary purposes of study historical phenomena have to be arranged.

As a matter of fact, however, not many of those chronological divisions which we call centuries are apt to present themselves to the mind of the general student in the light of separate entities (if I may so say), each with characteristics proper to itself. Most of them are too far off to detach themselves to our eyes from the nebulous clusters into which they seem absorbed; others are too near at hand to admit of our surveying their conditions of life and the motive forces which determined them as detached from the surroundings in which we ourselves have our being. Yet it is not always comparative nearness or remoteness which makes one of these conventional divisions of time fitter or less fit for such special treatment. Some centuries seem the mere brooding-times of history, and while watching them we can only speculate as to

> 'the main chance of things
> As yet not come to life, which in their seeds
> And weak beginnings lie intreasured.'

Others again appear to us as it were broken up, like the ground near the seats of the oracles of the Gods, by the very magnitude and force of some of the historical movements which have occurred in them, and which have so to speak changed the face of the century itself. You will I think as a rule find that there is some inner reason for a literary usage that effectually establishes itself; and I cannot recall any century which more adequately lends itself to treatment as a whole than the eighteenth of our era, which is constantly on our lips as a term carrying with it a definite and distinct political, intellectual and moral significance. With regard at all events to the political history of Europe and that of other parts of the world whose affairs were brought into direct contact with those of our own continent—notably the New World and the East Indies—in few other centuries do the main issues seem so clear, or does the logic of their connexion with one another appear so palpable ; and again in few others, as they pass onwards to their close, is the coming of a new age so unmistakably announced by the downfall of old ideas of government and traditions of social life.

Whether, when a few generations hence—and generations pass rapidly in this little academical world of ours to which we bid all our visitors the heartiest of welcomes—whether, when the time has come to sum up the characteristic movements, and the ideas informing them, of the nineteenth century, they will be found possessed of a coherence of bearing and a definiteness of aim such as I have ascribed to those of its predecessor, I will not now enquire. Of this, however, I am quite sure that we still stand too near to the nineteenth century to judge of it as a whole ; that the present stage of dealing with its history should still be primarily one of investigation, and to a large extent not more than tentatively one of criticism. For this reason I look with satisfaction on the programme, full of variety as well as of other elements of interest, which has been prepared for the Historical Section of this Summer

Meeting, and which I understand to aim at an examination of classified material, rather than to aspire to a premature attempt at a synthesis of results. And this I say without any fear of 'being misunderstood. The study of quite modern history is in my humble opinion—and if I am guilty of heresy, I am in no great fear of having to go to the stake alone—quite as profitable as is that of any other kind of history, so long as it is carried on with a consciousness of its special drawbacks as well as of its special advantages. Among the latter the chief of course is the quicker insight of the student into the various bearings of the problems presented to him—a readiness inseparable from the greater intensity of the interest excited. On the other hand, the student of recent history is at a relative disadvantage, not so much because much of the evidence he requires is still kept from him, for alas! time and the worm are obscurantists as well as princes and officials; but also because the danger of misunderstanding the evidence actually at hand and the temptation towards perverting it is greatest for those who are inclined to look upon themselves as witnesses. The historian, we know, has prophetical functions; but his prophesying must come to naught if he is in any way personally associated with the inspirations which he reveals.

This experience was not spared to a very high-minded as well as clear-thinking and well-equipped writer who about the middle of the last century undertook to write its history, from the Treaties of Vienna onwards. The name of GERVINUS deserves to be held in honour in England; but my reason for saying this is not the fact that like so many Continental liberals of the second quarter of the nineteenth century he cherished an admiration for our institutions to which not all remained like himself faithful in their later years. At all events his regard for this country and his interest in her public life was not chargeable with the facile enthusiasm of those who, as the Czar, Nicholas I, said—some time before his thoughts of England had changed into gall—because they had paid a single visit to London, heard something about *Magna Charta*, and shaved with an English razor, could thenceforth never turn away their thoughts from our incomparable constitution. Gervinus was, as I need not remind many of my hearers, deeply imbued with the spirit of Germanic literature which in his eyes found its supreme embodiment in Shakspere, and not less profoundly with that of Germanic Art, of which as he held a true type was with the same certainty recognisable in Handel, whom we may without presumption claim as an Englishman by adoption. These things we are not likely to overlook— least of all in this University, where we take pride in following the great teacher of history whom we have recently lost in believing that historical progress is not most conclusively traceable in the domain of politics. To the principle, ignored by some of Gervinus' successors, that political history cannot, and ought not to, be isolated from the history of general national and human progress, he steadily adhered in his great work, which may thus claim to be a contribution to the philosophy of history as well as a successful digest of a large section of its political material, besides furnishing an abundance of characterisation, and thus illustrating that imaginative side of historical composition which vindicates one among the uses of the study of Shakspere and his precursors. But of the work itself I must not essay to speak within the narrow framework of my present address, nor can I more than allude to the causes of its having been broken off at what might seem the height of its progress. The eighth and last volume of the *History of the Nineteenth Century* deals with the July Revolution of 1830 and its immediate consequences, including the severance of Belgium from Holland—the removal, in Louis-Philippe's phrase, of that stumbling-block of Europe which her representatives at Vienna had in their fear of France thought to set up once and for ever. Yet it was not the Revolution of 1830 or its sequel of 1848—9 which troubled Gervinus; but his knowledge that at home in Germany—at the beginning

of that era of which most of us have been contemporaries—
events were taking a turn contradictory to the ideals of self-
development and self-reorganisation to which as a historian
and as a politician he had so consistently adhered. But
though no writer of history is called upon to exclude himself
from taking part in the making of it, he ought at his peril to
keep the two functions distinct from one another.

And in truth I was on the present occasion thinking less
of Gervinus' *History* itself than of the Introduction to it—an
essay once so well known that I have felt a kind of familiar
tremor in turning over its well-marked pages—which meant so
much more to us than they ever can mean to you of a later
generation. Yet, for all that, this brief but pregnant disserta-
tion might, perhaps, taking it as a whole, prove not less interesting and useful to an enquirer into the historical sequences
of the century as a whole, than it could have been to Gervinus'
first readers, placed like himself in the midst of its eddying
currents and conflicting interests. The great truth which this
essay teaches, and which to my mind it succeeds in enforcing
without any pedantic insistence upon the momentousness of
any particular step in the argument, is that, from the point of
view of political growth or development, the nineteenth century
is, like all the periods which have succeeded one another since
the Middle Ages drew towards their close, itself but a stage—
an act, if you will, in the drama—of one great and still unfinished
struggle. This struggle may be summarised as concerned with
the transference of power from the few to the many, with the
contention in other words between the democratic and the
oligarchic principle—absolute government or monarchy proper
intervening again and again in the conflict, siding now with
the one and now with the other combatant, at one time
seeming to accelerate the movement towards a final solution
or settlement, at another, with the aid of many instincts and
interests contriving to block the path, but without ever ultimately proving itself more than a passing phase in the history

of the unending strife. Though this great struggle between principles of government, by which almost every kind of social principle is likewise largely affected, might have seemed to be approaching its termination towards the end of the eighteenth century, it renewed itself with fresh impetus in the nineteenth, after the transitory phase of the Napoleonic era—transitory even to contemporary eyes that remained undazzled by the sun of Austerlitz. What may be the prospects of solution, what may be the issue which so many voices are proclaiming to us as plainly written on the wall, it may or may not be for the historian of the twentieth century to determine. In the meantime, the most instructive portion of Gervinus' essay is beyond all question that longer portion of which I fear many an impatient hand will in this age (in no sense the age of introductions) incline rapidly to turn the pages—where in a masterly survey of the general progress of modern history since the close of the Middle Ages the author shows how each succeeding century has a share in the movement, without deflecting its main current, or preventing it from a nearer approach to the unseen goal.

But Gervinus was well aware, and indeed he explicitly reminds his readers, that though such a movement is discernible by those capable of surveying the entire course of modern political history—much as an analogous current was observed by Aristotle in the political life of the ancient Mediterranean world—yet it is not thus that it would be either possible or expedient for the historical enquirer to look upon the briefer periods, with which he has in the first instance to deal, and of which it behoves him to make clear to himself the significance. In such periods as these it is necessary for him in the first instance to distinguish clearly what may be described as the successive oscillations of ebb and tide ; and there are still narrower limits, yet limits beyond which the consciousness of those whose lives fall within them often fails to range, in which a single potent force, one group of ideas and conceptions, perhaps the influence of one great individuality, seems irresistibly to direct and control the life and progress of a nation or a group of nations. More than ever are we impressed by the fact of such periodical predominances in an age like our own, in which political ideas, intellectual tendencies and artistic conceptions assert their mastery over the whole civilised world with the mysterious rapidity of a panic terror or a new fashion in millinery. The historian of modern times is privileged to command a wealth of material of every kind ; and his first task is to find the true signature of whatever period, however short it be, which is immediately under his ken. The true history of the English Commonwealth and of the Great War which brought it forth, could as their late venerated historian Samuel Rawson Gardiner well knew, never be written truthfully until it had been written carefully, and until it had been followed through each of its successive stages, year by year. How much more must this be the case with the history of the quickly-moved and quickly-moving times near to our own, to whose immediate impulses the oldest and most self-contained of us must perforce in a large measure respond.

The task which the student of nineteenth century history has before him is therefore a laborious one ; but it is not labours such as these which weary the mind alive to interests of which none is alien to it. May I, within the half hour during which I may still venture to trespass on your patience, attempt to recall a passage or two in the history of nineteenth century Europe, exhibiting the contemporary political world, or prominent sections of it, as intent upon a settlement, more or less final and complete, of its problems, and hopeful of a consummation which alas ! it needs no prophet looking backwards to announce to us as unachieved ? My observations will almost entirely refer to the earlier half of the century and for the most part to a single stage of that period, partly because of the exigencies of time, and partly because I know that it is the later half which is to be chiefly discussed in a full and well-arranged series of special lectures that are to follow.

If, then, as we are surely justified in doing, we regard the Napoleonic age as the necessary complement of the Revolutionary, and accept the position in which Napoleon himself was willing to acquiesce, that with his first overthrow the period of the fundamental unsettlement of Europe was at an end, we can have no difficulty in understanding the hopes and expectations with which her populations watched the assembling of the Congress of Vienna in 1814. The process of disenchantment was no doubt to be rapid; and under the dictatorial influence of an epigram or two posterity has been inclined to minimise not only the actual results of the Congress but also the labours by which those results were produced—as if at any time the real work of a large assembly were done by more than a small and select body; and the necessary few were not wanting at Vienna. I doubt whether more than one or two of the names of the statesmen who were the real working-bees of the Congress would carry any particular significance to modern ears; but such is often the fate of those who are content to take a continuous part in the constructive work of statesmanship and to forego the applause which as a rule must inevitably attach itself to the arena. At the outset of the Congress, the hopes set on the issue of its deliberations were unprecedented alike in their height and in their variety. While the pacifications concluded within the last twenty years had, as it were, but dotted the surface of the sea of war, none of those earlier compacts which had long been accounted landmarks in the political history of Europe—not even the Treaties of Westphalia or the Peace of Utrecht—had attempted more than to regulate the relations between a definite number of important States; at Vienna every country in Europe, with the sole exception of Turkey, knew that its interests would be drawn under discussion. It is true that the bases of the territorial resettlement had already been laid down at Paris, though Talleyrand, whose influence thus made itself felt even before the assembling of the Congress, had managed to have them kept secret in order to spare the susceptibilities of defeated France; and on the other hand it was not known how far from complete was the agreement which had been reached, and how questions were still left open, destined in the very midst of negotiations for peace to bring the chief Powers to the verge of a new war. Thus it came to pass that not only romantic journalists—and in the early decades of the nineteenth century there were romantic journalists who occupied posts of honour in their profession and in contemporary literature—but practical politicians reckoned on the establishment by the Congress of a system of States, capable of maintaining a positive balance of power, and not merely of satisfying that quasi-negative interpretation of the term which means a combination against the preponderance of any single Power,—be its name Habsburg, or France, or Russia. Such hopes as these were undeceived by the operations of the Congress itself, or rather by those of the Committee of Powers acting on its behalf, who speedily enough made it evident that their scheme of territorial reconstruction began and ended in patchwork; and that even as to the negative principle of not leaving France too strong they were prepared for compromise. It is too much to say, as has been repeatedly said, that the principle of territorial readjustment followed in the Vienna Treaties was statistical or more properly speaking numerical only—*i.e.* that the apportionment of dominions and the assignment of frontiers was made out by a comparison of the number of subjects or 'souls' allotted to each government. Still it was numerical almost or quite as much as it was historical or linguistic or religious or, to use the word of magic sound in whose significance that of all the rest is wont to enter —national. Thus the Congress accorded its sanction to a long series of arrangements which seem to us to fly in the face of that principle of nationality destined so soon to become one of the active forces of European politics, but which were in reality by their very arbitrariness and rigour to help to hasten the assertion of that principle. If we turn to the South, we find Austria securing to herself an uncontested conpensation in that Lombardo-Venetian Kingdom which a government far worse than hers might under other conditions have far more easily conciliated to its rule. If we pass to the North, we see Norway, cut off from Denmark, who spoke her tongue, and coupled against her will with Sweden, while Denmark is thus driven to seek to make up for her loss by forcing her German Provinces into political union with herself; or we see Finland apathetically left in the grasp of Russia, which in our own day is in defiance of historical tradition, and in defiance of sworn rights, at last closing upon the victim of tendencies against which neither protest nor scruple seems of avail. Or again, if we glance at the Northern border provinces between France and Germany—the Belgian and the Dutch—which after separating from one another in the hour of common stress had come to agree to differ in their material interests, in their religious traditions and in other respects, we find them, to no real purpose so far as the peace of Europe was concerned, forced into an arbitrary union. Everywhere the settlement was a settlement *de par le Congrès*—and often one palpably opposed to history and against kind.

But the Congress had been expected to accomplish other things besides the establishment of that comprehensive political system of States which, as Gentz had the sublime assurance to declare, only missed being perfected by it because Napoleon chose to break loose from Elba. I need not dwell in particular on the expectation of a systematic encouragement by the Congress of constitutional forms of government, due not so much to the wishes of the leading statesmen of the Congress itself, as to the situation of which European public opinion regarded them as the trustees. Metternich, to do him justice, consistently kept Austria out of the competition, and Castlereagh in the House of Lords, using one of those simpler figures of irony which suited him, expressed himself as by no means convinced that, had he gone about like a missionary to preach the excellency and the fitness of our constitution, all countries would have been found ripe for profiting by his endeavours. The action in this direction of Great Britain, whose own parliamentary constitution was we remember still unreformed— had as yet been little more than incidental, and had by no means assumed that sympathetic provocativeness of bearing with which our policy was credited in later days, when Palmerston sought to better the instructions of Canning. On the other hand, the granting or promising of constitutions had already become an expedient of the collapsing tyranny of Great Britain's archfoe, Napoleon ; nor can there be any doubt but that to his Warsaw constitution was due the suggestion of the grand scheme of a constitutional Poland so warmly cherished for a time by the fluctuating idealism of the Czar Alexander. As for the Congress itself, though it showed small solicitude, more especially where the inherited or traditional rights of oligarchical bodies whether in Switzerland or else-where were concerned, for preserving the growth of chartered rights, it showed no unwillingness to favour the establishment of new constitutions, more especially on the motion of the governments themselves. In its very first article, the Final Act of the Congress guaranteed their national institutions and representation to those Poles who had respectively become the subjects of the three so-called Partitioning Powers, and it proceeded to make special provision for the security of a constitution of such vanishing importance as that of Cracow. It guaranteed the new German federal constitution, which in its turn explicitly promised the grant of constitutions to all the States composing the federation (though of course the Austrian government never fulfilled its part of the compact), and elsewhere, in Norway, in Spain, and in France itself, the grant or expectation of constitutional forms of government was declared or understood to have the sanction of the concert of the European Powers.

The imperfect success of these constitutional hopes and expectations in some instances, in others the resistance offered to them openly or secretly by the governments directly concerned with their fulfilment, and the conflicts, the conspiracies, the insurrections which in consequence filled the earlier half of the century, till they culminated in the general revolutionary outbreak of 1848–9 cannot be dwelt upon here. I do not see why the Congress should be made chargeable with all these failures; for its actual commission—the commission with which it had been charged at Paris, and which was the only definite commission that it had at any time received—did not include the regeneration of the public life of the States of Europe on constitutional lines. But public opinion had expected this from so unusual a gathering of representative statesmen, and it had expected a great deal more than this.

Hopes—more or less vague—had been cherished that at Vienna, after a real equilibrium had been established among the States of Europe, and after their internal tranquillity had been assured by the grant or the prospect of representative institutions, the foundations would be laid of a legally established international community,—perhaps by the establishment of a great Court of arbitration, and perhaps by the adoption of common binding principles of future disarmament, however remote and however gradual might be its actual consummation. We need not wonder that such aspirations should have attended the termination of an age of war and the assembling of the statesmen of Europe, whose primary task it was to elaborate the terms of the pacification which had at last put an end to it; indeed, it would have been strange had an invariable sequence not repeated itself on so exceptional an occasion. The Peace of Utrecht had been followed by the announcement of Bernardin de Ste Pierre's utopian peace-project

' *Une fable aussi belle:*
La paix universelle:'

Jeremy Bentham's project of an international Court for the
decision of international differences was probably suggested by
Catharine II's in another way almost equally abortive Armed
Neutrality of 1780; and Kant's more famous plan of a Universal Peace, not the less interesting to us because it was
confuted by Hegel from the point of view of the modern conception of the State, unmistakably had an origin less noble
than itself in the ill-fated attempt to safeguard the neutrality
of Northern Germany in the shameless Peace of Basel.

The problem of a proportionate disarmament of the chief
European Powers, it must not be forgotten, could hardly be
solved by them even in principle when Four of them held
themselves obliged for an indefinite period of time to occupy
the territory of a Fifth. But though the reductions of the
military strength of the several European Powers both in 1814
and in 1815—except in the case of Great Britain, who may be
said to have reduced her army fighting power by little short
of one half,—were far less considerable than had been hoped,
neither the Powers nor the peoples of Europe in the period
which followed upon the close of the Napoleonic Age acquiesced
in the policy of an armed peace—or in other words were
prepared to maintain themselves in a constant state of preparation for war. It is not to be denied that any system of separate
alliances between particular Powers—be they dual or triple or
other—is far more likely to lead to the maintenance of such
a policy than was the system of an alliance of all the Great
Powers, which the statesmanship of the Congressional period
sought to put into operation.

You are aware how both in the matter of disarmament, and
more especially in that of the establishment of some common
tribunal for the settlement of international differences, the
disappointment of the hopes founded upon direct action on
the part of the Congress of Vienna by no means damped the

ardour of those who, whether in the Old World or in the New, had at heart a cause of so perennial an interest for Europe and for humanity. The task of protesting against War, and against the avowal by statesmanship and by society of their impotence to find any way of systematically averting it, was now—and this again was characteristic of the new century—taken up by combinations and Societies. Often no doubt aided by the potent influence of personality—for the spirit of William Penn had survived into the ninth and tenth generations—these associations as a rule sought strength in numbers, and gradually overcame that impression of futile dogmatism which had been created by isolated efforts. No more interesting statement was ever put on record than that drawn up by the late Johann von Bloch in the last volume of his monumental work on *The War of the Future*—the text-book as I may call it of the Hague Congress—with the purpose of showing how the endeavours of which I speak gradually took possession of public opinion, and through public opinion impressed their significance upon the governments. In course of time Napoleon III took notice of these efforts—though unhappily his ears, like those of the rider in the legend, were open to inspirations and insinuations both on the left hand and on the right. At Paris in 1856 the late Lord Clarendon honoured himself and his country by proposing a declaration which was adopted by the Powers, that it was their desire in the event of serious international differences to seek to avert war by arbitration before actually resorting to arms. In this last clause, of course, lay the novelty of the Paris Declaration, for there was nothing new in the resort to arbitration in the case of boundary questions and other difficulties which were not of a nature to threaten a warlike issue. Whether or not such an issue was actually within measurable distance, when in 1871 the British government over which Mr Gladstone presided resolved on signing the Treaty of Washington, which referred to arbitration the so-called *Alabama* and cognate claims, moral courage of an unusual kind was no doubt required to make possible both that signature and the acceptance of the American view, which treated these claims as national and not merely as private. Resort has since been had with increasing frequency to arbitration for the solution of international difficulties; and though the application of it has at times been baulked, its progressive use seems assured.

The Congress of Vienna, it may be worth remembering, took an important step in the direction of securing the blessings of peace to certain European territories peculiarly exposed to the dangers of war, and for the same reasons specially liable themselves to give rise to conflicts between other nations. The neutrality of Switzerland, which had been violated both in the Revolutionary and Napoleonic Wars and was again violated immediately after the first overthrow of Napoleon, was now placed under the most formal guarantees; and you know how this precedent was followed in the instance of Belgium in 1831, in that of Servia in 1856, and in that of Luxemburg in 1867. You are probably also aware that it was not long afterwards —in the course of the great Franco-German War—that the question arose in connexion with the last-named guarantee, whether the principle was generally accepted that any one of the guaranteeing Powers was entitled to judge for itself as to any supposed offence against the terms of the neutrality conceded, and consequently to decide for itself as to withdrawal from the guarantee, or whether such questions were for the decision of all the signatories. The latter principle, if it had been definitively accepted, would have added another security, so far as it went, for the peace of Europe. The general system, I may add, of interposing weak States between strong—buffer-States as they are sometimes, though not I think very felicitously called—was itself a not very happy adaptation of a Napoleonic device, adopted by him with a very different purpose; nor was it to prove successful in the case of Sardinia, or in that of Saxony, or so far as I can remember in any other case.

It would take me too far to advert to those aspirations towards an international treatment of international interests which addressed themselves not so much to the aversion of War, as to its incidence and management. The days of the Congress of Vienna and the period ensuing were unfavourable to a discussion of the rights of neutrals by sea; and Great Britain who at the time of the opening of the Congress was actually still at war with the United States on behalf of her navigation laws, was not likely for some time to consent to entertain proposals in favour of their modifications. Other questions were in the interests of humanity at large to be taken up by a much later generation, and to these I advert only in order that they may not seem to have been left unremembered. The Geneva Convention of 1863 was only the first of a beneficent series of agreements; for when the war of 1866 had demonstrated its incompleteness, it was supplemented by another Convention in 1868 which was held in time to be in force in the great war of 1870. The reaction produced by that War against the propaganda of peace and the various schemes for giving more definite shape to it which had again and again appeared on the horizon since the days of the Congress of Vienna itself is not to be denied; but the experience is one which in one way or another we have gone through before and since. In this case there was much coolness shown especially in Germany in response to the sympathy displayed in Russia, and in the highest quarters there, with objects for the promotion of which the Conference at the Hague was ultimately summoned in the last year of the century. From the regions of diplomacy and administration, this antipathy found its way into the academic chair and into the history-books, where it was characteristically transformed into a direct enthusiasm for war and its value as a moral agency. This strange gospel, too, was not then preached either for the first or the last time. For the rest, whatever may be the results of the Hague Conference, its main object, the promotion of a better understanding between the nations, will assuredly be hastened by the series of subsidiary conferences on subjects of private international law, which thanks to the high-minded energy of the Dutch government, have been carried on in the same capital during the last quarter of the century, and in which most of the States of Europe have taken part—our own, for perhaps hardly sufficient reasons, not being included in their number.

I may perhaps be thought to have strayed outside the limits which I had proposed to myself for my remarks ; but it seemed permissible to indicate how some at least of those aspirations which long appeared to have in vain found expression at the time of the assembling of the Congress of Vienna were far from extinguished by their failure to advance visibly towards fulfilment on this unprecedented, and indeed unparalleled international occasion. It would, of course, be an error to conclude that no advance was made at the Congress and in the period of European history which followed, towards better securities than had previously existed for the endurance of the European system of States and superior facilities for its development or improvement. The Four Great Powers which (no doubt each at the time and under the conditions best suiting its own interests) had entered into the decisive struggle against Napoleonic France, and had carried it to a successful issue, deliberately took it upon themselves by their action at Vienna to establish and maintain in the name and in the interest of Europe at large the political system elaborated at the Congress. The Four Powers were indeed, by the dexterous audacity of Talleyrand on his arrival at Vienna, obliged to include the representatives of the whole of the Eight Powers who had signed the Peace of Paris in the Preliminary Committee of the Congress—and in its work there was really nothing that was not preliminary except the Final Act. Even this Final Act was technically only the Act of the Eight Powers and the rest of the States of Europe were simply invited to adhere to it. But everyone knew that Spain and Portugal and Sweden were only included so that France might not come in alone—though both Spain and Sweden still cherished a remembrance of the days when they had been numbered among the Great Powers—a remembrance which the eighteenth century had not quite taken away from the Swedish throne, and which perhaps not even the nineteenth has ended by extinguishing in the hearts of the Spanish people. And even this Committee of the Eight was not very often summoned, especially in the earlier months of the Congress, when its chief task was the appointment of the Special or Sub-Committees to whom the various branches of the business of the Congress were assigned; and the plenipotentiaries of the Five Great Powers occasionally took it upon themselves to meet without the three supernumeraries. Thus, then, during the all-important months of deliberations preceding Napoleon's return from Elba, the Four Allied Powers, by the side of whom Talleyrand had contrived to establish France as a working fifth wheel of the machine, controlled the destinies of Europe. How completely the remaining States were prepared to follow their lead, was shown by their adhesion to the action taken by the Four Powers on Napoleon's return—the exceptions to the unanimity being Spain and Sweden, whose hesitation only emphasised their actual insignificance. It was again shown by the adhesion of all the European States to the Final Act— with the exception again of Spain, this time associated (though his protest was more formal than real) with the Pope.

Whatever may be thought of the way in which this European Committee exercised the authority assumed by it—and I am convinced that the extent, variety and importance of its labours have been alike undervalued—it cannot be gainsaid that a new method had been set on foot, a new departure had been made, in the interests of the balance of power, or in other words of the peace of Europe, or in other words of the increased prosperity and happiness of its populations. The origin of this innovation has been much mistaken, though nothing can be more certain;

and its purposes—I do not say its results—have been consequently misjudged. The Treaty of Chaumont, signed on March 1, 1814, by Lord Castlereagh and the other plenipotentiaries of the Four Powers who were then, arms in hand, intent upon accomplishing Napoleon's overthrow, not only declared the peace of Europe to be dependent on the maintenance by their augmented armies of the order of things which they had resolved on establishing in France, but it provided that in order to arrange future measures for the preservation of peace and to promote a good understanding between the Four Powers, periodical meetings should take place between the Sovereigns in person, or their plenipotentiaries. This was the system to which the method of procedure at Vienna just described gave practical effect, and which was stereotyped on the same day as that on which the Second Peace of Paris was signed (November 20, 1815) by a further agreement between the Four Powers. This agreement, while it maintained the exclusion from the French throne of Napoleon and the Napoleonic dynasty, renewed the mutual undertaking of the Allied Sovereigns not only to unite if necessary in common measures of war, but also to meet at stated intervals either in person or through their representatives, for the purpose of dealing with matters of interest to them all, and of discussing measures conducive to the tranquillity and prosperity of their peoples, and to the preservation of the peace of Europe. This Paris compact, based on the Treaty of Chaumont, was the actual beginning of the Congressional epoch of nineteenth century European history—a period as well-marked and some will say as barren of results in political as the Conciliar period of the 14th and 15th centuries is in ecclesiastical history. But, as I ventured to say before, we must guard against judging within cycles; and we must guard, I may add, against turning the pages of the book of history with too rapid a hand. The Congressional epoch had been practically begun at Vienna, when as has been noted France, whose frontiers the concert of

the Allies was to regulate and over whose destinies it was to
retain control, was as a matter of fact admitted to that concert,
though not unreservedly or unintermittently.   The new epoch
was formally opened at Aix-la-Chapelle in 1818, when France
was solemnly introduced into the Alliance originally formed
against her power; but even then on the very day when this
admission was proclaimed the plenipotentiaries of the Four
Powers signed a secret protocol, binding them if necessary to
consider measures for anticipating the disastrous effects of any
new revolutionary agitation which might menace France.

The nations and nationalities which, before the century
had passed out of its decades of hope and promise, had lost
all faith in the Congressional panacea for their troubles, took
a singular revenge upon the system which Metternich christened
the Moral Pentarchy of Europe.   They taught themselves to
mistake and misrepresent its origin, and to confound the
cautious stipulations set down by Metternich, Castlereagh,
Nesselrode and Hardenberg for the Quadruple Alliance of
the future with what the first-named of these statesmen called
the *verbiage* of the Holy Alliance.   The principles of the Holy
Alliance, which are supposed to have regulated the policy of
the Great Powers during a momentous period of European
history (and not only poets and journalists, but historians and
diplomatists—even such a diplomatist as Bismarck—have encouraged this misapprehension), were the personal aspirations
of a single potentate, the Czar Alexander, expressed in a
document to which his fellow-sovereigns, the Emperor Francis
and King Frederick William of Prussia, had only reluctantly
signified their assent, without so much as communicating it
to their cabinets, though Metternich had read it, corrected it
here and there, and disliked it as a whole.   In a general way,
this programme or prospectus (for its character was such rather
than that of a definite plan or scheme) was due to the self-
consciousness of Alexander I, which had been inevitably increased by the prominence, again inevitable, of the part played

by him at Vienna. Russia's share in the final struggle against Napoleon had in some respects been unique in its conditions, and the Czar's personal power was autocratic in a sense in which this could be predicated of no other sovereign at Vienna. But above all he had an insatiable ambition to intervene where he could as a beneficent Providence to which no nation or nationality—Polish, Swiss, German, Hellenic—need appeal in vain and, while Russia pursued all the time the policy of her traditions and the policy of her interests, to colour the outline with hues of his own. The particular design of the Holy Alliance, however, was inspired in him by Madame de Krudener, a fascinating woman, who without the intervening stage of penance common in the lives of saints, had passed from the character of a fashionable beauty into that of a prophetess. When Alexander met her, thereby fulfilling her first prophecy, he had already been prepared for her revelations by the philosopher Franz von Baader's theories as to the necessity of intensifying the Christian element in the government of States, in contravention of the principles of government identified with the French Revolution. I cannot here enter into the more precise bearing of these theories, the reverse of ignoble or unpatriotic in themselves, though tinged by a theosophy which may account for their having been held to point to the necessity of a union between the spiritual and the temporal headship of Christian communities. They certainly fell upon ground responsive in more senses than one, and accorded with national religious conceptions inherited by the Czar, as well as with the promptings of personal vanity and jealousy and the dictates of a political interest, which to instance but a single phase of it, in the East was Christian or nothing. Nothing could be simpler than the fundamental document of the Alliance signed by the Czar's own hand. Using scriptural phraseology, its signatories undertook in conjunction with one another to uphold religion, peace and justice; acknowledging themselves the mere delegates of the one sovereign of Christendom—the Holy Trinity, devoting themselves to making their peoples happy by enabling them to obey the Divine Will, and welcoming into the Alliance all Powers who accepted its principles.

Besides the Emperor Francis and King Frederick William, King Louis XVIII afterwards added his signature to this document—a curious agent in the proposed religious regeneration of France; and the Prince Regent of Great Britain, though debarred by the constitution of his country from entering into personal engagements with foreign sovereigns, felt himself able to write a letter expressive of his thorough agreement with the principles of the Holy Alliance. But notwithstanding these edifying signatures and communications, it is the Treaty of Chaumont and the Declaration accompanying the Second Treaty of Paris, and not the Holy Alliance, which represents the outcome of the endeavour permanently to control the re-settlement of Europe after the close of the Napoleonic Wars, by means of a Committee of Great Powers. For Englishmen at least, the distinction, which I may seem to you to have unnecessarily laboured, is historically not insignificant; we may disclaim any national responsibility for the Holy Alliance, in spite of the Prince Regent's approval of it; but into the Congressional policy the British government consciously entered, and no European Power had a more direct and a more conspicuous share in setting it on foot. We, therefore, as a nation have a share in its honour and dishonour, in its endeavour to follow aims and satisfy aspirations which have approved themselves to the judgment of history, or which the friends of humanity and the believers in the ultimate progress of our race still continue to cherish,— and in its failures, its self-delusions and its perversity.

Among the benefits which the Congressional system at the very outset directly helped to confer upon mankind, I will only mention one, whose chief credit belongs to our own country, though it was undoubtedly expedited by the machinery of the Congress, which extracted a theoretical assent to our demands even from the most reluctant of the Powers to whom they were addressed. The declaration expressing the desire of the Eight Powers to put a stop to the scourge which had so long desolated Africa, degraded Europe and afflicted the human race, was accompanied by an expression of their intention to carry out the universal abolition of the African Slave-trade with the utmost promptitude possible. The choice of time and season was indeed left to each Power concerned; but the effectiveness of so formal an appeal to public opinion was shown before the Congress of Vienna separated, when Napoleon on his return from Elba decreed the immediate abolition of the Slave-trade throughout the dominions of France, and when Louis XVIII from Ghent, in order not to be outdone by the usurper, empowered Talleyrand to make the same announcement in the royal name. The question was even so by no means settled; but Great Britain had succeeded in identifying the acknowledged organ of European political action with the progress of its settlement.

I had intended to carry these comments a little further, and to enquire what in the period of the successive Congresses—Aix-la-Chapelle, Troppau, Laibach, Verona—were the aims and aspirations which it was sought to meet, to influence or to evade under the newly organised *tutela* of the Great Powers, which had succeeded to the autocracy of the Napoleonic will. In studying these transactions, we may do well to notice how, as a rule, it is a divergence of interests rather than a preconception of principle which accounts for the inadequacy of the system—an inadequacy which in the end becomes hopeless. Even at Aix-la-Chapelle the attention of the Powers was by no means absorbed by the most pressing tasks of safeguarding the Restoration in France, and of correcting the imperfections of the Germanic Confederation; but though the accord of the Great Powers still seemed unbroken, and Metternich was for the time satisfied with the Czar, the question

of the relations between Spain and her Colonies, which had
been ignored at Vienna, already gave rise to differences of
view between Russia and Great Britain, and a grouping of the
Powers—the incipient negation of the Congressional concert—
had begun.   Before the next Congress the inevitable had
happened.   The Revolution had broken out in Spain, in Portugal and in Sicily ; and at Laibach in 1821 the determination
of the Eastern Powers to intervene directly—in other words
their logical assertion of the right of the Powers (or their
majority) to assume the character of an international police—
led to a schism between the three Eastern and the two Western,
and the great protective and representative Alliance was already
on the eve of disruption.   A year later, at Verona—where the
Eastern Powers dealt with Italian affairs throughout the
Peninsula entirely on the principles on which they had agreed,
and where Canning's instructions (not perhaps altogether
relished by Wellington) completely severed Great Britain from
the other Powers in the matter of the Spanish-American
Colonies—the Greek Insurrection, and with it the Eastern
Question, knocked at the door.   It knocked as yet in vain ;
but a harmonious treatment of these new issues on the part of
Russia and Austria was impossible, and a new epoch in the
history of Europe opens with the self-assertion of the Hellenic
nationality.

The character of that epoch is first conspicuously marked
by the French July Revolution of 1830 and the Belgian Insurrection, ending in the separation of Belgium from Holland,
which ensued in close connexion with it.   The Powers had to
submit to the undoing of the union which had been one of the
most elaborately devised of the pieces of constructive work done
at Vienna, and as to the right of the French nation to determine its own government there was now no longer any attempt
at European control.   In Spain and Portugal the 'legitimate'
claimants—for Talleyrand's catchword still held out, though it
had lost much of its magic—were now mere pretenders, sup-

ported not by the sanction of Congresses, but by voluntary contributions. In Poland, which notwithstanding the specious promises of the Czar had remained a Russian province and a conquered territory, a nation rose within half-a-dozen days ; and neither the insurrection nor its suppression left any doubt as to the issue to which they were alike single-mindedly directed.

In the lectures to which you are about to listen and in the studies which these lectures will, I trust, stimulate you to pursue with increasing assiduity and thoroughness, you may not by preference occupy yourselves with the period of the political history of modern Europe on which I have touched this morning, with the Congressional machinery which, originally at first with no purpose either visionary or sinister, it sought to set in motion, and with the aims and aspirations which those who worked this machinery sought to advance, modify or defeat. You may not even find much leisure to spare for a close enquiry into the period of political history which began with the collapse of the Congressional system, and which after witnessing the early triumphs of 1830, came to an end with the collapse of the Revolution of 1848—9.

This epoch, however, was likewise full of aspirations proper to itself, and the field of its history is likewise strewn with memories of insufficient methods and of baffled hopes. The eminent author whom I cited earlier in this address, closes his *Introduction to the History of the Nineteenth Century*, composed by him when that century had run half its course and when to less comprehensive minds it might have seemed doomed to begin its endeavours over again, with the expression of a hope that Germany, for whom it might eventually be reserved to exercise an influence in Europe such as had formerly been exercised by France, would follow the example of England in renouncing all ambition to play the part of a conquering State. Her true ideal of action, as it seemed to him, was on the contrary the dissolution into federations of those vast State-unities by which the progress of liberty and of culture were alike endangered. Even without anticipating the comments which will be offered to you on the history of the application of the federal principle of government to European politics in the nineteenth century;—even without, on the other hand, betraying any nervous alarm as to the spectres of Panslavism and Pangermanism which daily walk in sheets;—even without venturing on any speculations as to the ultimate results of the tendencies towards imperial expansion which have derived so extraordinary an impulse in our own land and elsewhere from patriotic sentiment, from literary demonstration, and from that most powerful of teachers, actual achievement—which of us can be blind to the irony of the answer which the last years of the nineteenth century seem to have returned to the aspirations of the historian of its earlier decades? It is less easy to speculate on the measure of fulfilment which will be granted to the aspirations that have taken their place. But I think that such speculations are scarcely incumbent upon ourselves, and that in the meantime we may be content to rest our faith, as historical students, on laws which the experiences of a century can neither make nor unmake. Our primary task is after all to observe, to compare, to record.

To some measure of participation in that task we, being all of us fellow-workers in the same field, most cordially invite you; and though your leisure we know is limited (but then whose is not?) we would gladly help you to turn it to good account. A little advice and a little guidance cannot go a very long way, but how far they will go, depends most upon the learner. For my part, I could do nothing this morning beyond asking you to accompany me for a brief hour while I recalled a passage or two of my own studies. Others will address you whom you will follow with more pleasure and with more profit; but we all alike have at heart the twofold purpose of this Summer Meeting, that you should spend some pleasant weeks at Cambridge, and that you should leave this ancient home of learning for its own sake more resolved than ever to be and remain students in the true sense of the word.

INTRODUCTION TO THE INTERNATIONAL HISTORY OF EUROPE DURING THE NINETEENTH CENTURY.

By Prof. J. Westlake, LL.D.

In studying the international history of Europe during the nineteenth century the first step should be to compare the map of Europe at the beginning and at the end of the period. The end is marked for us by this year 1902 in which we are : for the beginning we ought to take the year 1792, that in which the great war commenced, which lasted almost continuously to the battle of Waterloo in 1815. Comparing the map of 1902 with that of 1792 we are struck by two great facts, unification and transfer. Unification is seen in Italy and Germany. In 1792 Italy was divided between a dozen independent sovereignties, and Germany comprised several hundred princes and cities having distinct international existence, grouped indeed under the Holy Roman Empire, but by a tie so loose as to be scarcely perceptible. There are now the one kingdom of Italy and the one German empire, in the latter of which are grouped twenty-five states, of which it is the distinct international existence that has in its turn become scarcely perceptible. Austria, which lay within the Holy Roman Empire, is outside the German one; but that single circumstance cannot obscure the great fact of unification.

When we come to the difference between the map of 1902 and that of 1792 as resulting from transfers, including the separation of parts which have become independent, it is almost over the whole of Europe that our view must range. Let us make the tour of Europe in a circle. Poland has ceased to exist: its dismembered sovereignty has been transferred to Russia, Prussia, and Austria. Not attempting to express with nicety the various modes in which territories may be associated while remaining autonomous, we may say broadly that Finland has been transferred from Sweden to Russia, Norway from Denmark to Sweden, and Sleswick-Holstein from Denmark to Prussia, that is to Germany. The Austrian Netherlands, after a passing union with Holland, have become the kingdom of Belgium. Alsace-Lorraine has been transferred from France to Germany; Savoy and Nice from Sardinia to France. Lombardy has been transferred from Austria to Italy. Venice has disappeared, and after a varied intermediate history her Italian territory has been merged, with the willing assent of its population, in the kingdom of Italy, while her possessions on the other side of the Adriatic have ended by becoming parts of Austria and Greece. Greece herself, Servia, and Roumania are three kingdoms which have been carved out of Turkey, with which decaying empire Bulgaria, Crete, and Samos retain but a slight connection, while Bosnia and Herzegovina have been transferred from it, nominally to the administration but really to the rule of Austria. To sum this up, one-fifth of the population of Europe may now be called on to fight *against* flags *under* which the grandfathers of men not yet old might have been called on to fight, and this without reckoning anything for the separation of Austria from Germany, or for transfers from one German or Italian flag to another. I wish to impress on you the magnitude of this fact. Do not misinterpret it, as if one-fifth of Europe was living under a rule felt to be alien. Many of the changes have been made with the goodwill of the peoples concerned. But the fact is a great one nevertheless. We are apt to forget it when both in current politics, and in following history through the ages, we use the same names of states without thinking of the variations in their composition and boundaries. An Englishman is especially apt to forget it, slumbering in the security of his unchanging islands. Yet no practical politician, nor any-one who speculates on the ties which may bind a state together, can afford to forget it.

Now how are you, as students of history, to deal with the period which has wrought such changes in the map? There is not one historical method suited to the study of all ages. From the ages more properly called prehistorical no records have come down, and their events are therefore irrecoverably lost. All that can be done for them is to construct some broadly outlined picture of society, with here and there an approach to an event, such as the succession of a shortheaded race to a longheaded race in a particular country, within possible limits of time ranging perhaps over a thousand years. Then there is history properly so called, that of events, but for which the records are scanty. There you must be diligent in augmenting the available records as far as possible, by searching in libraries, record offices, and even in Egyptian ruins; and you must exercise the historic imagination. That is a faculty to be spoken of with the highest respect. As men of science show you in phenomena what few could have found out in them, but all can see when found out, so the historic imagination can supplement records and link them together, producing results of which a large part receive general assent. But of the nineteenth century the records all exist and are mostly known. Any that are not yet accessible are not likely to affect our judgment on important matters, though they may throw new light on the characters of individuals and on particular incidents. Discovery and the historic imagination are not therefore so much called for as diligent study and just and sympathetic appreciation of what we possess. And I re-commend you to address that study and appreciation to the following points.

First, learn the wars and treaties, which have been, let us not say the causes, but the instruments by which the map has been revolutionised. By them you will know not merely the final change in the map but the process of change : you will know what was the external situation in which the personages of the historical epic were placed at any moment during the period, a knowledge without which the course of the epic cannot be intelligently followed. From the instruments of change you must rise to the immediate causes, the popular feeling, the ambition or statecraft, which prompted the moves in the game of battle and diplomacy. These immediate causes you must learn both as they really existed and as they were expressed in state papers. When statesmen express or justify their policy they are seldom wholly cynical. Their policy usually represents to their own minds some general view—it might be too laudatory always to call it a principle—of which perhaps we may disapprove, but which can be held with no more insincerity than goes with the actions of common men. The general views of statesmen are sometimes sound, sometimes the most plausible expression which can be given to popular feelings or to dynastic or personal ambitions, sometimes mere catchwords expressing only routine and meaningless habits of thought. In any case they are among the most important factors in international affairs, so great is the influence of statesmen on those affairs, secretly conducted as they commonly are in their most important stages.

Behind these immediate causes there are remoter ones. The course of human action is like that of the tides, setting steadily in certain directions for a time, and rising or falling on the coasts which they pass in their flood or ebb ; mass movements, distinct from the waves which the wind raises on the surface. These streams of tendency give to some periods of history characters more visible in retrospect than at the time, as the set of the tide is not to be seen in the waves, but by the marks which are submerged or uncovered. Of course such streams of tendency are only the summation of the thoughts and acts of men, but of millions of men, often less apparent on the surface than those of the few who guide national action or give a voice to public opinion. Take for example what we can now see to have been one of the greatest issues in the international politics of the eighteenth century, the question whether England or France should prove to be the more expansive power, the power which, for itself and the states which might arise from its colonies, should take the lead in America and Asia. There are large tracts of the diplomatic history of the eighteenth century in which that question does not make much show, either in the public opinion bearing on them or in the utterances to be found in state papers, but the rivalry was there all the time, and operated in the backs of men's minds to shape what they said and did.

When we have learnt the international events of a period and their immediate and remoter causes, we shall know its international history; and when the period is so recent a one as the century just ended, the prolongation of the lines which we have been following may guide our eyes a little way into the future. On that borderland of the past and the future the duty is especially urgent which lies on all students of history, not to be content with the interest of the spectacle, but to judge the real value, the rights and wrongs, of the story. Perhaps, when you close the history of a period which has been marked by such great transfers of population, you may be led to reflect on the nature of the state tie, the conditions which make it possible or fitting that men should live together as a state. But in that or in any other line of reflection you will enjoy a rare opportunity. The international history of the nineteenth century will be presented to you by leading authorities of different countries, between whom you may be sure that no important aspect of it or consideration about it will be omitted. Again a spectacle for you of the highest interest, but again a call for you to judge.

The Europe on which the storm of the French Revolution burst read the *Contrat Social* of Rousseau and speculated on the foundations of government, but in practice demanded no other test of the legitimacy of a government than its settled existence. The absolute monarchies of France and Austria ruling by divine right, the limited monarchy of England ruling by a parliamentary title, the aristocratic republics of Venice and Bern ruling with severity whole subject populations, and the simple democracies of the Forest Cantons, were all accepted as equally legitimate. Subject populations and classes without a voice in government seemed a part of the order of nature; not less so did political liberty where it existed. What we call the question of nationalities had not arisen; it had occurred to no one that the proper basis of political unity was essential unity in race, language, or ideas. Provinces of the most diverse character in those respects found a sufficient tie in loyalty to a common sovereign or dynasty: they felt no want of a common language in which to discuss together affairs which they were not allowed to discuss at all; their gentlemen were welcomed as courtiers and officials at the common capital, and their peasants marched side by side as food for powder. India, with its picturesque varieties of creeds, laws and habits, based on custom, may help us to realise the old Europe. Yet the Europe of the eighteenth century was not really old. No long time, as periods in the history of the world are counted, had elapsed since the decline of feudalism and the upheavals caused by the Renaissance and the Reformation had substituted a new world for that of the Middle Ages. But a great lassitude had succeeded to those upheavals, and to the wars which were needed in order to check the domination of Spain and France; and that lassitude naturally led to reposing with acquiescent respect on any arrangement that existed. It must not however be supposed that the age was a quiet one. Lassitude in respect of public aims left the door open for the ambitions and resentments of sovereigns and their favourites, which never caused more superfluous wars than in the eighteenth century. Never have the state papers of an age explained its wars and treaties on grounds with which a modern student feels that he has less concern. At the back of them, however, three of those remoter causes of events to which I have called your attention were operating: the pressure of England for expansion over the world, necessarily resisted by her great rival, France; the pressure of Prussia towards the constitution of North Germany into a great Protestant power; and the pressure of Russia towards the west. But those pressures were comparatively little heard of in diplomacy: often they worked by allying themselves with the far pettier immediate ends which agitated the courts of the sovereigns.

Into the Europe which I have pictured to you, the closing years of the eighteenth century introduced the idea of liberty as an explosive agent. That idea comprises two forms of liberty. One is the internal form, popular government; the government of a state, not by an autocrat or by a privileged class, but by the mass of the nation. The other is external liberty, the freedom of the state itself from control by its neighbours, whether over its internal institutions or over its relations with foreign states. These two forms of liberty are not necessarily found together. States enjoying at home no shred of popular government may be so great that, far from being controlled by any foreign power, they rank among the controlling powers of the world. Such, for example, is Russia. On the other hand, territories or cities which a foreign control excludes from all independent action beyond their borders may have popular government at home. Such were the subject cities in the Athenian empire of the days of Pericles, democracies subject to Athens, and relying on Athenian support for the maintenance of their democratic governments. But in spite of their occasional separation there is a close connection between the two forms of liberty. The free exercise of its activities which every energetic and independent character demands leads to both, and whenever a people endowed with such a character is possessed of one of the forms of liberty, it will not fail, sooner or later, to demand the other.

Now in 1792, the inevitable starting-point of the international relations of the nineteenth century, the idea of liberty was bursting forth at three different points in Europe, with a vividness which contrasted forcibly with the neutral tints of the eighteenth century. England had set an example of internal liberty, far from perfect, but a sufficiently large part of her people shared in the government to give the nation at large the feeling of being self-governed. Still, in England, the leading political motive during the eighteenth century was not government by a larger or smaller section of the people but good government, doing justice to all and fostering the development of the national resources; and settled existence, or what we call precedent, was the criterion to which the legitimacy of the forms of her government was generally subjected. Her American colonies, repudiating taxation not based on representation, followed her example in practice, but raised it in thought to an idea, which their circumstances led them to present in its fulness by uniting national independence with internal liberty. The idea recrossed the Atlantic. In the France of the Revolution internal liberty, the government of the state by the mass of the nation, was preached, not merely as a remedy for the misgovernment from which the country had grievously suffered, but as the only legitimate system. Whatever may be due to the thinkers of any time or language, whatever may have happened in ancient Athens or medieval Florence, or even within the eighteenth century at Geneva, France was the first great European country to act consciously on the principle that the legitimacy of government rests on the participation of the governed. And that principle became a faith. It was the faith embodied in the revolutionary declaration of the rights of man, and from its birth it was propagandist, as every faith must be.

Neither England, nor at the commencement of the Revolution France, had anything to fear on the head of the freedom of the state from foreign control; but in that form the idea of liberty, at the same time, burst forth strongly in Poland. In that country the want of an adequate middle class and the backward condition of the lower classes made popular government out of the question; but the constitution, in which the king had no real power and the diet could be prevented from passing any resolution by a single nobleman's interposing his veto, was nothing better than anarchy made legal; and every attempt to reform it led to invasion and forcible repression by Russia, who, with Prussia and Austria as her allies, reckoned on the continuance of the anarchy for bringing about the extinction of the state and the partition of its territory between them. The imminence of the danger aroused a high-spirited people to a struggle for reform and national independence, undertaken too late to avert their doom.

In a third European country a flame, which had broken out a little earlier than the French Revolution but in 1792 was still smouldering, presented the name of liberty from a third point of view. That country was what is now the kingdom of Belgium, then a part of the vast dominions of the House of Hapsburg, and known as the Austrian Netherlands or the Belgian provinces. The House of Hapsburg had produced an autocrat of liberal ideas, the emperor Joseph II, who tried to introduce reforms and diminish the excessive power of the Church in those Netherlands, where his plans were distasteful to a rich but ultra-Catholic population. Their opposition was entrenched behind the ancient rights of provinces and cities, on which the emperor in his reforming zeal had trampled, but it could not fail to be tinged with the ideas on the rights of the people that were current across the French border. And to that mixture of old and new principles, enlisted against such reforms as on the same principles were demanded elsewhere, was added a growing and already powerful national consciousness. Separate in language, in character and in habits from their Austrian masters, as they had been from the Spanish masters who preceded the Austrian, they had long been drawn together, and

were feeling their way towards the national unity which they
now enjoy.

To the revolutions which were thus blazing out under the
impulse of the same or closely allied sentiments the old
Europe, at least on the Continent, made the answer known as
the first coalition. That coalition was formed between nearly
all the rulers of monarchical states on the Continent, in the
name of what they called the common interest of sovereigns,
for maintaining what they called the sacred rights of the French
king and monarchy. The king's freedom of action was to be
secured to him, first in agreeing to a constitution and afterwards in working the constitution to which he had agreed, and
the emigrated nobility were allowed in fact, in spite of plausible
excuses, to keep up threatening assemblages on the French
frontier. France declared war; the king became the captive of
the insurgents; a republic was established which successfully
repelled invasion and carried the war into the enemies'
countries, thereby bringing England on the scene. The navigation of the Scheldt to Antwerp had been prohibited by treaty
in the interest of the commerce of Holland, England's ally.
The French, on making themselves masters of the Austrian
Netherlands, declared the Scheldt open, and England objected.
England had not officially recognised the republic, indeed she
could not have been expected to do so till the new system had
given more proof of internal stability, but diplomatic relations
between the two countries had not been broken off until the
horror caused by the execution of the king caused George III
to withdraw his ambassador from Paris, and thereupon, and in
consequence of the difference about the Scheldt, France declared war. From that moment England, which had taken no
part in the original design of interference in the internal affairs
of France, became the most active member of the first coalition.
But the success of France on land, though at times chequered,
was on the whole so great that the original design of interference in her internal affairs soon ceased to be seriously

entertained even by the continental allies. England indeed aided the royalist insurgents on several points of the French coast, and her ignorance of the state of opinion in France led her to form exaggerated hopes of the political effect to be so produced, but in any case such aid would probably have been given as a measure of military diversion.

It is not too much to say that after 1794 at the latest the war had lost all real connection, on the one side with the alarm caused to the sovereigns by the outburst of liberty in France, and on the other with the French propagandism of liberty. The interested motives and routine political maxims which had so long governed men's minds, and which seemed for a time to vanish out of sight in a conflict of ideas, again took possession of them. On land it was on the side of France a war for her old ambitions of the Rhine frontier and aggrandisement in Italy: annexations to the republic took the place of the aid which had been promised to oppressed populations. The resistance to those ambitions was soon left to Austria, which had the most to lose by them. Prussia had not for an instant laid aside her old ambition of completing the destruction and partition of Poland. The part she took in the French war was consequently feeble, and she early made her peace. Russia, clinging to her schemes of conquest both in Turkey and in Poland, had not taken the field in the west, though a member of the coalition. Between France and England the struggle had become another act in their drama of rivalry for the position of the leading world power. England pursued it by her fleets, and by her old system of subsidizing those continental sovereigns who carried on the war. Spain turned into an ally of France, renewing with the republic the family compact of the Bourbons. The one important feature that seemed still to differentiate European politics from those of the century drawing to a close was that Holland, overrun by the French armies which had placed the democratic party in power, was now an ally of France against England.

But the great upheaval in the name of liberty was not destined to fall back into the old welter of interested ambitions, even though among them deeper causes were slowly making themselves felt. Four years after the commencement of the war the brilliant successes of General Bonaparte in Italy again gave it a new character. In that peninsula the ground had been prepared in a manner different from any that we have yet had to notice. The breath of liberty was stirring, but Italy was not a state within which a people might demand self-government, or. which might demand for itself to be emancipated from foreign interference. It was not a state but a geographical expression, covering the large dominions of the pope, governed absolutely; Bourbon and Hapsburg kingdoms and duchies, and at Milan the Hapsburg emperor, all absolute ; the House of Savoy, from beyond the Alps, ruling absolutely, but with some Italian feeling, in a corner of the country; and the republics of Genoa and Venice, in the latter of which, a republic only because not a monarchy, the strictly limited and jealous aristocracy of a single city governed despotically other considerable cities and rich districts. But this geographical expression enjoyed a common language, with the oldest of modern literatures, which had helped to call into being and to give refinement to the more recent literatures north of the Alps. It could look back to a past in which, if many of the chief glories belonged to different cities, they had all been made common by the common literature. Between the different provinces the differences in character and habits were not greater than are often found within a country which no one seeks to dismember. A common sentiment had arisen, and the better minds of Italy felt as Italians rather than as the subjects of this or that potentate. In such circumstances, wherever they occur, the largest of all fields is closed to the greatest of all human activities, unless political unity be also attained. That aim may be realised either by federation or, if the particular governments resist too obstinately the curtailment of their powers which federation would require, then by the establishment of a single consolidated state. And so the spirit of liberty in the largest sense of that word, as denoting the free exercise of all wholesome human activities, became for the Italians that of nationality ; it demanded the creation of a state in which the two forms of liberty which we began by considering, external independence and popular government at home, might be fittingly enjoyed together.

Bonaparte, as the general of the French republic, broke into Italy so prepared. The national sentiment which he found already born there, and which has since grown continuously, was too valuable an ally to be wholly ignored by him, but the jealous policy of France would not allow it any great scope. Some satisfaction was given to it by the creation of the Cisalpine republic, which however was immediately placed in a position of abject dependence on France, but Austria was permitted to annex Venice and most of her territory, and with these events the war of the first Coalition ended on the Continent by the close of 1797. In five years the Austrian Netherlands, Germany west of the Rhine, Savoy, Nice and the Ionian Islands had passed into the possession of France, besides the authority which she had acquired in Italy ; Poland and Venice had been annihilated as states, and the chiefs of the coalition hoped that by their spoils the balance of power had been preserved ; but the idea of nationality had been introduced as a new factor into European politics. England refused to comply with the demand that she should surrender all the acquisitions which she had made during the hostilities, and continued at war.

Even on the Continent the peace was short. Of the twenty-three years between the commencement of our period and Waterloo, eighteen still remained to be chiefly spent in war. You will have to follow with care the kaleidoscopic changes which the map of Europe underwent in the course of them, and you will have to note two great personal ambitions as their dominant features. One, that of Napoleon, is almost un-rivalled in history by the splendid military talents and genius for civil organisation on which it was based, by the height of success to which it attained, and by the tragic vengeance of its fall. France prided herself in the glories of Napoleon as she had prided herself in those of Lewis the Fourteenth : the emancipated nation followed its chief along the old ruts worn by the wars of dynastic ambition. And you will have to note the immense scale on which the genius of one man, seconded by the energy of one nation, was able to operate on the world, in a time which, though literature and art flourished in it, was remarkable in most countries, till near its close, for a weakness of individual character. The other great personal ambition to which I have referred, that of the Czar Alexander, coincided in its effects with the secular pressure of Russia on the west and south ; and thus the period, so far as represented by its principal actors, shows us little that is new except in scale and brilliancy. But of the remoter causes of events which operated at the back of the principal actors, others besides those which we have yet had occasion to notice were making themselves felt.

The first great practical example of unification was given on the European scene when the immediate nobility of the Holy Roman Empire, as the old German empire was officially called, hundreds of princelets who had possessed for ages a certain international existence, were reduced to the condition of subjects of larger German states, though allowed certain honours expressed by calling them mediatized princes. The process of their mediatization was begun in 1803, not with any general views, but solely through the greed of the larger potentates, with Bavaria and Prussia at their head, and was completed in 1806 as a part of the measures by which the short-lived Confederation of the Rhine was established under the protection of Napoleon. But it fell in with the needs of the age, the multitude of petty sovereignties being a hindrance to increasing intercourse, and the mediatized princelets were not restored to any international position when the confused ledger of the revolutionary quarter of a century was liquidated at the Congress of Vienna.

But most important of all the pages in that ledger was the one which was opened by the awakening of the German people to political self-consciousness and activity. The division of the old empire into a multitude of states and fiefs had not been a great hindrance to intellectual and artistic progress, except so far as, by denying the opportunity of great deeds to that large part of the German people who lived in the smaller states and fiefs, it denied them one of the strongest intellectual and artistic stimuli. There had been liberty enough for following such impulses as the nature of the case admitted. But the empire had been quite ineffectual as a protection against foreign oppression, and it ceased to exist in 1806, Francis the Second, the last of its emperors, abdicating that character in consequence of the establishment of the Confederation of the Rhine, and assuming instead the title of emperor of Austria. The Napoleonic rule which followed in Germany was deeply felt both as an injury and as a humiliation. States nominally independent were violated by systematic spying and arrests made by French officers on their soil. Under banners which bore the vain names of Austria, Prussia, and the states forming the Confederation of the Rhine—many, under the banners of France herself, which continually extended her annexations—the youth of Germany were obliged to fight in the cause of Napoleon against the causes which were really their own. And this had befallen a people once dominant, and who felt it in them, in their natural strength of limb and character, to renew, if but once free and united, the dominance of which they had scarcely dreamed since Barbarossa. The result was the great outburst of German political feeling in the final struggle against Napoleon, known in Germany as the war of liberation.

The German sentiment which was thus launched into the
world of European politics must be distinguished from the idea
of nationality which was contributed by Italy. We have seen
that that idea pointed to the political unification of populations
having a language and literature, a character and memories, in
common; but, being an idea, it set corresponding limits to
the unification which it demanded, it forbade the attempt to
incorporate by force populations not sharing those characteristics. The German sentiment on the other hand, being merely
the self-consciousness of a great and strong people, was
primarily connected with the feeling of race, which admits the
existence of ruling and subject races, and never for a moment
did it dream of relaxing the German hold on Poles or Italians.
Though not claiming to incorporate these in a German empire
or federation, it coincided with and supported the dynastic
interests of the Austrian and Prussian sovereigns in demanding
what was accomplished at the Congress of Vienna, the retention
or absorption in Austria and Prussia of as much of Poland
and Italy as could be secured, with the consequent effort to
Germanise their inhabitants as far as possible. But how did
it fare in the settlement at Vienna of the territories formerly
part of the old empire, which during the Napoleonic convulsions had finally disappeared in 1806? Here the German
sentiment, which naturally tended towards a closer unity, was
unable to extort any considerable sacrifice of power from the
sovereigns who, by the fall of the old empire on the one hand
and of the French empire on the other hand, were left without
even a nominal superior. It was indeed a sentiment too new
to cope with the loyalty, founded on long possession and
in many cases on memorable deeds, which defended those
sovereigns and their houses. It was not over them but over
the foreigner that the German triumphs had been won, and
the result was the establishment, for thirty-eight German states,
not including those dominions of Austria and Prussia which
had not been included in the Holy Roman Empire, of the

loosest of loose confederations, incapable of providing an effective unity even for purposes of defence.

Such were some of the causes which contributed to the resettlement of Germany in 1814 and 1815, but we have still to examine the general spirit of the resettlement, not only of Germany but of Europe. After twenty-three years of violence an earnest desire was felt for some basis on which the work of reconstruction might rest securely. Back to 1792, to the arrangements and modes of thought which then existed, and let the interval be treated as a bad dream that has passed away, was an obvious thought. But in political modes of thought return is not possible—only an onward movement, good or bad, is possible—and as to the arrangements which existed in 1792, what about Italy, Poland and Finland? Some notion of legitimacy is demanded by the human mind, which will not acquiesce in a state of possession avowedly resting on force, but in 1815 it could not be the old legitimacy of use and wont, if the restitution was not to be general, but the conquerors were to keep what they had gained. A new conception of legitimacy emerged, to which expression was given by Metternich and Talleyrand, and which was widely accepted for a time in the more conservative classes of European society. The contest with Napoleon had been carried on by sovereigns, and no republic might claim the benefit of the new idea. A restoration in the name of legitimacy was not vouchsafed to Venice or Genoa; to Hamburg and the other free cities of Germany it was not conceded without opposition, and only because the rights on which they re-entered were founded in the old German constitution. Restricted to sovereigns, the new legitimacy belonged to them internally as well as externally. As no transfer of a sovereign's territory could rest on a title by conquest, so no constitution could be set up without his consent: his cession or his grant was necessary to the validity of either. Thus linked to personal rule, the new legitimacy had an undefined tincture of divine right, which put on its deepest colour in the principles of Austrian and Prussian autocrats and their chancellors. French statesmen, though under the restoration agreeing in the main, could not be equally averse to a considerable amount of pressure for extorting constitutional liberties. Only Alexander, solitary and dreaming, could oscillate in his preference between liberalism and autocracy, while led in fact by more consistent if smaller natures.

In the Europe which thus emerged from the Congress of Vienna and from Waterloo the wishes of the populations had been left out of account. The new legitimacy had been applied to restore those sovereigns whose territories had during the revolutionary and Napoleonic periods been wrested from them without cession, and the mass which still remained in the hands of the triumphant allies was used in various interests, especially to reward Prussia for the great share which she had had in the war of liberation. All Italy was placed under the rule or influence of Austria, which, by Dalmatia, was also firmly established on the eastern coast of the Adriatic. Belgium was united to Holland in order to form a strong power of the second class as a barrier against France. It had been intended to transfer Norway from Denmark to Sweden, as a compensation to the latter for the loss of Finland to Russia, and in order to secure her from an attack by land while fighting for the allies, but the brave attitude of the Norwegian people had resulted in their free and by no means close union with Sweden under one king.

Russia had won Finland from Sweden, but the Finlanders had rallied to Alexander in return for his confirmation of their ancient representative constitution as that of a separate grand-duchy. Russia had also acquired a large part of Poland, under the title of a separate kingdom, to which Alexander had promised a representative constitution, and had acquired Bessarabia from Turkey. Insurrection in Servia and unrest in her other Christian provinces threatened Turkey with dismemberment.

In sum the continental Europe of the eighteenth century had disappeared, largely in its arrangements, entirely in its spirit. The new arrangements, whether territorial or internal, had to rest on repression instead of on acquiescence. *Stare super antiquas vias*, to stand on the old ways unassailed by importunate questionings, neither was nor could be any more the happy lot of governments. The old ways were broken up or deserted. The governments in Central, Southern and Eastern Europe were mostly absolute, and in France the very high qualification both for electors and elected reduced parliament to little more than a form. The masses beneath all these governments were stirred by the ferments of which we have seen the successive introduction, and the governments, united in their resistance, formed what is known as the Holy Alliance, though that name strictly belonged only to a vague and sentimental paper signed by the sovereigns, of no direct importance. The spirit of liberty demanded both popular control at home and international independence, the latter constantly violated by the interference of the more powerful sovereigns of the Holy Alliance, in support of absolutism in the weaker states. The idea of nationality worked towards rearranging territorial boundaries, and the German patriotic sentiment, while assisting the work of the sovereigns in repressing the idea of nationality among other populations, aided the ferment by persistently claiming freedom for Germans in Germany.

From continental Europe we must now turn to England. Her perseverance in the twenty-three years' war was due to the conviction that no peace with Napoleon could be safe for her, a conviction which had its counterpart and justification in that of Napoleon. So fully was he persuaded that no extent of domination on the continent of Europe could be secure for him so long as England was not brought low, that one main object of the mad enterprise which led to his fall was to force Russia to maintain the continental system directed against her. She however issued from the struggle with a great extension of her Indian and colonial dominions, a prodigious increase of her manufactures and trade, and a reputation enhanced by her indomitable persistence, maintained though at more than one period of the struggle she had stood alone, and by the willingness of her people to endure sacrifices for national objects. But she suffered severely from the increase of her national debt, bad commercial legislation and a bad poor law, the crowding into new manufacturing centres of a population not adapted for them either by temperance or by providence, and the dislocation by the peace of a vicious agricultural system of mortgages and high rents which during the war had become general. There was much distress, which, combined with the growth of political theory, gave a force, little known in the England of the eighteenth century, to the demand for increased popular control over the government.

But while passing through a period of unrest at home, England could not dissociate herself from continental politics. She had in them two great interests, one that of peace, the other that of the balance of power in the Mediterranean, her position in which was essential to the security of her dominion in India. Bonaparte had emphasized that truth by his expedition to Egypt, undertaken with an ulterior view to India, and by other and subsequent parts of his policy. To these interests, as the aspirations for reform at home grew in strength, was added a sympathy with the cause of liberal institutions throughout the world, nor did commercial motives fail to be combined. France, as the instrument of the Holy Alliance, suppressed by her intervention in Spain the constitution of which the Spanish liberals had been able to compel the king's acceptance, and while the liberal cause and the Mediterranean question were thus directly involved, a further danger arose. The Spanish colonies in North and South America had declared their independence and practically established it, and there was danger lest a similar intervention should be resorted to in order to restore the royal authority over these new republics, from the commerce and future political importance of which great expectations were entertained. The English statesmen, with Castlereagh at their head, who had been as it were the comrades of the sovereigns in the war of liberation, had abstained from condemning the interventions of the Holy Alliance in Italy, although they had held aloof from them. But now Canning openly carried England into an opposite camp, acknowledged the Spanish-American republics, and, by inviting the United States to join in a declaration in their favour, gave occasion to the famous declaration of President Monroe by which the American continent was for ever excluded from the field of operation of European political systems.

Concurrently with these events the Greek insurrection against the Sultan was splitting up the Holy Alliance itself. To Metternich that insurrection was a political event, to be no more countenanced than any insurrection in Western Europe. To Alexander and to Russians in general it appealed on its religious side, as an uprising of oppressed Christians against their infidel masters. In England and France it excited much sympathy, backed by personal and pecuniary aid, largely on the ground of the glories of ancient Greece; and in the end Greek independence was established, by the aid of England, Russia, and France, even before the government of the restored Bourbons was overthrown in France by the revolution of 1830. That revolution placed Louis Philippe, the representative of the younger or Orleans branch of the Bourbons, on a constitutional throne, with enlarged popular liberties, though still with a very restricted suffrage for the election of the Chamber of Deputies. And it completed the rearrangement of the powers into an Eastern and Western group. The former comprised Austria and Prussia, with Russia, which, the Greek question being in the main settled, had nothing further to separate her from the absolutist circle.

She celebrated her restoration to it by putting down relentlessly the Polish insurrection of 1830, since which the only distinctions between Alexander's kingdom of Poland and the rest of the Russian empire have been such as are maintained to the disadvantage of the former. The Western group comprised England and France, with the powers of the second order which constitutional government might place on their side.

First among the chief instances of the co-operation of England and France in this new grouping came the support given by them to the Belgian revolution of 1830, by which the Belgians liberated themselves from their union with the Dutch, from whom they differed in religion, character, and historical associations, to a large extent also in language, only one half of Belgium speaking Flemish, a language almost the same as Dutch, while the other half speaks French. Belgium was established, with the ultimate but reluctant assent of the absolute powers, as an independent and constitutional kingdom, bound to perpetual neutrality under an international guarantee. Next came the Quadruple Alliance between England, France, Spain and Portugal, for the maintenance on the thrones of the two latter countries of those branches of their dynasties that were willing to give effect to liberal constitutions; an object which may be said to have been on the whole successfully attained, notwithstanding the vicissitudes through which Spain has since passed. The cordial understanding between England and France which thus arose was improved by common action of less importance in various parts of the world, but it was unhappily impaired by incidents which took place in the latter part of Louis Philippe's reign, and when he was swept away by the revolution of 1848 a new chapter of European history was opened.

You will learn in detail the convulsions which that revolution caused in most European countries, and the unrest and violence which followed it, making in the whole, from 1848 to 1871, a period of twenty-three years, equal in duration to that from 1792 to 1815, and comparable if not quite equal to it in the frequency of war and in the total amount of international change produced. In 1848 the territorial arrangements of Europe were the same as in 1815, except in Belgium and Greece. In 1871 they had become what they are now, except in the Balkan Peninsula. All I can do to-day is to put the principal changes before you in what I conceive to have been their connection with the great moving forces of the time.

In Italy the true idea of nationality seems to have been fairly carried out, resting as it does on the national sentiment actually entertained by a population, and not on circumstances of race and language on which theorists may choose to think that its being entertained ought to depend. The kingdom of Sardinia with its gallant and patriotic dynasty, most truly representative of Italian feeling, has become that of entire Italy, though it has lost to France Savoy, of which the language is French, and Nice, of which the popular language is a dialect intermediate to French and Italian. That in both these districts a popular vote approved the transfer is not a circumstance of much account, considering how the vote is taken in such cases, but there is no reason to think that the general feeling was adverse to the transfer. Neither district had any share in Italian literature or in the historic glories of the Italian cities. They no doubt felt a personal attachment to the dynasty of which Savoy was the cradle, but that dynasty now flourishes in a remote capital and amid quite other associations.

On the other hand, of the Italian-speaking districts which have not been incorporated in the kingdom, the Swiss canton of Ticino is Swiss in feeling, the southern part of Tyrol is loyal to Tyrol and Austria, and the narrow Istrian and Dalmatian coast region could scarcely be separated politically from the Slavonic inland country even if, which is not certain, such separation were desired by it.

But the international processes by which the unity of Italy was brought about present no agreeable retrospect. The

assistance for which France was paid by the cession of Savoy
and Nice was marred by the persistent attempts of Napoleon
the Third to maintain the sovereignty of the pope at Rome and
to limit Italian unity to a federation, attempts due to jealousy
of a power which could have no reason to be hostile to France,
but of which the unity would put an end to the influence
France might exercise over the rulers of minor states. Austria
naturally fought in defence of the Italian territory which she
possessed : it would be asking too much from human nature to
expect that any power should do otherwise. But Prussia and
the German governments generally, hostile to a cause which
had in any degree the support of France, and alleging that the
Austrian fortresses in Venetia were necessary to the defence of
Germany, compelled by their attitude the premature close of
the liberating campaign of 1859. Only in 1866, when engaged
in turning Austria out of Germany, Prussia accepted the Italian
alliance, which was rewarded with Venice. England, alone of
the great powers, was frankly sympathetic, and prevented any
interference with Garibaldi's crossing to the mainland after his
victorious campaign in Sicily. But the spirit of the Italian
people was the most powerful factor. Freedom, as well from
absolute government at home as from foreign interference, and
the realisation of a deeply felt nationality, were all combined in
the object contended for; and although republicans and constitutional monarchists differed at first about the means, every
motive was soon blended in one wave of enthusiasm. On that
wave Cavour and his successors piloted their cause with consummate skill amid the cross currents of European politics.

North of the Alps the unity of Germany was opposed by
France under Napoleon the Third with the same jealousy which
she displayed in Italy, but with results calamitous to her and to
him. We may hope that in future, under her better republican
guidance, she will be content, as she now seems to be, with
such influence in Europe as the development of her own great
resources and genius will assure her. But this was not the

only difficulty. In Germany herself the liberals and the sovereigns, the latter supported by the conservative classes, were almost to the last at variance about the constitutional character with which the unity desired should be clothed. In the failure of the first attempt to set up a united empire, that made by the Frankfort parliament in 1849, and in the defiance of parliamentary authority by Bismarck while creating the military power of Prussia which he used against Austria and France, you will learn through what internal dissensions the attainment of external unity was pursued. Nor can it be said that in the end the German patriotic sentiment, such as it embarked on the enterprise, has been fully satisfied. It has probably not been deeply wounded by the Prussian conquest of the kingdom of Hanover and some others of the states which belonged to the confederation of 1815. And it has been a great victory for it that most of the remaining members of that confederation, with the addition of those Prussian dominions which did not before belong to Germany, have been united in an empire centralised enough, both theoretically in its form of government and practically in the feelings of the mass of its population, to start at once into life as one of the greatest powers of the world. But the exclusion of Austria, so long the leading state of the old Germany, cannot be counted otherwise than as a great sacrifice by which the victory has been bought.

Coming now to examine the composition of the new German empire more closely we must trace, on its western side, how the transfer of Alsace from France stood connected with certain theories. One is that of natural boundaries, which used to be invoked by France when she claimed the frontier of the Rhine, was forgotten by her when the first Napoleon did not content himself with the Rhine frontier, and was revived when Napoleon the Third intrigued for it again. It is now quoted, only in favour not of rivers but of mountains, the chain of the Vosges, in the southern part of its extent, being the new

Franco-German boundary. In the mean time, as I have already had occasion to mention, we used to hear that not even the Alps, but the quadrilateral of fortresses in the plains of Venetia, were the true defence of Germany. The truth is that no good result will be reached by treating men as appendages to rivers, to mountains or to fortresses. The international history of Europe during the nineteenth century teaches no plainer lesson than that, if once we allow ourselves to consider anything but the people as the primary factor in the determination of boundaries, there is no natural boundary except the furthest limit of what we can get.

The other theory which was more or less concerned with the transfer of Alsace, speaking German as that province does, treats indeed the people as the primary element, but looks, not at the actual preferences of the people, but at those which from their language and supposed race it is thought that they ought to entertain. The idea of nationality, as we have thus far come in contact with it to-day, is that of the entire spiritual idiosyncrasy of a people, to which language can never be wholly indifferent, though in particular cases other characteristics may mould the total idiosyncrasy more powerfully. The theory we have now to deal with, growing as it has been during the nineteenth century by hasty generalisation and by the effect of a literary treatment of politics, would reduce nationality to a question of language, and of race presumed on the very insecure foundation of language. Its application to Alsace would not need much remark here, were it not that the tenacious hold which Germany keeps on her share of the Poles brings her into opposite relations with it in the east.

The Poles are Slavs, and I hope that you will hear more about Panslavism from the able and well-known lecturers of Slavonic nationality to whom you will listen this summer. I have made no such study of the politics of Eastern Europe as to be entitled to speak of it with any authority. But it falls within my province to-day to point it out to you as already a feature not to be ignored in the international history of the closing part of the nineteenth century. That Germany should have so easily acquiesced in the necessity of founding her new imperial organisation on the exclusion of Austria is hardly to be explained except by the knowledge that the large Slavonic population contained in Austria would not be easy to assimilate. And the turmoil in which Austria is kept to-day by the contests of German and Slav, bearing as it does on the relations of that very important part of Europe to its neighbours, has placed the growing self-consciousness of the Slavonic peoples in the foreground of international politics. So far as I can hazard an opinion, Panslavism appears to me to differ from Pangermanism in that its aspirations do not always and necessarily point to any one state as representing it, not even to Russia. Pangermanism can have no meaning apart from the German empire and its future. But the populations speaking Slavonic languages, for I will not say anything about a Slavonic race, are numerous and varied outside Russia—in Germany, in Austria, in Hungary, and in the Balkan Peninsula. They are not wanting in independence of character, and having been accustomed to representative institutions in the different states to which they belong, they are little likely to throw themselves blindly into the hands of any state, however powerful, in which popular control is unknown. But the consciousness of their common Slavonic character to which they have awakened has not yet, so far as I know, given rise to any definite common aspirations, and whether it will ultimately strengthen or modify the secular pressure of Russia on the west is one of the most important riddles which the twentieth century will have to solve.

Perhaps the greatest difference between the international aspect of the two twenty-three years' periods of convulsion is that, whereas England was the backbone of the contest with France between 1792 and 1815, she took no part in arms, and little in diplomacy, in the affairs of Christian Europe between 1848 and 1871. Her alliance with France in the war against Russia, known as the Crimean War, 1854 to 1856, was, at least so far as England was concerned, a thing apart from the dissensions of Christian Europe. That war was necessary in order to save Turkey from falling into a state of vassalage to Russia, a point which deeply concerned the balance of power in the Mediterranean, that constant interest of England. At its successful close Turkey was formally "admitted to participate in the advantages of the public law and system of Europe," which was equivalent to saying that in future any aggression on her should be regarded as a matter of common interest to the Christian powers, whereas before that date her wars with Russia and Austria had had only an occasional and casual connection with general European politics. When in 1878 the Russian forces, this time the instruments of a widespread indignation caused by great massacres and outrages, extorted from the Sultan the treaty of San Stefano at the gates of Constantinople, Turkey received the benefit of her admission to the system of Europe by the narrower limit which the great powers, assembled in congress at Berlin, placed on the concessions which she was obliged to make. But neither in 1856 nor in 1878 was she made to pay by any real reforms for the support thus given her. On each occasion the liberties of some provinces were guaranteed by the powers, but for the rest of the empire the powers in 1856 merely took note of a promise of reform, in 1878 they stipulated reforms which they have not since insisted on being carried into effect. At the former period more might have been done with comparative ease, for the Christian subjects of Turkey were then so backward in condition that they might have accepted at the hands of the Sultan reforms which would now be distasteful to them as strengthening his rule. At present it seems as though the further emancipation of the Balkan Christians must await the day when the mutual jealousies and hatreds of Serbs, Bulgarians, Albanians, and Greeks shall no longer prevent their forming a union which it would be difficult for Turkey to resist, and morally impossible for Europe to discountenance. In the mean time the future of the Balkan Peninsula and of Constantinople itself has become of less importance to England, owing to her occupation of Egypt. Before the Crimean War the Emperor Nicholas of Russia had proposed to England a partition of the dominions of the sick man, as he called the Sultan, in which she should have Egypt ; but not to mention that an acceptance by England would have embroiled her with France, and whether or not the Sultan's misgovernment had then reached such a point as to justify the step against him, it would certainly have been unjust to his Christian subjects, whose claim to be his autonomous heirs it would have set aside. In 1882 the anarchy of Egypt consequent on the revolt of Arabi Pasha had made European intervention inevitable, France and Italy refused the invitations which England addressed to them successively to take part in one, and England was left to restore alone the order, and to multiply alone the prosperity, of the country.

That England figured so little in the history of the convulsions of Christian Europe between 1848 and 1871 was due in part to their scene lying chiefly outside the range of her Mediterranean interests. But there are other causes which marked that period, and which tend still to keep the interests and active sympathies of England out of continental politics. Wars do not tend in our day to the creation of any colossal power, unbalanced by others, and likely to be a danger to her, as was that of the first Napoleon. Nor again is she concerned, otherwise than as a speculative onlooker, in questions of unification, of natural frontiers, of nationality, of German domination over Slavs and Magyars on the one hand, or of Magyar independence and Panslavism on the other hand. She was at one time accustomed to see her natural friends in constitutional governments, but that consideration has lost much of its force for two reasons. All the great powers except Russia, which was not touched by the great uprising of 1848—not excepting even Austria, during her temporary triumph over Hungary—have ever since that uprising admitted the necessity of conceding some amount of power to the people, and so constitutional government has become a question of degree and form. And were that otherwise, it is doubtful how far popular government can in our times be regarded as favouring peace. The most active moving forces of disturbance seem to be no longer those of dynastic or personal ambition, but the popular desires for unity, for the realisation of nationality, for the maintenance of racial domination or the emancipation from it, all likely to thrill most powerfully through an assembly. The dominions of England, and the spheres of influence, like Egypt, which are connected with them, are amply sufficient to occupy her attention, and she administers them on a system in which such desires have no place.

The tie by which we seek to keep the British empire united is that of loyalty to the throne, under good government, without favour to any race, language, or religion. I need not tell you what we believe to be the chief conditions of good government, although I must mention them for the completeness of my subject, if only by way of contrast to what I have referred to as existing elsewhere. Recognising that India requires a different system, and that in the smaller British possessions some greater power may have to be reserved to the mother country, we believe in self-government for possessions inhabited by a white population, too remote from the mother country for incorporate union with it, and not torn by internal discord. If populations differing in language and character are found in the same possession, but geographically separate, we allow them, as in Canada, to be politically separate under a federal tie. If such populations are not geographically separate, as we may find in our new colonies of the Transvaal and Orange River, still we see no reason why they should not accept the principle of equality of race, language, and religion, and pursue their common interests as citizens under a single system of self-government. If they are prevented from doing so either by old memories tenaciously cherished, or by a desire in one or both sections of the people for predominance, the regrettable but unavoidable remedy for discord is government from above; only such government must in its turn be impartial in questions of race, language, and religion. We believe that within the British empire these principles, if faithfully and patiently carried out, will end by overcoming any alien feeling arising from the fact that a given possession was originally acquired by conquest; except indeed in the case last put, where permanent discord is unaccompanied by geographical separation, in which case the discord would not be cured by abandoning the conquest.

I have said that we believe the result will be such within the British empire, because the conditions for overcoming an original alien feeling are more favourable in possessions divided by oceans from the states from which they may have been acquired, than in a continent like Europe, where a province annexed against its will may be in close contact with the populations with which it would unite if it could. The one thing which may be predicted in such a case with some confidence is that the attempt to extirpate alien feelings by force will fail. It is less easy to be confident that the impartial treatment of all differences would succeed. Here we have to face that speculation on the ties which may bind a state together to which I intimated to you in the beginning of this lecture that a view of the nineteenth century as a whole, great century of transfers as it has been, would lead. I cannot enter into that speculation : the twentieth century may throw light on it. And to the twentieth century must also be left to show what will be the effect on international relations of that industrial and commercial rivalry, with the passion for colonial expansion and spheres of influence, of which the close of the nineteenth century has seen the dawn. The antagonistic pressures of

England and France for expansion over the world were among the great causes operating in the eighteenth century, though comparatively in the background. After a long intermission a similar pressure, on the part not of two only but of nearly all the great states, has started into activity, and loudly claims a foremost place. It also is a popular pressure, which parliamentary institutions and a free press tend rather to promote than to moderate. Assuredly the twentieth century will not be wanting in interest.

ENGLAND'S COMMERCIAL STRUGGLE WITH NAPOLEON.

By J. Holland Rose, M.A.

We are all more or less acquainted with the chief external events of the great war with Napoleon. They bulk so large in the hazy middle distance of history that even boys who are trained in our public schools, and for whom the year 1815 is the end of all historical study, know nearly as much of the military and naval events of the greatest war of all time as they do of the Peloponnesian War. The man in the street, also, aided by some outstanding landmarks of London topography, remembers that Nelson beat the French and Spaniards at Trafalgar. Then a mist settles down over his historical consciousness, until it is dispelled by the ring of those magical words, "Up Guards and at them"; and he then remembers with a thrill of pride that when those words were uttered the French turned their backs on Wellington at Waterloo, and the power of Napoleon was no more.

But what was all that fighting about? I fear that if that question were put to the average public school-boy (unless he were of the mental stature of that prodigy whom Macaulay used to invoke for our general discomfiture) it would prove very embarrassing. The very well-trained boy would perhaps say that it was caused by a dispute about Malta ; or else, seeking safety in generalities, he would hazard the guess that it was due to Napoleon's ambition. But when we came to press our examinee hard, and ask him why Malta was so important to both parties, and what were the objects on which Napoleon's ambition centred, we should receive extemporized versions of history that would only show the ingenuity and ignorance of their contriver.   If we further enquired why the Spaniards opposed us at Trafalgar and four years later fought by our side at Talavera ; or why Russia and Prussia veered round from enmity to friendship in the course of the years 1812–13, the replies would be at best only bewildered half-truths.

There is, indeed, much that is puzzling in the sudden changes of policy of those years ; and the perplexity of the examinee who has been trained merely on superficial text-books is in part excusable ; for few of these books attempt at giving any clue to the diplomatic maze of that period ; and they leave the reader plodding among masses of seemingly disconnected facts.   This is probably the reason why so many persons approach the study of the Napoleonic era as a duty which patriotism demands, but from which flesh and blood shrinks as from a penance scarcely to be borne, unless the historian leads his reader full often aside into oases of mendacious anecdotes and conjugal scandals.

And yet surely there is no period in all the world's history fraught with a more profound interest—an interest so dramatic at times that it no more needs these petty distractions than the *Agamemnon* and *Hamlet* stand in need of forced jokes and puns.   The Napoleonic period, I make bold to say, is the greatest drama of secular history.   It is a world-drama in the widest sense ; for the fortunes of all the continents were then deeply at stake, and nation was hurled against nation in a way which had never happened before and can scarcely happen again.   Moreover, the man about whom this vast cyclone revolved was essentially a dramatic figure.   He was endowed with gifts so commanding that he must have left his mark deep on any period, however stagnant, and on any people however unreceptive.   Place him side by side with the heroes of other ages ; and in respect of intellectual grasp and force of will (I am not speaking of moral qualities, for of these he had scant store,) he outstrips them all. His schemes of Empire were vaster than those of Alexander, and were pursued with an equally inflexible will. We can scarcely think of Caesar, even had he lived out his life, reorganizing the Roman State and Roman society with the startling success that Napoleon achieved for France in the four momentous years of the Consulate. Frederick the Great, brilliant though he was as a leader and organiser, never showed quite the same breadth of view and overmastering power in the camp and in the Cabinet as the man who tamed a revolution and all but conquered Europe. Furthermore, we must remember that the other great rulers whom I have named were heirs to mighty names and fortunes; while Napoleon entered on life as an orphan, educated at the expense of the French Monarchy : he owed nothing to family or position : he climbed the dizzy heights of fame by sheer force of will and transcendent genius.

It is the combination of mental powers that made Napoleon so formidable and so attractive. The scion of a race that viewed public life from the standpoint of the *vendetta*, he early matured all the fighting and scheming faculties ; and, thanks to his poverty and his early Republican zeal, he reinforced these Corsican aptitudes by an eager study of civil and military history of diverse times and peoples. Fired with zeal by the French Revolution, he set himself to understand that strange people whom at first he so much hated. And he succeeded. He won the hearts of the soldiery by his wondrous exploits in Italy. The other generals, even burly veterans like Masséna and Augereau, owned at once that there was a something in those hawk-like eyes that bespoke the master ; and they grumblingly yielded the first place to the slim, sallow-faced youth whom they had at first derided. The victory of genius over talent was even more marked in the case of the civilian rulers of France. Their little schemes to keep him away from

France and to ruin him were futile.   The glamour of the
Egyptian Campaign held France spell-bound; and the *soi-
disant* Conqueror of the East on his return from Egypt had
the easiest of tasks to oust the Directory and make himself
master of France.

For most men this success would have brought satisfaction
or repose.   For him it meant a new and vast opportunity of
curbing the Revolution and building its more lasting results
into a political system of which he was the keystone.   Again
he conquered: and the fundamental institutions of Modern
France were the result of this absorption of the Revolution by
the Napoleonic *régime*.   And this almost miraculous absorption
of a great movement by a single personality was the outcome,
not of force (for how could 40,000,000 men be coerced by one
man) but rather of a persuasive, persistent, and occasionally
unscrupulous statecraft.   He outwitted the Liberal Opposition
as he outwitted the Roman Cardinals: he hoisted Royalist and
Jacobinical plotters with their own petards: he found work for
every man and saw to it that every man worked: in brief, he
infused into France his own prodigious energy so that the
strifes of the Revolution were forgotten in the new passion for
organization and for mighty undertakings.   The ablest Ministers thought it a privilege to slave for him twelve hours a day
and then to bear his reproaches for slackness ; and the whole
nation rose to a sense of new and bounding life, just as a high-
mettled steed responds to the touch of a master-hand.   It was
this power of calling out the fullest energies of a nation that
enabled him to triumph over Jacobins and Royalists, just as it
was his subtle Italian grace that fascinated men even while they
feared his sterner qualities.   Such a character, at once seduc-
tive and coercive, by turns pleasing and terrifying, imaginative
and practical, a veritable god of war and yet unequalled in the
arts and activities of peace, is certain to leave his mark deep
on a sensitive Celtic people, above all when it has struggled
through a Revolution and stands in need of rest.

Alas! these great gifts were used for selfish ends. He deliberately sought to arouse the old military instincts, as also the kindred desire for strong personal government; and France speedily became under his hands the most perfect military machine that the world has ever seen.

What brought this terrible engine of war into deadly conflict with Great Britain? Had its founder and director an ineradicable hatred of us as a people? I find few signs of this. On the whole Napoleon respected us for our activity, enterprise, and tenacity of purpose. No! He was possessed by no silly dislike of us as a people. He only came to hate us because we were always in the way of his most cherished design; and this was to found a great colonial Empire, above all, an Empire in India. Alexander the Great appealed to him more than any other hero of antiquity. Ah! What a genius—he exclaimed to Gourgaud at St Helena,—to have founded a mighty Empire before he was 33 years of age, and to have gained the love of his subjects! How wise of him to visit the temple of Ammon, and to cast aside merely Greek ideas.—"If I had remained in the East, I would probably have founded an Empire like Alexander: I would have gone on a pilgrimage to Mecca[1]." And then, again, he said that if he had taken the turban, as he meant to do after capturing Acre, he would have been at the head of 200,000 good troops. He concludes with these significant words, "The East only awaits a man[2]."

And that was the dream of his youth, as it was the keenest regret of his last years. Look at his early letters. In Oct. 1797 when he is about to sign peace with Austria, his thoughts centre on the Ionian Islands, Malta, and Egypt. By blotting out the Venetian Republic he secures the Ionian Isles for France: he sends a political agent to Malta to intrigue with the French Knights of St John; and he advises the Directory

---

[1] Gourgaud, *Journal de Ste. Hélène*, II. p. 435.

[2] *Ib.* I. 165.

to concentrate all its activity on the French navy "and destroy England. That done, Europe is at our feet." In the month of February following he inspects the flotilla at Boulogne, and declares that an invasion of England is for the present impossible. As alternatives to this he recommends the Directory either to turn their attention to the North-German coast-line and shut out English goods from Hanover and Hamburg, or else to prepare to attack her in India[1]. It is important to note that he always kept these alternatives before him ; and chose one or other of them as the conditions of the time prescribed. The latter plan was that to which he strongly inclined ; and the Egyptian Expedition was to furnish the means of ruining our commerce and our possessions in India. For, as he never tired of asserting, "the power that is master of Egypt, is master of India[2]." Thus, even as early as the year 1798, he resolved on a career of Asiatic conquest. But, if he was to reach the banks of the Indus, he must first cripple England or distract her by a blow at Ireland. Then, at last, when he reached Lahore and Delhi, he could satisfy the dictates of an oriental ambition, and also dry up the wealth of those "active and intriguing islanders." Ambition and statecraft therefore brought him into conflict with us ; and hostility to our commerce became one of the axioms of his policy.

In this respect, then, Bonaparte's Eastern Expedition was the first of his persistent attempts to found an Eastern Empire on the ruins of our own ; for he believed, in common with most of the French merchants and economists, that our expulsion from the markets of the East would speedily lead to our commercial ruin and to national bankruptcy.

I have no space in which to add complete proofs of the tenacity with which he cherished these designs. There can, however, be no doubt that he determined to secure half of

---

[1] Letter of Feb. 23, 1798.
[2] Gourgaud, *op. cit.* II. 315.

Australia for France; for a French official map of 1807 designates all the central parts as *Terre Napoléon*. And in that same year he made a treaty with the Shah of Persia, and sent out a Commissioner to arrange plans for a Franco-Persian invasion of India. Even as late as March, 1811, he gives orders for the equipment of squadrons that were to seize the Cape of Good Hope and Egypt, as half-way houses between France and India; and he clearly hoped that when England was choked to death by the grip of his Continental System he would at last be free for the completion of his long-cherished oriental designs.

All great conquerors are remarkable for doggedness of purpose; but I think no man has ever been so dogged as he who, amidst all the turmoil of European strifes, ever kept his mind's eye on the grander arena of the East. And this quality was fed by the conviction that his great enemy, England, lacked the elements of real strength and must therefore soon give way. There was some reason for his underrating our vitality. He shared the opinion of the Jacobins that tillage of the soil was the only sure foundation of a nation's strength. Foreign commerce, said they, might add to national wealth, but it enervated and degraded the people. Furthermore, it could easily be destroyed by war; and they pointed to the many examples where the ruin of commerce in time of war brought with it the decadence of the State. Tyre and Carthage, Venice and Genoa, served them with effective texts on the instability of maritime and commercial States; whence they readily inferred that Britain, the modern Carthage, must succumb under a vigorous and well-sustained onset on her mercantile marine. There was much to be said in favour of this view. Foreign commerce is, of course, a less secure basis for national life than agriculture. Three or four times in our modern history we have been on the verge of ruin owing to this cause; and our continental friends have sagely wagged their heads in token that our last hour had come, until that miraculous organism, the British

Empire, set all probabilities at defiance, and rose triumphant over dangers.

Early in the nineteenth century there seemed special reasons for deeming the decadence of England to have set in. Despite our successes at sea, our Ministers allowed themselves to be cajoled into a most disadvantageous peace, the Peace of Amiens, whereby we gave up all our conquests, except Trinidad and Ceylon, which Napoleon compelled his allies, the Spaniards and Dutch, to surrender to us; France was left in possession of her immense conquests in Europe, and received back the colonies which we had wrested from her. No word was said as to the resumption of our commercial relations with France; and we soon found our goods excluded not only from France and her colonies, but also from lands over which she held control. Furthermore, we were soon informed by Napoleon that the extension of his influence in the lands bordering on France was no business of ours; and we were expected to acquiesce in his annexations of Piedmont and Elba as also in his plans for securing Louisiana and parts of Australia and India.

His reason for expecting this tame acquiescence on our part was that he had found our negotiators singularly weak at Amiens; and he believed, after the retirement of Pitt early in 1801, that weakness might confidently be expected from the Addington Ministry which took his place. Added to this, no small part of the English Opposition was in the habit of carping at every act of the Cabinet, and extolling the wisdom and power of Napoleon. As a result of these deplorable events England's prestige steadily waned while that of Napoleon as surely waxed with every diplomatic success.

But when he ventured to assert that the reconquest of Egypt would be an easy matter, and let it be seen that the mastery of the Mediterranean would be but the prelude to an attack on our Eastern possessions, even the Addington Ministry held firm. It refused to evacuate Malta, for that island was now a post of vital importance to us ; and war broke forth on this Maltese question, closely linked as it was with the wider imperial questions that I have outlined.

In a word, the decline of British prestige hurried Napoleon into world-wide schemes, for the realisation of which he was not in that year (1803) fully prepared. Had he waited, as he really wanted to do, for another year, when the new French navy would be ready, the blow might have fallen with crushing effect. As it was, his excess of confidence and the final firmness of Addington were our salvation. Apparently he intended to attack us in India in the autumn of 1804[1]. And it seems probable that, if we had given him time to bring the growing maritime resources of France fully to bear upon us, the results might have been fatal to our commerce, our Colonial Empire, and therefore to our existence as a great nation.

For at the very time when Napoleon was excluding British goods from lands that came under his control Great Britain was rapidly increasing her manufacturing output, and therefore needed markets for that output more than ever before. The years which in French history are marked by the great Revolution and the ascendency of Napoleon are memorable in our more prosaic annals as the period when the inventions of Hargreaves, Arkwright, Crompton, Cartwright, and Watt, began to revolutionise industry. The end of the eighteenth century saw spinning machinery driven by steam ; in the first years of the nineteenth century the power-loom became a practical success ; and the manufacturing power of Lanarkshire, Lancashire, Yorkshire, and the Midlands increased by leaps and bounds. Robert Owen at a somewhat later date computed the number of cotton-workers at 800,000, each of whom by means of machinery could produce forty times as much as in the old days of hand-labour[2]. The output, then, in that single

---

[1] See his secret instructions to General Decaen concerning India printed in the *Revue historique* of 1879 and of 1881.

[2] *Life of Robert Owen*, written by himself (Appendix S).

industry equalled that of 32,000,000 of hand-workers. And when we remember that on the Continent of Europe these labour-saving inventions were unknown, and that manufacturers there soon had the greatest difficulty in procuring raw material, the reasons for the commercial supremacy of England are obvious. The Continent needed English goods, quite as much as we needed their markets. But it was vitally important for us to have those markets kept open; otherwise we should speedily have been choked by the excess of our new vitality: we should have manufactured goods only to see them accumulate in our warehouses. It was essential that we should have fair play commercially from Napoleon; and instead of giving us fair play he threatened us even during the year of peace with the prospect of commercial exclusion from nearly one-half of Europe and from many of the new lands. This was the reason why the war which began in 1803 was fought with such deadly earnestness. On Napoleon's side it was a struggle for world-wide empire: on our side it was a struggle to save our colonies and commerce from the ruin which Napoleon's triumph would infallibly have inflicted on us.

There was very little chance of a peaceful compromise. An effort was made by Fox in 1806 to come to an understanding with the French Emperor. But it was soon evident that he meant to have Sicily under his control; and on this question Fox was inflexible, and quite rightly so. To have allowed Napoleon to gain Sicily would have been a fatal mistake. It would have handed over to him the command of the Mediterranean and endangered our communications with India. The negotiations virtually broke down on this question before Fox passed away. The statement that the death of the great Whig Minister put an end to all hopes of peace with Napoleon is one of those pleasing fictions which die hard. French historians and Whig historians have written eloquently on this theme, until they almost came to believe it themselves.

There is not a particle of truth in it. Read Fox's own confession of his despair of peace as he lay on his death-bed ; and those sad words of the generous peace-loving Minister must convince you of the inevitableness of the great struggle. No ! The war could only end with the overthrow or exhaustion of one of the combatants. The cast-iron nature of Napoleon forbade him abating one iota of his plans ; and those plans were inconsistent with the greatness of England and with the manufacturing activity which she was then developing.

We have seen that the methods of attack by which he meant to bring us to our knees were threefold. Either (1) a direct invasion, or (2) the exclusion of our goods from a large portion of Europe, or (3) an expedition to ruin our colonies and commerce in the East. That was his conclusion in 1798; and, with the inflexibility that is one of his chief mental characteristics, he clung to this governing conception throughout the struggle—at any rate up to the year 1811. In 1803, when his navy was as yet unprepared for distant enterprises an Eastern expedition was almost impossible. He only used the threat of it to distract Nelson and weaken our forces in the Channel. For a time he cherished the hope of invading England. That hope was dashed by Nelson and Cornwallis ; and after Trafalgar only the third alternative was available, that of excluding our goods from the Continent and thus assuring our financial exhaustion. This scheme soon became feasible. In 1805 he vanquished Austria. In 1806 he trampled Prussia underfoot after Jena ; and, when safely installed at Berlin, he issued the famous Berlin Decree. It excluded our ships and goods from all lands under his control and forbade entry to any ship whatsoever that had touched at a British port.

This famous decree was the first evident sign of his resolve to banish our commerce from the Continent. But his correspondence, as also his merciless pressure on Prussia early in 1806, proves that for months past he had been preparing for this measure. It formed the basis of his *Continental System*—a name applied to the many decrees by which he sought to cut off all relations between England and the Continent.

The events of the following months enabled him to impose his will on other Powers. Russia and Prussia accepted the System by the terms of the Treaties of Tilsit. Denmark, Portugal, the Papal States, Austria, and Sweden were in turn swept into his net; and by the year 1809 British commerce was officially banned in every European country but Turkey, Sicily, and Portugal.

It is difficult for us now to realise how terrible an engine of war the Continental System was. We now depend so largely on our trade with Canada, South Africa, Australia, China, and Japan, and other distant lands, that we are apt to think complacently of the exclusion of commerce from nearly the whole of Europe. The commercial hostility, to which we are now exposed by the chief of the Continental States, has reduced the volume of our trade with those countries as compared with that which we have developed with trans-oceanic lands. Since the days of Bismarck we have learnt to look farther afield for markets, seeing that those of the Continent are almost closed against many of our goods by stringently protective tariffs. In fact, it is worth noting that this has been one of the forces compelling us to expand the Empire. Just as Napoleon's Continental System drove us to the colonial conquests which mark the years after Trafalgar; so too the fiscal barriers which have been piled up against us in Europe have had the inevitable result of driving our exports more and more to other lands which would trade with us on something like fair terms. Commerce follows the lines of least resistance. Bar it out from the old countries and it will seek new lands : above all it will find out British colonies and will pour fresh life-blood into them. Whence it would appear that, after all, we owe a debt of gratitude to Napoleon and to the contrivers of modern protectionist tariffs. To him, and to them, we may perhaps rightly award the title *Reichsmehrer*, though in a sense which he and they would scarcely have appreciated.

But, to return to our theme, we must remember that in the year 1806, when our commercial struggle with Napoleon definitely began, our exclusion from the Continent might well seem a fatal blow at our prosperity. Canada was then in its infancy; the two or three half-starved penal settlements of New Holland gave no promise of the mighty Commonwealth of Australia; Cape Town was passing into our possession, but it was looked upon much as we look upon Aden now, an important naval station with an almost barren and useless *Hinterland*. The only colonial possessions to which we attached any great value were the East and West Indies. To these we clung desperately as to the very pillars of the Empire. But elsewhere there seemed, at first sight, little chance of making up for the loss of the European markets. Our trade with the United States was important, but our relations with our kinsfolk were at best precarious; and when we insisted on the right of searching neutral ships and subjected them to restraints that were deemed desirable as a counterblast to Napoleon's orders our trade with North America ceased almost entirely.

I have no space in which to examine, or even to state, the various devices set forth in our Orders in Council to compel neutrals to observe our maritime code. They have caused almost as many headaches to students of law and of naval affairs as they caused heartburnings and strifes in those days. But I think we may fairly say this of our Orders in Council, that they were provoked by Napoleon's action. As his Continental System was rendered stricter and stricter by the decrees signed at Milan, Fontainebleau and the Trianon in the years 1807–10, so the British Government increased the rigour of our maritime code. The more he tried to prevent neutrals trading with England by threats of confiscation of ships and wares, so much the more were we determined that neutrals should not trade with his States except by way of our ports. Both Napoleon and England violated the principles of international law: but I think it can be proved that he took the initiative in every step, whereupon the British Government followed with the measure of retaliation which it deemed most effective. I know that on the ground of morality it is a very poor excuse to urge, "My enemy did it first; and I followed his example." One could pursue that line of argument with the same childish futility that marked the recriminations of our first parents in the Garden of Eden. But, in all seriousness, I maintain that in a struggle such as that which Napoleon waged against us in 1806–12, the question of morality hardly comes in at all. Because he could not attack us directly, he devised this plan of commercial strangulation; and we, as we felt his grip extending and tightening, adopted such expedients as would relax his hold and would give us a chance of gripping him in turn. In a struggle for sheer life neither combatant thinks about the morality of the expedients adopted, but only of their effectiveness. And we may further remark, that Napoleon in his private conversations never blamed us much for our retaliation: he seemed to consider it quite natural.

Leaving on one side, then, the question as to the morality or immorality of the acts of the two combatants, we may inquire which of their engines of war was the more effective. Did the Land-Power throttle the Sea-Power, or *vice versâ*? Outwardly it seemed as though the Land-Power must succeed. By the middle of the year 1807 Napoleon counted on having the whole of the Continent on his side. After signing the Peace of Tilsit he was sure of Russia, Prussia and Austria. Smaller States, like Denmark, Sweden and Portugal, could be coerced: and these States, added to his Dutch, German, Italian and Spanish allies, would place Europe absolutely at his feet. At once he framed his plans for coercing Denmark and Portugal; and great was his chagrin when we anticipated him by seizing the Danish fleet. This action of ours very naturally exposed us to the severest censure: but, viewing it in the light of facts that have now been ascertained, it is difficult to see what else the British Ministry could have done[1]. Canning strove by all the means in his power to persuade the Danes to accept our alliance and to give the fleet in deposit ; and in face of their resolve to accept Napoleon's alliance there was practically no other alternative than that which our Foreign Minister adopted. None the less we must deplore this event as one of the most lamentable in our annals.

It is, I think, generally forgotten that when the French Imperial Press was upbraiding us with our rapacity at Copenhagen, Napoleon was preparing to do the very same thing at Lisbon. Because the Portuguese Regent refused to confiscate British merchandise, Napoleon sent Junot with a *corps d'armée* in hot haste to the banks of the Tagus, and instructed him to give out that he came as a friend, so that he might the more readily seize the Royal Family and the fleet. Again, however, we thwarted him : that family sailed away on the fleet to Brazil; and he contented himself with seizing the little kingdom.

The French military occupation of Portugal, however, proved to be a snare. It tempted the French Emperor on to his design of dethroning the Spanish Bourbons ; and the insidious manner in which he carried this out drove that proud and brave people into the ranks of his enemies. In the spring of 1808 the Spaniards rose against the French ; and so there came about that firm alliance between Spain and England that safeguarded the national independence of both peoples. Here again Napoleon's action was due, in part at least, to commercial motives. Not only did he owe the Spanish Bourbons a grudge for their flash of hostility during the campaign of Jena, but it is clear that he believed he was completing his Continental System by gaining direct control of Spain and her fleet, and her vast Colonial Empire. Shortly before the Spanish insurrection he wrote jubilantly of the naval resources that would be

---

[1] See my articles in the *English Historical Review* for Jan. 1896, and Oct. 1901.

his, with Cadiz and Carthagena as naval bases for expeditions. The command of the Mediterranean would now be assured, and half of the New World would pass under his sway. What chance then could there be for battered and discredited England ?

Never did he commit a worse blunder. Far from adding to his naval and mercantile resources by the seizure of Spain, he brought on a struggle that was to busy a quarter of a million, or more, of his best troops for five years to come, that was to empty his coffers, and—worst of all in his sight—was to give most timely relief to England. Not only English soldiers but English goods began to pour into Spain, whence they had hitherto been excluded. More important still for the well-nigh bankrupt merchants of Lancashire, the Spanish colonies (that is, all the lands from Mexico to Valparaiso and Buenos Ayres) began to take our merchandise, and that too for the first time in their history. Thus, not only was a foothold gained for Sir Arthur Wellesley in Spain, but ruin was staved off from the manufacturing districts of England by the very enterprise whereby Napoleon thought he had assured that ruin.

I think we may assert that, but for the welcome outlet to our energies, both commercial and military, afforded by our alliance with Spain, we must have succumbed from sheer exhaustion. I judge this to be the case because, after the first flush of commercial activity, due to this cause, was past, we experienced in the years 1810–11 the severest depression through which we have ever struggled. The Spanish markets being for a time glutted with our goods, we had no adequate outlet for our great productive power. True, our merchants showed great ingenuity in smuggling goods into the Continent ; and from our posts of vantage—the Ionian Isles, Malta, parts of Spain, the Channel Islands, and Heligoland—we managed to get merchandise into many parts of the Continent. But this did not make up for the loss of direct and regular access to the great ports, all of which, from Riga right round to Trieste were closed to our goods. The distress in our manufacturing districts was terrible; and it is difficult to see how we could have struggled through that black year 1811 but for the relief fitfully afforded by commerce with Spain, Portugal, and their colonies. Our own colonial trade was growing: but it was not enough then to support our large manufacturing population.

We must also be thankful for another strange blunder committed by Napoleon. Throughout the greater part of the years 1810–11 bread was at famine prices; and it would have been easy to starve us into surrender. Our own harvests were lamentably bad. North America then sent us only a few shiploads a year; and we depended on the Baltic lands to make good any shortage in our home-supply. Napoleon's word was law in the Baltic lands. Then why was it that he did not stop all export of corn by sea, and thus intensify our miseries? So far from doing that, he allowed 2,000,000 quarters of wheat to come to us in the year 1810. The only explanation of this strange blindness of his, in presence of the most favourable opportunity of his life, seems to be this. He clung to the crude old mercantilist theory that imports weakened a State, while exports strengthened it. There are one or two letters of his which harp on that strange delusion—especially the letter of Aug. 6, 1810, to Eugène Beauharnais, whence it would seem that he believed he was weakening us by letting us buy corn at the extravagant rates then ruling. Whatever the cause of this very strange fact, there is no doubt that we were allowed to buy corn from our enemies at the time when we most needed it. There still seem to be some official persons at Westminster whose minds are so firmly cast after the Micawber and Mark Tapley type, as to believe that our enemies are always going to be equally obliging. I venture to say that if these gentlemen would spend part of their recess in looking into our economic condition in the years 1810–11, they would find that they, and the whole nation as well, are living in a Fool's Paradise on this question. So extraordinary a piece of good fortune as that of having an enemy who knew nothing of Political Economy is not likely to happen again[1].

Napoleon staked his Empire on the success of this vast commercial experiment of cutting off our exports. It mattered comparatively little, he thought, what we imported; for imports had to be paid for, and therefore drained a country of gold. In order to perfect his system and compass our ruin he made those hazardous experiments of the years 1810–12. He annexed the North Sea coastlands: he tightened the cords of the Continental System on all his subject lands, and ordered the seizure and burning of all goods of British origin. A wail of despair and indignation went up from German manufacturers: even those of France ventured to point out the hardships to which they were exposed, with raw cotton 10 francs the lb. and indigo 21 francs the lb. He rebuked them for their faintheartedness, and bade them do as best they might; for England was exhausted and would soon give up the game.

But now trouble loomed in the East. The Czar would no longer see the ruin of his trading classes, and began timidly to resume trade with England. We, on our side, withdrew the obnoxious Orders in Council, and saw our export trade improve; while Napoleon, in order to rivet his System on Russia, prepared for that Moscow Campaign which, as Talleyrand finely said, was the beginning of the end. And then, in the days of disaster, the great Emperor realised how mad he had been to drive the patient German people to despair by rapacious decrees and hordes of inquisitive *douaniers*. The day of reckoning came, and the *Völkerschlacht* at Leipzig was the judgment of Central Europe on the Continental System.

Whether that System might not have succeeded in the hands of a more tactful ruler than Napoleon I will not venture

---

[1] See my article in the *Monthly Review* for March 1902, on this question.

to say. But I do say that it came very near to success in the years 1810–11. No one can look into our records without noting very many signs of exhaustion and despair. Had Wellington given Masséna a chance at Torres Vedras ; had our own people been less dogged than they always are in time of adversity ; above all, had Napoleon not committed that "Spanish blunder" of 1808, I think it very doubtful whether he might not have drained away our life-blood. But the Spanish blunder was fundamental. It lost him the unanimous vote of the Continent, which up to then he seemed fairly sure of winning against England. With a unanimous feeling in his favour he could have done with us what he listed.

What would then have been the upshot? Britain would probably have been stripped of her colonies,—certainly of Canada, the Cape, and India—and allowed to exist almost on sufferance as Carthage did after the Second Punic War. Napoleonic France would then have been the great World-Power, giving laws to Europe and developing the resources of a vast Colonial Empire with the untiring energy that marked her terrible ruler. The arts and sciences would have prospered prodigiously, and the world would have advanced with giant strides at the behest of the autocrat. Material progress would have been more orderly and more rapid than has been the case under the lead of the easy-going Anglo-Saxon. In place of individual initiative, we should see State control ; and the best parts of the earth would be ordered after the fashion of a huge labour colony. We may also be sure that all that material advancement would have been ordered with a view to the glory of France and the Napoleonic dynasty. Napoleon had no conception of the maxim—"Live and let live." His commercial ideas were narrowly national. His first idea on the gaining of any new colony was to push on French commerce to the exclusion of that of every other nation. He had no conception of Free Trade : he was for Prohibition if possible, or failing that, for stringent Protection. A proof of this is seen in his remark to Gourgaud at St Helena, when he heard of our giving back Java and Sumatra to the Dutch, and L'Île de Bourbon to France in 1815 : "The English are stupid : if I "were in their place I would have stipulated in the last treaties "that I alone should be able to navigate and trade in the seas "of India and of China. It is ridiculous for them to leave "Batavia [*i.e.* Java] to the Dutch, and the Isle of Bourbon to "the French.... The Americans ought no longer to navigate "in the China Sea. What can they do against England?"[1]

This is fairly typical of his utterances on these questions. "The spoils to the victors : woe to the vanquished "—these were his maxims in commerce as in politics. As one of his Ministers phrased it, Napoleon thought he could make commerce "manœuvre like a battalion".[2] There you have the inner cause of the failure of his great commercial experiment. He looked on commerce as an engine of war for assuring the predominance of one nation, not as a means for promoting the wealth of nations.

While, therefore, we as Britons rejoice that this great struggle ended as it did, we may do so on more than merely national grounds. The triumph of Napoleon must have led to the founding of a world-wide Empire, in which power and prosperity would have been dearly bought at the expense of individual liberty and private enterprise. The triumph of Great Britain has built up a Commonwealth whose citizens are in every sense free men, whose industries develop the grit and fibre of the individual, and whose commerce is open to all the world.

[1] *Journal de Ste. Hélène*, II. p. 315. Mollien, *Mémoires*, vol. III. pp. 287—296, 314—318.

[2] Chaptal, *Mes Souvenirs sur Napoléon*, p. 275.

BRITAIN'S NAVAL POLICY.

By Professor J. K. Laughton, M.A.

It is not many years ago that a political agitator, addressing a meeting in the north of England, urged on his audience the iniquity and injustice of their being taxed for the maintenance of a navy whose only possible use was to defend the interests of the south. At the present time, in view of the recent growth of imperial sentiment, the most brazen-throated demagogue might think twice before he ventured to talk such blatant nonsense; but it is worth asking whether the objection to it would be one of knowledge or of mere sentiment. Sentiment is a noble thing in its way, but unless it is based on knowledge and common sense, it will not endure; and I am not at all certain that even now our demagogue might not find an audience who could not explain the faith that is in them; the faith—quoting the words of an old Act of Parliament—that "it is on the navy, through the good Providence of God, that our wealth, safety and strength do chiefly depend"; or, in a still older phrase, dating back to the time of the Plantagenets, that "the navy is the wall and fence of the kingdom." These old declarations are my text for this evening. They are as true or perhaps truer now than ever they were, and really prescribe in outline the whole of our naval policy. Details may vary with varying conditions; the broad principle remains constant and unchanged.

The geographical fact that this country is an island is one that does not appear to have been intelligently grasped by our popular historians, the writers of text-books. They model the accounts of our great wars on those of continental nations, with whom the army is everything, the navy is non-existent; and thus—as I know by every-day experience—it is very common for a young student to have been through a course of English history without having been led to any appreciation of the part which—for good or bad—our navy has taken in the life of the kingdom, the growth and establishment of the Empire. The reign of Edward III, for instance, is generally illustrated with long descriptions and highly-imaginative plans of Crécy and Poitiers; our subsequent reverses are cut very short indeed; and not a word is said to show that, to a very great extent, Crécy and Calais and Poitiers were corollaries of Sluys and Les Espagnols-sur-Mer, and that the reverses resulted from the signal defeat we sustained off Rochelle. It is not my business now to dwell on this neglect of our historians, but rather to put you in the way of supplying the omission by thinking the matter out for yourselves; asking yourselves—to revert to the instance I have just used—what would probably have happened if the English fleet, instead of the French, had been destroyed at Sluys, or similar questions for any of our great wars. I think the answers to which you will be forced will give some of you new ideas on many of the salient points of our history.

But what I now wish to impress on you is that, in time of war, the position of this country is essentially different from that of any other. It has to trust for its defence almost wholly to its navy; the work of the army, important as it is, is attack. What the navy has to do is to occupy the seas in such force as may prevent the enemy's ships from passing, whether for purposes of commerce or of aggression. You will easily understand that—as a rule—ships do not go roaming promiscuously about the ocean, but proceed to their destination by the shortest possible way; that is, for sailing ships, by routes forced on them by the prevailing winds, and for steamers, either direct or as the conditions of the voyage may dictate. Within certain broad limits, these routes are marked on the map as clearly as the Great North Road itself. It is conceivable that ships or even fleets may stray from these tracks, and—with a view to evade an enemy—may take a circuitous route; but such instances will always be exceptional, and ships carrying cargo, whether merchandise or soldiers, will prefer the fixed route.

It is the duty, then, of our ships of war to occupy these routes so that the enemy's ships may not pass, and—which is still more important—that his ships of war may not block the routes so as to hinder the passing of our ships. The first-named object is the stoppage of the enemy's trade, and the preventing any attempt to invade our country or any of its dependencies. In presence of any serious risk, commerce stops itself; beyond a certain limit, owners will not chance it; and there is no cargo more precious, more costly, and as to which the owners are more sensitive, than a cargo of troops. Hence it is an axiom in naval war that territorial aggression— that is, invasion—cannot pass over a sea that is not perfectly commanded; and that the only way to gain that command of the sea is by utterly smashing the enemy's fleet, or by driving it off and shutting it up. So long as it is free and—even though worsted in fight—able to give annoyance, it has been spoken of as "a fleet in being," and no invasion can take place.

From the mere abstract point of view, it might be thought that this prevention of invasion is the most important duty of our navy: in the concrete, however, considering the particular circumstances of these islands, their absolute dependence on sea-borne commerce for daily food and for the raw materials of many of our manufactures, as also the extreme improbability of any enemy undertaking the prolonged, the difficult and needless task of invasion, if his navy is able to stop our commerce, it is difficult not to think that the protection of our commerce is the first and most important duty which our navy will have to perform.

For us, at least, the conditions are now quite different from those of former wars. Even in the great Napoleonic war our population was much smaller, our production of food-stuffs was much greater, agriculture was by far our most important industry; we were practically a self-supporting country. The repeal of the corn laws, the adoption of free trade has altogether changed this independent state. We are no longer self-supporting. Our population, crowding into the towns and engaged in other more lucrative industries, is dependent for its food on corn and flesh—even for eggs, butter and cheese—brought from our colonies or from foreign countries. It is outside my present purpose to enlarge on the possible consequences of war with those countries from which we draw large supplies of corn—Russia, say, or the United States. In any case, Canada should be able to make good the deficiency. I doubt, however, if she could do it without several months or perhaps a year's warning, which she would not have ; it would be a matter of instant urgency ; though I understand she has professed her willingness to undertake the whole contract, and to grow enough wheat for the wants of the United Kingdom, subject to the arrangement of a preferential tariff—an insult to the fetish of free trade which our politicians are not disposed to consider in time of peace. With this, however, I am not now concerned.

But, independent of the source of supply, it would be a question, depending on the relative strength of our navy, whether the corn or any other food-stuffs would be allowed to come at all. And not only food-stuffs. The stopping of the raw materials of manufacture would stop the factories, would stop the wages of the industrial population, and would equally deprive them of their daily bread. I daresay there are many here who have heard their fathers or grandfathers tell of the terrible Lancashire cotton famine of forty years ago, when the

American Civil War put a sharp and sudden stop to the importation of cotton. What that famine of 1862 was to the Lancashire district and the cotton industry, the cutting of our lines of commercial communication would extend to the whole kingdom and, more or less severely, to every branch of manufacture.

This danger of wholesale starvation—direct or indirect— and the necessity of guarding against it is, in fact, the price we pay for the many advantages of free trade. I fancy there are some people who have imagined and do imagine that free trade is all advantage; that it has no countervailing disadvantages. Well, it has, if having to pay something over thirty millions a year for the up-keep of the navy instead of four or five, is a disadvantage. No doubt there are other reasons for this tremendous increase; it is not wholly due to free trade, but it is very largely so; and beyond all question it is to free trade that we owe the absolute dependence of our population on sea-borne food, and of our industrial population on sea-borne staples of manufacture.

It is this that makes me say that the first and most important duty of our navy is absolutely to command and keep open our communications, and to close those of the enemy. Great fights at sea are merely incidents of these main duties; most important and interesting incidents, but still incidents; they are the means to an end, not the end itself. No doubt to many of you, who have read something of our naval history merely as a record of brave fighting and brilliant adventure, this may seem a very prosaic view of these glories of the past, and you may try to believe that the great battles were fought mainly to show how much finer fellow an Englishman is than a Frenchman, or a Spaniard, or a Dutchman. The belief is wholesome enough in its way and I am not going to object to it, only it has nothing to do with the matter in hand. The battles are fought to prevent the enemy occupying or using the water-ways; and, apart from these incidents, the daily work of the navy is to enforce this, not by actual fighting, but by the mere silent threat of its presence—just as the mere presence of a policeman will very commonly prevent a street row; and to say, after a war is over, that—owing to the weakness of the enemy—the navy had no part in it, is very much like saying that the police had no part in preventing a row because they had not to break any heads.

And yet this, or something like it, has been said over and over again. I will not now dwell on the fact—which, however, may give you something to think of by-and-by—that during the late war in South Africa the mere existence and prepared state of our navy kept the communications clear, and prevented any interference on the part of some of our not too friendly neighbours, who might have been quite willing to find their opportunity in any appearance of our weakness. I will ask you rather to refer to the history of a war that took place about the middle of last century and has been generally spoken of as the "Crimean War." It was, of course, a war with Russia, in which—by the action of our navy—the fighting was almost entirely confined to the Crimea; so much so that our popular histories seem to give the idea that that, or something like it, was the natural and necessary course of such a war. If they make any mention of our fleet in the Baltic it is only to say that it accomplished nothing. In reality, it accomplished a very great deal. At that time the Russians had in the Gulf of Finland some thirty ships of the line of battle, besides smaller vessels, which had all the will in the world to come into the North Sea or the open ocean and work all possible havoc, but were unable or unwilling to face the allied fleet—mostly English—which during the open seasons of 1854 and 1855 kept the Russian ships closely bottled up in Cronstadt. The rendering this large Russian fleet absolutely innocuous during the whole time of the war, and the finding employment for a very considerable land army scattered along the coasts, was the important work of that Baltic fleet which your histories will tell you did little or nothing.

I bring this forward as a marked illustration of what I mean in saying that by far the larger and more important work of the navy is of a kind which the popular historian does not understand and cannot recognise. Now that I have shown you how to look for it you will find it an exercise both interesting and profitable to examine—for instance—the share of the navy in the Peninsular War, or in the celebrated conquest of Canada; and how entirely the loss of our North American Colonies—in the military, not in the political sense—was due to the inefficiency of the navy and its temporary forgetfulness of the maxim handed down from the lips of Blake, "It is not for us to meddle with State affairs, but to keep foreigners from fooling us."

You will now, I hope, be able fully to realise that it is not in a mere sentimental sense, or as asserting the theoretical unity of the Empire, but in the direct, practical, bread-and-beef, £ s. d. sense, that I say that the condition and well-being of the navy is of interest and importance to every living soul within our boundaries; not only within the shores of this island, or of our near sister on the other side of St George's Channel, but of our vast trans-oceanic dependencies—the Dominion of Canada, the Commonwealth of Australia, the Empire of India, and all islands and territories, wherever situated. If any of you happen to have lived for any length of time in one of our remote islands—Hong Kong, say, or Suva, or even Vancouver—this will seem common-place; for it has already been borne in on you that the navy is the chain which binds and holds together the whole Empire; that without that chain the Empire would fall to pieces on the first whisper of war; and that with that chain insufficiently strong and liable to be broken the Empire would again be disintegrated, even as it was in the American Revolution, 120 years ago.

And now that we understand what it is that our navy has to do—the keeping open the sea routes for our own ships and blocking them for those of the enemy—we have to consider how it has to do it. If the enemy attempts to hold one of these routes by main force, that is by a fleet of great ships, such as are now commonly called battle-ships, the immediate duty of our navy, or rather of such part of it as is appointed to the task, is to find that fleet, to defeat it, to destroy it, or to drive it back to its own or some friendly harbour, and there to keep it; to ensure, as far as possible, that it does not come out again. In this you will recognise an operation that has been very conspicuous in most modern wars—the blockade of an enemy's port, as Brest, Toulon, Cadiz, Cronstadt. But the term blockade is liable to misconception. Nelson always insisted that he never blockaded Toulon; that, on the contrary, he gave the French every opportunity of coming out. And this must be taken as the meaning of a naval blockade—the watching a port so that the enemy cannot come out without fighting. If they do not feel equal to fighting they remain inside, under cover of their fortifications.

There they have been safe, or comparatively so. Against the fortifications with which the great continental nations guard the approaches to their military ports, ships can do nothing. This has been recognised by all our great admirals for the last 200 years. Hawke, Boscawen, Howe, St Vincent, Cornwallis, Nelson, closely watched Brest, or Toulon, or Cadiz, for months and years, longing for the enemy to come out, but never conceiving a possibility of going in to bring them out. And yet, when Napier went up the Baltic in 1854, people took it into their heads that he was going immediately to force his way in past the batteries of Cronstadt—the most formidable in existence—and railed bitterly against him when they found that he had no intention of trying to do so. How silly it would have been was shown the same season in the Black Sea, where the ships off Sebastopol, attempting a diversion in support of the army, were very roughly handled, without being able to accomplish anything.

It is now much debated whether blockades in any way resembling those of the past will be possible in the future. No doubt the conditions will be very different. It is not only that steam complicates the problem; that on a dark night a fast, full-powered steamer may slip out of the watched port, followed by another and another, in a way that was not possible for a sailing ship, which was not under such perfect control and whose spread of canvas would be more likely to betray her; it is—much more—that by the use, or the dread of the use of modern inventions—sea mines, torpedoes, submarines—the watching fleet will be compelled to keep at such a distance that, on a dark night, the whole inside fleet, together or in detachments, may get away, and the morning dawn on an empty harbour. It is impossible for anyone to say in advance how this problem will be solved; but it may be held for certain that in the next naval war the solution will be sought for in the most practical ways. It would be rash to assert that it will be found without many abortive attempts and failures; on which, and on the decay of British seamanship, or on the want of intelligence of British naval officers, the halfpenny newspapers will have much to say.

In any case, however, there is no reason to suppose that the blockade of an enemy's coast will be more stringent in the future than ever it was in the past. The war with Russia was exceptional, both from the paucity of the enemy's ships and—still more—from the situation of the harbours and the formation of the coast lines. But the French coast, lying exposed to a stormy sea, has always proved difficult; and though the escape of a large fleet could generally be prevented, evasions were sometimes found possible, and small squadrons often got to sea without much difficulty; frigates and smaller vessels without any. And when these got well away they might do, and indeed very often did do an enormous amount of mischief before they could be caught. I think we may count it as certain that, should we be again at war with France, history would repeat itself in many of its phases; and the particular phase which may be expected to repeat itself is the escape of many commerce destroyers and their consequent attack on our commerce. It is then a problem of the most serious importance how, in a future war—I am speaking only of a war with a great naval power—how, in a war, say, with France, our commerce is to be protected.

There are many who assert that all the conditions are so different from anything hitherto known that past experience is no guide, and that the problem has to be attacked as a perfectly new thing. There are others, among whom I would range myself, who incline to the opinion that—where man is the agent—there is nothing new under the sun, and that if you want to consider how a thing is to be done in the future the first and best guide to consult is the history of the past. Now on this point the history of the past is remarkably clear and definite. In our old wars—it is perhaps unnecessary here to go farther back than the French Revolution—merchant ships divided themselves roughly into two classes—"runners" and "the trade." Ships forming "the trade" assembled at the appointed place—the Downs, for instance, or St Helen's, at home—and there waited till one or more ships of war, of such size and number as were judged necessary, took charge of them, sailed in company with them, defended them against attack, and if overpowered, made—or were expected to make— such resistance as to give the trade time to escape. Such a fleet of merchant ships and the protecting men-of-war was called a convoy.

Now, in time of war, by far the largest part of our trade sailed in convoy—to Lisbon and the Mediterranean, North America, the West Indies, East Indies, or China; the details of the arrangements for convoys were fully recorded and are perfectly well known. As a general rule they answered very satisfactorily; and though at least two, perhaps three gigantic disasters are on record, they were of an earlier date than the

French Revolution. On a smaller scale mishaps were not unfrequent. In a fleet of three or four hundred merchant ships of different sizes and different rates of sailing, commanded by men unused to discipline and each wishing to show that he was captain of his own ship, it was difficult, or rather impossible to keep them all together, in their appointed stations. The more weatherly ships would get to windward; the faster, eager to anticipate the market, would get ahead as far as they could; the slower or more leewardly would drop astern or to leeward; and the enemy's cruisers or privateers, closely attending on them, like sharks attending on a slaver, picked up a good many. It was, of course, the object of the commander of the convoy to prevent this as much as possible; but it was most commonly a thankless office, which entailed on the unfortunate man a great deal of abuse from the merchant skippers whose vagaries he restrained, bitter complaints from the merchants whose ships and cargoes were snapped up and carried off; and after all, when the voyage was happily brought to an end, he seldom obtained promotion or acknowledgment. Naturally the service was not popular, but it was necessary; it had to be done, and was done well; so well, that the war risks of ships sailing in convoy were held by the underwriters as not greater than the ordinary risks from perils of the sea, that is to say, they about doubled the insurance in time of peace. But then the conditions as to the convoy were strict, and ships which could be shown to have been captured in consequence of their neglect of regulations forfeited the insurance.

There were, however, many inconveniences. It was the object of a merchant to get his cargo out, and his ship, with the return cargo, home again; it was the skipper's object to push on and show what a splendid ship he had and that he was just the man for her. The loss of time in waiting for the trade to assemble, and afterwards by the slow sailing of the convoy, was extremely irritating to the owner and master of a fast ship; so that it is not to be wondered at that many were willing to take their chance as "runners," and trust to "a clean pair of heels" and their own armament to escape from or beat off the enemy's cruisers. The insurance offices did not look on this plan of independent sailing with any favour, and either refused point-blank to have anything to do with ships so sailing, or placed the premium so high as to be virtually prohibitive; and thus, as a rule, "runners" took the risks themselves. Sometimes it answered fairly well: sometimes it proved a ghastly failure. When two or three clever Frenchmen, with good fast ships, worked in company, runners had a poor chance. The historic instance of this is the partnership of Surcouf in the *Revenant*, a privateer, and Epron in the *Piémontaise*, a national frigate, who, working together in the Bay of Bengal in 1807, scourged the Calcutta commerce to an enormous extent. Running proved quite ineffectual, and of the ships they captured then none was able to attempt any defence. But even a heavier armament was found unavailing. The *Kent*, an East-Indiaman, with about 150 fighting men on board, was captured without much difficulty by the *Confiance*, a small French privateer; and the *Warren Hastings*, another East-Indiaman, with the nominal armament of a heavy frigate, was taken by the *Piémontaise*, which was not specially efficient as a fighting ship.

Here then we have the teachings of history:

Convoy:—Much loss of time; small risks.

Running:—Possible gain of time; risks great; insurance prohibitive.

Self-defence:—Quite inefficient.

How do these apply to the present time? It is very commonly urged that merchants and ship-owners, now or in the future, will not consent to the delays of a system of convoy. There is no doubt that hurry is a principal feature of modern trade, but the wisdom of ages is embodied in two words—*festina lente*; and it is impossible to say what, under stress, ship-owners may or may not consent to. They will certainly wish to reduce their losses to a minimum; and if they find that the insurance offices insist on convoy, that a ship captured without convoy is all loss, that a runner is very likely to be captured, then, I think, they will accept convoy as the least of the threatening evils; and indeed, when all competition is in the same boat, the loss is relatively reduced.

But, it is urged, our large mail steamers, the so-called "ocean greyhounds," are faster and of greater endurance than any cruisers, and would be safe from their pursuit. From the pursuit of one, perhaps, though not necessarily; less probably from the pursuit of two or three, coming on them from different points of the compass; in running from one, the chase might be running into the clutches of another. As to self-defence, it would be very right and proper for any such steamer to have some armament, so as not to be at the mercy of any insignificant vessel, which, by craft or otherwise, could manage to get alongside her; but I do not believe in the possibility of a merchant ship defending herself with success against an efficient ship of war.

Against all this, however, it is urged that it must be rendered impossible, or at any rate highly improbable, for a runner to have to escape from two or three enemy's cruisers; they must be swept out of the way; and this is to be done by a system of patrols, in almost the same manner that a piece of road may be patrolled by policemen. I would not for a moment say that this is impossible; on the contrary, I think that in some circumstances, and within strict limitations, such a system may be extremely valuable; but that, in general, the cost would be prohibitive. Bear in mind that it is a measure of relative not of absolute defence, and especially for the protection of commerce. Now, logically, the protection of commerce is as much a question of money as the commerce itself. The nation cannot be called on to pay more for the protection of commerce than the commerce is worth; and of two methods, equally efficient, the one which costs least is the best.

The idea of effectively patrolling the great ocean routes, in their entire length, may be dismissed as impossible; but the patrolling of short routes, over which the traffic is relatively large, such, for instance, as the route down the coast of Portugal, from Cape Finisterre to Cape St Vincent, would be economically possible; the Red Sea, again, could be secured at a very small cost; as also the track from Aden to Bombay; and the more distant eastern routes—to Calcutta, China, and Australia or New Zealand, would be largely secured on this side of the Cape of Good Hope. Every French ship—if we were at war with France—that got past the Cape of Good Hope ought to be, would have to be specially looked after, shadowed and provided for. From this point of view the recent French acquisitions in Tonquin and Cochin China may be considered as valuable allies; they will hive, so to speak, the French ships, and our work will be made so much the easier; though, indeed, without these territories it is difficult to see how French ships could venture east of the Cape. In the old war they could only do so when the French held Mauritius and the Dutch islands; when these fell into our hands the French depredations in the eastern seas came to an end.

The English Channel and the Mediterranean fall into a somewhat different category. Every possible care should be taken to prevent the appearance of an enemy's ship in the Channel, or, to repeat the language and the thoughts of our forefathers, the invasion of English territory; for in time of war—and indeed in time of peace too—they were accustomed to maintain that the boundary of English territory was the high-water mark on the coast of France. We know how, in the old wars, French privateers swarmed in the narrow seas— from Dungeness to the Naze. These were often of the most paltry descriptions; sometimes in the guise of fishing-boats, pilot-boats, which were allowed to get alongside without suspicion that a thing so insignificant could be dangerous. Of course we all know that by the Declaration of Paris "privateering is and remains abolished"; but the Declaration of Paris does not say that the French Government is not at liberty to take up every coasting or river steamer in the north of France, put a one-, or two- or three-pounder on board her, with a dozen or twenty men, and call her a man-of-war; that is, if they feel bound by the Declaration of Paris, which is far from certain if they find it inconvenient. We certainly do feel ourselves bound by the Declaration of Paris; but, as well as the French, we are at full liberty to turn all the small steamers on the Thames into men-of-war sufficient to overpower those I have just been speaking of, giving them of course a backbone of efficient ships—gunboats and third or second class cruisers—so as to give them an undoubted superiority. I see no difficulty in the way of making the Channel and the narrow seas absolutely safe.

The Mediterranean is different. It has frequently been urged that the commanding the seas and the protecting our commerce, as I have sketched it, is quite beyond the power of our navy, and that on the outbreak of war the first consideration must be the limiting of our efforts by withdrawing from the Mediterranean. It is said that, with the French at Toulon and Biserta, the position of a British fleet at Malta would be extremely perilous, and that our proper course would be to get out of that perilous position, leave Malta to defend itself, and relinquish the commerce of the Mediterranean and the route by the Suez Canal. This is really a question of strategy rather than of policy, and with strategy I have now no business; though I will so far deviate from my strict course as to say that, in my opinion, the suggested strategy is based on false conceptions and is altogether absurd. Speaking of it as policy, I will go farther and say it is iniquitous; that the commerce of the Mediterranean and the route by the Canal are necessary to us; and that if we are to be beaten out of them our best traditions teach us to take our beating fighting, not lying down. But in fact, there is no strategical reason why we should be beaten out of them; and with our line of cruisers or occasional battle-ships resting on Gibraltar and Malta and our Mediterranean fleet, the weak strategical position seems to me that of the French, not of the English, and the protection of our commerce does not present any abnormal difficulties.

Patrolling in the open ocean is a very different thing, and for the great ocean routes a perfect system thereof is—as I have already said—impossible; but I think they may be so far guarded as to render it economically possible for the "ocean greyhounds" to take the risk of independent voyages; for others, for slower vessels, I see no effective substitute for the old-fashioned system of convoy, though it may be modified by dividing the trade into detachments, according to the speed of the steamers—classifying them in fact. In this way the loss of time would be greatly reduced; the temptation for the fast steamers to leave the slower would be done away with, and the protective power of the escort greatly increased.

Sailing vessels still form an appreciable part of our merchant shipping, but it has been very commonly asserted that, on the first breath of war, these would all be laid up. I do not know that this would be necessary: from the purely naval point of view I do not think it would be. I think it would be entirely a question of money. Though the initial cost of sailing vessels is less than that of steamers, they are in reality more costly, from the greater number of men they require, and still more from the very much longer time they take on the voyage. When the delays of convoy largely increase this "longer time," it is very possible that the increased cost will render it economically better to lay the sailing vessels up till the return of peace. The question is not one of naval protection, for that could be better now than ever; it is simply a question of the economics of trade.

But the whole problem of protection is based on the assumption that we have the superior strength at sea. With that we are safe. Without it the work which I have outlined cannot be done; our coasts cannot be secured from insult; our territories from invasion; our commerce from ruin. There is an old familiar story of a cat which had but one way to safety, and by taking that way was safe, whilst the fox, that knew of fifty ways, was caught by the hounds and broken up. It is for us to see that our one way to safety is secure; that our navy is superior in strength to any possible enemy. That is the whole essence of our naval policy: Keep well the sea!

THE TRANSFORMATION OF GERMANY
BY PRUSSIA.

BY PROFESSOR ERICH MARCKS, PH.D.

You are reviewing here the progress and events of the nineteenth century, and you want to hear something about Germany from the lips of a German. I am to tell you what has been, as far as I can judge, most important and characteristic for my country. I will do so, and, as the time is short, I will direct my attention to this subject alone. And here let me say at once: the political history of Germany, indeed the whole development of Germany, is summed up in the title of this lecture, "The Transformation of Germany by Prussia." I shall have to answer the following questions:—What was the old Germany like at the beginning of the century, and what was Prussia? Then what did Prussia do in and for Germany? How strong did Prussia's influence on the nation finally become? How does it act at the present day, and what are its limits? For one thing is obvious: Germany has changed tremendously. It has risen from disruption to unity, from weakness to strength; the whole national character seems to have altered. The nation of poets and thinkers has become a nation of power and business. And, as far as it is possible to squeeze this process into a single sentence, you can say, "Prussia has effected this." Germany has become Prussian.

The great difficulty of German history for a foreigner is that it has so many local centres. It has them even to-day, but to-day it has in Berlin one more important than all the others. In earlier times there were always some common features and interests, but the disruptive tendencies used to predominate. And a hundred years ago it seemed almost as though there was nothing but disruption in the country.

It was the old process of German history that the Empire grew weak and the national state broke up; on its ruins had arisen in the course of many centuries the separate states, of ever-increasing strength; a crowd of states differing from each other as widely as possible in form, covered the German soil. They were most motley in the South and West of the Empire; small states, spiritual and temporal, bishoprics and abbeys, duchies, principalities, counties, cities, were there mixed up together; and even when Napoleon the First had stamped out most of the smallest, and had secularised the ecclesiastical ones, there still remained a considerable number of small, but especially of medium and larger-sized states. Among them were Hanover, Saxony, Bavaria, Würtemberg, Baden, Hessen; states of great self-confidence, especially Bavaria; states of active internal government, of ancient intellectual life; many of them had distinctive features, and a rich past; but none of them possessed great strength of their own as states. It was for the most part a little world, full of life and colour, important as regards culture, but with no strong and steady impulse, and, taken together, of no assured position or importance in Europe. One of the two great states which emerged from this swarm, Austria, was more outside Germany than in, and for the most part not German at all. The one and only state that led a vital existence as such, striving greatly after power at home and abroad, and concentrating in itself all the strength of the people, was the kingdom of Prussia.

Beside this world of midgets Prussia had long posed as something special. While German culture developed elsewhere under cramped and often unenlightened conditions, in Prussia the glorious house of Hohenzollern trained a poor population

up to the strength that befits a state. Out of isolated, powerless provinces, it formed a great, united state; it breathed
into this state energy, ambition, compactness, and discipline;
frugally, amid privations, it created by rigid perseverance the
strongest army in Germany, and side by side with it the best
and most reliable bureaucracy. The independence of the
separate provinces and the political power of the nobility were
broken; the monarchy, bureaucracy, and army, as unifying
forces, were set above everything. Frederick William the First
and Frederick the Second built up an enlightened despotism
which was the best government on the Continent in the eighteenth century; the nobility obligingly fell in with the scheme;
there arose the conception of a Prussian state, a Prussian patriotism of a special and powerful kind, which became a historic
power on the battlefields of the Seven Years' War. Everything
culminated in the king and his will, in international activity, in
the politics of a great power; Prussia was directed from above.
In the separate provinces the nobles certainly remained strong;
submissive though they were in affairs of state, they retained
a large share of self-government; in the east they were the
prevailing class, the magistrates and governors in their districts.
The absolutism did not tend to downright centralisation, such
as was sought by France : royal absolutism was combined with
aristocratic self-government. And after the defeat of 1806
a new element entered this world of monarchy and aristocracy:
the new civil ideas of the time. Ideals of French and English
origin, ideals of the freedom of the individual, found their
opportunity, in the epoch of the reformers, in the epoch of
Stein, Hardenberg, and Scharnhorst, to set free all the forces of
the land which Napoleon had reduced in size. The universal
obligation to military service was created, the emancipation
of the peasants was completed, the barriers between classes
were broken down, privileges were done away with, the individual was fully respected and allowed self-control; Stein
aimed at complete self-government, and was actually able to

grant it to the cities. The Crown and the aristocracy were limited; the state was to be brought nearer to the whole people. There was still no Constitution, but the popular elements penetrated deep into the structure of the old state. The most important innovation of all was the universal obligation to military service. The old army of foreign mercenaries and forced levies was replaced by the national army, that respected the dignity of the individual, and made all the forces of the state available. It was easier to introduce the system here because Prussia was still chiefly agrarian: the other countries of Europe which followed suit later, found it more difficult. Thus an organism was created which blended itself at all points intimately with Prussian life in all its aspects; army and people became one unity, the national spirit responded cheerfully to the military drill and was itself trained by it; the new army was more humane, freer, more contented by far than the old, and at the same time an extraordinary source of power for a state that was still small. This military law of 1814 together with the city self-government, remained the best and most vital heritage from the period of Reform: at once thoroughly modern and thoroughly Prussian, the most characteristic and important law of the Prussian and German world, and one of the most important of the nineteenth century altogether. After the defeat of France, after 1815, the old polity certainly predominated in Prussia; the reforms remained standing, but did not develop further. The Crown and aristocracy came once more to the front, and the period of new creations was followed by a quieter period of gradual working. The East and the West, the old and the new provinces of the wide-reaching dominion grew gradually united, but the brilliant life of 1807 gave way to a less lively period. Prussia fell back again into its North-German separate existence.

Even at that time, both before and after Napoleon's overthrow, clear-thinking individuals in Germany saw that only this Prussian state, strong in arms and full of character, harsh and bluff though it might be, only this German great power would be able to form a future united Germany. But it is not by chance that a half-century elapsed before this came about. The rest of Germany was at that time by no means prepared to submit to Prussian leadership, or indeed to any leadership whatever. For many generations the Germans had lived apart in small groups; the tribes, the provinces, but especially the individual states with their own firmly-rooted dynasties, insisted on their independence. And now the modern Liberalism permeated the small states of South Germany, and filled their Parliaments. Prussia was still without a Constitution; from 1815 to 1840 South and North drifted only further and further apart. Prussia was again, in spite of many innovations, remarkable for its army, administration, and political power; the rest of Germany lacked power, and possessed all the more strongly the spirit especially characteristic of the old Germany: the spirit of an idealism not conversant with politics and unable to grasp realities.

There were various great currents which prepared and then brought on the union of Germany: at the end they all worked together, but only late and with difficulty were they brought together into the same channel. There was a political, an intellectual, an economic current. The political union was based on the strength of Prussia, as we shall see later on. The intellectual union was of another origin. When Germany was still politically quite divided she had created her great literature; when Napoleon's fist subjugated the German states, Goethe and Schiller were ours, we possessed the wealth of a creative half-century, we possessed a great poetry, a great philosophy; these intellectual possessions showed the Germans that they were a nation, a rich and distinguished nation, notwithstanding their want of power in the world. And this feeling of the unity and greatness of our culture contributed enormously towards fostering the desire for a further unity of political life. Then came the doctrines of the French Revolution and Liberalism, the doctrine of freedom, of the right of every nation to be its own master, to make its own arrangements, and order its life according to its needs. In Germany also an idealism of national aspiration grew up; Germany also pressed forward, filled with a belief in national sovereignty; she yearned for unity, not only because it meant power, but because also all the internal forces of the nation, each individual citizen even, would thereby gain moral emancipation, and be made nobler, freer, better. There was a strongly abstract and dogmatic character about this idealising of unity: it was dominated by theory. And this was just the peculiarity of all German thought from 1800 to 1850: it was theoretical, idealistic, metaphysical. The Germans did not live in really powerful states; they had no constitutions, or only narrow, insignificant ones; they had no acquaintance whatever with political actualities; their highest performance and their deepest pride was their poetry and philosophy, splendid, pure, and rich; but their thought was directed towards the universal and the ideal; it sought the upper air, and did not keep to firm ground; even now, when it became political, it was as a rule more like French than English thought: it was literary, abstract, *doctrinaire*, universal.

The increasing strength of this national idealism contributed enormously towards making German unity possible, and necessary. But idealism could not create unity. Realities stood in its way—the old states, and organised power; idealism could condemn them, but not set them aside, and it condemned them far too hurriedly.

Besides this there was a new movement, also making for unity, but quite different in essence—the economic and social movement. Unity was not only the aspiration of the German intellect, but the economic life of Germany demanded it and laid the first foundations. While the theorists were looking for national sovereignty and a national constitution, Prussia founded the German Customs Union (*Zollverein*). For the division of Germany into forty different customs districts meant economic death. Surrounded on all sides by great nations with customs boundaries, each a self-contained economic organism, Germany was obliged to create a common customs tariff and make itself an economic organism too, if it wished to remain or to become economic at all. The politics of Prussia as a state, combined with the general want felt by all Germans, created a corporate organism, the Customs Union, which finally covered almost the same limits as the present Empire. Austria remained outside, because she was still economically backward, but Germany, from about 1830 onwards, when she was still politically divided, constituted a unity as far as customs-duties were concerned, a unity under Prussia, a unity for trade and commerce, for agrarian and industrial production, a unity within and without. Then came the railways, from 1840 onwards, and welded the bonds of union closer and closer. And on this soil there grew up, as the chief supporter of the economic coherence, a powerful working citizen class. It needed a wide area for production and consumption, it filled Germany with its activity, and became universally German.

But while a new Germany, civic and economic, was thus growing up, a new order of thought sprang up at the same time. The one-sided idealistic thought peculiar to Germany was gradually supplemented and at last supplanted by a new kind of thought which I may call realistic. This transition to realism is of course not merely German. In England and France from 1820 and 1830 onwards literature turned more and more decidedly towards realism; the lofty poetry of Lord Byron's generation was followed by the splendid series of novelists of the Victorian Age; French Romanticism gave way to the period of Balzac; and if the drama and the novel in Germany took to realism, they were only obeying the general tendency of the times. But this change of direction meant far more for Germany than for the neighbouring countries, because the whole life of Germany, as we have seen, had hitherto had such a strong bias towards idealism. The metaphysical philosophy now went to pieces; the natural sciences sprang up, and the practical arts became a leading force. In Germany they were still more fertile of innovation than elsewhere. In Germany the rise of the economic movement was the transition to a new period; the economic agitation attracted attention; the development of German industry created quite new objects and directions of interest, almost recreated the general view of things; men's minds began to break loose from the universal and the ideal, and to grasp everywhere more firmly the objective. And by this means the spirit of Germany gradually, of its own accord, drew nearer to the Prussian polity—and thus we are brought back to our subject.

For the Prussian state had always been filled with a sense of reality. That which was unattainable at Stuttgart, Frankfort, Weimar, or Dresden, had here been predominant: the sense of great political actuality, that is the sense of *power*. France and England had long had this spirit; in Germany it was possessed by Prussia alone; and the Germans had complained of the cut-and-dry severity of the Prussian state. If the appreciation of material forces now increased in Germany, then was also Germany inwardly approximating towards the Prussian state as the corner-stone of concrete political energy. Prussia supported the Customs Union; Prussia's old, intense way of thinking, and her character as a great power, became something more intelligible and akin to the new Germany that was becoming "realistic" too. And only the power of Prussia was able to satisfy the desire and the need of unity felt by the German people. This Prussia did.

It is not my business to relate how it was done. I had to sketch the contrasts in German life: here the old Germany, divided, unpolitical, literary, there the old Prussia, sturdy, unamiable, political, "realistic"; and you see, the two have begun to draw closer together. I will just remind you, in a word or two, of the stages on the way.

In 1848 the German political idealists sought union. They did so, as was their wont, with much thought, ardour, and splendid inspiration, but abstractly. They wanted unconditional unity, democratic and integral, on the basis of the sovereignty of the people, the nation. They ignored the old states; and their attempt, with all its high and noble motives, tragically failed at the outset.

The old states and dynasties were too strong, the new thing was too impracticable; the old separate states rose up afresh soon after 1848. The Revolutionists had wanted to place Prussia at the head, but only as the servant of the nation; Prussia also was to cease to be a state by itself, a power on its own account. She was to create the nation's ideal—complete unity—and then merge itself in the nation. But Prussia would not and could not do this. She was far too great a power herself; she could very well rule Germany, but not serve. The Revolutionists had wanted to attack Austria because there was only room for one great power in the German polity, if it was to be united, and because Austria was not German. In 1850 Austria had defended herself with vigour and success; she had won back her hegemony; for ten years she was the prevailing power; all thoughts of German unity were crushed, and even Prussia was prostrate.

And yet Prussia remained the state of the future in Germany. She was already the basis of the economic unity and greatness of the nation; the Prussian citizen class became gradually the first in Germany. But above all, the Prussian state, as a state, was the only one that was mighty enough to carry through the unification in the face of Europe and to compel the Germans themselves thereto. It was indeed the only great power of the German world proper. And from 1860 onwards it rose higher and higher. King William the

First made good once more the stability of the old Prussia. He reorganised and enlarged the army, making it stronger and readier to fight; he reduced the militia (*Landwehr*) and strengthened the regiments of the line; he insisted on discipline and technical training above everything. In internal affairs he kept a firm grasp on the power of the Crown, in spite of the liberal constitution; he placed Prussia, as a stout military power, in the hands of the sovereign. And then came the one strong man who knew how to use this power, who with indomitable will set the Prussian state its old task again, the task which Frederick the Great had left behind him, the task of expanding its power. Prince Bismarck induced Prussia to undertake to improve her position in Germany. While in the German Federation, her hands had been tied by Austria, by the kingdoms of Bavaria, Saxony, and so on; the others had held her down. Out of this position she was raised by Bismarck. He determined to decide the old rivalry with Austria by force of arms; brimful of the great political egoism of Prussia, an out-and-out "realist," he set Prussia on to fight for power. He wanted to bring Prussia to the top—that was his solution of the German question—not under commission from the German nation, but as the servant of the Prussian executive. And he did so. As an independent great power Prussia defeated Austria, and destroyed the infirm old German Confederation. Round the nucleus of the power of Prussia a new beginning was made to organise the German polity. Such was the origin of the North German Confederation of 1866; Prussia was the predominant partner; the other North German states joined it with fixed rights, but still only as additional members. For Prussia and for the new Confederation the leading power remained the Prussian Crown. Side by side with it the dynasties of Saxony, Mecklenburg, the Thuringian Princes, and so on, remained as they had been; it was the old Germany with its different states, but they had become subject to the Confederate state; the old was not taken away, but preserved, and yet subordinated to the new. On exactly the same principles Bismarck constructed the new German Empire in 1870–71. The Southern states, Bavaria, Würtemberg, Baden, Hessen, entered the existing Confederation ; they retained their own governments, they surrendered to the community only the necessary minimum of their rights. Within the Empire the states remained as they were ; Prussia above all remained as she was. She swayed the North German Confederation and the German Empire, she did not dissolve herself ; she had become stronger than before, and had completely asserted her special character. Prussia had put an iron girdle round the whole of German life ; the old Prussia of Frederick the Second had become the lord or at least the leader of the new Germany; only thus, through stable power, had unity been attainable, through stern strength and force of arms, through political energy ; not without the preparatory work of German idealism ; not through idealism, however, but through the determination and compulsion of the old Prussian power.

And what is this new Germany like, that was created between 1862 and 1871, the Germany of the last 30 years ?

I must not here analyse the complex Imperial Constitution, which is not easily described. It includes three elements : Prussia, the monarchical leader through whom unity was realised ; the aristocracy of the separate states of Germany, the basis of the political fabric ; and the great mass of the German people as the united, democratic community : that is, Emperor, Federal Council (*Bundesrat*), and Imperial Parliament (*Reichstag*). Prussia with her King is strictly only the strongest of the separate states ; the Emperor does not properly stand above the other Princes ; in the Federal Council he has only a minority of votes ; and yet, much as formal appearances are against it, as a matter of fact Germany is ruled principally by the Emperor. Such things are often judged more clearly abroad than at home ; it would sound absurd to an Englishman if anybody tried to describe the German Empire to him as something different from a monarchy. Well, politically it *is* a monarchy, and the Emperor is its monarch. So it was brought into being by William the First and Prince Bismarck, and so it has remained, almost more clearly even than before, under William the Second.

And more than this. In very important respects the old Germany has been psychically transformed, after the Prussian model, by Prussian, Bismarckian "realism." The tendency to actuality has become completely victorious since 1871. The ideal has receded into the background; power has come to the front. The old political idealism of the Germans had aimed at a liberal constitution, if possible with a sovereign Parliament. Since 1860 and 1870 and 1880 this ideal has more and more completely broken down. Germany, surrounded by rivals, and still internally divided into numerous parties and groups, is ruled by the Government, by the monarchy, and not by a Parliamentary majority. The weighty mass of monarchy has conquered; and I believe.that without this support it would be impossible for Germany to exist. And the interest in forms of constitution and constitutional ideals has become less; actuality, strength has become more important to Germans than the form. In place of the constitutional struggle, the conflict between Liberal, Conservative, and Monarchistic opinion, came a new struggle over the material import of political life. Social development has pushed social problems to the fore; Liberalism, which, for the most part, left social and economic processes to take their course, was crowded out by the reviving old Prussian tradition. Frederick the Second had taught, and it was repeated by Bismarck, that the state must seek also to influence and control social development, economic development, and cut off the excrescences : the state is in every respect responsible for the whole life of the population. The state and the bureaucracy have again become stronger in modern Germany than before 1870 ; the customs policy, the transition to protective duties, has given the Empire new means and powers; tariff questions, economic questions, social questions have formed the staple of political strife in Germany since 1880. And economic life itself, both economic sense and economic success, has grown greatly. Under the protection of a united and victorious national state German industry and commerce have at length risen, not without fluctuations, certainly, but in spite of them, to a position of world-wide importance; the progress is patent to all eyes. This extraordinary leap upward is not due to Prussia alone; the whole of Germany has contributed to it; but we may well say that the peculiar character of the Prussian system has played a great part in the upward movement. German economic enterprise of the last thirty years has been praised by many foreigners—your countrymen not excepted—for its educational methods, good technical training, and intelligent and united direction of forces: German labour has learnt a lesson from the Prussian army.

In fact, universal military service has won Germany over to itself and the Prussian genius. Even in England you perceive well enough that one of the decisive points lies here, though the two great Teutonic nations stand so wide apart on this question, and find it so difficult to understand each other. Germany, it has been often said, has been militarised by Prussia. Outwardly the country has adopted armaments, and barracks, and warlike exercises; inwardly it has imbued itself with the military spirit, which previously had been cultivated only in Prussia. The military spirit has educated the Germans; through its school—a school of intelligence, will, organisation—the majority of our manhood pass; economic efficiency has been increased thereby; we have been disciplined politically; we have been made keener and sturdier. Think of Swabia in the first thirty years of the nineteenth century, and see how this world of philosophers and poets, standing aloof in obstinate independence, has changed. Thought has been turned towards realities, organisation, the systematic co-operation of forces, the material objects of life. Above all, thinkers have come round to esteem political power. The character of the Germans, both as a people and as individuals, has become, through their common membership of one powerful unity, stronger and loftier; their views of the world have become broader and wider. The sense of nationality, which has long been second nature to the earlier developed peoples of Western Europe, was late in developing here, but it has developed. The feeling for the honour of the country, the appreciation of its power, and of power in general as one of the greatest factors in the life of the nations, all these, and the race for power, have become stronger and more conscious. We have learnt to look forth into the world and to pursue our interests not only in Europe but also beyond the seas; Prince Bismarck taught us this, and William the Second has continued expanding his work. In this respect the old Prussian impulse has spread over Germany, and has itself become more universal. The new Germany is impelled to make itself of account among the nations of the earth by its commerce and power; the old style may have been pleasanter, but this new development was, as every critic must admit, natural and inevitable for a nation capable of life. I recognise fully that this transition has not been accomplished without losses. We have become poorer in pure and high idealism, in calm and collected repose, introspection, and the old poetry of German life; but then the new period, this age of masses and expanding will, has a poetry and inspiration of its own, personified in the Emperor William. Manhood always must give up something of the sweetness of childhood.

But really, is the Old so completely buried by the New in Germany to-day? I said that Germany has become Prussian, united, "realistic," monarchical. But it would be a gross misconception, a misconception into which foreigners, I believe, often fall, to suppose that Germany lives under the dominion of a centralised autocracy. On the contrary, the features just described are everywhere strongly counterbalanced: everywhere in Germany there is variety and independence. It would be wrong to form a too narrow estimate of the efficiency of German Parliamentary institutions. Our great parties all, supported by universal suffrage, exercise, directly or indirectly, considerable influence on public life and on Government, in this world which grows more and more democratic. I have pointed out, that a sovereign Parliament of the English type would not do for Germany; but everywhere the influence of the Chambers is great on the legislation, administration, and policy both of the Empire and of the separate states—greater than it appears at first sight. These political bodies are important. So too is the independence of the separate states and of the separate provinces and districts. The confederate states, even if the most important functions of state have passed over to the Empire, have retained plenty of individual life; they have never ceased to watch over the interests of culture; the Empire has entrusted them with new and ample tasks, for instance through its social legislation; their administration has become greater, not smaller, since 1871. And they have themselves remained special centres of culture, of a strong individual character, which is consciously, even jealously, guarded. How different Bavaria and Würtemberg have remained from Prussia; how different, too, Baden. How different, again, Hamburg and Bremen. Everywhere the local life has remained strong, without injury hitherto to the unity of the Empire. All the tribes and states work together in the new Germany. Deeper down, moreover, in the provinces of Prussia and of the other larger states, in the counties, in the districts and parishes of town and country, everywhere a local administration exists by the side of the powerful bureaucracy; and everywhere since the sixties, and not least in Prussia itself, this self-government has undergone further marked development. Our towns, watched over by the state, form lively and individualised unities in themselves. Everywhere besides the tendency towards unity there is maintained the tendency towards diversity, towards independence. It cannot be said that centralisation is progressing at a dangerous rate. The old Germany, stripped of its old extravagances and onesidedness, lives still—the multiform Germany. And the intellectual Germany of the old days also continues to live, or is coming to life again. It is true that "realism"—and often a barren materialism—has waxed strong amongst us; the great political and economic epoch which we so urgently needed, has not remained free from unhealthy excrescences. But on the other hand German Science has remained alive all the time, and continues to flourish in a host of different centres; and at the present day it is rising once more in conscious flight towards the ideal. And so in like manner for the last ten or twenty years Art, both literary and pictorial, has been everywhere springing up and blossoming anew. There is a fresh and vigorous feeling for Art, while Art itself shows a new activity in seeking, under stimulus from abroad, but with its own national impulse, new paths of progress, and this in all kinds of places, in North, and West, and South, and in all kinds of ways. Round a number of able masters, round a few great artists everywhere flocks a fill of cheerful life.

Indeed, anyone visiting the smaller German states, especially Bavaria and Swabia, could easily get an exaggerated impression of diversity, an impression that the South is passionately opposed to the leadership of Prussia. This opposition exists, but yet the influence of Prussia in Germany since 1871 has progressed, quietly and continuously. Undoubtedly the old Germany has reacted against the onesidedness of this Prussian tendency; our polity and culture incline more than formerly towards unification, but they have not become centralised. What is German and old, continues to thrive, along with the new and the Prussian. I am well aware and will here expressly observe that Prussia itself is by no means merely a land of discipline and of the sword. Prussia has also long been a land of culture, the seat of many of our most celebrated Universities, the cradle of an ancient native Art, as it was and is the home of German self-government; and the rest of Germany has also exercised in many respects a broadening and vivifying counter-influence on Prussia. Yet let me name here for once as specifically Prussian the power of unifying, of discipline, and of realism. And then can we truly say: The Prussian and German elements still stand side by side to-day, neither the one nor the other unduly preponderating. Beside the needful new elements, vigour and unity, there comes everywhere into play the old Teutonic impulse towards independence, which brings our culture essentially so near the English. And a German—since you want to hear the frank and characteristic opinion of a German about the modern history of his people—a German must thankfully proclaim this blending of old and new, unity and plurality, a *blessing.* He must, even if he remains conscious how much is still only begun and in progress, and what seriously urgent problems await his people, what dangers threaten them within and without, even then he must praise the progress of this century, which, I say it again, made a weak, divided people strong and important. He rejoices that the old has remained undestroyed and is still influential; but the great thing about our modern development is still that on which I have laid principal stress in this short sketch: Germany became strong in herself and in the world in the nineteenth century through Prussia, through Prussian politics and Prussian military service, through Prussian sense for actualities and Prussian cult of power; and therefore the truest and highest embodiment of what is creative and decisive, really new and vital in this epoch of German history is the man who was a Prussian and became a German, who transfused Prussia into Germany—Prince Otto von Bismarck.

PRINCE BISMARCK.

BY PROFESSOR ERICH MARCKS, PH.D.

IT was perhaps rather a rough road that I led you yesterday, through the history of the development of Germany in the nineteenth century; I spoke of the unification of Germany, of the part that Prussia played in it, of the influence which she exercises at present, but I could not do more than sketch the barest general outline. To-day I am permitted to give life to the picture by portraying the great man whose career was the best reflection of this development of his country. You will meet the same subjects as before, but in a personal form—a great man, in touch with all the forces, both Prussian, German, and universal, of his century, one who moved the world, but was above all a world in himself.

Otto von Bismarck sprang from an old Brandenburg family of rank. His ancestors had lived for four centuries in the Altmark (Old Mark), not far from Stendal: they had resisted and afterwards served the Hohenzollerns, and had done good work as warriors and civil officials, but especially as cultivators of the soil. As a race they faithfully reflected all the variations of succeeding epochs, roughness, industry, warlike glory, and enlightened civilisation, but they were always a knightly race, attached to their ancestral lands, long since devoted to the ruling dynasty, but with all the proud self-reliance of a noble house—in their own sphere a historic power in miniature. Bismarck's mother, being a commoner, infused new blood into

this knightly strain. Her father was a statesman, her forefathers were scholars, she herself a cool, clever, ambitious
woman. Her son grew up on the parental estates, chiefly in
Pomerania, but was early sent to school at Berlin. Thus he
learnt to know both town and country, and in the town became familiar with the criticism, philosophy, and the political
tendencies, German and Liberal, of the day. He studied law
at Göttingen and Berlin, and began the regular judicial and
administrative career. In these years he acquired the essentials
of legal knowledge, and a great deal of historical knowledge; at
Aachen (Aix-la-Chapelle) he saw the great world and conformed
to its social amenities more like a young nobleman than a
young official. But then in 1838 he left the public service. We
know why: he did not want to adjust himself as a part of the
bureaucratic machine. He cherished the secret ambition of
a highly-gifted, yet at the same time of an independent man—
the nobleman's ambition. He wished to live free and independent on his own land, his own master, the lord of his
estate, owning no constraint and no command. In a state
with a free Constitution public life would attract him, "but,"
he says, "I will play the music which *I* think good, or none
at all." It was not so much theoretical Liberalism which
actuated him as the impulse of the aristocracy for self-manage-
ment. And then for the space of ten years he worked hard
as an agriculturist in Pomerania, saving the estates from debt,
and becoming thoroughly acquainted with country, and climate,
cultivation of grain, and cattle-breeding. But he was not a
narrow-minded country squire. He travelled in western Europe,
England, and France, and looked round him with very open
eyes indeed. He read and meditated in the quiet of his estate.
But he was no more satisfied than young Oliver Cromwell was
when he was still a country gentleman. Bismarck's giant
powers also demanded harder work, in him too everything was
in a seething ferment, he too fought his way painfully through
a religious crisis. The son of a Christian, though rationalistic

family, but born in a critical age, he had lost positive belief in God, and now he strove for knowledge, read philosophy, ancient and modern, and remained still unanswered. His soul needed a personal God as a staff to support his powerful and weighty personality; for a long time he was unable to find Him again, but at last he did. He was helped in this by the ardent exhortations of a friend of his youth, who, having entered the ranks of the Pietists in Pomerania, professed a strict, warm, somewhat sectarian faith. He was further helped by his love for Johanna von Puttkamer, a lady who belonged to the same circles, simple, warm-hearted, lively, of true and natural womanliness, who gave him her hand in marriage in 1847, and who remained for almost 50 years the modest, indispensable companion of his career. His own home, and deepest positive belief, first raised him out of distraction into peace, from the poetry of Byron to the study of the New Testament; he did not become a Pietist, a religious dreamer, a man of quiet; his religion remained masculine, independent, the strengthening faith of a man of action, who needed support for the enormous responsibility of his resolutions.

Soon after this deliverance of soul the task of his life took possession of him. The preludes of the Revolution of 1848, and then the Revolution itself, came on. Bismarck, who held the post of Captain of the Dykes on the Elbe, came forward to keep out the floods of democracy from his country. He became the ally of King Frederick William the Fourth and his Christian Conservative friends. He, the convert, professed also in politics the orthodox doctrine of the Christian-aristocratic-monarchical state. As a country gentleman in the Prussian Parliament from 1847 to 1851 he fought with biting weapons, with defiant, spirited speeches against the unbelief and restlessness of the new age and the new citizen class, against Liberalism, and the national, German ideals. But if he preached the doctrine of these Conservatives, his feelings were different from theirs. His blood was up when his state, the Prussian state, was threatened in its independence and individuality; in the depths of his gifts he possessed the one sense which his contemporaries in Germany lacked, a sense for political power. It was his desire to procure free scope and suzerainty for his Prussia, for that Prussia which we have seen fettered in the German Confederation, dominated and hindered by her rival Austria and by the hostile intermediate states, such as Bavaria and Saxony. He gazed beyond the internal party strife into the wide world, towards Germany, towards Europe.

Hence he was the born diplomatist, the born statesman of a great state; hence also his real political career begins first in 1851, when he was sent by his King and party to Frankfort to represent Prussia at the Diet of the German Confederation, at the focus of German politics. It is one of the most remarkable spectacles ever presented by a great career, how Bismarck developed into himself at Frankfort (1851 to 1859). He put off the party-man; the local Parliament at home became indifferent to him; the champion of the reaction disappears; even the Conservative disappears; the theory of his friends is forgotten. Yet in the future, too, he is guided by a creed, a general idea; but this idea, which he serves, is Prussia, the community, the state, the strength and power of his state. No one, not even the King, feels the community in himself as Bismarck does; from henceforward Bismarck *is* Prussia. His personal ambition and feeling for power are strong, but fully merged in consideration for his state. It is his state he wants to free, to deliver from the Austrian hegemony, and to set up great and strong; that becomes the object of his whole passion. He becomes acquainted with the German political world, courts, and parties—the European also. When the Crimean War comes, he preaches to the Government a free, independent, purely Prussian policy. No sympathy either for liberal England or for conservative Russia. No inclinations or disinclinations. And also no detestation of the crowned revolutionary, the democratic Cæsar, Napoleon the Third—only clear weighing of Prussian political interests, only matter-of-factness, calmness, clearness, firm and manly determination. He turns over everything in his mind, all possible means of a future emancipation; Prussia will have to force Austria back and draw Germany to herself; she will also be able to call up a Liberal policy, but above all she will rely on power, arms, and combat. And all this for the greatness of his state, in the spirit of Frederick the Second. At Frankfort he foresees the war of 1866. And he lays down that Prussia will have to seek her path in Europe between Austria and France, and must play her game between and with both countries. And for all this he equips himself during these years of preparation, full of deep thoughts of his own, already in daily strife with Austria, proud and keen, but not yet laden with the responsibility of the leading Minister, still joyful and free, a young husband and father, happy, unconstrained, but very much in earnest; a man of strength, indefatigable in bodily vigour, fond of shooting, swimming and riding, full of indomitable courage, the thorough *grand seigneur*, self-possessed and distinguished, tall and stately, a survival from the old days of the heroes, radiant and conquering by strength and valour, fearless and pious, a man of triumphs, the rising victor and hero of future battles.

Then Frederick William the Fourth fell ill; the Prince Regent William tried to rule according to Liberal principles; and Bismarck, being mistrusted, was banished to St Petersburg in 1859. There too he learnt something, and did some preparatory work; then he went for a few short months to Paris in 1862. But then his destiny summoned him. The attempt of William the First had failed. The Crown of Prussia, the Crown of the Hohenzollerns, which had created Prussia, had come into conflict with the representation of the country on the question of army reform. The object of contention was power: Who should direct Prussia, the King or the Parliament? And the German question, too, had taken a new course. The nationalist parties, fettered since 1850, now again demanded unity; Austria and the intermediate states tried to use the movement for their own purposes. Prussia—I spoke about it yesterday—had to face the question whether she would create unity for herself, with a Prussian hegemony, in the Prussian interest. If so, war was inevitable. King William hesitated to take the risk. In internal affairs he held firmly to the power of the Crown; but the Liberal opposition rose up powerfully; the royal Ministers shrank before it; it seemed that the old King would never find a Minister again. For years his attention had been called to Bismarck, especially by the War Minister, General von Roon. It was an open secret that Bismarck was a fighting man, the representative of kingly power and Prussian ambition. King William did not want to summon him: the paths of this venturesome man projected too far into the dark for him. Only when all fell away from him, in September, 1862, did he take Bismarck's hand—and Bismarck promised him to defend the Crown in the struggle against Parliament. Bismarck did so from conviction: he knew that Prussia had need of the Crown. He did so as a servant of his master, reckless and ready for strife; he has gone through the domestic struggle, and hurled back the deputies: in doing so he seemed to be the old fighter, the old squire of 1847. He took on himself the breach of the laws— the due course of the life of the state had already been violently disturbed before Bismarck appeared. But he did all this principally in order to gain room for his foreign policy. He wanted to set to work from outside, to disentangle the disordered skein of internal contraries, to disarm opposition at home by conquest abroad. He had to fight the "conflict" out to the end, and did so gladly, because by this internal struggle the King became indispensably bound to the Minister. But his own personal work had been planned out long before at Frankfort. What were his wishes, now that he became Minister? Not the establishment of German unity, not the satisfaction of the national desires. He was not the servant of national sovereignty. He took his stand on the separate state, the Prussian state. He had to pursue a Prussian, not a German policy. He wanted to set free and then increase the power of Prussia—now as before. Did he want war with Austria? Well, he wanted what was possible. He had not got an abstract programme; he wanted as much profit, as much health for his state as possible: and he knew, as a statesman, that he must obey circumstances. If circumstances allowed Prussia's position to be improved, though only to an equality with Austria, he was—for the present, at least—content; he was ready to share with Austria the leadership of Germany—if he must. If he could gain more, that is the whole of Germany, so much the better. He certainly on all accounts preferred war with Austria as the sound, clear solution of the old German question—a thorough purging once for all. He was resolved to seize the present best for his country, without sentimentality, without dogmatism, without obstinacy. The best of all for Prussia's greatness was the unity of the whole of Germany under Prussia alone, and he considered whether he could attain it.

And, as you know, he did attain this best of all. He did so by a diplomacy beyond compare. He found Prussia and Germany excited, feverish, full of yearnings, full of parties, full of ideals. He knew only one ideal: the welfare of his state. His instrument was not national sentiment: he reserved that for the hour of fulfilment. Diplomacy was his instrument: a sober attempt of what was possible, on the basis of European relations. For the elevation of Germany could only be played for among the great powers. He won over Russia and courted France; at the same time he balanced Austria against France. At last he directed his attacks continuously and exclusively against the rival at Vienna; but he also made use of him as often as he could and must. He showed the Austrians the danger of their anti-Prussian policy; he repulsed unhesitatingly Francis Joseph's political aggression in Germany in

1863; but on the other side he stretched out a hand to Austria against the enmity of Napoleon. It was the most brilliant of his masterpieces, that he succeeded in linking Austria with Prussia on the Schleswig-Holstein question. I must not trace in detail how he did so, how he made use of things European and German, how he even made use of Austrian jealousy, how he steered the Imperial state towards Schleswig, how he held the two great powers of Germany together against Europe, and yet always maintained a position of independent leadership towards Austria, always ready to ring the changes also on the Paris chimes, always remaining also in a good understanding with the Czar. In 1864 he won back the two German duchies from Danish rule, in opposition to the public opinion of Germany, which feared that he would betray the duchies to Denmark; in opposition to Austria, which did not desire the reconquest at all; in opposition to Europe, which did not and could not desire the rise of a strong Germany. He did so in spite of attacks and jeers—uncertain even of his own King— and he triumphed over all. He had made the two liberated provinces the joint booty of Austria and Prussia: this booty became the object of strife. He must have known beforehand that it would be so. He would have maintained a friendly attitude towards Austria if he had been compelled—but how could that be? Their opposition must one day come to a clash. King William, serious, slow and honest, was not the man for a risky game, and did not want war. The new quarrel with Austria over Schleswig-Holstein enabled Bismarck in a certain degree to compel his sovereign to fight. And the iron die was cast; as the heir of Frederick the Great Bismarck led the Prussian state in 1866 before the gates of Vienna.

It was a success achieved by tremendous personal exertion: it was achieved at the cost of his nerves. And in the midst of victory, soon after Sadowa, Napoleon seized his arms, and Bismarck had to be content to take only North Germany for the present, leaving South Germany outside. He did so ; he won over his King to this limitation. And now he set up the North-German Confederation, based on an alliance of the states, led by Prussia. Prussia and her Throne were the framework, the Prussian military system was the cement ; the new state was monarchical and Prussian, not democratic and national. It was founded, not by the sovereignty of the nation, but by the power of the old dynasties. But now the nation must come forward to complete it; the Imperial Parliament, based on universal suffrage, was established beside the Federal Council of the Governments. Thus was formed the skeleton of the new national polity ; though the South was not yet included, yet already with a view to the inclusion of the South; and Bismarck was now Chancellor of the North-German Confederation, and not merely a Prussian Minister. His task henceforward was to fill the new and larger circle ; he served Prussia indeed, but also the whole of North-Germany, which he now represented, and he now advanced further towards the establishment of the complete Empire itself.

His victories had made him the indispensable assistant of his venerable Sovereign. He succeeded in gradually drawing the conservative Monarch, not without difficulties, into a freer course. He now needed the national party in order to win over and animate the new Germany through and through ; and this party was middle-class and Liberal. He made his treaty with Liberalism ; he led the old Prussia into new ways, but always so that Crown and Minister remained masters of the situation. But he himself became the nation's man. His personality became the symbol of the power and progressive unity of the whole ; his victory decided the constitutional struggle in favour of the monarchy; but also his whole self and his political methods became decisive for the nation. He educated the Germans up to the practical view of politics ; he was the central figure round which the process I described yesterday turned. The nation then discovered that it possessed a great man, and began to submit to his guidance—guidance and influence.

He fulfilled the nation's expectations of him. The semi-Germany allowed him by France and Austria in 1866 could not endure for ever. Economic considerations, considerations of national spirit and power, made it necessary to attract the South. Austria and France put themselves in the way. France would not tolerate the entry of a strong neighbour in place of the chaos which for four centuries had been so convenient to the French. If France forbade the lawful and necessary unification of the Germans, she thereby acted as a great power unwilling to submit to a restriction of power,—but she thereby forced Germany into war. The fact that he brought on the settlement that could hardly be avoided, and his manner of doing so, constitute one of Bismarck's highest achievements. It is beyond doubt that he, in 1870, pressed the Spanish candidature with all his might, and that he did so against France. That in doing so he wanted to provoke war, and nothing but war, is obviously *not* true; but he was ready, if France wanted war, to fight on the occasion of this candidature. I cannot, unfortunately, narrate to-day how the government of the Duc de Gramont after all kinds of episodes and dangers put the game into Bismarck's hands. In the highest sense of statesmanship he did his duty as a patriot by compelling France through the Ems despatch to put her threats into effect; he forced France to a declaration of war; as in 1866, he took up the indispensable decision heroically, for the welfare of his state and his nation. And the greatest days of modern Germany dawned. Bismarck succeeded in fighting out the war to the end without interference from Europe. He brought about the declaration of the Empire at Versailles. The bounds of the North-German Confederation were merely enlarged; the new Empire also became not indeed a single state but a Confederate state, made up of voluntary associates, not centralised, but provided with strict rights for the separate states; on the

power of the states he based also the great new state; but
unity was riveted firmly enough; and above all stood in 1871
as in 1866, the power of Prussia, the Prussian monarchy with
its army and authority.

I described yesterday how peculiar life was poured into
the mould of the Empire, so that plurality and unity became
amalgamated. To-day I glance only at the man in whose
personality the Empire was embodied. Now indeed he was
the hero of the nation; he entered the ranks of its greatest,
and took his place beside Martin Luther, beside and above
Frederick the Second and Goethe. His influence became
immense. But there still remained violent conflicts. He had
to bear ceaseless personal opposition at Court; only the loyalty
of his Emperor upheld him through all these frictions. All
the great parties in the country opposed him; the Conservatives, because he had fallen away from them; the Clericals,
because they hated the Protestant Empire; the Liberals,
though his allies, were always struggling with him for political
power; the Radicals clung to the democratic ideals of 1848
which he had overthrown; the new Labour party looked on
him as an autocrat, the stern representative of the old political
forces. The enthusiasm for unity came in his favour again
and again; but he had to make his own path daily amid
exhausting struggles. And he himself was irritated, in bad
health, a man of wrath and strength, a born ruler, but not a
flexible Parliamentary leader; he was by nature above all parties,
and therefore a stranger to them. It was his difficult task
to rule *over*, not with them. He remained, as he had always
been, the representative of the monarchy, but he was at the
same time the representative of the whole. He identified himself with the whole nation, and with its new polity, the Empire;
his personality and the interests of the state which he had
founded were fused together. He looked outwards; he saw
his state surrounded by possible enemies; he feared an alliance of all the neighbours against the inconvenient upstart.

With wonderful virtuosity he succeeded in averting this alliance; he obtained support in Russia, then in Austria, and gradually accustomed Europe to the new power. At the same time he tried to give it greater cohesion. The various organs of the new Empire grew; beside the Imperial Chancellor there appeared gradually new assistant and subordinate authorities. The tasks of the Empire increased. It gradually drew the various departments of life into its sphere of work and legislation. And the champion here, too, was always Prince Bismarck. Until 1878 he acted with the Liberals, in spite of all their border warfare. With them he turned against the Catholic party, which denied the fundamentals of his Empire. He carried on the "Kultur-Kampf" with all his passion for fighting. But before he could end it—and it was difficult to tackle the Church with his political resources—new tasks sprang up for him. The social conditions altered; a Fourth Estate grew up below the middle-class and knocked threateningly at the gates of society. To Bismarck the old Conservative, the Liberals and the middle class were not exactly agreeable confederates. And now economic necessities pressed upon him; the circumstances of the world's trade altered: industry and agriculture implored his protection. And in increasing the customs tariff he at the same time obtained larger revenues for his Empire. The customs were made to render the Empire financially independent, whereas up to the present it had chiefly been supported by proportional contributions from the separate states. The customs were also made to strengthen the Government greatly, to strengthen the bureaucracy, to strengthen the state which should now act upon all the relations of life. This was then a new prop for the Empire; and if he shut off the Empire against outsiders by a high wall of protective duties, the inner unity of the area was increased. Finally the new policy was highly beneficial to the agriculturists—that is the Conservatives.

Thus from 1877 onwards the Chancellor was suddenly confronted by a quite new combination. Separation from the Liberals, alliance with the Conservatives, protective duties, a strengthening of the Empire and monarchy, a change of all parties, a new system of economic and political activity. This extremely many-sided new programme was thought out by him in 1877 in long months of loneliness and shaped into unity by his mind. He changed all the relations of public life in Germany. And then he even drew the new social movement into this extensive programme. As an old fighter for the monarchy he wanted to oppose with all his might the social revolution heralded by the two attempts on the life of the Emperor William in 1878. But he wanted to satisfy the crying needs and well-grounded complaints of the proletariate, as far as it was possible for the state to do so. He wanted to oppose force to force, but he wanted to reconcile the millions of the working-classes to the national state, to make them feel at home in the Commonwealth, whose creator and representative he himself was. It was he who thought out the gigantic scheme of workmen's insurance against illness, accident, disablement, and old age.

Thus it was for prosperity and power that he wanted to strive. In doing so he had renewed the traditions of the old Prussian state. I spoke yesterday of Frederick the Second's system of the strong state's care for all classes and all vital interests of society. Power and prosperity, authority and social welfare, imperial, social, and party politics—everything was comprised in this change. Whatever the individual judgment may be, it was certainly a grand design, embracing all departments of life, the plan of a genius ; then first Prince Bismarck entered the real domestic politics of his state, actually innovating and renovating on his own account. He began a second life-work. To an Englishman this work, with its strong accentuation of the power of the state and the monarchy, will of course seem to a certain degree Continental. I willingly admit that the political traditions of Continental absolutism underlie it, and I am well aware that it is not without drawbacks; especially in the repression of socialism lie many expressly Continental features. And yet I praise these Bismarckian innovations highly: they opened the way for a new and deeper conception of the state among us; they carried over desires and ideas of social reform from the region of theory into the living present; they attacked tremendous problems for the first time with adequate force; they broke the ice for far-reaching future reforms.

To carry them through required the whole giant strength of their promoter. He concluded peace with Rome, not without serious losses, but also not without gains for the state; he completed his tariff reform with the aid of Conservatives, moderate Liberals, and Clericals; and he established the insurance system for workmen with a strong appeal to moral and religious feelings. At the same time he clung to the repressive Socialist law down to 1890. In the Imperial Parliament (*Reichstag*) he wrestled against hostile majorities; his new ideas penetrated through to the people but slowly. But the younger generation enthusiastically joined the great pioneer. He realised the essential, he strengthened the army, the finances, and the administration of his Empire, made the monarchy once more a leading power inwardly and outwardly, and at least once (from 1887 to 1890) possessed also a continuous majority in Parliament. At the end nothing could obstruct him.

While at home he made his way only with difficulty, amid constant strife and opposition, by exerting his whole forces as orator and agitator, his foreign policy, on the other hand, quickly won him the unquestioning admiration of the nation. After 1871 he changed front very often indeed, but his leading idea remained always the same: to prevent coalitions against Germany, or to counterbalance them by other coalitions. He went with Russia and Austria against France (1871), with Austria against Russia (1879) when Russia began to fall away, and drew Italy, and, in a certain sense, perhaps also England after him. He sought, even as Austria's ally, to recover the understanding with St Petersburg. In 1887 he had cause to fear war with France and perhaps with Russia, and was prepared to carry it through. From 1871 he strove for peace, but he sharpened his weapons; he did not want fresh conquests, but he wanted, by power and alliances, to protect what he had gained. He did so with the skill of a perfect master, with the authority of one holding a matchless position as a diplomatist. He gave his young state a full position in Europe.

And he gave it a position in the world. When the economic power of Germany arose, after unity had been secured, and strove to assure itself outlets into the wide world, it turned to him for his patronage. He followed the colonial movement of his people heedfully, and protected it with his power. With all the prudence of mature experience, without enthusiasm, but without feebleness, he laid the first foundations of a colonial and world-wide policy; here also he showed the way for the future.

Never was Germany so guided and enriched by a single hand. This hand held home and foreign affairs in its grasp, educated the nation up to unity, strength, and matter-of-factness, and summoned up the enthusiasm for its work, so sober and yet so vast. The eighties elevated the great Chancellor and his aged Emperor to a great eminence, and Prince Bismarck, the Prussian, was then, both in reality and in the people's heart, the embodiment of the new Germany. He became in the deepest sense a spiritual force for his people.

His very personality presented a unique appearance. He was a powerful man if ever there was: a sovereign nature of intense passion, always giving his whole soul to the matter in hand, fiery and abrupt, a giant in anger, hate, and conflict; not a precisian, and not too convenient for others—a ruler of the great Germanic type, lion-like in temperament as in the glance of his powerful eyes; dangerous to enemies and allies, demoniacally defiant in his strength, crushing, pitiless. And yet bending—autocratic and reckless as he was in his choice of practical means—yet bending in the service of general forces: full of a deep faith till the end, supported by his religion, though his was not a religion of mildness and "love your enemies"; a servant of the Emperor and King and monarchy, but a proud servant, who stood upright and spoke home-truths like one ruler to another; a servant of the state and of the political sense, full of devotion to the community, the nation, its unity, and its power; although in him the servant of the state and the man of individual greatness were blended. Thus he was closely connected with the great ideal forces, and yet regarded everything as reality, nothing abstractly; everywhere he saw details, individuals, things within reach. How different he was from the greatest leader of the Liberal idea of his time, Mr Gladstone, whom he neither understood nor respected. But even beneath Bismarck's defiant colossality lay the general forces and ideas of his country and his age.

And what was he to the Germans, not only through the endless amount of gratitude due to and shown him; not only through the streams of new life which continually proceeded from him: but also through his very existence! We saw him in the fight, trembling with wrath, in his nerve-consuming work, and saw him as the host of his guests, the lord of his castle, the head of his family; we saw him in his woods and fields, closely intimate to the soil; loving, spirited, kind, and simple; we saw in his eyes the lightning-flash of demoniacal wrath, and the warmth of a deep, clear heart. Thus the love of his people has regarded and conceived him, an ardent, deep-seated love, which penetrated the souls of hundreds of thousands. What we —for here too you wish to hear a full and personal testimony from the lips of a German—what we Germans celebrate as best in the German character when we idealise our nation, that appeared to us living in this great man, and when he raised his voice we heard the echo of long centuries of our history. He seemed to us without parallel in richness and strength of soul, an equal of Luther and Goethe; his moral influence was enormous. The Englishman may regard it all with cooler criticism

—or does he, too, see in Bismarck a piece of Teutonic greatness?—in any case what I have just said is the opinion of large sections in Germany. He educated us—I showed that yesterday; he may have acted crushingly on many; he urged men perhaps all too exclusively to power, work, and practical issues; well, these shortcomings have since then corrected themselves in the natural course of time; but what he is to us, what he gave and gives us, that remains indispensable to us; he made us strong and manly.

After 1887 possibly the first breath of old age fell on this gigantic force. When his old master died, and the young Emperor sought for himself paths and distinction of his own—ways the length of which Prince Bismarck did not wish to go with him—then there came into his government a disrupted dual element; and it is well known how William the Second in March, 1890, abruptly dismissed the man of seventy-five. At present it is still difficult to determine the distribution of right and wrong in this action. But it was a tragic spectacle—few more so. The great German withdrew in bitter resentment to his estate; that he raised a voice of warning, blame, and opposition, will seem more natural to the Englishman, to whom otherwise perhaps so much in Bismarck is alien, than to the monarchical German. Bismarck was and remained the nobleman, who walks haughtily even beside his Prince; the passion and anxiety he felt for his work were with him stronger than his sense of propriety. From 1890 on he was an inconvenient personage to the German Government; he, whose nature constrained him to work, could now only criticise; but he obtained a hearing in many important matters, and saw his paths therein being sought out anew. And above all he still remained, whatever the parties thought of his warnings and appeals, the herald of the Empire, the genius of unity, even after his dismissal. Thousands and thousands made pilgrimage to him to the Sachsenwald, and his voice had for them an ever-sacred ring; they brought him gratitude, admiration, mourning, they brought him fidelity and undying love. They carried back into their daily life a reflection of imperishable greatness, and they felt as though blessed when they had seen the greatest man of their day.

Bismarck died in July, 1898. To the Germans he remained the symbol of their best possessions. The perishable, the unavoidable misproportions in single epochs and individuals pass away under the solvent action of new aims and ideas; but the greatest among the dead live on still after that, not only as names, not only in the memory, but as forces in the will and conscience of a people. This great man gave his nation a polity of his creation, steeped in his being; he was with unparalleled grandness the representative of all that was or is to become common to his nation. His figure is so prominent, four-square, lofty, and sharp-cut, it will never be overlooked and forgotten by posterity. To the world in general he will always remain at least *one* of the greatest figures which the nineteenth century exhibits—personally the strongest of them all, I believe, though not perhaps the most beloved by the rest of nations. You will not find fault with us Germans if we believe, and joyfully confess the belief, that he will be to *our* people immortal in the special sense of which I spoke. The idea of his native country continues to live in him, and whenever his nation, in days of happiness or of need, recalls her good and great men, then will the name of Bismarck stand out, far above all other names. Such men, however, in whom a single people finds its best enshrined in great and characteristic form, certainly belong, above praise and blame, above love and hate, also to the eternal collective property of mankind.

NOTE. I wish to express my best thanks to Mr Lionel Strachan, M.A., Lector of the English language at Heidelberg University, for his excellent translation of my two lectures; also to Professor Johannes Hoops of Heidelberg and Mr Eberhard Focke of Sydenham for much supplementary advice.

AUSTRIA AND HUNGARY IN THE
NINETEENTH CENTURY.

By Dr Emil Reich.

THE past weighs heavily on most countries. Some nations glory in their uninterrupted connection with long bygone ages; others complain of it. But there are few peoples with whom events long buried have still such an influence, an actuality as intense as past events have on the history of Austria. In a sense it may be said, that with regard to Austria the dead do not bury the dead, they bury rather the living. The diplomatic and military events of 1526 and 1741 are still the dominating factors of all Austrian policy; and since the local distribution of the Slav and Magyar races in Austria-Hungary happened in 300 B.C. and 900 A.D. respectively, the nationalist factor of Austria goes back to times almost beyond well-authenticated history.

To this, the element of Time, there is in Austrian history an equally strong element of Space. The geographical situation of the various peoples destined to form the empire of Austria-Hungary is one making for disunion rather than union. There is, it is true, a common stream, the Danube. However, the Cechs and Moravians belong, hydrographically, to the Elbe or Oder River systems, and not to the Danube. Moreover Austria had up to 1797 no sea-board to speak of. It was entirely an inland empire; its provinces were not given that powerful stimulus for unity which the sea has at all times exercised on the inhabitants of peninsulas or islands. The sea unites; mountains disaggregate.

In order to seize clearly the potent influence of the element of Time—that of Space scarcely needing here further explanation—let us briefly recapitulate the story of the building-up of Austria.

From the thirteenth century upward there were four different monarchs and rulers bidding and struggling for the supremacy in the valley of the Danube : the Kings of Hungary; the Kings of Bohemia ; the Dukes of Bavaria ; and the Archdukes of Austria proper. In 1526 the decision of this secular struggle was made in favour of the Austrian Archdukes. True, they had been very frequently beaten and worsted in battles and on the diplomatic field by their rivals. Yet, in the end, they secured the great prize; and in 1526 the crowns both of Bohemia and Hungary, *i.e.* vast territories comprising Bohemia proper, Moravia, Silesia, Lusatia, Hungary proper, Transylvania, Croatia, Slavonia, Dalmatia, etc. were, partly *de facto,* partly only *de lege* transferred to the rulers of Austria. The causes of this astounding accession of power do not concern us here ; suffice it to say, that the Archdukes, although deficient in military and financial resources, were superior to their rivals in point of sound and persistent foreign policy, then (end of the fifteenth and throughout the sixteenth century) the directing power of political affairs in Central and Western Europe.

In 1526, then, as well as in 1860, Austria consisted of a very large number of heterogeneous peoples and races, each having aspirations of its own, each trying to occupy a prominent place amongst the rest, each clinging firmly to its language, traditions, religion, political institutions and privileges. Yet, during the sixteenth century, the Archdukes had troubles rather with the Turk than with their own subjects ; and in the seventeenth century, troubles with the Bohemians were removed by a victorious campaign of two years' duration, from 1618 to 1620 ; while the troubles with Hungary were largely a secondary

feature of the wars with the Turk, and were finally ended in
1711 by the peace of Szathmár. All during the eighteenth
century, the Austrian Empire, although adding to its inner
discordance by incorporating new and alien peoples, did not
suffer from its present internal disturbances at all. This seems
very strange. For it must not be overlooked that far from
being amazed at the present unrest of the Austrian races, one
ought rather to wonder about the long period of internal calm
that Austria enjoyed, with insignificant interruptions, from 1711
to 1848. The reason of this calm is the broad fact that Austria
was all through the seventeenth and eighteenth centuries, up
to the downfall of Napoleon, engaged in the most tremendous and international wars, ranging from Gibraltar to the
northern end of Denmark, and from Belgium to Servia, against
the Turks, the Swedes, Louis XIV, Louis XV, Frederick the
Great, the French Revolution, and Napoleon. Those wars
brought such an outside pressure to bear upon all the peoples
of Austria as to act with them as their strongest bond of unity.
Austria's centre of gravity was outside her own territory. The
disruptive elements at home could not easily pursue their own
individual aims, while their very existence was daily threatened
by powers from the outside. We find, for instance, that only
one generation after the last of the Rákóczy rebellions in
Hungary the Magyars did everything in their power to save
Austria from the Prussians, Bavarians, and French, in 1741 ;
likewise in the period of the Revolutionary and Napoleonic
wars.

However, the benefit derived by Austria from her great
international contests could not possibly survive the period of
history when alone such contests were possible. It is well
known that since 1815 there have been no international wars at
all. All wars, since that time, have been local and limited.
No sooner had this new phase of European politics become
manifest than Austria began to shift her centre of gravity.
The great home-problems, which had long been settled by the

other powers, either in the sixteenth century, as in Spain; in
the seventeenth (1688—1689), as in England; or in the
eighteenth, as in France and Prussia, now demanded their
solution in Austria too. For this, however, Austria found
herself without any preparation at all. The attempt at unifying
the Empire by a violent process of Germanization, under
Joseph II (1780—1790), had completely failed. Nor could
that process be repeated under Francis or Ferdinand in the
nineteenth century. For, since 1741, the balance between the
German and non-German peoples of the Empire had been
considerably altered in favour of the non-German races. By
the battle of Mollwitz (1741, April), Frederick the Great
possessed himself of Austrian Silesia, a rich province, inhabited
mostly by Germans. Silesia, together with Eastern Moravia,
Lower and Upper Austria, Styria and Carinthia, formed, before
1741, a series of provinces inhabited almost exclusively by
German-speaking Austrian subjects, who thus formed a German
wedge between the Magyars on the eastern, the Cechs on the
western, and the Slovenes on the southern side of the Empire.
By being shorn, after 1741, of Silesia, the German element in
Austria lost considerably of its former leverage; and when in
1772, 1775, 1797, and 1814 still more and non-German peoples
were incorporated with Austria (Poles, Ruthenians, and Italians,
by the acquisition of Galicia, Bukovina, Dalmatia, Lombardy
respectively), the German element came very near being out-
weighed, as it certainly was outnumbered, by the other nationalities. Any attempt at wholesale Germanization of Austria
was therefore, since 1814, entirely out of the question.

The various constituent nations of Austria now undertook
to solve the problem in their own fashion. Hungary, already
in 1825, led by men of the most exalted patriotism, such as
Count Széchenyi and Baron Wesselényi, had taken up the
questions of home-reform as well as that of Hungary's relation
to Austria, in the most serious manner. The frequent Diets at
Pozsony witnessed the animated discussions of these subjects

by Louis Kossúth, Francis Deák, Count Apponyi, and many others, who had clearly seized the fact that the old-standing vital problems of the Magyar polity had then reached the period when solutions favourable to the ideals of the Hungarians might very well be realized. Accordingly, Deák, the Timoleon of Hungary, a small country-squire whose admirable grasp of Hungarian law, both private and constitutional, was equalled by his perfect temper and self-possession, Deák at once set to reforming first the criminal legislation, then the county-administration, working, however, mainly at the realization of that Dualism which he both formulated first and, in 1867, established as the fundamental law of both halves of the Austro-Hungarian empire.

But while the Magyars fully entered upon the spirit of the time which, as already remarked, had since 1815 necessitated a shifting of the historic forces of Austria, the Austrian monarchs and their ministers, chiefly Prince Metternich, had no sympathy for nor understanding of the new phase of Austrian history. As in the period of the great international wars, Metternich and his colleagues still thought of being able to dominate the ever-rising surge of Nationalism by drastic or draconic police-measures. In that, of course, he signally failed. Rebellions may be stemmed and suppressed by dragonnades and police-ordinances ; revolutions can only be amended. In 1848 the Magyars rose against Austria. That famous revolution quickly led to the expulsion of all Austrian soldiers and officials from Hungary by the victorious Magyar generals, Klapka, Perczel, Görgey, and others. Kossúth, in public assembly at Debreczen, declared the Hapsburgs to have, by the unanimous will of the Hungarian nation, lost their claim to the crown of St Stephen for ever. Austria now appealed to Czar Nicholas, who readily sent a considerable Russian army, under Paskievich, into Hungary, in order there to restore Austrian supremacy. Paskievich succeeded in forcing Görgey to surrender with his entire army at Világos, August 13, 1849.

The smaller risings in Austria proper had likewise been put down, so that the first attempt of the Austrian nationalities to solve the home-problem by means of revolutions had failed. It will be remarked that up to 1850 neither the efforts of the Crown nor those of the peoples had led to any satisfactory organization of the distracted forces and heterogeneous elements of the Danubian empire. Nor can we now doubt that in the failure of all such efforts, from 1780 to 1850, the same law may be observed that has at all times dominated the history of Austro-Hungary: the law, that as in Prussia all political development starts from the monarch and his cabinet, so in Austria home-policy is directed mainly by the international position of the empire. The reforms that neither the monarch nor the people alone were able to bring about were initiated by several great events, deeply affecting the foreign policy of Austria.

Before the advent of these events, however, the Austrian Government placed for ten years (1850—1860) every province of the empire, including Hungary, under a reactionary *régime* of the most stringent kind, suppressing the very slightest symptom of liberal ideas or cravings for autonomy with an iron hand. The singing of the Rákóczy-march in public; the wearing of a "Kossúth-hat"; the whistling of the Marseillaise; the most innocent or indifferent remarks on politics were sufficient to cause the offender to be locked up at Munkács or Kufstein, two of the state prisons of Austria-Hungary. Hungary, whose revolutionary leaders had all fled to Turkey or to England, was flooded with a host of German officials. Everything was Germanized, and Minister Bach and his "Bach-Hussars" fondly hoped to stamp out a nationality that had withstood, for then nearly a thousand years, the terrible onslaughts of Turk, Slav, and German without impairing its spirit or courage.

During that miserable period, the "sage of the nation," Deák, lived in close retirement, first on his estate in the county of Zala, then at Pest, in the hotel "Queen of England." He had not taken an active part in the military events of 1848–49, and preferred to bide his time until the fit moment for political action would come, as come it must. The nation looked up to him for advice in this their most vital difficulty, and nobody doubted that in Deák there was the requisite force of insight, moderation, and bold perseverance by which alone the all-important question could be brought to a satisfactory issue.

As already remarked, foreign events helped Hungary in the critical moment. As Magna Charta was largely won on the battlefield of Bouvines, in north-eastern France, so the famous Diploma of October, 1860, or the first sign of the downfall of the reactionary system in Austria, was obtained on the battlefields of Magenta and Solferino, in 1859. The Italian campaign, in which Austria was defeated by Napoleon III, ended with the peace of Villafranca, constituting the loss of Lombardy to Austria and inflicting on her a deep humiliation. As is always the case in moments of great national disaster, the ruler of Austria became conscious that the Bach system was not the panacea of all evil that its supporters had proclaimed it to be. A new system was to be tried; and in October, 1860, the so-called "October Diploma" was issued, in which representative government was introduced on a federal basis. In other words, *all* the "provinces" of the "Austrian Empire" were to send their representatives to a Diet in Vienna, the Diet to decide on many of the important issues of current and constitutional policy. Together with that new move, new personalities were introduced, of whom the most remarkable was Schmerling, the new premier. Born and bred in the atmosphere of bureaucratism, Schmerling was, like so many an Austrian statesman, both very clever and very inefficient. His undoubted gifts enabled him to keep himself in power for a few years; his utter misreading of the real powers and tendencies of the Hungarian, Cech and the other leading nationalities frustrated all his efforts. He was a centralist in a polity that would, as above explained, make for no form other than federal. He was ardently in favour of complete administrative and political union with Hungary against the manifest impossibility of persuading the Hungarians to unite with the polities of Cisleithania. Accordingly he failed. His famous word " *Wir können warten* " ("We can afford to wait") only shows that he had no grasp of the urgency and precipitation of events in the early sixties. The answer of the nations, more especially of Hungary, was, implied if not explicit, "We have been waiting long enough."

The Hungarians, far from accepting the federal Reichsrath as established by the October Diploma, and somewhat modified by the "Patent" of February, 1861, abstained from sending representative members of theirs to Vienna. They were soon followed by the Cechs and Poles. Nobody cared for such a federal Diet. The political agitation of Hungary from 1861 to 1865 culminated in two events : one the striking, passive resistance of the people, the other the political pamphlets, articles and discourses of Deák. As the passive resistance was the unmistakable evidence that the Hungarian nation had fully and definitively made up their mind, so Deák's writings and speeches clearly formulated the constitutional demands and thoughts of the Hungarian people. In a lengthy controversy with Professor Lustkandl, of Vienna, who maintained that Hungary had always formed part of the Austrian Empire, being united with Cisleithania in "real", and not only in personal union, Deák, in a manner as clear as it was elaborate, proved that Hungary had never been in the legal status of a "province" of Austria, and that by the sacred principle of the continuity of law, Hungary still (1865) claimed her ancient independence for all matters concerning her home affairs, including a Parliament of her own, her ancient county-system with elective annual officials, her own law, her old provinces (Transylvania, Croatia, Slavonia, and Dalmatia), and, first of all, her inalienable right to acknowledge the ruler of Austria as King of Hungary only on condition of his being previously crowned as King at Pest, after having formally sworn to observe the ancient constitution of Hungary. Such were the leading points of Deák's writings, discourses, and especially of his famous article in the newspaper *Pesti Napló* of April, 1865 ("Easter Sunday article"). It will be seen that Deák would not admit at all that the Hungarians had by their revolution and by being ultimately defeated in 1848–49, lost their privileges and constitution as established by the treaties and laws previous to the Revolution. This, the chief argument of the Austrian statesman, and one for which, from the strictly legal standpoint, there is indeed something to say, lost all its power, if not by Deák's otherwise irrefutable argumentation, by the "passive resistance" of the nation. In that remarkable phenomenon, probably the most important of all the events of the period from 1861 to 1865, although less noticed than the brilliant speeches and political moves of Count Julius Andrássy, M. Lónyay, Coloman Tisza, and, of course, Deák; in that "passive resistance" must be found the final cause of the success crowning the efforts of the Magyar statesmen. Without any preconcerted measure whatever, the Hungarian nation, on learning that the Austrian Government had, in the summer of 1861, rejected the *felirat* or memorial of the Hungarian Diet, in which the principles of Deák had been expressed in language as moderate as it was forcible, at once organized itself into an "opposition" of a striking kind. Suddenly nobody disposed of the smallest funds for paying his taxes; suddenly the number of law-suits, or any other proceedings requiring intervention of officials, dwindled down with astounding rapidity; the officials found themselves hampered on all sides by the sullen antagonism of noblemen, bourgeois, and peasants alike, and no official order, even of the slightest kind, was sure to be carried out. The situation became unbearable. In many a state-office not a penny was to be found for the most urgent needs of the families of the officials. The whole public life of the country had come to a standstill, to an ill-boding stagnation. A change became imperative. In September, 1865, the Schmerling ministry fell, after Francis Joseph had by a visit to Hungary acquired the conviction that nothing short of the Dualism proposed by Deák would satisfy the Hungarians, and restore order in the empire. In this case, too, an external event came to the help of the Hungarians; for this is one of the most patent, if sadly neglected lessons of the history of Hungary, too, that as their greatest national disaster, the terrible defeat at Mohács, in 1526, at the hands of the Turks, was owing mainly to Hungary's being deserted by the rest of Central Europe, even so Hungary's greatest triumph was largely owing to the decisive victory of Prussia at Königgrätz, July 3, 1866, over Austria. The utterly altered international position of Austria necessitated, after 1866, a complete overhauling of her internal situation, and the most essential portion of that change of *régime* was the introduction of Dualism as long insisted upon by Deák. After 1866, Austria was finally and probably for ever severed from the States of Germany and the "German Empire," and also forced to quit the Italian peninsula for good. This could not but profoundly alter Austria's international position. She ceased to be a neighbour of France, a power in Italy, a rival of Prussia. Reduced in territory; very considerably shorn of her influence as a Great Power in Europe, she was inevitably driven to the task of gaining by more intense growth at home what she had lost in her territorial and moral expansion abroad. Deák's "moment" had come. He knew how to utilise it. At one with the other leaders of Hungary, he carried out his system of "Dualism," aided by Count Beust, the new foreign minister, in 1867.

The Dualism of Austria and Hungary is still little understood in France, England, or America. It is indeed a form of polity so alien to the traditional systems of these western countries, that a clear understanding of it cannot be easily reached by a Frenchman imbued with the secular unity of

France, by an Englishman accustomed to systems of compromise baffling all definite formulae, or by an American inured to a confederacy in which there is no possible room for Dualism. Yet Sweden and Norway offer the same example as Austria-Hungary; and inevitable events will sooner or later prompt Russia and Germany to imitate the Austro-Hungarian system with regard to Poles and Finns. One of the chief misleading factors consists probably in the false idea that Austria is by far the larger, and the more influential of the two sections. As a matter of fact, however, the kingdom of Hungary is larger than Austria, as it is larger than Italy, and larger than the United Kingdom. More remarkable still is the fact, that there is an Austria-Hungary; there is a Hungary; but there is, legally, no Austria. In terms of constitutional law, Cisleithania is called "*Die im Reichsrath vertretenen Laender,*" "The countries represented in the Reichsrath." The term "Austria" is a mere *façon de parler*; whereas the countries united under the crown of St Stephen bear the legal common name of Hungary, *Magyarország*. This alone indicates and proves that in the case of Hungary we are dealing with an old historic individuality, nay personality, while "Austria" has never been able to clothe her different peoples with the unity of a homogeneous historic individuality. This vast difference at once explains both the untiring opposition offered by the people of Hungary to all the attempts of the rulers of Austria to incorporate them as a "province" with the rest of the Hapsburg dominions, and their final success in establishing the Dualism. The Hapsburgs, until 1806, were also Emperors of the Holy Roman Empire; yet Hungary never formed part of the Empire. As against the Roman Empire, so against Austria, the Hungarians invariably manifested that unconquerable desire of every true individuality to be left to itself. For many a purpose of culture, commerce or industry it might have been better had the Hungarians agreed to be made an integral portion of Germany in the time of the Empire. Yet with regard to the highest of all historic purposes, with regard to the building up of a great and fully differentiated historic individuality, the persistent abhorrence of all union with German ideas and institutions, could not but strengthen the political force and increase the dignity of the historic *rôle* of Hungary. Or has not History long taught us that its powers always followed the intense impulses of small but highly individualized polities? The *rôle* of Athens, Rome, or Florence is infinitely more important than that of vast India or China. Nations that have long felt in them a vocation for a distinct political personality can under no circumstances abandon their evident destiny. *Sint ut sunt aut non sint*—these words apply not only to the artificial personality organized by Loyola, but with infinitely greater force to old historic personalities, such as Hungary. A hundred times beaten down, a hundred times the Magyars rose up to recommence the struggle for what made existence alone acceptable, for their independent individuality.

In that absolute resolution not to part with their individuality lay also, as already remarked, their greatest leverage and power. The other nations of Cisleithania were, on the whole, devoid of that intense and resolute determination to keep their historic existence uninterfered with. Contests between two adversaries, of whom one is lukewarm and not sufficiently equipped with clear notions about his own ends, while the other is filled with the intensest energy focused distinctly on a definite end, cannot but end in favour of the latter. That is what happened in the case of Hungary. The leading Magyar statesmen, fully conversant with German and with the people, customs, and tendencies of Austria, had, in that, in addition to their greater resolution, union, and address, an enormous advantage over the Austrian statesmen, who did not know Hungarian, nor Hungary's people, constitution, or customs. The result could only be one. Hungary finally compelled Austria to recognize the absolute independence of the countries united under the crown of St Stephen. No Austrian official can put a foot on Hungarian soil. Austrian citizenship does not imply Hungarian citizenship, and the latter must be obtained, if needed, by an Austrian citizen in the same way in which it is obtained eventually by an Englishman or Frenchman. The sole official language of Hungary is Magyar, which is, it is scarcely necessary to add, neither a Slav nor a German idiom, but a Turanian language, akin to Finnish on the one hand, and Turkish on the other. The law of Hungary is quite different from that of Austria; so is, and in a still greater degree, her provincial organization in counties and *járások*, or subdivision of counties. The Parliament of Hungary, consisting of two Houses, the House of Magnates and the House of Representatives, is historically and technically quite different from the Reichsrath in Austria.

For such purposes as are, from the international position of Austria and Hungary, common to both halves of the Empire, there is a common "Parliament," the so-called Delegations, selected from the Austrian Reichsrath and the Hungarian Parliament respectively. Such purposes are (1) Foreign policy; (2) the common army, as distinct from Hungary's own army formed by the *honvédség*; (3) the common finances, that is, the common debt, the customs, and expenditure for the preceding common causes; and (4) Bosnia and Herzegovina, which both are an imperial territory of the Austro-Hungarian Empire. Before approaching the financial questions, or the *Ausgleich*, it is very important to remark, that the influence exercised by either the Austrian or the Hungarian peoples on the foreign policy of their country, is both feeble and quite inadequately organized. As a matter of fact, questions of foreign policy cannot very well be mooted and discussed in either the Cisleithanian or the Transleithanian Parliament. Such discussions are left to the Delegations, where from sheer lack of time they can receive only purely academic treatment in the rare, short, and moreover separate meetings of the

Austrian and Magyar Delegations.   Now in this, if in nothing else, is to be found one of the causes of the unrest and anarchy of Austria.   An Empire which, as seen above, is largely the product of international factors; or to put that more correctly (no nation being really self-made), an Empire whose political health and power depend so largely on its foreign policy, cannot afford to leave that policy untouched by the select and hence presumably best fitted political intellect of the country.   To deprive Parliaments of all real influence on foreign policy is to open the door to petty local influences, to a policy of municipal or provincial backstair intrigues. Foreign policy has, amongst other wholesome influences on Parliaments, especially the well-known effect of reducing party-formations to two or three broad and clearly crystallized parties, and thus to obviate the cropping up of those countless little party-centres and factions that have, in Austria particularly, quite disorganized and as it were atomized political life.   At present there are over twenty-five parties in the Reichsrath of Austria.   Hungary, it is true, does not suffer from similar morbid excrescences in her party-organizations.   There too, however, the absence of any appreciable influence of Parliament on the foreign policy of the Empire, has had an undesirable effect on party life; and it is uncertain what it may still lead to in the near future.   At any rate, foreign policy has in the Austrian Empire been carried on in a spirit decidedly injurious to the welfare of the Empire and to its international position.   The Hungarians, it must be admitted, are not free from their share of guilt in that mistaken course adopted by Austria in her foreign policy since 1866.   Count Andrássy, whose prime motives were undoubtedly those of a Hungarian patriot, opposed all sympathy with France, that is, the very course that Austria ought to have followed during the Franco-German war.   In his opinion, an Austria that ceased to play a great *rôle* in the great European conflicts of the time, was more likely to surrender to Hungary all that he,

Deák and the Hungarians in general demanded. In that he
may have been right. However that may be, it remains true
that Austria, by abstaining from any interference in the Franco-
German war, practically abdicated from her former position as
a Great Power. The worst, and after all unlikely defeat at the
hands of the Germans, had Austria interfered in 1870, could
not have left her in a position more reduced in international
prestige than that in which her inactivity had landed her after
the peace of Frankfort on the Maine in 1871. The fear of
Russia, then (1870) the ally of Germany, is one of those
legendary nightmares that the innumerable victories of a small
nation like the Turks over Russia ought to have dispelled long
ago. When finally in 1879, a close alliance was made with
Germany, and in 1883 widened into a Triple Alliance of
Germany, Austria-Hungary, and Italy, Austria definitively
abdicated from her former international position, although
apparently she was placed on a basis offering more security
than she enjoyed before. The utterly misleading view of the
alleged beneficial effects of the *Triplice* on Austria-Hungary is
shared by all those who have carefully omitted to study the
history of the Danubian Empire and its just claims to a first-
class position in Europe. The Triple Alliance, by averting for
a given number of years in advance, any danger of attack
from Germany and Italy, the only two neighbours possibly
threatening Austria with war (Russia being quite absorbed
in her Asiatic policy), most effectively contributed to cripple
all independent or energetic foreign policy in Austria, where, as
we have seen, foreign policy is anyhow suffering from a want of
adequate organization. In reality, Austria-Hungary has for the
last twenty years had no foreign policy at all. In that she committed an error that the most stupid of the Hapsburgs in the
seventeenth or eighteenth century avoided doing. Better a
thousand mistakes than to abstain from making any mistake
at all. Death alone is the end of all mistakes; life means
errors. The anarchy in modern Austria is due neither to the

unreasonableness or conceit of this or that nation or party alone; it is neither indicative of sheer wickedness, nor caused by mere ignorance. It is largely due to a hopelessly wrong foreign policy. The ballast of a spirited foreign policy being indispensable for Austria, no wonder her vessel is tossed and buffeted about in a somewhat helpless manner. Her foreign policy is, or ought to be, quite clear. It is dictated by her history, and by her geographical position. Its chief axis runs through the near east. It is Austria, not Germany, that ought to have built and acquired the Baghdad railway. As long as Austrian foreign policy remains on its present lines of inertia and barren alliances, the old historic life of the Empire must largely remain toned down, if not more and more weakened.

In turning now to the third common feature of both halves of the Dual Empire, to the *Ausgleich* proper (the second feature, the common army, needing no special comment), it is necessary to note that that famous term refers to financial questions only. *Ausgleich*, in German, may seem to include political or constitutional matters too. The *Ausgleich* between Austria and Hungary, however, refers only to the quota to be paid by the two halves towards their common expenditure. The financial arrangement called *Ausgleich* is indeed of the utmost importance for both monarchies, and forms an integral portion of the Dualism as established by Deák. It is generally agreed to for a period of ten years. Roughly speaking, the Hungarians contribute 32 to 34 per cent., the Austrians 66 to 68 per cent. to the common expenses. The Hungarians, although much wealthier now than they were in 1867, do not want to accept a greater share of the common expenses; and this together with a natural jealousy of Austria's distracted parties against united Hungary, has rendered the renewal of the *Ausgleich* increasingly difficult.

As to the future of the Austro-Hungarian Empire it is safe to state, that the pessimistic predictions of the near downfall and partition of the Empire are unworthy of any serious discussion.   Austria, like France, has a hundred times been predicted to be nearing her final dissolution; every time falsely. Austria is as necessary to the balance of Europe, as is France; and the vitality of both has been probed and not found wanting in hundreds of campaigns and in numberless trials of strength from 1527 to 1866.   With all the vaunted strength of the Prussian system Austria has never known a period of collapse as ignominious as that which degraded the realm of Frederick the Great only twenty years after his death, in consequence of one double-battle lost.   The fighting material, the natural wealth, the strategic position of the Austro-Hungarian monarchy are such as to warrant her a dominant place in European politics for a very long time to come, provided her statesmen learn the lessons of her history and act up to it.   The present turbulence of the Austrian Parliament; the numerous scandalous scenes of which we read in the papers; the disruptive tendencies of the extreme Cech or German parties in Austria, all that must not blind us to the fact, that far from being symptoms of decay, they are rather welcome indications of a rising interest in public life, an interest which previous to 1875 was practically absent among large classes of Austria.   Like all people, the Austrians too have to learn the business of representative government by long and painful experience.   The English behaved just as badly in their time of apprenticeship, say at the Parliament of Oxford in 1681, and even very much later.   It might rather be suggested that the present turbulence of Austrian parties is probably too academic, and that the flinging of inkstands is too tame a procedure to inculcate political lessons with.   Austria will scarcely reach political manhood without internal disturbances very much more acute than all that we have heard of so far.   But far from misreading such disturbances into signs of the approaching end; far from thinking that the life of the present Emperor and King is the only mainstay of the Empire, it will be both more prudent and more in keeping with the facts not to prognosticate rashly a dismemberment of a realm that has, these three hundred years, directed many a principal current of European history, and has in that secular struggle acquired powers, latent and explicit, too great to be rendered useless or inefficient by the brawlings of a few agitators. As the Alps, the Carpathians, and the Danube now form, after prehistoric geological revolutions, the natural Triple Basis of the Dual Empire, so the Germans, the Magyars, and the Slavs are destined to form her true political Triple Alliance, each of them, if by a few catastrophes, finding in the end their proper sphere for the common weal of Austria-Hungary.

FRANCE AS THE LAND OF THE REVOLUTION.

By Professor Paul Mantoux.

A century of Revolution: so Mr Bodley, in his able book on modern France, describes the French history of the last hundred years. But what does that word Revolution mean? Does it mean mere disorder, barricades, kings flying from their palace through the back door, while provisional governments are hailed by equally provisional supporters in the hall of some Hôtel de Ville? If it means nothing more, why is France more interesting than any South American Republic, the modern history of which would show a more continuous series of Revolutions? Mr Bodley does not really answer this question. He seems to have come to the conclusion that the French people, as he has seen them in most provinces, are a quiet, home-keeping, hard-working sort of people, who have no taste whatever for Revolution, and who would like a strong Government to preserve them for ever from revolutionary agitation.— But Revolution means something else and something better than disturbance and civil war. The French Revolution has not been, as Mr Bodley hints, a great tragedy, followed in the course of a century by accessory little plays, the chief benefit of which would have been to supply mankind, in a dull and unpoetical age, with fresh elements of picturesque. If we give that word Revolution the substantial meaning it did and does convey to a French mind, if we show that Revolutions have not been futile dramatic incidents in modern French history, but are part of one great Revolution which is still going on at this very hour, and the final consequences of which have not been reached yet, then, I think, we shall understand much better many events of the past and of the present time. France is not only a land of Revolutions, but *the land of the Revolution*, the same spirit, which led the nation a hundred years ago, being still and always at work.

I.

A very easy and misleading explanation of the many changes which have occurred in France within a century is supplied by the fickleness of the French nation. In opposition to this ready-made explanation I shall quote some eloquent English verses, which may be conveniently used as an illustration of my own un-English prose. I take them from the sixth book of *Aurora Leigh*:

> The English have a scornful insular way
> Of calling the French light. The levity
> Is in the judgment only, which yet stands,
> For say a foolish thing but oft enough
> (And here's the secret of a hundred creeds,
> Men get opinions as boys learn to spell
> By reiteration chiefly), the same thing
> Shall pass at last for absolutely wise
> And not with fools exclusively. And so
> We say the French are light, as if we said
> The cat mews or the milch-cow gives us milk:
> Say rather, cats are milked and milch-cows mew:
> For what is lightness but inconsequence,
> Vague fluctuation 'twixt effect and cause,
> Compelled by neither? Is a bullet light
> That dashes from the gun-mouth, while the eye
> Winks, and the heart beats one, to flatten itself

To a wafer on the white speck on a wall
A hundred paces off? Even so direct,
So sternly undivertible of aim,
Is this French people.
All, idealists
Even too absolute and earnest, *with them all
The idea of a knife cuts real flesh;*
And still, devouring the safe interval
Which Nature placed between the thought and act,
With those too fiery and impatient souls,
They threaten conflagration to the world,
And rush with most unscrupulous logic on
Impossible practice.

The tendency which Elizabeth Browning thus noticed among the French is a double one. First, the French logic is unscrupulous: it carries principles to their extreme conclusions. French people are fearless before the logical consequences of free thought, whatever they are. They will never be stopped by any reverential feeling, if logic urges them on. Not only religion has been more boldly criticised in France than in any other country; but what survives every particular denomination, what philosophers like Kant would set apart, above the reach of reasoning, moral obligation, has been questioned by French thinkers with even more audacity than by Hume or Stuart Mill. Let us simply mention the telling title of Guyau's book, *Sketch of a moral philosophy excluding the ideas of obligation and reward.* If on the contrary a Frenchman undertakes to uphold tradition against critical reason, he will go straight to Tertullian's motto: *Credo quia absurdum.* Joseph de Maistre, in his *Evenings spent in St Petersburg,* is led, by an unsparing logical process, to the same sort of conclusions which illiterate sectarians credit by blind faith and enthusiasm. He will, for instance, maintain that there is no medicine, and will sneer at the doctor who answers something about tried remedies. "What is quinine?" he writes. "The bark of a tree. Whoever heard of bark doing anything, curing anybody, but by leave, in each particular case, of the Almighty God?"

Now—and this is the very essence of the French Revolution —the French do not only carry principles to their last conclusions, however subversive or absurd, but they want to force such conclusions into immediate effect. The French monarchy, and the whole structure of French society before 1789, were the produce of centuries; they had been modelled by force and settled by tradition. The French Revolution, as prepared by the writers of the 18th century, was a challenge to tradition and force, and an attempt to rebuild society from top to bottom according to the rules of abstract reason and theoretical justice. There was no claiming of historical rights, embodied in ancient charters: the Revolution was to establish the prevalence of natural rights, nature being understood, not as to what does now exist, but as what ought to exist. Throughout the dark story of the Revolution, among the tragical incidents of its necessary struggle against privilege, which unhappily gave occasion to unnecessary crimes, above that dreadful uproar of hope and despair, enthusiasm and rage, we hear ringing for ever the famous words once delivered by Mirabeau's mighty voice: *Le droit est le souverain du monde*[1].

Let us go now to some of the Parisian suburbs, where white-bearded workmen still remember the terrible fighting of February and June, 1848, where every man of fifty remembers the dark days of 1871. Let us go to the villages of Nivernais or Provence, which rose in 1851 against Louis Napoleon's usurpation, and where hundreds of persons were in consequence sentenced and transported. You will hear the people there still using the words of the great Revolution, speaking of the rights of the people, of political and social justice, and of the long-expected reign of reason, with the same deep and earnest feeling as in the old days, and you will think of live

---

[1] A translation is not easy, owing to the wide meaning of the French word *droit*: "Right is the sovereign of the world" would be literal, but by no means equivalent.

embers beneath mouldering ashes : you will almost forget that so many years have passed since 1789.

But how is it—here comes the unavoidable question—that the Revolution, after a whole century, seems to have achieved so little? Mr Bodley makes a pitiless dissection of the Republican motto: Liberty, Equality, Fraternity. He is right when he says it is not enough when you engrave them on the walls. Liberty? but a French citizen is far less secure against official molestation than the meanest British subject. Equality? but in no country you would observe such a rush for titles and decorations. Fraternity? but nowhere else you could witness such a merciless strife between parties, such violent attacks in the press against persons, such an unrelenting and unsparing criticism of men, institutions, and of the nation itself. So that, in Hobbes's words, the French may be said to be a wolf to the French: *Gallus Gallo lupus.*

The objection is not so difficult to answer as it would at first seem. The Revolution, except perhaps during the short idyllic period of its beginnings, never was a unanimous movement. Its immediate result could not possibly be to reconcile men together, but on the contrary to create a sharp division of interests and opinions, which has lasted down to the present day. The development of the Revolution is a struggle between hostile forces and doctrines : how could you expect it to result into fraternity as long as it is not concluded? How could you expect liberty to exist without any restraint, when it has to be fought for every day? how could equality be perfect, when privilege is still standing and resisting? The struggle is a hard one: the enemies of the Revolution, being French people, have shown themselves as extreme in their theory and practice of reaction as the Revolutionists had been in radical reform. They were led by the body of men who can best represent tradition against rational criticism, the spirit of reverence and obedience against the spirit of rebellion, the preservation of the established orders of things against change and novelty; an ancient and powerful body too, the Catholic Church itself. This again is typically French: the party of reaction, finding in the Church and its dogmas the very root of authority and social conservation, were led by their "unscrupulous" logic to forget the Church's exclusively ethical and religious character, and often to throw it as it were to the front of the political battle. That battle was begun more than a hundred years ago, and the end is not in view.

It is a great mistake to pass sentence on the Revolution as if its progress was concluded and its final results attained. Liberty, Equality, Fraternity, this does not pretend to be a description of the present state of things in the French Republic, or even a command to be enforced at once. It is the ever-receding summit of a long and steep ascent, every inch of which has to be won by an effort and a struggle. As for the division of French opinion, we must admit it has very often made the nation unhappy. But here lies the true greatness and glory of modern France. During a century idealist France has been showing to the world, at the cost of many sufferings, how the abstract conflict between tradition and reason, social justice and social privilege, can be translated into facts; she has turned dialectics into history: so that what you would sometimes call inconsistency is the result of logical opposition, and the succession of events which have filled the 19th century with their apparent haphazard and disorder, their sudden and startling changes, can be explained by the continuous action of a few main principles and causes.

II.

I am afraid the above considerations illustrate rather too well how French people indulge in abstraction. Let us come now, if not to the facts in their detail, at least to the general development of a few leading facts in the course of the 19th century.

1814—the beginning of the Restoration—is a most important date in French history. France had been invaded, Napoleon overwhelmed by the coalition's forces, and the fallen dynasty of Bourbon brought back with an escort of foreign soldiers.—How is it, that something of the Revolution could survive such a catastrophe? Louis XVIII, the brother of unhappy Louis XVI, was compelled by the Russian Emperor to declare that his return would not be the return of despotism. But he spoke of "linking again the chain of tradition, which had been broken during a period of nefarious crimes," and to him the year 1814 was the nineteenth of his reign. Being an old man and an invalid he was rather averse to passion and violence; he was, moreover, endowed with a keen political sense, which soon enabled him to perceive the nature of the changes which had taken place since 1789, and to understand that there could be no question of reviving the whole *Ancien Régime*. But he was surrounded by a party of rabid Royalists, who thirsted for revenge. They were noblemen who had fought during twenty years against the Revolution and against their own country with a hope of recovering their forfeited estates and feudal privileges; country squires from Brittany or Languedoc as fanatical as peasants, and ready to die for Church and King; clergymen who held the same views on the French Revolution as Bossuet once on Charles the First's fall, considering it as an ordeal and a punishment inflicted by an angry God on impious and reprobate France. After the rising of 1815, when the country, fascinated again by Napoleon's genius, had been subdued at last with him at Waterloo, those men, who were said to be "more royalist than the King," showed how violent their hate against modern institutions was. The movement known as the "White Terror" broke out in various parts of the country, and could not be excused, as the Red Terror of 1793, on account of misled patriotism. While the invading armies were greeted by royalist mobs with abject demonstrations, while the Government ordered trials and executions, a sort of religious war broke out in the South, and hideous murders were committed in the name of Religion and Loyalism.

But the cause of the Revolution had material forces on its side. The forfeited land, which the Revolutionary Governments had sold, had become the property of a class of people, who were thus personally interested in the duration of the new state of things. Louis XVIII understood that he could not afford to turn them against his authority; he felt obliged to remove their apprehension and to declare that the social conditions would not be changed again. He not only could not think of going back to the *Ancien Régime*, but, as he wanted to ingratiate himself with the middle class, he had from the beginning to assume the character of a restorer of liberty, which Buonaparte, the Corsican ogre, had suppressed. As a matter of fact, the Restoration was a period of free institutions and free speech: not a democratic government by any means, but not an illiberal one. Thus, when the White Terror was over, eloquent voices were allowed to ask for more liberty and more equality, and to remind the nation of its recent history. The Royalist party organised itself strongly and resisted the movement; relying upon the principles put forth by the *traditionalist* writers, de Maistre, de Bonald, they formed a great half-civil, half-religious association known as the Congregation, which controlled the elections, forced appointments upon the Cabinets, and pretended to direct the King himself; their propaganda was very active, they sent preaching missions to the provinces and hoped to bring back the whole of France under the sway of militant Catholicism. But the Liberals had on their side, against such a powerful action, not only the interest of the majority, but a passionate and almost unanimous national feeling.

A special stress must be laid upon the latter point. The national feeling, which plays such an important part in the modern history of every European country, had the greatest influence over the development of the French Revolution. In 1792 the Revolution and the Nation in danger seemed to be one thing; the tricolour flag was at the same time the emblem of French liberty, and the Standard which led the French armies to an unheard-of succession of victories. With Napoleon—and even some time before him—national defence had ceased, and a period of conquest had begun; it was no more France, but the neighbouring nations, who had to fight for independence. But when the French territory was being invaded, the glory of twenty years crushed and insulted, the very existence of the nation in question, the feeling of 1792 reappeared as strong as ever. You can imagine the indignation of the people, when they saw in the ranks of the invading forces some of their countrymen, triumphing over the ruin of their own country. The Government of the Restoration was thus hated and branded as being forced upon conquered France by the foreign conqueror, "brought back in the waggons of the foreign armies." The loss of the tricolour, which had thus been replaced by the old white flag of Henri IV, was considered as a symbol of national humiliation.

All these ideas of wounded patriotism centred round the memory of the wonderful man whose despotism and disastrous ambition were forgotten or forgiven by the nation his genius had mastered. In the popular recollection he remained as he had shown himself in 1814, when revolutionists like Carnot helped him in defending the frontier, and in 1815, when he embodied against the monarchy the nation and the revolution together. After his final defeat, when he lived, as in another world, on the distant rock of St Helena, his legend began to grow, mixing the idea of liberty with the idea of glory, the taking of the Bastille with Austerlitz and Wagram. The Liberals of the Restoration were all of them more or less Bonapartists, the national feeling was on their side, the tricolour was their flag, and this goes far to explain the Revolution of 1830.

III.

The Charter of 1814 had been looked upon by the
Restoration men as the real conclusion of the French Revolution. Just in the same way the ministers and prominent
supporters of Louis Philippe believed in earnest that 1830
was a final date. Among them we must mention Guizot, who,
being a historian as well as a statesman, erected his political
theory on a historical basis. Long before 1830 he had been
studying the English Revolution of the 17th century : his
Collection of Memoirs relating to the English Revolution was
begun in 1823 : his remarkable *History of the English Revolution* was published in 1827. The purpose of his work was
never merely scientific : he was led very soon to institute a
comparison between French and English history, which became more striking after the second fall of the French monarchy.
On both sides a double revolution, the Bourbons committing
the same faults and doomed to the same fate as the Stuarts :
such comparisons had been used, on the eve of the July
Revolution, for preparing the public mind to the idea of a
French 1688. After 1830 it was admitted by Guizot that the
era of Revolutions—as in England after 1688—was closed.
France had but to enjoy her permanent *régime* : the constitutional monarchy, controlled by the middle classes, was to be
her government for centuries to come—1848 gave him the lie
in a rather brutal way.

Let us consider with more attention the Revolution of 1830.
The classical view is that it was caused by the outrage committed by Charles X against the Constitution : the people rose
in defence of law and liberty, and the logical end of the
struggle was to restore the Charter under a sovereign holding
his royal office from the nation. But a careful study of the
events shows more clearly their close connection with the
tendencies of public opinion since 1814. It is true, that the
occasion of the rising was Charles X's *ordonnances*, which dis-

solved the Chamber just after its re-election, and put down the liberty of the press; it is equally true, that the insurrection was led at first with the cry of *Vive la Charte*. But the Charter concerned chiefly the middle and wealthy classes. The people as a whole desired liberty, but did not care much for a constitution which had given them no political rights. Their enmity against Charles X and his government had less definite and more powerful causes. The King had challenged public opinion by the appointment of the Polignac ministry: his choice roused at the same time the revolutionary feeling, the hate of the *Ancien Régime* and of clerical influence, and the national feeling. Bourmont, the new Minister of War, was a general who had gone over to the enemy two days before Waterloo; Marmont, who was to keep down the popular movement, had been charged with treason by Napoleon. The rising was begun in defence of the Charter; but what made it general, what stirred the crowds, was the reappearance of the proscribed tricolour. The insurgents of 1830 were led by the flag which recalled to their mind the Revolution and the Empire: their national feeling reinforced their revolutionary feeling. Old soldiers were fighting on the barricades: round aged Lafayette, who represented the spirit of 1789, young Polytechnicians, whose uniform had become popular on account of the part their school had taken in the defence of Paris against the Prussian and Russian armies, were the staff of the Revolution. The three days of July, 1830, were but the bursting out of the disappointment and hate which had been kept under during fifteen years.

As for the result, it cannot be considered as the logical consequence of the popular tendency: it was simply a compromise between parties. The middle class had already more to lose than to get by a Revolution, and was afraid of its own work. Charles X's return was impossible: but how to avoid demagogy, the red demagogy of '93, or the more imminent danger of a warlike government and European war? It was proved by recent researches that men like Talleyrand, conservative statesmen and *status quo* diplomatists, had much to do with the solution of the July problem. The result was the accession of Louis Philippe, Duke of Orleans; Lafayette accepted him, because he also wished to preserve peace, while most republicans dreamed of war: the misunderstanding was beginning already between the ideals of 1789 and 1804, between the passion for liberty and the passion for glory. The people who had fought and conquered in July won nothing but the flag they loved: the whole substantial benefit was for the rich middle-class, for the trading and peace-seeking *bourgeoisie*.

As soon as the people understood their Revolution had been juggled away a new movement sprang up at once. The popular feeling took three principal directions. First, the republican feeling was revived. Lafayette soon criticised and afterwards opposed the Government he had helped to establish, when he hoped to make it "the best of Republics." The younger men were ardent and enthusiastic, and believed in violent action. The first ten years of Louis Philippe's reign were disturbed by several republican risings: in 1832, 1834, 1839, secret societies were formed under men like chivalrous Barbès, the knight-errant of democracy, and mysterious Blanqui, the eternal conspirer whom all governments in succession dreaded, and who spent forty years of his life in state prisons. The Republicans were represented in Parliament, and while the most energetic Liberals of 1825 never dreamt of anything more than the British constitution of their own time, Ledru Rollin and Raspail remembered the Convention of 1792, and boldly advocated manhood suffrage.—The republican and democratic ideas did not apply exclusively to political questions: they were extended to a wider field of action. Fifty years had elapsed since 1789, and the principles of the *Déclaration des Droits de l'Homme* had to be applied to a new state of society. The growing of the factory system had effected a deep transformation of the nation's economic conditions; the towns were rapidly increasing in population, and a numerous class of factory operatives, different from the craftsmen of the foregoing times, was springing up, at the same time as a small and powerful body of industrial capitalists. The modern social question arose in consequence. The workpeople being overworked and underpaid, discontent was spreading and new Revolutions were brewing: in 1832 and 1834 terrible riots broke out among the Lyons silkweavers, who fought, not for Republic or Empire, but for their daily bread. The revolutionary doctrine assumed a new form in order to deal with these new problems: French Socialism, which had been anticipated by Gracchus Babeuf as early as 1796, practically dates from the time of the July Monarchy. There was an extraordinary growth of systems: St Simon's and Fourier's disciples, Louis Blanc, with his plans for the Organisation of Labour, found enthusiastic supporters among the young generation. A young man who would have termed himself a Liberal if he had lived in 1825, was a Socialist in 1845. What was Socialism, as it was then understood, but the revolutionary principle of justice by equality, being extended from the political to the social question?

Another great movement was due to the permanence of the national feeling, the influence of which had been so strong in 1830. Louis Philippe was bound to a peace policy: that policy can be said to have been his special task, and it was undoubtedly beneficial to France and Europe. But peace often was not easy to preserve against the passion of the crowds. After the July Revolution, when Belgium, Italy, Poland rose against their foreign masters, there was a great stir among the population; would France do nothing? would not she resume the work of armed propaganda begun by the Convention? On other occasions it was international difficulties which endangered peace and embittered public opinion. In 1840 a sudden development of the Eastern question left

France isolated against diffident or hostile Powers; there was a feeling of humiliation and anger in the country, and the situation was most dangerous for the Government, which avoided the conflict but at the expense of its popularity. Louis Philippe was also sharply taken to task for his alleged weakness towards England.—All this favoured the spreading of the Napoleonic legend, which helped as much as Socialism to subvert the "popular throne" of 1830.

If from the side of Revolution we turn to the side of conservatism and reaction we shall find that important changes had taken place. The party of the *Ancien Régime* had hardly survived their crushing defeat. But the majority of the middle-class had ceased to belong to the Liberal opposition, and were more and more opposing reform. The capitalistic *bourgeoisie* was growing wealthy: it was the golden age of commercial and industrial undertakings to which the great railway boom, about 1840, gave a tremendous push. Louis Philippe's monarchy was the best *régime* for the middle-class, as the monarchy of the white flag had been for noblemen and landowners. The progress of democracy, which takes the government from the hands of the middle-class people, and still more the progress of Socialism, which threatens their property, were dreaded by the sons of the *Tiers État*, who had in their turn become a privileged class.

The *bourgeoisie* used several means of defence against Revolution. They understood they could turn on their side the force of the national—or rather nationalist—feeling. Louis Philippe led the way, and his only mistake was to believe his own monarchy would benefit by it. Napoleon's statue was reinstated on the Colonne Vendôme: the King was present, and lifting his hat shouted "Vive l'Empereur." Versailles Palace became a military Museum, and was dedicated "To all the glories of France." The Emperor's remains were brought back from St Helena, and a triumphal funeral took place, the coffin being led to the Invalides, where it now rests under the gilt dome. The danger of such ceremonies was perceived by a few clear-sighted men : Lamartine, in a beautiful speech which was a sort of prophecy, protested against the apotheosis of unscrupulous genius, and said : "At least write on the tombstone : To Napoleon, and nobody else." So the Napoleonic movement was becoming distinct from the liberal and democratic movement, and was soon to be used against it.—A still more momentous change took place in the attitude of a great part of the French middle-class towards the Church. During the Restoration the middle-class as a whole was rather hostile to clericalism. Immediately after 1830 there was still a violent anti-clerical feeling. But when the "subversive" doctrines of Socialism made their appearance, the *bourgeoisie* became afraid. The Catholic party, being led with marvellous skill, understood at once there was an opportunity of taking hold of the coming generation. They claimed the right of teaching, the "liberty of teaching" as they called it : great men like Montalembert and Lacordaire were among them, and conducted their tactics. They were followed : their schools, brotherhoods, congregations became flourishing, and were mighty weapons against the spirit of Revolution. So everything was prepared for a struggle which was to make more evident than ever the radical opposition between hostile principles : on one side tradition, represented by the Catholic Church, and force, represented by Napoleon's worship ; on the other side Revolution, that is, rational criticism and government by rational laws.

IV.

The conflict broke into a crisis in 1848, and the crisis was such a grave one that nearly all Europe felt the shock. Its first cause was the question of suffrage. The parliamentary system, such as it had been established in 1814 and revised in 1830, rested upon a very narrow basis : the Chambers did not really represent the nation, but a very small minority of wealthy ratepayers. The republicans urged a reform, and advocated manhood suffrage. Guizot refused, and went as far as to maintain that manhood suffrage was absurd and impossible, and would never exist. Then began the agitation : the republican leaders, Ledru Rollin, Lamartine, held political banquets and delivered eloquent speeches. The interdiction of one of those banquets in Paris led to further agitation and riots ; the national guards sympathised with the rioters ; everything seemed to be at an end with Guizot's resignation. The quite accidental occurrence of a regiment firing at the mob kindled the dying flame into a blaze again. Then all the passions we have described simultaneously burst out, and the Revolution resumed its irresistible progress.

1848 resembles 1789 as the son does the father. The same enthusiasm, with which the whole nation for a short time seemed to be transported ; the *Assemblée Constituante*, the first assembly elected by manhood suffrage, was almost unanimously Republican, and trees of Liberty were planted on each village's market-place, and solemnly consecrated by the Catholic clergy. The same unbounded confidence in the efficiency of justice and reason: societies and clubs were swarming, and entertained unbounded hopes of improving the world and mankind ; a characteristic book of the time is Cabet's utopian novel entitled *Icarie*. There was no lack of great men, though they failed to appeal to the popular imagination as much as the men of the first Revolution did. There is hardly a nobler character in history than that of the poet Lamartine, facing the mob alone with the bare power of lofty eloquence, pacifying the country and removing Europe's fears. As for the results of the Revolution of 1848, they were most positive and important : the principle, one man one vote, which had been declared to be absurd a very short time before, was then established : a permanent acquisition, which even the despotic government of Napoleon III did not try to suppress. Slavery in the French colonies was abolished: so was the capital punishment for political offences. Much of our present liberty is due to the men of 1848.

But the question was: when and where will the Revolution stop? The whole of society was in an unsettled state, and fear began to prevail: some were afraid of war, most were afraid of Socialism. Business was disturbed, and a dangerous commercial crisis ensued. The working classes suffered very much, and called for help. The political problem being solved, the Revolution now came to a social problem. The preaching of Socialism had given occasion to vague and deluding hopes: the Republican Government finding itself unable to do much, it was a terrible disappointment to the working population. The National Workshops, where some sort of work was given to the unemployed, were but a shift, but they were still too much tainted with socialism in the eyes of the reactionaries, who urged their immediate suppression. The result was the rising of June, 1848, four days' fighting in Paris, with all the implacable fury of a civil war. Nothing so grave had occurred in half a century: it seemed to be a question of life or death to the Republic and the country. The middle-classes were defending their property against the desperate attack of the hungry crowds: the peasantry, afraid of losing their land, were anxious to take part in the struggle also, and helped in crushing the rebellion. Victory at last remained with the tricolour against the red flag, and peace—if not concord—was restored.

After June, 1848, the parties which under Louis Philippe had been resisting the revolutionary tendency were supreme in their turn. Had not they been right when they denounced the dangers of change? France, being frightened, threw herself on their side, on the side of reaction. General Cavaignac, who had put down the rising, was not thought to be conservative enough. The country rallied round the name which was the very symbol of strength and order: liberty might suffer, but there would be some compensation allowed to the nation's pride and to the popular craving for glory.—Louis Napoleon in 1847 was nothing : if he was known at all, it was rather as a ridiculous person, whose attempts against the Government had twice excited more laughter than indignation. But the spell of his magical name worked miracles : every enemy and many a candid friend of the Revolution hailed him as a heaven-sent leader, and, the 10th of December, 1848, he was elected President of the Republic by five million votes.

The tide was now on the side of reaction. Louis Napoleon at first seemed to be a mere tool in the hands of the Clerical party. He sent an army to Rome, against the Roman Republic which was claiming sisterhood with the French Republic, to restore the Pope's temporal power. The *Assemblée Législative,* which succeeded the *Constituante,* had a Monarchist and Clerical majority. Among many typical votes we may mention the passing of the Falloux Act. Viscount de Falloux was an ardent Catholic, who had written a Life of St Pius V, some lines of which, extolling the Holy Inquisition, have remained famous. His and his followers' watchword was liberty of teaching. As a matter of fact he obtained for the Church a real privilege over education, which according to his party's views was the best means of checking both intellectual and social Revolution. So the middle-class understood it : its spokesman, Thiers, though he was himself a professed Voltairian, supported the Bill on account of its probable action against subversive doctrines. The years 1849 and 1850 are as characteristic as 1848, in the opposite direction : the Government's policy was one of fear and hatred against democracy and social progress.

But the Clerical reaction was never popular. Louis Napoleon was popular, on account of his glorious name. The national feeling, hurt or disappointed so many times, was alive and awake, and entertained untold hopes and dreams about the new Napoleon. He knew it, and did not care for any abstract cause, but only for his own: he had been willing to serve the Assembly, but he expected the Assembly to be grateful and obedient. The conflict was bound to come. The Constitution of 1848 contained a most dangerous clause: the President, being elected by the direct suffrage of the whole nation, had as much or more power than the Assembly which was supposed to control his ministers' acts. When Louis Napoleon found himself strong enough he broke the oath he had solemnly taken of "remaining loyal to the Democratic Republic, and defending the Constitution." By the criminal *Coup d'État* of 1851 he instituted his own personal government. Only a minority of advanced republicans resisted, and terrible reprisals silenced their protest. The danger which had been foreseen by Lamartine in 1840 had destroyed liberty. The two feelings, which being still mixed together in 1830, had been roused alike by the reappearance of the tricolour flag, had now parted, and the opposition was stronger than ever between the two irreconcilable principles, the struggle of which had filled the first half of the century.

V.

The history of the Second Empire is not, it must be admitted, a history of principles. A more unprincipled gang of adventurers never took office than the people who surrounded Napoleon III. But the same causes, which had brought France to that dangerous turning of her career, were still at work.— A noticeable fact is that the Imperial Government was really popular with a large part of the nation: it would be childish to deny it, and to try, as it has been done sometimes, to represent France as having been tyrannised over by a hated usurper. The system appealed to every conservative instinct: the men of property, the tradespeople, the landowning peasantry, were naturally on the side of the police, and felt comforted under a government which was the very reign of policemen and gendarmes. With compulsory order and silence an era of material prosperity began : Napoleon and his ministers understood very well that it was their own interest to help in the economic progress of the times. The Emperor personally took part in the negotiations which resulted in the treaty of commerce of 1860 with England, and he patronised the doctrine of free trade. The natural development of industry and commerce after the great crisis of 1848, and the general increase of wealth, contributed very much to the Emperor's popularity.

At the same time as the material interests of a great part of the nation were satisfied, satisfactions of the immaterial order were offered to all, such as had been long expected and waited for by French Jingoism. Was not Napoleon III the nephew and successor of Napoleon I ? The longing for glory, the memory of victories and conquests, and the galling remembrance of the invasions of 1814 and 1815 had undermined the Restoration, and had been checked with great difficulty by Louis Philippe's cautious methods : but at last the time had come. War after war, in Crimea, in Italy, in Mexico, succeeded to the long period of peace which had followed Waterloo ; cheap triumphs appealed to the nation's vanity. While by his aggressive and improvident policy the Emperor prepared irretrievable disaster, his subjects and himself were deluded by outward appearances of *prestige* and glory.

For such dangerous delusions the country had given up the cause of liberty. The system of internal government was the contrary of a liberal one : universal suffrage was domesticated, the press muzzled, every idea of social reform forbidden and prosecuted.—But the Revolution could not be stopped for ever. Like steam in a boiler, it was sure to find some outlet, or burst out. The exiles at first could alone raise their voices against despotism : but they were heard in France, and when Victor Hugo, on Guernsey's rock, wrote his immortal *Châtiments*, the book's dedication was : "Book, may the wind take thee—To France, where I was born...." After some years, the opposition became strong enough to be represented in the Legislative body. The Italian war, which estranged the extreme Clericals, obliged the Emperor to offer some sort of compromise to the moderate Liberals, and the republicans and democrats were enabled to make further progress. Socialism, which had nearly disappeared after 1848, was reviving under the influence of Karl Marx, and the new generation were dreaming again their fathers' dreams. Napoleon III at last, after making an ineffectual experiment of what was called the "Liberal Empire," committed his dynasty's future to the hazard of a foreign war.

We have not to deal with the war of 1870, but only to consider how it influenced the development of internal history. It was a terrible lesson, which taught the nation the real meaning of Caesarism—which had been forgotten so soon after 1815. The fatherland being invaded, the memory of the Revolution was recalled at once. The name of the Republic was recurred to as a magic weapon: had not the first Republic raised fourteen armies in the midst of national distress, and defeated a coalition which included the whole of Europe? The national passion this time was on the side of liberty and Revolution again, and Gambetta's eloquence, which before the Emperor's fall had boldly denounced the crime committed in 1851, was now encouraging resistance against the German conqueror. A tumultuous wave of national and social hopes arose: not only victory was expected, but the establishment of an ideal Republic, which was to fulfil the promises of many Revolutions. Never was public opinion more sanguine than in that dark hour.

A terrible disappointment fell upon the country after the final collapse, and this explains the Commune of 1871, that frightful rising, which mixed enraged patriots with violent Socialists, those who thought the nation was betrayed with those who believed a short effort would put down iniquity and establish the millennium of justice. Civil war succeeded foreign war, and the world for some months thought it was all over with France.—But after the storm we distinguish the same elements, still opposing each other in the same way as before. This time the lessons seem to have borne fruit, and the progress of democracy will be regular and almost uninterrupted. Every attempt against the spirit of the Revolution, however formidable, will end in failure; Boulangism after Marshal Mac Mahon's Moral Order, Nationalism after Boulangism, will be defeated, and the result will be the more and more secure establishment of democratic institutions.

VI.

For the conflict between contradictory principles we have just tried to relate in its main lines is slowly advancing towards a settlement. French democracy does exist, and the growth of a genuine democratic feeling is an undeniable fact. Take the desire for equality: this may be called a democratic feeling, the democratic feeling *par excellence*. The French military system has been altered four times, under the pressure of that desire. Conscription had been in existence ever since the beginning of the first Empire: but the replacing of recruits by paid substitutes was allowed, the result being that not one young man of the wealthier class had to go to the army. After 1870 every man was bound to serve as a soldier: but if you could pay £60 and undergo a very easy examination, you were sent to the barracks for one year only, while the others remained there five years. In 1889 a new Act instituted the three years' compulsory service: only a few students, or the widows' eldest sons, still enjoyed the privilege of serving one year. Many abuses having crept into that system, which has become inconsistent with the public need for equality, a new Act is now in progress, which will take every man to the army for two years, all alike, making no difference between work-

man and gentleman, rich and poor. Thus the poorest classes
will not be allowed to bear the heavier part of the common
burden. I think this is a fair instance of democratic progress.
The spreading of education is democracy: the present Republic has made elementary teaching compulsory, and millions
of children have been educated in consequence. One man
one vote is undoubtedly a democratic motto: France is the
first country where manhood suffrage has been in existence,
and what her most reactionary governments have done has
been to turn it to account according to their wishes, but they
never could destroy it. French democracy is fighting, but
advancing while it fights.

The last question is, whether the Revolution has still its broad
cosmopolitan character of a hundred years ago, whether we
could trace throughout the century the revolutionary influence
of France outside her borders? This ought to be studied,
and would be a most interesting subject. The conflict between
past and present is nearly the same at bottom in every civilised
country: but nowhere is the logical opposition of principles
as clear and decided as in France, and this is enough to
maintain the influence of the French Revolution. France is
like a theatre, in which the interests and passions which the
looker-on feels confusedly struggling in his own bosom are
arranged into a striking and pathetic drama. The Marseillaise
is a revolutionary song for all countries. The three days of
July, 1848, set the half of Europe on fire; in 1848 not a State
on the Continent remained untouched by Revolution, and
reaction in France was the beginning of reaction all round.
This influence may have diminished to-day, but I notice how
anxiously the public abroad observes whatever happens in
France, how for instance a French judicial case lately became
the very symbol of judicial iniquity in every country. And
why did that case rouse interest in all parts of the world?
because it illustrated another critical stage in the great struggle,
which has sometimes wronged the nation, but for the nation's

true glory, which is not to be sought in war, but in sacrifices made for civilisation, human progress, and justice. And so, in the poet's words,

> And so, I am strong to love this noble France,
> This poet of the nations, who dreams on
> For ever, after some ideal good,
> Some equal poise of sex, some unvowed love
> Inviolate, some spontaneous brotherhood,
> Some wealth that leaves none poor and finds none tired,
> Some freedom of the many that respects
> The wisdom of the few. Heroic dreams!

As long as such dreams are dreamt in France, as her inhabitants are never content with dreaming only, she will remain, as she has been for more than a hundred years, the land of the Revolution.

TWO STATESMEN OF THE THIRD REPUBLIC.

By Professor Paul Mantoux.

No government was ever born under such tragical circumstances as the Third Republic. On the 3rd of September, 1870, the first news from Sedan began to reach anxious and excited Paris : something about a great battle, Marshal Mac Mahon wounded or killed, the whole army in danger of being surrounded by the enemy. Soon after, the whole truth, the naked, terrible truth became known : the Emperor had surrendered with ninety thousand men, and the road to Paris was laid open to the invader. Under such circumstances, on the 4th of September, public indignation swept away the ruined Empire, and the Republic was established. Its beginnings were hardly less trying than the occasion of its birth : after a desperate resistance, France had to submit to the conqueror's will, while a dreadful rising was adding to the evils of war the horrors of the most infuriated civil strife. There are still two generations of Parisian people who remember the dark days of April and May 1871, when the red flag of the Commune was waving over Paris, the tricolour over Versailles; and over St Denis, at three miles distance from the capital, the new flag of the German Empire : for the victorious German troops were still there, looking at the great city, to which some of her inhabitants had set fire, and which, with its hideous crown of smoke and flames, was like a circle of Dante's Inferno.

I think it would be a mistaken feeling for a Frenchman to feel uneasy about the recollection of those times. On the contrary, a Frenchman ought to be proud when he considers that his country has survived such an ordeal; that France not only was not destroyed, but soon reappeared as strong and prosperous as ever, resuming her position among nations, and her work of civilisation and progress. This is certainly due to the vital forces of the nation, but also to a few men who deserved the title of restorers of the country as well as that of founders of the Republic. Thiers and Gambetta were most prominent among them. Thiers was like a cunning old physician, who cured the wounds of France and managed to keep aside the monarchical quack-doctors. Gambetta, after organising national defence in 1870, led the democratic movement between 1875 and 1883. The history of both their careers will not only make us acquainted with two of the most interesting characters in recent times; it goes far to explain how the Republic, being born among such dangers, was able in spite of all to live and thrive.

I.

No portrait is more popularly known than that of old Thiers, as he was in the latter days of his life: a short, very short old man, in an eternal black frock-coat, with a shrewd, clean-shaven face, a funny little tuft of white hair over it, and sparkling eyes behind a pair of round spectacles. That was at the time when he used to say about himself: "I am an old, old umbrella which has become used to rain, from having seen so many showers." Many, indeed, for his experience of political meteorology had begun more than fifty years before, even before the stormy days of July 1830.

He was born in 1797, at Marseilles, and he always kept the quick gestures and speech of the Southerner, and also the accent, which gave an amusing tone to his fluty voice. He became known as early as 1823 or 1824 by his contributions to liberal papers, and soon undertook an important historical work : a *History of the Revolution*, which was, with Mignet's shorter book, the first attempt to deal with the subject. He had been encouraged in his beginnings by somebody who was a clear-sighted judge of talent, the old diplomatist Talleyrand. In January, 1830, a new Opposition paper was published against the Polignac Ministry : its title was *Le National*. It was secretly patronised by Talleyrand, and in carefully chosen words advocated a revolution similar to the English revolution of 1688 : nobody could be mistaken about the new William the Third, who was the Duke of Orleans. Thiers, who ran that paper, was then a young man of a rather enthusiastic temper : he took a very active part in the events of July 1830.

The Monarchy of July was a most favourable time to the development of his political fortunes. It was the reign of the middle-class, and he was most distinctly a middle-class man, with middle-class views and even prejudices. He soon became a parliamentary leader, and took office several times, being twice Prime Minister. His rivalry with Guizot has remained famous. The difference between them was perhaps a difference of temper more than of principles : Guizot was cold, haughty, somewhat pedantic, and could not become easily popular ; Thiers, on the contrary, was good-natured, talkative, and of easy access, more open to the currents and counter-currents of opinion than his rival, more liberal at least in appearance—for he was convinced as much as Guizot that the government of the middle-class was the best possible. Above all, he sympathised with the popular feeling concerning national glory : during his leisures he compiled his huge *History of the Consulate and Empire*, paying thus his tribute to Napoleon's memory.

Whether in office or in opposition, he equally distinguished himself by his deep knowledge of public business, the admirable clearness of his mind, which seemed to unravel without the least effort the most intricate questions, and by his peculiar eloquence, which was that of an unrivalled debater : never appealing strongly to the feelings of his audience, but persuading them by skilful arguments, as distinct and easy in his reasoning as the sound of his shrill Southern voice, and making figures themselves attractive. He was loved by the *bourgeoisie* of 1840; he was a favourite with the jolly national guards, whose pot-bellies and peaceful whiskers have been so often portrayed in the amusing cartoons of Daumier and Gavarni.

In 1848 the evolution of his opinions was most significant. As a man of the middle class he hated and was afraid of Socialism : he not only opposed its progress as a politician, but also as an economist. About that time he wrote his little book on Property, which was an attempt to justify Capitalism by reducing political economy into Franklin's advice: "Take care of your pence, and your pounds will take care of themselves." It is curious enough that, while he explained the right of property by admitting that wealth is identical with work, he was preparing the way to the theory of Karl Marx on the origin of Capital. He was of course indignant against the rising of June, 1848, and very bitter against the labouring classes : he went as far as to call them, in a public debate, "a vile mob," which was not entitled to retain the franchise. He sided with the anti-liberal reaction in 1849 and 1850, and supported the Falloux Act in favour of Clerical education. But his hatred of socialism and advanced democracy did not obscure his perception of the dangers of despotism : he denounced Louis Napoleon's ambition, and soon led the opposition against his suspected schemes : "If this House," he said on one occasion, "does not maintain its right, the Empire is as good as made."

After years of forced silence, when parliamentary discussion became possible again, he was the most unrelenting and the most competent critic of Napoleon III's faults. There was hardly an important debate in which he did not express the protest of liberal and enlightened opinion against the Imperial *régime.* He criticised everything : the financial policy, which consisted in spending money without end for objectionable wars, and in burdening the nation with loans, without any care for the future; the foreign policy, when Denmark was sacrificed to the German Powers, or when Napoleon III undertook the nonsensical establishment of a Mexican Empire. When, in spite of Thiers's advice, France contented herself with looking on the struggle between Austria and Prussia, and by her inactivity made possible and sanctioned as it were the Prussian victory at Sadowa, Thiers bitterly exclaimed : " There is not a blunder which has not been committed." There was still another most dangerous blunder in store, which was committed when war was declared against Prussia in July, 1870.

Had the French ambassador been insulted by William I's refusing to discuss any more with him on the question of the Spanish succession, which seemed to be settled by Leopold von Hohenzollern's retirement? Did Bismarck alone create the sensation by his altered edition of the telegram from Ems relating the interview? Anyhow the French ministers, who knew the truth, contrived, as much as Bismarck did, to keep the genuine report in the dark : they wanted to incense the national feeling and have war. Thiers then delivered the most eloquent speech of his life, among the furious ejaculations of rabid Bonapartists, for whom a man who dared oppose the War policy was no better than a traitor : " If you can't understand," he said, turning to them, "if you can't understand that I am now performing a duty, and the most painful one in my life, I pity you indeed. I am ready to suffer anything for preserving my countrymen's blood, which you are so heedlessly going to spill. You may insult me, I don't care." On that day he deserved the nation's gratitude, and the power which was committed to him immediately after that unhappy war.

He had still another painful duty to perform. The Government of National Defence sent him, though he was an old man of over seventy-three, on a general embassy to the courts of Europe. He visited London, Vienna, Florence, Petersburg, asking for help, trying to rouse sympathy or interest : he was received everywhere as a distinguished guest, but how could he have induced any Government to associate its country's fortunes with those of overwhelmed France ? That mission put him as it were above political parties. When the general election for the National Assembly took place, in February, 1871, he was elected by twenty-four constituencies. As soon as the Assembly met, he was by common assent appointed Head of the Executive. Then began the most remarkable period in the course of his long political life.

He had to face the greatest difficulties a statesman ever met. Peace was not concluded yet ; everything in the country was destroyed or disturbed ; the advanced wing of democracy was ready to rebel against the Assembly ; and the Assembly, elected by special permission of Bismarck under German supervision, was full of monarchists who dreamed of a Restoration. The most urgent question was the question of peace. Thiers was perhaps the only man who could negotiate on equal terms with Bismarck : his keen practical sense was a match to Bismarck's cynicism. Jules Favre, an "old beard of 1848," had been a butt to the cruel sarcastic vein of the Chancellor, who used to hit hard. With Thiers it was quite different : Bismarck had to deal with a sharp business man, who questioned and discussed everything, and to whose prodigious knowledge of circumstances and men even a consummate statesman was obliged to bow. The victory won by Germany being a crushing one, the conditions of peace could not be much bettered by Thiers ; and yet he succeeded in keeping Belfort, which had never been taken by the enemy, and had been surrendered only by an article of the peace preliminaries. So a small district of Alsace has remained part of the French territory. And it must be observed that Belfort plays a most important part in the present system of defence of the Eastern frontier, being a key to one of the doors through which France might be invaded. The Assembly ratified the treaty without much opposition : most of its members had been sent there for the express purpose of making peace. The Extreme Left only, including Gambetta and Victor Hugo, advocated resistance to the bitter end, and reproached Thiers with not having exhausted the nation's last resources before consenting to the loss of Alsace and Lorraine.

After the treaty had been signed and ratified, another difficulty began. There was a terrible clause : France was to pay a war indemnity amounting to 200 million sterling, five thousand million francs ! The German troops were to be withdrawn gradually, in proportion to the sum paid after each fixed period. How to find the money ? The Treasury was empty, and the whole country north of the Loire had suffered from invasion. But Thiers did not despair : as early as the spring of 1872, he found himself able to undertake a loan. The public was asked to subscribe the £200,000,000 : more than a thousand millions were offered, such was the confidence which Thiers's name and policy had inspired. Then he began freeing the territory from foreign occupation : in October, 1873, there was not a German soldier within the new frontier.

Thiers had been elected Head of the Executive in February, 1871. In the course of the following month, on the 18th of March, the *Commune* broke out in Paris. It is difficult for a Frenchman, after thirty years only, to express an impartial opinion on the Commune. Those who fought against the rising still consider it as a heinous crime, an absurd and inhuman outburst of misery and ignorance, turned to account by a few villains. Those who fought on the side of the Commune, and most of the present Socialists, will tell you the Commune was a righteous Revolution for the attainment of social justice, which the selfish middle-class mercilessly suppressed ; and if they are reproached with the hostages' murder and the Tuileries' arson, they will answer by dreadful stories on the wholesale slaughter which undeniably took place during the "gory week" of May: for them Thiers was no better than a butcher in the service of the bloodthirsty *bourgeoisie*. I think we ought to consider what the people on both sides had suffered during the war: there lies the real explanation of both parties' violence and crimes. The Commune, far from being chiefly a social rising, was to a large extent a Chauvinistic movement, led by enraged patriots, who thought defeat had been caused by treason: on the other hand, the atrocities which were committed by the regular troops when the rebellion was crushed are explained, if not justified, by the indignation of having to subdue their own countrymen while the foreign conqueror was looking on.

What Thiers did was in his position the only thing to do. He did not try to resist the insurrection in Paris. He knew enough about Revolutions. Already in 1848 he had, we are told, advised the King to withdraw his forces from the capital, and to undertake a siege. That is what he did himself in 1871: not only the army, but every official or agent of the Government, down to the gaolers of the Paris prisons, were called back to Versailles, thus leaving the city to disorder and anarchy. Then the second siege of Paris began: at the end of May it was all over with the Commune. Whether the cruelty of the repression—thousands of persons being shot in Paris, thousands sentenced and transported—is to be ascribed to Thiers, it would be unfair to decide before the time for more impartial history has come. Anyhow peace and order were restored at last, and the new Government securely established.

Another danger still threatened that Government: there was a general belief that it could not escape being soon converted into a Monarchy. Thiers had been a Monarchist, and the Prime Minister of a King. But after so many Revolutions he had come to the conclusion that Monarchy had become impossible in France. It may be that his personal ambition was interested in such a conclusion; and yet we must observe that he professed still more Republican feelings after he had left office than when he held it. His Republic was not to be democratic in the extreme: he still styled himself a Conservative—a word which in his mind was not the opposite of Liberal —and he used to say: "The Republic will be Conservative, or it shall not exist."

Conservative as he was, the National Assembly of 1871 distrusted his advanced views. It was, like the Assembly of 1849, full of country gentlemen, either Legitimists—supporters of Henri V, grandson of Charles X—or Orleanists— supporters of the Count of Paris, grandson of Louis Philippe. They hated democracy, and were above all devoted to the Clerical cause. A typical fact was their vote consecrating France to the recent and idolatrous worship of the Sacred Heart, for which a large church was to be erected on the top of Montmartre Hill. If they had put Thiers at their head, it was because they could hardly compete with his immense and well-deserved popularity, and also because they were afraid of another man, Gambetta. The whole skill of the old statesman was required for remaining in office and maintaining the Republic in spite of the majority. By his services he had won an unequalled *prestige*. He knew the weakness of the monarchical parties, their prejudices and their mutual differences: he knew how to counterbalance them by each other. In the autumn of 1871 he changed his title for the more significant one of President of the French Republic. But he would not give up his right of taking part in parliamentary debates; he mastered the Assembly by the lucidity of his views, the weight of his experience and the cleverness of his political tactics. His enemies could not prevail before they had passed a standing order, under which the President could not address the House except on certain occasions: such was the direct influence of his person and his oratory!

The whole of the year 1872 was spent in reorganising the country. The army was reconstructed: military service was made compulsory for every man between twenty-one and forty years of age, with a time of actual service amounting to five years, the rest being spent in reserves more or less similar to the German *landwehr* and *landsturm*. Another important law, on local government, allowed more independent rights to local authorities than under the former *régimes*. Again and again the Monarchists tried to win Thiers to their side, but he kept his own ground, and went on organising the Republic. The bye-elections of 1873 were Republican, and even Radical. Thiers's own candidate in Paris, M. de Rémusat, did not succeed against an obscure Radical politician. This served as a pretext for Thiers's fall. All the men who had unwillingly followed and obeyed him during two years rose against him, charging him with being unable to stop the advance of demagogy. A man who belonged to a great Orleanist family, the Duke of Broglie, led the attack, and remonstrated about the expediency of checking the audacity of Radicalism and restoring "moral order" in the country. Thiers's administration was upset; and Marshal Mac Mahon, who was known to have monarchical sympathies, became President. From the date of the 24th of May, 1873, the Republic seemed to be doomed to destruction.

The four last years of Thiers's life showed the boundless gratitude, confidence, and respect, with which he was surrounded by the nation. As long as his age allowed him to do so, he sat in the Chamber, among the Republican party. He could no more assume the heavy duties of leadership, but his advice was asked for and followed like an oracle. He voted against the "moral order" Government of the Duke of Broglie, and opposed Clerical reaction. After a Republican constitution had been voted in 1875—by a majority of one vote—Marshal Mac Mahon and the Monarchists made a desperate attempt to govern against the new Assembly: Thiers was one of the 363 deputies who passed the famous resolution, refusing to acknowledge the Ministry appointed on the 16th of May, 1877. He was now reconciled with the more advanced Republicans. On one occasion, as a Reactionary Minister,

M. de Fourtou, had said in a speech : "Our Government has freed the national territory from foreign occupation," Gambetta sprang to his feet and exclaimed, pointing to Thiers : "The liberator of the territory, here you see him ! " And a storm of applause followed, while every man in the House turned to the little old man, who was sitting unmoved in his seat of the Left Centre.

He died in the same year, in the midst of public excite-ment and agitation. The Republican Chamber had been dissolved by President Mac Mahon, the general election was near, and the whole country was anxious about the result. Thiers's funeral was a huge Republican demonstration : a hundred thousand persons followed the hearse, and the mourning was universal. Persons who have seen other State funerals in Paris will tell you they never noticed such a striking silence, such signs of genuine and deep sorrow. Thiers in his old age had become the living standard of two causes equally dear to an immense majority of his country-men : the cause of fatherland and the cause of liberty. What he did for France in the most critical circumstances of her modern history will never be forgotten. And it is a most interesting fact, that the evolution of his political ideas was achieved under such circumstances, when he was an old man with fifty years' experience of politics : he always remained a man of the middle class, ready to suppress by force any attempt to alter the constitution of society, but he inclined more and more to Liberal and Republican principles. The Republic as he understood it was still a narrow one, but its being in existence made possible the wider and more democratic Republic of the future.

II.

Thiers's and Gambetta's names have become closely asso-ciated on account of the prominent part they took in politics at the same time, since the beginning of the Franco-German war ; the memory of one is nearly as remote as the memory of the other, Gambetta having survived Thiers but by a few years. It is hard to realise there was more than a generation's distance between them. Thiers was born in the eighteenth century, and his political career was one of the longest recorded in any country : for he was known as a journalist since 1823, and he died in 1877. Gambetta's career, which had begun as early, was on the contrary a very short one : when he died he was very far from being an old man, being hardly more than forty-four. As his death occurred in 1883, it is easy to calculate that if he had lived he would be now sixty-three, he would be Mr Chamberlain's junior. So he was more than forty years younger than Thiers : we must not be surprised if he was possessed with all the vigour and enthusiasm of youth, and if his democratic ideals were more modern than those of the aged statesman.

Both of them were Southerners, with the Southern talent of easy and fluent speech : but Nature, which had given to Thiers a short figure and a thin silvery voice, had endowed Gambetta with powerful shoulders, dark hair, and a beard which he used to shake like a lion's mane, a voice that rolled like thunder, and could express the strongest emotion, scorn, or anger. He was, much more than Thiers, the type of the orator ; oratory was his very life ; his enemies malignantly hinted that when he was not speaking he was not thinking either. Thiers's manners and style of life were those of a well-to-do old *bourgeois*. Gambetta led rather an artist's life, and was a slave to his wild passions as was another great orator whom he resembled in many ways, Mirabeau.

In 1867, the despotic system of the Second Empire, which had been somewhat relaxed already, was replaced by a sort of mitigated Liberalism, preparing the way for the so-called "Liberal" Empire. An Imperial decree gave back to deputies the right of asking questions ; public meetings were allowed to be held under certain conditions, and the press recovered a part of its former liberty. The Republicans at once made use of that liberty for uttering their long-silenced protest against the criminal *Coup d'État* of 1851. It was proposed to erect a monument to the memory of the victims, and more especially of the deputy Baudin, who had been shot while defending .the Constitution against the man who had sworn to respect and preserve it. The editor of the paper which had started the subscription was prosecuted, and took Gambetta for his counsel.

Gambetta was then a young, briefless barrister, his eloquence being known but to a few friends : but the day after the trial it was known to the whole country. His speech at the bar was an indignant charge against rampant usurpation : " On the 2nd of December a pretender rallied round him men without any ability, without any character...men who would have made themselves, at any time, the accomplices of the most hateful outrages upon the laws of the country....You have been for seventeen years possessed of absolute power ; well, you never dared to say : 'We will commemorate, we will reckon among national commemorations the 2nd of December.' And yet all the former *régimes* have prided themselves on the day of their birth : only two dates were omitted till now, the 18th of Brumaire and the 2nd of December : because you are well aware that if you dared to commemorate such days, the moral conscience of the world would rise against them and you ! "

The nation was thrilled by Gambetta's eloquence, and he soon became a leader of the rising Republican party. In 1869 he was returned to Parliament: his experience of practical politics had been a very short one, when the war of 1870 broke out.

On the 4th of September, 1870, after the Emperor's forfeiture had been proclaimed, a Provisional Government was hurriedly constituted : among its members was the young orator Gambetta. The name of the Republic, and the memory of the republican victories over invaders, had sent throughout the country a wave of enthusiastic feeling. Gambetta was the man of that feeling : he knew the better what enthusiasm can work in a French soul because he was himself intensely French in that respect. But he was not only the Government's speaker; he did not only stir the Parisian population by his proclamations and speeches. He left the beleaguered city, the inhabitants of which he had incited to endure every suffering before surrendering to the enemy, and, crossing the besiegers' lines in a balloon, he assumed the overwhelming, impossible task of organising resistance in the provinces.

Impossible, indeed, it seemed to be. Of the Imperial military system nothing was left. Out of two great armies one had been destroyed at Sedan, the other one was blockaded in Metz, where Marshal Bazaine soon surrendered after weeks of suspicious inaction. The few remaining regiments were shut up in Paris. When Gambetta began his work at Tours he had hardly a penny or a soldier to rely upon. He had not even lists of officers: we are told he heard for the first time of General d'Aurelles de Paladines in a conversation with a man he happened to meet in a railway carriage. What he contrived to do. is simply stupendous. Helped by technical men like the engineer de Freycinet he raised thousands of men, got clothes, arms, and ammunition for them, and food in the middle of the winter. Three armies were organised, one down the Loire under d'Aurelles and Chanzy, one in Northern France under Faidherbe, one in the East under Bourbaki. These armies won several victories: they were doomed to final disaster, the men being raw recruits, who suffered much from the exceptionally cold weather, and had to fight against well-trained and well-supplied troops, reinforced by inexhaustible reserves; but their resistance lasted nearly five months, from the beginning of September to the end of January, five months after Sedan, when the Prussian generals had thought the war would be at an end in a fortnight's time. If France at last fell, she did not disgrace herself by her fall: her honour had been saved owing to Gambetta's patriotism, enthusiasm, and indomitable will.

Gambetta was so sanguine about the work he had undertaken, he had such hopes of final success that he was indignant when he first heard of peace. He would have refused Bismarck's offer of a truce for a general election; his opinion was the struggle ought to be led with more energy and doggedness than ever. But his views were disapproved of by Thiers, and by his colleagues of the Provisional Government, Jules Simon, Garnier Pagès, etc. Before the polling-day he resigned, laying down the extraordinary power which for a few months had made him a sort of dictator. The Assembly, which met at Bordeaux in February, 1871, and in which he sat as a Radical deputy, could not possibly agree with him. The majority had been elected "in an evil hour" (an expression which Republicans afterwards ironically quoted) when the country was tired of war and afraid of Revolution : its tendency was a decidedly reactionary one. Garibaldi, who had been fighting with the French army, was not allowed to take his deputy's seat, because he was an alien ; Victor Hugo was hooted because he spoke against peace, and an unknown Breton bard told him he was not speaking French. An intense distrust of Republican Paris prevailed among the country squires and landowners who represented rural constituencies : the title of capital was transferred to Versailles, a measure which certainly was one of the causes of the Commune's rising. Gambetta to such people was no better than a Revolutionist and a firebrand. After protesting against the clauses of the treaty with Germany, he sent in his resignation, and left the Assembly.

Bye-elections took place in July, 1871 : Republicans were elected nearly everywhere. Peace being made and Revolution suppressed, the nation was no more in a state of panic, and was coming back to democracy. Gambetta, when he re-entered Parliament, was no more standing by himself, almost alone against a hostile majority : the rising movement of democracy was with him. But his position in the Assembly was still a difficult one, for he could support Thiers's general policy, but on many points he did not agree with the President's views. While his influence in Parliament was a weak one, he found another and a wider field for his un-impaired activity. He began travelling through the country, addressing meetings ; he denounced reaction and advocated reform. He jocularly called himself "the commercial traveller of the Republic." His unrelenting propaganda for Democracy was followed by the Radical bye-elections of 1873, which became the pretext of Thiers's fall.

The offensive move of the Monarchists brought about a close alliance between the moderate and the advanced Republicans. The young Republic was in danger. It was no mystery that Marshal Mac Mahon had Royalist connections, and the new Premier, the Duke of Broglie, was a professed Royalist. In the autumn of 1873 everything was ready for a Restoration, and the Count of Chambord would have become Henri V—it was reported the coronation carriage had been ordered—if he had not unexpectedly wrecked his own cause. With a remarkable devotion to his principles, and an astonishing lack of political sense, he declared he would never change the white flag of his ancestors for the tricolour, which in his eyes was but an emblem of Revolution. This was enough to make his accession impossible. France could not be brought as far back as 1829. But, if a Restoration could not be effected, the Monarchists were still in office, and, feeling public opinion was turning against them, they tried by stringent measures to stop the progress of Republican and Democratic ideas. The law on local government was altered; the Minister of the Interior was to appoint the mayors, as under Napoleon III: there was a clean sweep of Republican municipalities of course. While Republican demonstrations were hardly tolerated, the Reactionists, and even the Bonapartists, so justly unpopular after Sedan, were let loose: they used intimidation: Gambetta once was assaulted as he was coming back from Versailles. The parties of reaction knew he was their most dangerous opponent; and his eloquence was never more unwelcome to them than when it expressed the growing dissatisfaction of the nation.

He was still the leader of a parliamentary minority. But after the Constitution of 1875—the present French Constitution—had been voted owing to the disagreement between

Imperialists, Royalists, and Conservatives, the Republic was no more a provisional state of things, but the lawfully established *régime* under which the country was to live. The National Assembly broke up at last, and the popular vote returned to the new Chamber a strong Republican majority. Gambetta's position was a very peculiar one. As long as Marshal Mac Mahon's Presidency lasted there could be no question of his taking office : for the President was reluctant enough to appoint even Moderates like Jules Simon and Dufaure. But Gambetta's influence was so great that his enemies hinted he was playing the dictator again. He took every opportunity of showing he was not only an orator: as Chairman of the Budget Committee he gave proof of uncommon financial ability. And, as some extreme Radicals reproached him with being corrupted by success and deserting his former ideals, he answered by the famous Belleville speech, which expressed his views on practical statesmanship : "We have been accused of indulging in compromise : but men cannot be governed except by compromise. Some people will jeer at what they are pleased to call the policy of results. But the results are before you : it is for you to judge. A policy which would not take opportunity into account I call a policy of disaster. Opportunism ? what does the name matter, if the country approves of the thing ? "

The speech was much commented upon at home and abroad : it clearly meant that the French Republic was ready to begin its work of practical reform in a wise and conciliating spirit. But before this could be undertaken the Republic had to repel another assault against its very existence. Gambetta had denounced already the dangerous action of the Catholic party, when several bishops and preachers had tried to rouse public opinion against Italy in favour of the "captive" Pope. After showing how they wanted to control the foreign and home policy for their own clerical ends, Gambetta concluded by the famous words : "Le Cléricalisme, voilà l'ennemi ! " Clericalism soon had its revenge. On the 16th of May, 1877,

Marshal Mac Mahon under a trifling pretext dismissed his
Republican ministers, who had never lost the Chamber's confidence, and appointed a Clerical and Reactionary Cabinet, with
the Duke of Broglie as Prime Minister.

The majority resented the challenge, and a public protest
was at once issued by 363 deputies, Gambetta being one of
them, of course. During the agitated period which immediately followed, his eloquence, his unrivalled power as popular
tribune and propagandist, were more valuable than ever to his
party. It was in the Chamber at first that he led the attack
against "the parsons in office," who occupied the Ministerial
bench. The Chamber was then dissolved, and the Government
used every legal and illegal means for securing a majority.
Prefects were discharged wholesale, and changed for Bona-
partist or Royalist agents, and every kind of pressure was tried.
Thousands of prosecutions for political offences took place in
a few months. But the more an unpopular Government forced
itself upon the country, the more the country cheered the
deputies of the Republican majority, who each in his constituency were urging the voters to resistance. As for
Gambetta, his constituency on that occasion was France itself.
In every part of the country he had, not only supporters, but
men who had been working under him during the critical days
of 1875, and who were ready to work for him at any time. He
took his "commercial traveller's" bag again, and was received
everywhere with enthusiastic applause. Among his many
speeches the most celebrated one is the Lille speech, which
contained the threatening advice to Mac Mahon : "After the
nation's supreme voice shall have decided, the only choice will
be between submission and resignation." For this speech
Gambetta was prosecuted. But the general election was near,
and resulted in utter defeat for the Government. The President did not submit at once : he replaced the Duke of Broglie
by an obscure general, and contemplated a new Dissolution, or
a *Coup d'État*. But the country's hostile feeling compelled him
at last to submission. So the great and momentous struggle,

known as the 16th of May period, ended in victory for the
Republicans and their brilliant leader, Gambetta.

In the following years, when his friends were in office and
he himself had been elected to the Presidency of the Chamber,
everybody looked at him as the coming man. He did not
assume at first the burden of government, but Jules Ferry and
Freycinet were known to take his advice. His influence was
felt in every important measure or reform, especially when the
Chamber dealt with the Educational question, and, by the Act
of 1881, established elementary education for all children, at
the expense of the State. The older Republicans followed him
as the chief who had led them to many hard battles. Young
politicians swarmed round him and took lessons of him : men
like M. Waldeck Rousseau thus acquired their first knowledge
of politics. Gambetta was not sparing of his advice : he could
not have remained inactive or silent ; being President of the
Chamber, when he became too much interested in a debate, he
often committed the chair to a Vice-President, and, reappearing
in his private member's capacity, he delivered a speech in his
usual impassioned style, and then resumed his impartial functions again. He was the object of many attacks, from the
Right side, and from the Extreme Left, for some Radicals did
not approve of his ideas on political compromise, but he did
not care. Some of the charges made against him were rather
ludicrous : the Monarchists, for instance, accused him of playing the democrat, while he was living in a gorgeous country
seat, spending his nights in prodigal revelry, and using—
shame !—a golden bathing-tub ! Everybody now can visit his
villa at Ville d'Avray, near Paris, and see that palace of the
Arabian Nights, which is a rather small and quite unpretending
country-house.

After the election of 1880, he had become at last Prime
Minister : but his plans were too ambitious for immediate
success. His Bill for Constitutional Reform miscarried, and
his " Great Administration " did not last more than two months.
He had resigned without much regret : he thought his time

had not come yet: he was hardly more than forty years old. The future was his, and the hopes of democracy centred round him. He was more powerful, more hopeful than ever, when he suddenly died, on the last day of the year 1882. The public mourning was nearly as great and general as for Thiers's death. Even some of those who had been his most decided opponents during his lifetime remembered the terrible days when his eloquence had restored fortitude to the prostrated and despairing nation, when his political genius was not used against any party, but against the enemies of the country. The tricolour flag which was spread over his coffin was the flag of the nation he had represented in a time of danger, and the flag of the Revolution, the spirit of which he had been defending and propagating down to the last day of his life.

It has been a fashion lately to inveigh against his memory, as if he had started a sham democratic tradition, skilfully turned to account by selfish politicians. Such accusations are unjust. Gambetta was certainly not an Extreme Radical, and still less a Socialist: but he first taught many Radicals and Socialists what democracy means. While Thiers had remained a Conservative *bourgeois*, in the eyes of whom the Republic was no more than another experiment of the system which had ended in failure under King Louis Philippe, Gambetta understood the Republic as "the government of the people by the people, for the people." To Thiers it was the conclusion of a long, weary life; to Gambetta the beginning of bright hopes. But Gambetta's work would not have been possible without Thiers's action, and neither of them would have succeeded if they had not been made immensely popular by their services to France at the most critical moment of her history.

THE STRUGGLE FOR ITALIAN UNITY.

By Bolton King, M.A.

The unity of Italy was perhaps the highest political achievement of the last century; it was certainly the most difficult. The side, that we generally know most of,—the struggle with Austria, the conquest of Sicily, the pathos of Charles Albert's life, all the picturesque and brilliant movement that centres round Garibaldi,—was but one aspect of the story, and perhaps not the most arduous. The Italian movement has had five great questions to resolve;—how the Austrians should be driven out from their possessions in North Italy; how a country, parted among eight states, could be united; whether monarchy or republic should be its form of government; how the social question should be faced; and—last and thorniest problem of them all—what should be its relations with the Papacy. If we contrast its case with Germany's, where there was no foreigner to be expelled, no great religious power within its borders, we shall realize how much finer was Italy's achievement. To-day I propose to trace how far, and by what means, she has attained her end in the nationalist and social and religious problems; of the question of monarchy and republic I shall speak to-morrow, when treating of Mazzini.

Modern Italy begins under Napoleon's empire. In a sense he created the Italian ideal. Himself Italian by birth, in a large measure Italian in his sympathies, he knew enough of the tendencies of the time to see that the Unity of Italy was bound to come; and both in form and substance he took the country a long step forward towards unity and freedom. What was more, he shook the country out of its easy-going acquiescence with the existing fact. The exiled princes might return, but their prestige had gone; the Pope himself had been an exile, and the Temporal Power had lost its continuity; liberal ideas came in with the Revolution, and never quite deserted Napoleon's system; and in his wars Italians learnt that centuries of peace had not destroyed their ancient courage.

Thus the ideas he taught lived on, when his empire collapsed in 1814, and on the surface his work was all undone. Italy was again divided up, and became "a geographical expression." Piedmont and Austria divided the North; the Pope, the Grandduke of Tuscany and three petty dukes shared the Centre; the Bourbon King of Naples had the South and Sicily. The country was forced under a rule more illiberal than the old order which the Revolution had upset. The princes came back from exile, hardened and bigoted and hating progress; a brutal police and a corrupt bureaucracy terrorized and degraded the country; the Church got back much of the power, which it had lost under the freer influences of the eighteenth century. I propose to avoid as far as possible the details of the misrule; their interest is largely a pathological one. But it is necessary to remember that not only were the Italians denied all political liberty, that they had no parliamentary or public life, and little liberty of speech or writing, but that the barest personal rights—a man's home and honour and career— were at the mercy of a police that was always arbitrary, and often corrupt. Trade was crippled by out-of-date restrictions; popular education hardly existed in six out of the eight states; literary life, all sincere expression of thought, was stifled by the censorship. It was the middle classes who suffered most. Under the French rule they had come brilliantly to the front; now they were thrust back under almost feudal disabilities; and professional men and tradesmen found themselves cribbed by the political divisions of the land, that confined their energies to a handful of towns.

It was impossible, of course, that men, who had once tasted enlightened rule, would acquiesce. It was not that there was as yet any serious demand for unity, and there was little thought for the religious and social aspects of the national question. But among the great mass of the middle classes and a considerable section of the nobles, and here and there among the better educated artisans, there was one resolve,—that the Austrians must go from Lombardy and Venetia, and that, whatever might be the fate of the native princes, there must be an end to the misrule, and some kind of constitutional government to guard against its return. Austria must go, not because she ruled worse than the Italian princes, for on the whole her government was the best in Italy, but because it was her military strength that propped the existing order, because she threatened every movement for reform, because—more than all this—she was an alien power, which the new spirit of nationality could not tolerate.

The history of the thirty years from 1815 to 1845 is one of continuous but ill-fated national effort. Three parties in succession directed the nationalist movement, the Carbonari, Young Italy, the Moderates, whom, roughly speaking, we may distinguish as the liberal, the revolutionary, and the conservative nationalists. Of the second I shall speak chiefly to-morrow; of the first and third to-day.

The Carbonari were a secret society, that sprang out of the Freemasons of Southern Italy, and became a vast political organization. They had a strange, indefinite creed, a kind of vague democratic Christianity, with a fantastic ritual, that fascinated the imaginative populace of Southern Italy. Here they had a host of affiliates, especially among the lower middle classes; in the North their following was smaller, and hardly reached outside the educated classes. Their strength was in the armies of Piedmont and Naples. They made in fact the

13—2

last chapter of the Napoleonic period; they kept the traditions of a time when the army had stood on the whole for political and social liberty; they had the sentimentalism, the showiness, the political incapacity of a party that plotted revolution in barrack-rooms and took Byron for its literary idol. They had little programme beyond the demand for a constitution, of what kind they heeded little. For the unity of Italy, for any religious or social development they took small care. They wished to drive the Austrians out, but they did nothing to secure that co-operation of all the national forces by which alone they could defeat her. Hence the revolutions, which they made in Naples and Piedmont in 1820 and 1821, were foredoomed to failure. For the moment they carried all before them; but they soon quarrelled among themselves; they were betrayed by the kings whom they fondly hoped to win to their cause, they made speeches and disputed while Austria was collecting troops; and when the fighting came they marched to defeat.

The Carbonari, after another revolution ten years later, which failed as completely as the first, made way for Mazzini and Young Italy. Of that very noble movement I shall speak in detail to-morrow. From 1831 to 1843 it carried on the nationalist agitation; and, small as were its immediate results, it did two great things. For the first time it created a feeling for unity, as distinct from any scheme of federation. And it fired the young generation with Mazzini's own passionate patriotism, and created a spirit which no dangers could daunt, no difficulties discourage. The spirit survived, but the nationalist movement escaped Mazzini's direction. The Moderates, or Conservative Nationalists, sprang into prominence in the early forties, and eclipsed Young Italy. They came from three sources. Some of them were social reformers, men who were nationalists in a lukewarm way, but put politics in the background, and regarded the nationalist ideal as unattainable till the country had passed through a training of social improvement and more diffused education and moral reform. There were others, who gave themselves the name of New Guelfs, who looked for a reforming Pope to give some sort of unity to Italy and champion political and social progress. At that time the Papacy under Gregory XVI had sunk low; and it needed considerable faith to hope that it would declare for nationality and reform. But there was a large body of men, devoutly Catholic and genuinely nationalist, who hoped that the Papacy, as a great Italian institution, would plead the cause of Italy; that, as its consequence, Catholicism would find its reconciliation with modern life, that the nationalist movement would be saved from any free-thinking or anti-clerical colour, and a reformed Church and a liberated nation find strength in one another. Nay more, they caught at the idea of Italy's moral and intellectual primacy among the nations, which fascinated so many minds, and which, in a very different sense, Mazzini preached. Lastly, there was the school of the Piedmontese statesmen, cautious, calculating men, with a horror of utopias, whether clerical or revolutionary, men who liked to feel their way carefully before them. They had no faith in a reforming Pope, and set their hopes on Charles Albert, the King of Piedmont. Charles Albert's policy was a strange compound of irreconcilable ambitions. He had been a Liberal in his youth; but his court life had given him a narrow palace code of duty, and he was timidly anxious to stand well in the eyes of the Church and monarchical Europe. More and more, as he advanced in life, he fell under clerical influences, till he came to look on Liberalism as the enemy of throne and altar, to be fought and crushed without pity. And yet he loved popularity, and wished to be a reforming king, to purge his government of the medieval spirit that informed it, even in some degree to promote social equality and break down the rigid caste system that discredited his country. And he was always more or less a nationalist. He had his personal reasons for hating Austria; he inherited the historic policy of his House to creep on inch by inch till North Italy should own allegiance to the crown of Piedmont; he longed in his halting, indecisive way to lead Italy in a great nationalist war, which would leave the foreigner no foothold on Italian soil.

These three groups, the social reformers, the New Guelfs, the Piedmontese royalists, coalesced more or less to make the Moderate party. It inevitably attracted to it all the non-revolutionary nationalists,—the nationalist elements in the Church, then very strong, the nationalist nobles, the civil service, the vast crowd of men, who warmly or coldly shared the aspirations for independence and good government, but shrank from any effort that meant great sacrifice, and who dreaded democracy or any thorough-going social legislation. Events gave them their chance. In the summer of 1846 Gregory XVI died, and was succeeded by the Pope, whom we know best as Pio Nono. He was a man of excellent intentions, mildly liberal, mildly nationalist, dimly seeing that it was to the interest of the Papacy to ally itself with progress. But he was timid and irresolute, easily deflected by the influences nearest him, fearful of any democratic taint or aught that threatened the traditional position of the Papacy or its temporal dominion ; naturally anxious, too, that his Italian patriotism should not lead him into courses that would offend the Catholics of other countries. None the less the mass of nationalists and reformers hailed him with a wild acclaim. A great wave of patriotism swept through the country, breaking down old local barriers, healing social feuds, firing classes hitherto untouched by the nationalist spirit. When Austria showed its chagrin and threatened to occupy a part of Papal territory, Charles Albert sent word that his sword was at the service of the Pope. At the same time, too, for the nationalist and reform movements were always inextricably linked with one another, an irresistible cry went up, first for administrative reform, then for constitutional government. Slowly and reluctantly the governments gave way in Piedmont, Tuscany, and the Papal States, and granted freedom of the press and a national militia.

Thus matters drifted through 1846 and 1847. Then the year of revolution broke, and in a few weeks the face of Europe was changed. Early in January the Sicilians revolted from the intolerable tyranny of the King of Naples, and gave the signal to the reformers all through the country. At Naples King Ferdinand found that he must choose between constitutional government and civil war, and granted free institutions. Constitutions followed quickly in Piedmont and Tuscany and the Papal States ; and three-quarters of the country were under parliamentary government. At the same time there showed the faint beginnings of the anti-Papal and social movements. Everywhere the Jesuits, who had shown their Austrian sympathies, were driven from the country ; and not even the Pope's protection could save them at Rome. And the dim aspirations of the masses appeared in bread riots and a quasi-socialist revolt at Leghorn.

But all home questions went into the background again behind the imminence of the national war, to which all the hopes and efforts of the land were tending. An unexpected event precipitated it. At the end of February the Second Republic had been proclaimed in France, and its echo went through Europe. Less than three weeks later the students of Vienna rose in triumphant revolt, and the fabric of Austrian despotism seemed shattered at its centre. As the news spread through Lombardy and Venetia, it was everywhere the signal for war. At Milan, at Venice, in a score of other towns, there were scenes of splendid citizen heroism, and the Austrian garrisons retreated or capitulated to the almost unarmed populace. Within a week the Austrians had, outside five fortresses, no foot of ground left them in Italy. Their routed army took refuge in the fortresses of the Quadrilateral, and from all Italy the national forces were hastening to complete the victory. Piedmont and Tuscany declared war : the King of Naples and the Pope himself had perforce to let their armies march to the front. Some 20,000 volunteers hurried up, impatient for the final struggle. The great flood of patriotism swept along the mass of the people,—princes and nobles, Church and laity, middle classes and artisans, even a section of the peasantry. The Pope's patronage, unwilling as it was and exaggerated in the popular belief, made the war seem a crusade, where patriotism and religion went hand in hand, and dreams of class reconciliation and social peace promised a millennium when the enemy was crushed.

I have no time to trace how the splendid dream faded before the realities of war, how their own bad generalship and the grim Austrian tenacity lost the Italians their advantages, how all the courage and endurance of the four-months' struggle were in vain, how the brave renewal of the war in the following spring ended in the swift disaster of Novara, how the Roman Republic covered itself with glory, how Venice, heroically resisting for a year, made itself ever memorable for the courage of its people and the statesmanship of their great leader, Daniel Manin. For the moment it all failed, and I can only summarize the spirit and the consequences of the revolution. It was very noble in its spirit, pitifully ineffective in execution. The touch of religion that informed its patriotism, the fearlessness and devotedness, the trust in righteousness, the care for the bigger ends of life, that inspired its leaders and more or less filtered through the crowd, make it one of the purest and fairest movements that we read of. But it lacked the practical capacity that wins victories, whether on the battlefield or in parliament. Individualism ran riot ; outside the Piedmontese army and the Romans and Venetians there was no discipline. Royalists and Republicans alike forgot that independence was more important at the moment than the triumph of their theories. Local jealousies prevented any cordial co-operation of the different states. Parliamentary work was spoilt by oratory ; save at Venice and Rome there was no statesmanship worthy the name. There was too much emotionalism, too little perseverance; "too many songs about freeing Italy," too little practical grip and power. Well did Manin say, "the days of artistic Italy are over, let us see another Italy." It wanted an Italy that had its prose as well as its poetry, that knew the value of self-repression and organization, an Italy that kept its ideal high, and yet could face and cope with facts.

Still, Italy had permanently gained. She came out of the struggle unchanged in her territorial arrangements, but transformed in her political aspect. It is true the princes kept their thrones, and, except in Piedmont, repudiated their constitutions and destroyed almost every vestige of free government. Austria seemed more strong than ever; and on the surface it was a return to the old order that prevailed before the revolution. But there were three new facts, which in reality altered the whole position for better or for worse. Piedmont had leapt into a prominence it had never had before. When Charles Albert, again at the last true patriot and Liberal, abdicated heart-broken after Novara, he was succeeded by his son, Victor Emmanuel, and while the other princes made haste to break their constitutional oaths, he remained staunchly loyal to the free government, which his father had given, and to which himself had sworn. While the rest of Italy was groaning under a cruel, stupid reaction, there was free life and parliamentary government in Piedmont. The fact meant more than domestic progress; it meant that Piedmont, beaten in the field, was moral victor, that it had become the centre of Italian aspirations, that sooner or later it intended to lead the national forces again to battle. The peace was "a ten years' truce." And the little state, hitherto only half Italian in its language and customs, now was Italy itself in the eyes of the world. The exiles from the other states crowded to Turin and Genoa, and half the best intellect of Italy was gathered there. "Piedmont," said Cavour, "must gather round itself every living force in Italy, and lead our nation to the high destinies to which it is called." For the next ten years the history of Piedmont is the history of Italy.

The second great change was in the attitude of the Papacy. When the war broke out, Pius soon repented of his brief liberalism. By the end of 1848 the reactionary party had won him over. Frightened by the threats of the people and the murder of his prime-minister, Rossi, he had fled from Rome, and only returned when the French had cowed the Romans into sullen silence. Henceforth he is the bitter enemy of every Italian aspiration. And his passage to reaction coincided with a great change inside the Catholic Church. After the Pope's defection the Church lost ground rapidly in Italy, and the nationalist movement, hitherto so friendly to it, became more or less anti-clerical. But at the same time the Catholics strengthened their position outside Italy. The Jesuits, after their long eclipse, were now all-powerful within the Church, and their supremely skilful organization created a disciplined political party in almost every Catholic country. Of necessity therefore the Roman Court began to lose its specially Italian character, and the sense of its new political strength encouraged the Papacy to put out dormant claims. Through its popular and parliamentary forces it put pressure on Catholic governments to legislate in the interests of the Church and support the Papacy against the nationalists of Italy. It was now generally recognized that the contest there must end in a struggle for the Pope's temporal dominions. While the other Italian governments surrendered to the Church rights they had won from it in the eighteenth century, and Austria forgot her old suspicions of the Papacy, Piedmont marked the contrast between itself and them by anti-clerical legislation, abolishing the legal privileges of the clergy, and dissolving a large number of monasteries. Henceforth there could be no reconciliation between Piedmont and the Papacy.

The third new fact—closely connected with the last—was the intervention of the French in Italian politics. The tra-

ditional Italian policy of France had three ends in view, — to
check Austrian influence, to prevent the creation of a strong
Italian state, which might be France's rival in the Mediterranean,
and to secure the transference of Savoy from Piedmont to itself.
To these the new Catholic movement added the championing
of the Pope against Italian attacks. Louis Napoleon in his
bid for the French crown found the support of the Catholics
indispensable, and when in 1849 the French parliament voted
supplies for an expedition, which was intended to be a demonstration against Austria, he allowed it to be diverted from its
purpose in order to crush the republican government, which
had ruled Rome after the Pope's flight. For the next twenty
years French policy in Italy is dominated by the see-saw between
Catholic pressure and Napoleon's own more generous aims.
He had no love for the Pope, and was always anxious to withdraw the French garrison, which had been left at Rome to
protect the Pope from his own subjects. He had his big
schemes to remodel Europe on a basis of nationality ; and
though to some extent he shared the French prejudice against
Italian Unity, he wanted to see all North Italy annexed to Piedmont and some kind of federation connecting the different
Italian states. France was to have her pay by annexing Savoy,
and placing princes of his family on at least one Italian throne.

Such was the position in the early fifties. All now depended
on the capacity of Piedmont to use her chance. Fortunately
she found a man who had the finest stuff of statesmanship.
Cavour in normal times was a cautious, patient, parliamentary
leader and diplomatist, with a rare power of work and command
of details, on the surface somewhat of a cynic, contemptuous of
theories, a masterful man, but with almost perfect control of
his temper, and always ready to surrender a small end for
a big one ; absolutely unsparing of himself, but sometimes unscrupulous in his means, and forgetting that the honour of her
public policy is more precious to a country than any triumph.
But this cool, careful man was no commonplace politician.

As Manzoni, the novelist, said of him, he had the imprudence as well as the prudence of the true statesman. He had his passionate beliefs, his daring ideals; and though he could wait year after year for the moment to realize them, he could be, when the time came, a revolutionary, who threw diplomacy and conventionalities to the winds, and was ready to stake all for a great end.

He was a fervent nationalist, believing in Italian Unity with Rome for the capital. But, if he could not have that, he was content to annex as much of North and Central Italy as was possible to Victor Emmanuel's realm, and at all events make Piedmont the model state and champion of all Italy. At home his policy was to consolidate the new free constitution. He was a pure liberal. In words that his successors would have done well to keep before them, he said, " Italy must make herself by means of liberty, or we must give up trying to make her." He would have little or no coercion ; emancipation from clerical influences, free trade, the repeal of all restrictions on industry, the development of railways, pretty well sum up his domestic policy. With few and trifling exceptions he was true to it throughout, and it launched Piedmont on a new career of progress. Abroad, his immediate object was to secure the French alliance, in the certainty that, if this were done, Louis Napoleon would some day send his armies across the Alps to drive the Austrians out of Italy. Probably he had made up his mind to fight Austria in any case ; but he knew that without a foreign ally (and France was the only possible ally) the chance of victory was small. It was for this that he sent an Italian force to the Crimea, that he abased himself to trickery and unworthy condescension to satisfy the Emperor's exigencies.

Cavour, supremely skilful as he was, could not create opinion. He was an opportunist, and took opinion as it was and made the best of it. The man, who more than anyone else influenced Italian opinion in the fifties was Manin, the ex-Triumvir of Venice ; and it was the National Society, which he founded,

which did most to educate opinion in those years. Its programme was summed up in discipline and Italian Unity. There
must be no repetition of the divisions, which had paralysed the
country in 1848 and 1849—no feud of republicans and royalists,
no friction between the different Italian states. Therefore the
nationalists must rally to the one possible flag, must take Victor
Emmanuel for their figurehead and the Piedmontese statesmen
for their leaders. Manin had been a republican; but he was
willing to waive his preferences for the sake of harmony, and
with few exceptions and for the same reason the republicans
followed him into the royalist camp. But Manin asked that if
the republicans did this, the royalists should declare frankly for
unity. The movement of 1848 had been a federalist one, and
the cause of unity had gone into the background; but now that
Piedmont and its King stood out as the sole champions of Italy,
a great impetus had come again to the faith in Unity, and the
dangers of federalism appeared in their true light.

Cavour gladly encouraged the new movement. For diplomatic reasons he did not dare to pronounce openly for unity,
and perhaps he doubted the strength of the feeling for it; but
if others could convert the federalists, he was prepared to take
advantage of the fact. In 1858 he felt that it was safe to take
decisive steps. The great mass of nationalists were ready
to follow his lead, even in states like Tuscany, where the
autonomist feeling had been strongest. He knew that he could
count on the King. Garibaldi had joined the National Society
and given the royalists the benefit of his prestige. Louis
Napoleon, too, for various reasons was eager to go to war for
the liberation of Italy. In the summer of 1858 he met Cavour
secretly, and promised him to declare war with Austria at an
early date. But he would do nothing to countenance Unity.
Piedmont was to have the Austrian provinces and part of the
Papal territory, but the Centre and the South and the Pope's
remaining provinces were to be still three separate states, and
be forced into an Italian Federation under the Pope's presi-

dency. France was to be paid for her help by the cession of Savoy and perhaps of Nice. Cavour agreed to the terms, which perhaps were, under the circumstances, surprisingly good ; probably he knew that unity could not stop at any half-way house, and trusted to the force of events to do the rest. His business now was to keep the Emperor to his word, and complete his own preparations in Italy. He encouraged the formation of a volunteer force, that poured into Piedmont from the other states. By supremely adroit but quite unscrupulous diplomacy he dragged the hesitating Emperor after him, and parried every effort of the English government to prevent war. In the summer of 1859 the allied French and Piedmontese armies defeated the Austrians at Magenta and Solferino, and drove them out of Lombardy. Suddenly, in the midst of his triumph, Napoleon, fearing defeat in Venetia and a Prussian advance across the Rhine, lost courage, and concluded an armistice. Save for the surrender of Lombardy to Piedmont, the Preliminaries of Villafranca contemplated in all essentials a return to the old order that obtained before the war. Italy was maddened by the desertion and resolute not to be baulked of its will. Tuscany, the Po duchies, and the Northern part of the Pope's dominions had revolted and expelled their princes, soon after war was declared, and they were determined not to lose their new-won independence at the Emperor's bidding. They knew that Victor Emmanuel and Cavour were with them, and Tuscany had in Bettino Ricasoli an iron leader, whom no threats or difficulties could daunt. The revolted states refused to take the princes back, and prepared to defend themselves by arms. Cavour had resigned after the armistice, and feeble men had taken his place, but even they had to give their backing to the Central states. Napoleon, chagrined though he was at the opposition to his schemes, could not, for his own prestige's sake, allow Austria to restore the princes, and, despite the French Catholics, he loved the Pope too little to do much for him. His veto on any Austrian advance made a ring-fence round the revolted states, and they made good use of their position. They formed a military league; they declared boldly for annexation to Piedmont; they planned an invasion of Umbria, which the Pope's Swiss troops had recovered from the nationalists. Next January Cavour came back to office, determined to have a Kingdom of Italy, which should include most or all of the Centre. He offered to surrender Savoy and Nice as the price of Napoleon's endorsement, but he was determined at no cost to lose Tuscany and Romagna. The Emperor, borne down by his insistency and the passive resistance of the Italians, gave his consent to annexation, if a plebiscite of the inhabitants declared for it. The plebiscites were taken and showed a victorious majority for annexation. When the first Italian parliament met on April 2, 1860, it represented eleven millions of souls, or nearly half the population of the peninsula.

The nationalist wave hardly paused before it rolled on again. The events of the past year had changed the most moderate men to fervent advocates of Unity. All recognized that Central Italy was but a stepping-stone. Venetia and half the Pope's territory, Naples and Sicily, still stood outside, and there could be no rest nor peace till they were won. Venice, it was generally recognized, must wait. No one wanted to call the French armies in again, and, except in the event of a Hungarian rising, Austria was too formidable for the young country to challenge yet alone. It was madness, too, to attack Rome while the French garrison remained, and its winning therefore must depend on an understanding with France. But the Papal provinces of Umbria and the Marches and all the South were ripe for revolution. Even if diplomatic difficulties prevented the Italian government from freeing them, the volunteers could do the work, and the government could follow after. The old Mazzinian party, though most of them had accepted the monarchy, took up the task; and Garibaldi very reluctantly consented to lead 1,000 volunteers to Sicily. In a lecture, which has to deal more with political ideas and facts than deeds of war, there is small place for Garibaldi. Of heroic build and great achievement, his intellectual power was small, and he added nothing to the political thought of his country. But for the work now in hand he was supremely fitted. The magic of his personal influence, his courage, his superb talent for guerilla fighting, made him the one man in Italy who could conquer Sicily from the King of Naples' troops. It was a tremendous risk, for 1,000 men were attacking over 20,000, and but for the rottenness of the Neapolitan government and army, and the universal hatred of the Sicilians for the Bourbon rule, not all the heroism of his volunteers could have snatched victory from the heavy odds against them. As it was, a few weeks in May laid most of Sicily at his feet; three months later he was advancing rapidly on Naples, and the demoralized Bourbon army was surrendering by thousands without an attempt at resistance. Early in September he entered Naples, an easy conqueror.

Cavour had, with some misgivings, secretly encouraged and assisted him. While Garibaldi overran Sicily, he had been parrying any foreign interference, and taking his precautions that the South should be added to the kingdom. The situation was a very delicate one. In a sense Garibaldi had been too successful, for his fame was threatening to eclipse the King's; and though he was himself loyal to the King, he hated Cavour, and a man so easily influenced by those around him might become the centre of a movement to upset the one man capable of uniting Italy and even endanger the throne. Sometimes civil war seemed perilously near. It was necessary to repair the King's prestige by some striking triumph of the regular army; equally necessary to save Garibaldi from a disaster which might easily lose the South again. King Francis of Naples had still a formidable force with him. In the Papal States Catholic volunteers had gathered from half Europe, to protect the Pope from a nationalist invasion. If the two forces joined hands, they were only too likely to crush Garibaldi. Cavour determined to save the King's reputation and relieve Garibaldi by invading the Pope's territory, and, leaving Rome carefully alone, advancing through it to Naples. Again, the risk was a terrible one, for if Austria attacked while the King and his best troops were absent in the South, she could easily recover Lombardy. Once more Napoleon saved Italy by threatening Austria with war if she intervened. Cavour declared war on the Pope, and the Italian forces overran Umbria and the Marches, and, thence advancing Southwards, completed the discomfiture of King Francis' army. For the moment regular army and Garibaldi's men fronted each other sullenly, and the strain was dangerous. Thanks to Garibaldi's patriotism and the common-sense of the country, the friction wore down, and Naples and Sicily, which only wanted a quick settlement and unity, annexed themselves to the kingdom by majorities even more triumphant than those of Central Italy. In April, 1859, Victor Emmanuel reigned over less than five million subjects; in November, 1860, he was King of twenty-one millions.

Italian Unity was practically won, won by sheer audacity and through a sequence of tremendous perils. Sooner or later now another war would drive the Austrians from Venetia; sooner or later the ripening of the fates would give Italy her natural capital at Rome. Italy had come into being; and what a few years before had been laughed at as a utopian dream, was a solid European fact. But the young country had still to face tasks as important and perhaps more arduous. The social fabric had to be built from the foundations. Italy had to create her legal system, her civil service, her army, her finances, her local government; make commercial expansion possible by building railways and harbours, reclaim her great stretches of waste land, build schools for an almost illiterate country, lift the backward South to the level of the North. In the four years between 1861 and 1865 a series of great laws attempted a settlement of some of these matters, and on the whole the advance was very great. But the supreme problem of these years was how to win Rome and solve all the Church questions that were bound up with that. Italian Unity meant the destruction of the Temporal Power. Already the Pope had lost three-quarters of his territory, and Italy was a torso without Rome. But her determination to have the city brought her into sharp conflict with Catholic sentiment throughout the world. Catholic tradition held that territorial possession was essential to the Pope's dignity and independence, and Catholics naturally rallied to defend their Church's head from present and future dangers. The practical evidence of Catholic hostility lay in the presence of the French garrison at Rome. Louis Napoleon was keenly anxious to escape from the false position he had made for himself there, but he was afraid to strain overmuch the loyalty of his Catholic subjects, so he dared not let the Italians go to Rome, unless they offered concessions that would satisfy moderate Catholic opinion. Cavour, on his part, eager as he was to win Rome, was determined not to force it in despite of France and Catholic opinion ; he was, too, in his way a sincere Church reformer, and eager to reconcile Catholicism with modern life. He enlisted the very influential body of Catholic reformers in Italy in support of his scheme of the Free Church in the Free State. His plan was essentially a bargain between the Pope and Italy. The Pope was to surrender the Temporal Power. In return, the State would abandon all the control over the Church, which Concordats and ecclesiastical laws had given it. The Church, provided it conformed to the elementary conditions of a constitutional state, would have perfect freedom in its own internal government. The Pope would remain at Rome, with a nominal title of sovereignty, an ample endowment, and a guarantee that there would be no interference with his spiritual functions. The traditional policy of Catholic states had been to keep the Church in leading-strings. Cavour's scheme was an absolute reversal of it; but he was confident that State and Church alike stood to gain, that the Church would find fresh youth in an atmosphere of liberty, that new Italy would set a great example to the world. It was perhaps, however, considering the feeling on both sides, an impossible scheme at the time. Even Cavour failed, and a few weeks later died with his work half done.

The great statesman's death was an irreparable blow to Italy. He was only 51 years old (almost the same age as Mr Gladstone and the present Pope); and had he remained at the helm another twenty years, he might have saved his country much of its subsequent trouble. His more or less incompetent successors were powerless to solve the Roman question. Their position, indeed, was a very difficult one. The Pope refused to compromise; Napoleon, ageing and exhausted, surrendered more and more to the French clericals; Italian opinion, irritated by the delay and the Pope's hostility, was clamorous to defy both him and France. A foolhardy attempt of Garibaldi to march to Rome brought him into conflict with the Italian troops at Aspromonte. Two years later the government came to a feeble and dishonest compromise with France, in the September Convention. The French pledged themselves to withdraw from Rome within two years; the Italian government undertook to protect Papal territory from any attack by Garibaldi and his followers, and to move the capital to Florence, as evidence to the Catholic world that they had abandoned their claim to Rome. The treaty, as we know now, was intentionally insincere; it was secretly understood between the two governments that the Italians should take possession of Rome on the first decent pretext. Two years later, Ricasoli, during his second premiership, feeling acutely the danger to religion that came from the long strain, made another attempt to reconcile the Pope on Cavour's lines. But the Vatican would not yield on any essential, and feeling in the country was too hot to hear of compromise. Garibaldi made another

14—2

attempt to march to Rome, the government more or less con-
niving; and the French, who had withdrawn their garrison two
years before, sent troops again to defend the Pope. Garibaldi
was defeated at Mentana, and the country writhed in its impotence to avenge itself on the Pope and his French protectors.
There was no more thought among men in any party of
abandoning the claims to Rome; and less than three years
after Mentana the Franco-German war gave them their opportunity. France paid for her great blunder by losing the Italian,
and with it the Austrian alliance, and Italy seized the opportunity of the European turmoil to take possession of Rome.

Venice had been won four years before by the help of the
Prussian alliance, and save for the disputed frontier territories
of the Southern Tyrol and Istria, Italy was complete. Nearly
thirty-two years have passed since the capture of Rome, and we
unluckily have lost for Italy made the interest we felt for her
in the making. The heroic and picturesque have gone; there
has been disappointment and pessimism in her later history.
But these thirty years have had their solid prose, as instructive
as all the poetry of her *risorgimento*, and Italy stands to-day
higher morally, intellectually, socially than she did in the days
of Victor Emmanuel and Garibaldi. Underneath the blunder-
ing statesmanship and false ideals, the pinchbeck tyranny and
parliamentary corruption there has been a very real and steady
growth. Italians have cleared their ideas, have learnt the value
of details, have braced themselves to the earnest, serious, silent
work of a modern industrial community. In the few minutes
left me I will indicate the main lines of their recent development in their foreign policy, in their relations with the Vatican,
and in their social questions.

Though France paid for Mentana at Sedan, though there
was no French garrison now at Rome, the friction with her was
even more intense in the early days of the Third Republic
than under the Empire. The Republic was largely dominated
by clerical influences, and, down at all events to 1890, it was

the fixed idea of the French Catholics to restore the Temporal Power by French arms. At the same time the rise of Italy into a Great Power made her inevitably the rival of France in the Mediterranean, and both Powers were aiming at Tunis and Tripoli. With the hostility of the French Catholics on one side and the supreme unwisdom of the Italian statesmen on the other, with Bismarck watchful all the time to set the two countries by the ears, Italy and France have on more than one occasion been within measurable distance of war. To guard herself against the danger of a single-handed fight with France, Italy, in 1882, concluded the Triple Alliance with her old enemy, Austria, and her new ally, Germany. Five years later the strong protectionist current, both in France and Italy, together with Crispi's policy of pin-pricks, brought about a commercial rupture. Since 1890, however, there has been a steady reaction in favour of France. The disastrous results of the commercial war to both countries led to a new commercial treaty four years ago. French dreams of restoring the Temporal Power have passed away; Tunis has gone to France beyond recall, and Italy has probably secured the reversion of Tripoli; old influences, that naturally draw the two Latin countries together, have reasserted themselves; and they have now nearly or quite forgotten their feud. Concurrently, the alliance with Austria and Germany has lost what little popularity it had. Causes of friction with Austria, old and new, have come to the front; there are commercial differences with her and Germany; there is no longer any danger from France to justify the treaty; and above all the country knows that the Alliance has practically meant large armaments, and that large armaments are sucking its strength. I need hardly mention that the Triple Alliance has been renewed this year largely to save the commercial treaties with Germany and Austria, and that we know enough of its contents to be sure that they mean practically very little.

The controversy with the Vatican has, like the foreign

policy, run through its dangerous crises, and is now comparatively innocuous. It has done little credit to either side.
No doubt the position of both parties has been a difficult one.
The strong anti-clerical feeling in the country, the provocation of
the foreign Catholics, the fixed hostility of the late and present
Pope have not made it easy for the government to be con-
ciliatory. On the other side it was almost an impossibility
that the Vatican should break with its traditions, should
abandon at once its claim to the Temporal Power, which for
centuries had been regarded as indispensable to the Pope's
freedom, or meekly accept laws aimed against the Church.
After the capture of Rome the government made a well-meant
effort to conciliate by the Law of Guarantees. The law
carried out much of Cavour's scheme; it freed the Church in
many respects, and guaranteed the Pope his spiritual independence, but, unlike Cavour's project, it aimed at no corresponding
concession from the Pope. On the whole it has been loyally
observed; but it did little or nothing to reconcile the Vatican.
The Papal Court clung to its hope that foreign arms or foreign
diplomacy, whether from France or Germany, would restore
the Temporal Power. It has done its best to weaken the
young kingdom by an attempt, which has met with no great
success, to dissuade the Catholics from taking part in politics,
and thus keep out of public life men whose sincerity and
definite policy would have made them a very valuable element
in parliament. Latterly, however, the Vatican seems to have
recognized that the Temporal Power has gone for ever, that at
the best the Pope cannot hope to be sovereign over more than
a small part of Rome; and, though it will not explicitly
abandon the position of no surrender, in practice it is groping
after some *modus vivendi* with Italy. In minor matters there
is a good deal of mutual understanding between it and the
government; the veto on the Catholic vote is almost a dead
letter, and is not likely to survive the present Pope. Religious
animosity is softening on both sides; and the majority of

Catholics are eager for a political alliance with the Conservative Nationalists against the new and threatening democratic forces.

In fact every other question in Italy tends to be overshadowed by the social question. I shall not attempt to analyze the meaningless struggles between the Right and Left parties, which occupied parliamentary life for a quarter of a century. I would rather deal with the more coloured and fruitful period, which has followed the great disaster in Abyssinia, and Crispi's fall in 1896. A short period of reaction, which almost recalled the days of Austrian and Bourbon tyranny, has been followed by one of steady, peaceful growth. In place of the confused politics which ruled before, two great parliamentary parties are evolving themselves, one composed of Conservatives and Catholics with the army and capitalist influences, the other of the genuinely Liberal elements of the Left, the Radicals, and the Socialists. The master-fact of the period has been the rapid growth of the Socialists, and their evolution—already three parts accomplished—from a revolutionary to a parliamentary party. The Republicans, after gaining ground under the reaction, have rapidly lost it again, and are hardly more formidable than they were in Cavour's days. Meanwhile great social changes have been going on. Large industries are springing up; the towns of the north are becoming great manufacturing centres, and Genoa and Milan threaten to eclipse Marseilles and Lyons. The application of electricity to industry has opened up to Italy, the richest in water-power of all European countries, great industrial possibilities. Agriculture, at all events in the north, is being transformed with amazing rapidity by new methods of cultivation and the expansion of co-operation; and the peasant seems on the road to a prosperity that he has never known before. Thus, burdensome as taxation still is, serious as is still the poverty of Italy, wealth grows and spreads itself among all classes. The industrial development and the spread of socialism have been followed by a great labour movement. Before the advent of big industries, the artisans could hardly be an articulate class; and before the present reign the dead weight of the government was, though quite illegally, cast against any form of labour organization. The present government is the first of United Italy which has stood neutral in labour conflicts; and in consequence a strike movement—which for magnitude has had no parallel in any country—has swept through town and village in the last two years. Thus though the republican movement has largely died away, though Church and State are feeling their road to an understanding, Italy is passing through a social crisis, beside which perhaps the great times of her nationalist struggle will some day seem unimportant. Whatever may be its issue, it at all events proves that Italy is no decaying nation, but full, very full, of vitality and growth and far-reaching possibilities. She is richly gifted with common-sense, with perseverance and modesty, with keen scientific activity, and the desire to learn. Grievously loaded as she still is by poverty and illiteracy, she is perhaps advancing as fast as any European nation. Across the Atlantic she is building up in South America a Greater Italy, bound one day to play a big part in the world's history. It was not in vain then that her heroes and martyrs strove and died, that Mazzini, and Cavour, and Garibaldi, and many a known and many a forgotten patriot gave home and fortune and life for an ideal. Let us try to forget their rivalries, their blunders, their lapses; let us rather be thankful for that splendid record of faith and devotion, that lights up the hard nineteenth century, thankful that it has not been for nought, that its monument is with us in a nation re-born to life, destined perhaps to be a great factor in the progress of humanity.

MAZZINI.

By Bolton King, M.A.

The struggle for Italian Unity was fortunate in the men who inspired and led it. Perhaps no movement in the last century can boast three men as great in their respective ways as Cavour, Garibaldi, Mazzini;—Cavour, the consummate statesman, Garibaldi, the guerilla chieftain, Mazzini, the thinker and prophet. Mazzini is the greatest of the three, greater in character, greater intellectually, greater—most of all—because he lifted the politics of Italy to the height of a religious faith, and stamped them with his own moral grandeur.

Mazzini was born at Genoa in 1805, of a middle-class family. He grew up a thoughtful, studious man, now, as through all his life, of stainless nature, with a passionate love of moral good and public righteousness, fearless, impetuous, affectionate, possessing, even as a lad, a marvellous influence on those around him, a born leader from sheer force and purity of character. He had a good education, and his precocious brilliancy made him at twenty-five the first literary critic of Italy, one indeed of the greatest critics of the last century. His whole bent was towards literature, and it was with a painful wrench that he convinced himself that, in a country debased and enslaved as his own, literature was no patriot's call, and that the man, who loved his country, who wished to raise the men and women round him, must try to cleanse the social atmosphere, and for this must throw himself into politics. But politics under a despotism like that of Piedmont were necessarily secret, and Mazzini joined the one secret society of the time, the Carbonari. For this he was imprisoned and exiled just when the Carbonari were making their final attempt at revolution in 1831. He had quickly lost any hope in them, and before their movement had collapsed he had thought out the principles of a new society, which was to take their place.

To these principles he clung, with few changes, all his life. His intellect ripened young, and it was one of the defects of his qualities that he learnt little afterwards. We find in his writings, when he was a young man of twenty-six or twenty-seven the germ and generally the developed form of every doctrine that he preached. He intended Young Italy to lift Italian liberty and unity right out of the level of a mere political question, to make them part of a philosophy that embraced all sides of life, to give them the sanction of a great moral principle, to link them to the progress of mankind. He thought that any living political system was impossible, unless it reached down to a religious and ethical foundation. He wished to find for his Young Italy an energizing force, which would inspire its followers to endure and die, if need be, for their cause. Conspiracy under a despotism meant risking death or exile or imprisonment; a popular rising against Austria meant the loss of thousands of lives, the wrecking of thousands of homes, the wasting of the land. He knew that men would not face it for a selfish interest, that it was only when love of country and humanity merged itself in religion, when a sense of duty to God and man possessed their souls, that men would rise above themselves and their own small selfish aims to heroism and sacrifice. He sought for his followers the faith that gave victory to the Puritans, a faith that they were fighting on God's side and carrying out God's plan, that every man was called on to make the cause of righteousness his own, and work for it unrestingly, without thought of self or happiness, indifferent to his individual fate, so he helped in God's war with evil.

He made their country's cause the cause of right living both for themselves and for mankind. All through his aspirations for Italy his one supreme concern was that Italian men and women should grow in moral worth. But progress, moral and intellectual, was stopped by a misgovernment, which crushed the poor and discouraged education, and promoted corruption and servility and dishonesty. Only in a great, free, united Italy would Italians find room and light for moral growth, or learn the duties of citizenship and social service. And the cause of Italy was the cause of all the world. His intense and fiery patriotism never forgot the larger claims of humanity. The day would come, when Italy "radiant, purified by suffering, would move as an angel of light among the nations that thought her dead." Rome was the city destined by Providence to forward the cause of human unity. She had done so, when the Roman Empire united the civilized world by force of arms and majesty of law; she had done so again, when Catholic Rome united Christendom by spiritual authority. She would do so yet again and for ever, when "Rome of the People" taught the modern world a gospel of social duty and peace among the nations. Much of the belief was a fantastic one, a curious survival of the theories of the Holy Roman Empire ; he had learnt it from the classics, still more (as he learnt so many of his theories) from Dante. The spell of Rome's mighty past, the belief that Rome gave Italy a moral pre-eminence among the nations, was one that he shared with many another of his countrymen, and which inspired that inextinguishable resolve that Rome should be the capital of Italy. What possible germ of truth there lies in the belief we shall see later on.

This grounding of the national cause on a religious basis at once differentiated Mazzini's teaching from that of the earlier nationalists. Its other radical difference lies in its care for social progress. Amid the crying callousness to the lot of her poor, that has discredited Italy down almost to yesterday, Mazzini's voice rings out that no political change is worth making unless it takes the masses one step forward, that there is no true nation unless the state makes their condition its first care, unless there is a true national education and persistent legislative war with poverty. "I see the people pass before my eyes," he wrote, "in the livery of wretchedness and political subjection, ragged and hungry, painfully gathering the crumbs that wealth tosses insultingly to it, or lost and wandering in riot and the intoxication of a brutish, angry, savage joy; and I remember that those brutalized faces bear the finger-print of God, the mark of the same mission as our own. I lift myself to the vision of the future, and behold the people rising in its splendour, brothers in one faith, one bond of equality and love, one ideal of citizen virtue that ever grows in beauty and might; the people of the future, unspoilt by luxury, ungoaded by wretchedness, awed by the consciousness of its rights and duties. And in the presence of that vision my heart beats with anguish for the present and glorying for the future." Mazzini opposed socialism angrily and sometimes ignorantly; he always pleaded for class reconciliation. But he was the first to insist that Italy must be made by and for the people; and more and more he looked to the artisan classes to be the strength of the nationalist movement. He believed that united Italy would be the first country to solve the labour question by gradually substituting for capitalist industry a system of voluntary co-operative societies, helped by easy loans from the state.

You will see why Mazzini chose "God and the People" for the motto of Young Italy. His political programme, which was to enable Italy to reach his moral ideal, had three articles,— independence from Austria, Unity, the Republic. The first he held of course in common with all the nationalists; and his special contribution was to bring the question of Unity to the front. Before him only a few thinkers here and there had

dared to speak of a united Italy. To the majority the difficulties seemed insuperable. History and character divided
North and South. The great cities cherished their ancient
independence, and grudged to sink it in a common country.
All the official forces in each state, from prince to government
clerk, opposed a loss of their autonomy, which meant loss of
office. The diplomatic obstacles were very great. Above all,
the Papacy was fixedly hostile to a policy that doomed its
Temporal Power. It was a sense of the difficulties in the
way that now and for some time after prevented the mass of
nationalists from aiming at anything beyond a federation of
Italian states. It is Mazzini's chief claim to political foresight
that he saw that what was a utopia to his contemporaries was
a realizable ideal, that he inspired his countrymen with his own
passionate faith, and gave the power, which changed the seemingly impossible to fact. "And yet," said Carlyle long afterwards, "this idealist has conquered, he has transformed his
utopia into a patent and potent reality." I doubt whether
there is any other instance in modern times, where the same
man has both originated a great political idea and been the
chief instrument in realizing it. It gives Mazzini the claim to
rank among the makers of Modern Europe.

Mazzini's sagacity failed him when he added republicanism
to his programme. It was perhaps inevitable at the time. In
the days of the Holy Alliance, when despotic monarchies ruled
over two-thirds of Europe, and constitutional monarchy in
France was a byword for corruption, it was natural that men
should draw a sharp distinction between monarchies and
republics, and believe that honest, progressive popular government could flourish only under the latter. Mazzini's error lay
in clinging to the belief after it had ceased to be true. Since
1848 monarchy and republic make no longer an exact classification, and it is a commonplace that some monarchies approximate more to some republics than to other monarchies,
that the vital difference lies in the varying characters of

parliaments and the degree of their control over the executive. Mazzini came to understand this partially. In later life he had a strong admiration for English government, and on the other hand he refused his blessing to the Third Republic in France. But party spirit prevented him from ever really recognizing the truth in his own country, and we shall see, in tracing his after life, how his obstinate persistence in his republican faith damaged the bigger cause of unity. But his republican ideal was a very noble one. To him the republic meant perfect trust between government and people, the selection of the most virtuous and capable for office, a true national unity, free from any disturbing influence of dynasty or caste, that left no room for party friction, and allowed the country to devote its undivided forces to progress; in which "the whole community, strong, tranquil, happy, peaceful, bound in a solemn concord, stands on earth, as in a temple built to virtue and liberty, to progressive civilization and the laws that govern the moral world."

It was with these principles that Mazzini started his society of Young Italy. It was a secret society, not because Mazzini had any love, at all events then, for conspiracy in itself, but because under a despotic government public agitation was impossible. After his banishment from Italy the young exile (he was only twenty-six years old) settled at Marseilles, and gathering round him a few more exiles, started his society. It was a resolution of extraordinary hardihood for a few unknown young men, without any advantage of wealth, or birth, or influence, to calmly set to work to revolutionize Italy, and defy the powers that be of half Europe. Something of the Titan spirit of the French Revolution was still living then, and, as one of his schoolfellows wrote (the author in English of those charming novels, *Doctor Antonio* and *Lorenzo Benoni*), Mazzini's "confidence in men was great and in himself unlimited." From his press at Marseilles he poured into Italy a stream of revolutionary literature, ably written, passionate in its patriotism

and moral earnestness ; and though it was for the most part
too cultured to reach the illiterate working-classes, it fired the
educated youth with something of the writer's spirit.   In two
years branches of Young Italy had sprung up thick through
a large part of North and Central Italy, superseding the Carbonari, and drawing into their organization the great mass of
active nationalists.   Mazzini at once prepared for action, and
made two unsuccessful attempts at revolution.   Three years
later he came to England, and lived in London, with few
intervals, for the remainder of his life.   I am tempted to say
something of his English life,—his friendship with the Carlyles,
his closer friendship with the Stansfelds, the opening of his
letters in the English Post-Office, his letters to English working-
men on the Crimean War, his keen interest in English politics
and literature, his many English writings.   But my subject for-
bids me, and I must pass on to the early forties, when, after
a hard struggle with poverty and despair, he resumed his
revolutionary work.   As an organization, Young Italy had
practically broken up, but the spirit it had created lived on,
and for the next ten years it was slowly and quietly helping to
leaven Italian thought.   For the present at all events, however,
it did more to raise the general level of Italian politics than to
direct them towards Mazzini's own special theories.   It inspired
the nationalist movement with his own moral fervour and indomitable spirit, and deepened the resolve for independence.
But it made few republicans, and though it created among the
younger men a strong desire for unity, they held it rather as an
ideal to be realized at a future day than as an immediate political
object.   Besides, the men whom he influenced most deeply did
not come to the front till after 1849.   For the time being the
Moderates carried all before them, and Mazzini himself saw
that it was necessary to compromise with them.   When the
nationalist movement gathered in volume after Pio Nono's
accession, and war seemed imminent, he did not a little to get
republicans and royalists to work together, and promised to be

silent on domestic questions till the war was over. But though he was true to the letter of his promise, and at times had even short fits of trust in the Pope and Charles Albert, he could never work loyally with the Moderates or repress his republican preaching. He would not see that, as circumstances were, the republic and Unity were conflicting ideals, that if, as he himself acknowledged, independence was the first object, Unity the second, and the republic only third, it was his duty to be silent on the minor issues, and work with others, who were at one with him on the bigger points. Perhaps it was impossible for an exile to see facts in their true light, and Mazzini was too inflexible, too dogmatic, too wedded to every detail of his creed to be a useful or successful worker in practical politics. During the war of 1848 he did more hurt than help to the national cause.

Next year he had an opportunity to display all his essential greatness, and prove, when he could get rid of his partisanship, how much stuff of a statesman underlay the idealist. Two months after the Pope's flight from Rome, a parliament, elected on universal suffrage and drawn chiefly from the richer middle-classes, voted almost unanimously for a republic. It invited Mazzini to come to Rome, and after the catastrophe of Novara elected him a Triumvir. Mazzini's dream was realized in part. Rome was free and republican, the Papacy had left it; here, where his dearest aspirations had centred, he could create a government after his ideal, and prepare the ground for that mission to mankind, for which he had destined Rome. Perhaps, indeed, he realized from the first that the republic could not last, that the European reaction was too strong to let it live. But, even if it were doomed, it could set a noble example, which the future would not forget. With a power of adaptation, which Mazzini seldom showed, the idealist gave place to the statesman. His bigger social and religious hopes were put aside for a more quiet time. The immediate business was to defend the country from attack, to preserve order, and carry out such legislative changes as were practicable and necessary; above all, to inspire government and people with a new spirit of duty and patriotism. In a country, where coercion had been the every-day instrument of government, where political passion ran so high that in some towns assassination was habitually practised by both sides, he, in a time of utmost national peril, insisted on absolute liberty and tolerance. "Stiffness in principles, tolerance towards individuals" was his motto. Men, who were known to be plotting against the government, were hardly interfered with; the clergy were carefully protected from the people's threats. Two instances will illustrate Mazzini's love of tolerance and order, and his hold upon the people. When the French attack was threatening, the crowd, as a protest against clerical intrigues, took some confessional boxes from the churches to make barricades. It was impossible to discover the offenders, but Mazzini, who, it must be remembered, was no Catholic, appealed to the people to restore the confessionals, reminding them that at all events their mothers had heard words of comfort from them. Next day every confessional was brought back to its place. Afterwards, during the siege, some poor families, whose homes had been wrecked by shells, were lodged in the palaces of some fugitive nobles, on a promise that nothing should be stolen or injured. And though in the excitement of the siege it could have been done with easy impunity, not an article of the rich furniture was hurt or taken. Mazzini did not try to win the people by any appeal to their interests; such few attempts as were made to improve their condition were mostly initiated before he became Triumvir. He was true to his principle of appealing to their sense of duty; his ascendancy, which raised to heroism a people demoralized by bad government and charity, was a moral one, which asked them as men and Romans to be worthy of their fathers and their cause. His own noble life appealed to their best instincts. When, as head of the government, he had to live in the palace of the Quirinal (now the King of

Italy's abode), he hunted for a room "small enough to feel at home in." He dined in a cheap restaurant, afterwards in his own rooms on bread and raisins ; he gave away all the small stipend that he received as Triumvir. Fearless of assassination, he sat unguarded in his room, accessible to all who wished to see him, to working men as much as to his own officials, with the same smile and friendly grasp for every one.

All this, however, went for nothing in Europe. The press shamelessly misrepresented what was passing at Rome. "They lie, indeed they lie," said Clough, who was present all the time, of certain English and French papers. The Pope stiffly refused to compromise, though the Republic offered, if he returned, to guarantee perfect liberty for the exercise of his spiritual authority. It became a race among the Catholic Powers who should restore him to his Temporal Power. I mentioned yesterday how Louis Napoleon's government plotted the destruction of the Roman Republic by what is perhaps the meanest of modern political crimes. Oudinot, who commanded the French expedition, tried to get admission into Rome on false pretences; but the secret of his real intentions leaked out, and the Romans were unanimous in their determination to resist. The French troops attacked an equal number of raw Roman levies outside the city walls, and were routed. Their position was a critical one, and they put on the mask again ; Mazzini, earnestly anxious to avoid more fighting with France, and hoping that the genuine republicans at Paris would overthrow the ministry, allowed himself to be hoodwinked by negotiations till the French reinforcements arrived. When they came, Oudinot attacked again, and the Romans were now hopelessly outnumbered; but badly armed and badly-generalled though they were, they made a desperate defence and bore a three weeks' siege, till their poor defences were battered down. From all Italy men had gathered, drawn by the spell of Rome, to fight once more for the honour of Italy. Garibaldi and many another, who helped to unite Italy ten years later, fought with a splendid recklessness. Inside the city the people bore the bombardment, the scarcity, the hopelessness of victory with hardly a murmur, gripped by the love and reverence they felt for their great leader.

I have dwelt at length on the history of the Roman Republic, partly to illustrate Mazzini's policy and influence, partly because it shows at its best the spirit that made Italian Unity possible. The next period of Mazzini's life shows him and it on a weaker side, in the partisanship, the incapacity to see things in their true proportions. For the ten years between 1849 and 1859 Mazzini's energies were largely consumed in an unequal duél with Cavour. I spoke of Cavour yesterday, and you will recognize how sharp was the contrast between him and Mazzini in character and policy;—the one a patient, careful statesman, who hated theories, and seldom took a step till he had carefully prepared the ground;—the other a man of higher moral force and culture but much less practical capacity, an intolerant, impatient revolutionary, inspired by a very high ideal, but incapable of distinguishing the essential and the non-essential in it, and missing the road to attainment because he could not compromise or work with others. The antagonism between them was intensified by Mazzini's exile. If he had been living at Piedmont, taking a daily part in its public life, he would have learnt tolerance for men whose object had so much in common with his own. The shortsighted intolerance of the Piedmontese government, which kept in exile the greatest of living Italians, is most to blame for his incapacity to do justice to itself. Mazzini's attacks on Cavour turned mainly on three points. First there was the question of the republic. Again and again he promised to give up his republican agitation if the royalists declared for Unity. But, as in 1848, he kept his promise in the letter, not in the spirit. Cavour could not at this time pronounce explicitly for Unity; but had Mazzini cared to look below the surface of his professed ambitions, he might have known, as others knew, that Cavour was quietly encouraging the movement for Unity, and would gladly stand openly for it as soon as circumstances made it safe. Secondly, his criticism fastened on the time and method of the next war. Cavour's delay seemed to him mere cowardice. He clung to his old policy of little local risings, believing that if the tinder was once alight, all Italy would soon be in flames, and the united strength of the country, regular armies and volunteers alike, would pour down on Lombardy. On this point, however, each was willing to take something from the other's programme; and both here and on the question of Unity the two men, with goodwill on both sides, might have come to an understanding. On the third point—that of the French alliance—compromise was impossible. Mazzini attacked it on two grounds; it was dishonouring to a young country, he thought, to win its independence otherwise than by its own unaided strength; it was guilty to ask help of the man who had crushed the Roman Republic and made the *coup d'état.* Mazzini never more than faintly recognized that Louis Napoleon had much of his own faith in nationality. He felt an honourable man's disgust at the steps by which the Emperor had climbed to power, and he hated the man who had bombarded Rome as he hated no one else. All through his life, too, he had an unconquerable dislike of France and Frenchmen. Cavour recognized, as Mazzini never did, the hard fact that Italy must either accept the French alliance, or wait indefinitely for the expulsion of Austria. His own less fine nature was prepared to accept the humiliating conditions of the alliance, the trickery and dishonour to which it so easily led. One is bound to condemn Cavour, not for the French alliance, but for the methods by which he fixed it. But when one remembers that his diplomacy was for no common end, that it sought the emancipation of millions of his countrymen, that it aimed at the good of Europe as well as of his own country, one will not readily cast stones at him.

We may pass rapidly over Mazzini's remaining life. His

influence steadily declined after 1849. Something he always did to brace his countrymen to active patriotism, but his later policy is a story of high-minded effort wasted by obstinacy and incapacity to see the facts. His part in the struggle of 1859 and 1860 was not a big one. The spirit of his teaching was indeed still at work; he helped to push on the movement which sent Garibaldi to Sicily; but it is doubtful whether his action made any appreciable difference to the events of those years. During the early sixties he incessantly preached war for the liberation of Venetia, wisely recognizing that it was folly to attack Rome while the French garrison was there. He tried to win Garibaldi to his policy, and to a small extent succeeded; but Garibaldi's umbrageous mind harboured unworthy suspicions and, partly from sheer rivalry with Mazzini, he clung to his impossible scheme of attacking Rome. Mazzini had a curious intrigue with the King, who was equally desirous to conquer Venetia and leave Rome alone at present. Both men cherished the idea of destroying the Austrian power, by encouraging the Hungarians and Slavs to rise, while Italy attacked from the West. The negotiations came to nothing, in spite of the real liking which the two had for one another; it proves their common carelessness for constitutional propriety, that they should have attempted the personal treaty over the heads of the King's ministers. In 1866 Venetia was won, thanks to the Prussian victories. Italy for her part had, in spite of her superior forces, been defeated both by land and sea, and she had had to abandon her claim to the Southern Tyrol. The country was maddened by the humiliation of defeat; there had been abundant incapacity and some corruption; the King's popularity was gone, and there was an acute, however unreasonable, disappointment that Unity had not brought at once all the economic and social gain that had been looked for. All this feeling turned against the Crown. Mazzini abandoned his semi-acceptance of the monarchy, and most of the remainder of his life was spent in vain attempts at

republican insurrection. Sometimes he thought now that the
Republic was more important than Unity, and would rather that
Rome should remain to the Pope than that it should be the
capital of a monarchy. It was a pitiful ending to the great
patriot's life, that he closed it with deliberate appeals to civil
war, and intrigued with Bismarck against his own country's
government. When the Italians entered Rome, his only feeling
was one of grief that Rome was "polluted" by the monarchy.
Eighteen months later, working, preaching to the end, he died.

Let us turn from his life's sad close to that splendid body
of teaching which made Italy. For it was Mazzini who made
Italy. Whether without him Italy would be united to-day, it
is of course impossible to tell. But he it was, who created the
faith that Unity was possible, who, while others doubted or fell
away, kept that faith ever living, whose influence to lift men up
to strong and selfless love of country carried Italians through
defeat and disappointment and tremendous risks to the national
end. He did this because he was a great moral teacher. His
philosophy, imposing and embracing and suggestive as it is,
covering most provinces of human thought—theology, ethics,
politics, art, literature—is too loosely constructed, sometimes
too little in touch with modern thought, to rank among great
contributions to intellectual progress. But as a prophet he
stands unrivalled in the nineteenth century, and his code of
ethics is perhaps the noblest which has applied itself to the
problems of modern life. I want here, at the risk of some
repetition, to touch on two of his theories, the theory of duty,
which gave the Italian movement much of its moral greatness,
the theory of nationality, which gave it its political justification.

In Mazzini's early years the doctrine of individual rights,
which had been the mainspring of the French Revolution, was
the accepted principle of European and American Liberals,
save for a handful of thinkers, such as Carlyle and Emerson.
Bentham and the Utilitarians, though they rejected the false

historical basis of the theory, preserved its spirit—its insistence on happiness as the end of life, its appeal to the self-seeking side of man. Mazzini loved to quote Carlyle's dictum that man's end is not the greatest possible happiness but the greatest possible nobleness, and George Sand's complementary tenet that "there is only one virtue—the eternal sacrifice of self." Any belief in the right to happiness, he said, however much men might be taught to aim at the happiness of the many, must lead inevitably to selfishness, to each man's fighting for himself, to conflict and anarchy, to struggle of class against class, of nation against nation, and the inevitable worsting of the weak. It admitted no ideal, and therefore had no guide for human conduct. It made self-sacrifice an absurdity, it could create no martyrs, and no political any more than a religious creed could triumph without the spirit that made martyrs. Men needed a principle that would take them right away from the selfish side of their nature, that would ever keep in sight a great ideal. Life, he said, is a mission; the individual man is called by God to work, and suffer, and die, if need be, for his fellows. The law of life is duty, duty that thinks not of difficulty or danger, of results or personal reward, but makes a man work earnestly, unceasingly, in his appointed sphere, work all the more when evil is strong and the path is dark, looking only to God's final question, "How many souls hast thou saved on earth?" Mazzini's own life, with its utter forgetfulness of self, its unremitting toil, its self-imposed poverty, its acceptance of the exile's homeless lot, was splendidly true to his creed. You will understand how the same creed helped to fortify and hallow the Italian struggle.

Mazzini, as I have said, was pre-eminently a moralist. Everything to him was a question of character, and men's motives were more important than any political or social system. But no man felt more strongly how much morality depends on education and surroundings, how intimately therefore it is connected with political and social life. This it was that sent him reluctantly from literature to politics, and kept him constant to the weariness and danger of his public life, despite his lifelong yearning to return to his books. It made him necessarily apply his moral principles to political and social questions. He deduced from his theory of duty a doctrine on which he built an elaborate political system. If the value of a man's life depends on its devotion to the good of others, its share in the common life, the true man will be inevitably drawn to work not only for but with others. And because the individual is weak, and the force of evil strong, and the ideal so immense, a man will not dare to face his duty, unless he knows that not only God but other men are working with him. Hence the true principle of social and political life is Association, and Mazzini thought that it was the recognition of this that marked the chief advance in the political theories of the century over earlier ones. He hated the whole individualist theory of the French Revolution and the economists. The waste and discord of the time, its class and national antagonisms, were supremely distasteful to him, and he sought to lessen the friction and promote unity of belief and conduct. And so he judged political systems by the extent to which they carried out the principle of Association. It was because he believed that republican government would best give it play, that he pleaded so earnestly for the republic.

It is the application of the principle to nationality that I am chiefly concerned with here. In Mazzini's view nations were groups of mankind, associated for their own good and for humanity's. Humanity took precedence, but the work of the world's civilization and moral growth needed a division of labour, and this division was best made among communities cemented by strong natural ties. Men would do for country what they would not do for mankind; their work was more effective when it was done for and with the men to whom they were related by the intimate and affectionate bonds of a common country. I am bound to say that Mazzini is not always quite consistent in defining the marks of nationality, but on the whole he is true to its only real foundation,—the free will of the inhabitants of a certain territory to unite themselves into a nation. Long before Bismarck perverted the national idea, Mazzini insisted that race and language were at the best only its minor characteristics. He believed indeed that great geographical boundaries, as the Alps, were set by Providence to indicate the natural limits of the nations. Community of language and literature, of customs and traditions helped to make a nation ; and no one felt more strongly than he did what Dante had done to make Italy. But these were not the essentials. The true mark of a nationality was the free consent of its members. Italy was called to be a nation because Italians wished it. He was fiercely indignant at Cavour's cession of Savoy, not because he thought that Savoy naturally belonged to Italy, but because the Savoyards had no voice in settling their own fate. Italy herself has been true to his principles. The plebiscites which annexed Central and South Italy to the Italian Kingdom (and here let me say that, in spite of oft-refuted denials, the plebiscites were free and genuine expressions of the national will) have been the highest manifestations of the national spirit in Modern Europe. It is the glory of United Italy that she recognized that the popular consent, freely and publicly expressed, must be her moral and legal justification.

Mazzini had another test of nationality, which I fear is less accepted. There is no true nationality, he thought, save where a people has a clear and bounden service to render to the world. He, patriot of patriots, based his love of country on the faith that the claims of humanity come first, that a country is false to itself, if it does not ever keep in view the good of all mankind. "Nationality," he said, "is sacred to me, because I see in it the instrument of labour for the good and progress of all men." It is not merely that a country is guilty (he would have called it irreligious) if it wrongs another people, or finds its strength in others' weakness; beyond all that, a country has its definite, positive duty to render to the world. And this in two ways. A true nation can never be neutral in the strife of right and wrong, wherever it is fought. He framed a tremendous indictment against English foreign policy for its indifference to the cause of struggling nationalities; and he looked to his own Italy to be friend and protectress of oppressed peoples. He wrote to an American friend after the close of the Civil War: "You have become a leading nation. You may act as such. In the great battle which is fought throughout the world between right and wrong, justice and arbitrary rule, equality and privilege, duty and egotism, republic and monarchy, truth and lies, God and idols, your part is marked; you must accept it." And, besides this, he believed that every country had its divinely appointed function to perform in humanity's service. England's was to spread commerce and colonize, Russia's was to civilize Asia, Poland's to fight the cause of the Slav peoples. Germany's sign was thought, France's was action.

And what was Italy's? I have spoken of his supreme faith in Italy and Rome, his confidence that Rome had yet another part to play, greater than any she had played in the past. I shall do no more than refer to his belief that a new religion would issue from her. But he had a more modest and practicable ideal for his country and her capital. He was confident that when Europe was settled on a nationalist basis, when national aspirations were satisfied and the chief cause of war had thereby disappeared (for he did not foresee what antagonisms would arise from colonial expansion), the nations would federate in a United States of Europe, with a common Diet to regulate international relations, and in some undefined way stimulate social progress. The natural seat of the Diet would be at Rome, and Rome would be the centre of the cause of peace. Is this an impossible ideal? A modern publicist, M. Novicow, has recently put out the same idea,

almost in Mazzini's words. Italy, which has practically no
territorial ambitions, no colonial empire, whose geographical
position makes it the mediator between the two great European
alliances, is the natural champion of peace and disarmament;
and if current rumours may be believed, the present King of
Italy, a man of big views and high principles, is not unmindful
of the fact. Italy has behind her a moral prestige such as no
other nation possesses. The spell of Rome reaches through
the world. Europe can never forget that it owes more to Italy
than to any other country, and it is still true in a sense that
every man has two countries, his own and Italy. Should the
European nations ever establish a true international tribunal,
Rome, rather than The Hague, would be its natural seat; and
should that day come, may the world remember that Mazzini
was not only the great moral teacher of the century and the
maker of modern Italy, but was also the prophet of the new
international law.

In concluding these two lectures, I should like to say one
word as to Modern Italy's contribution to the world's progress.
I have to some extent indicated it already. If, as most of us
believe, there can be no final settlement of Europe till states
are conterminous with nationalities,—nationalities that is in the
true and democratic sense,—the making of Italy is an achievement whose importance it is difficult to exaggerate. Among
the nationalist aspirations of the last hundred years Italy is
the one country that has truly attained. She has founded her
national existence on the will of the people; she—unlike
Germany—has done it without wronging another nation; and
all through her national movement she has remembered that a
country has duties to the world as well as to itself. Mazzini
looked to Italy and Rome to introduce a new moral order for
humanity; Gioberti looked for an Italian Pope to champion
Christian reform and peace among the nations; Cavour hoped
"to sign a new religious peace from the Capitol"; Ricasoli

believed that the destinies of Italy were pregnant with in-
calculable results for all humanity. The impossible and
fantastic in their teaching passed ; but the spirit of it stayed,
and new Italy stamped herself with the truest mark of a great
people, national altruism. Even under the feeble statesmanship of the last thirty years she has stood on the whole in the
European polity for justice and freedom more than any other
leading nation. I have indicated how in the future she may
do still more. Italy and the Italian race have a great part to
play. And it is permitted to believe that that part will be not
only a great but a beneficent one, that when, as she will do,
Italy makes her power felt, it will be a power not of armies and
fleets, but one that comes of industrial expansion and scientific
discovery and social pioneering, and above all of a high sense
of national mission for the good of all men.

THE REFORMING WORK OF THE TZAR ALEXANDER II.

By Professor Paul Vinogradoff, D.C.L.

No age in the history of Russia has a greater claim to glory than the time of Alexander II. The reign of Peter the Great may have been of more moment for the development of the Empire, the reigns of Catherine II and Alexander I may have brought more brilliant successes : the epoch of Alexander II will ever stand forward as an unparalleled effort towards the inward regeneration of society. To speak with a contemporary : it was a grand time, and death has no terror for one who has seen it.

The monarch with whose name these pages of our history are inscribed was in many respects a worthy leader of history. Not that his personality was marked by inventive genius or far-sighted statesmanship, by unbending will or a special ability to profit by circumstances. His was more a representative than a commanding character, but he was thoroughly imbued with the sense of his great historical task, and aimed rather at good will towards men than at power and glory. Education had given him a characteristic bent : he grew up under the stern discipline of his father's military rule and, whatever drawbacks may have attended this rule, it certainly went far to develop the sense of duty. The culture of his mind had been entrusted, on the other hand, to the care of a romantic poet, Joukovsky, and from this quarter came a softer influence, a humanitarian feeling which entered a kind of protest against the harsh spirit of Nicholas' court.

"I am almost afraid," the poet wrote to the young prince's mother, "that all these military playthings may spoil in him what ought to be his chief calling. Must he grow up to be only a soldier, to act in the narrow horizon of a general? When shall we come to look with respect on the real needs of the people, on the laws, on civilization and morals? The passion for military things is likely to harden his soul, to teach him to see in his people a regiment, in his country—barracks."

The great merit of the grown-up man and of the Emperor comes from the fact that he was in touch with the aspirations of the most enlightened men of his time during the decisive crisis of the sixties, and that he stood to a course which in his immediate surroundings was distrusted and opposed by most people. The secret of this spirit of resolution is to be found even more in the heart than in the mind, more in a sensitive nature than in a clear perception of contingencies. This may explain how it came, that when the chief effort had been made, and the most dangerous cape had been rounded, the helmsman relaxed, as it were, in his steering, and could not find his true course in the midst of conflicting currents of society. The seventies were as marked by contradictions and uncertain drifting as the sixties had been full of manly purpose and hopeful activity. The Tzar himself fell a victim to this troubled time, and from the point of view of historical fatality, his terrible death is not difficult to explain—he had called forth a movement which he was unable either to follow or to stay. Of course, such considerations are not meant to do away with the moral verdict of history : the murder of the benefactor of his country has indeed proved the truth of Talleyrand's saying : it was more than a crime, it was a mistake. It defeated its object, and during more than twenty years the whole country has had to suffer from its consequences.

My aim in the present lecture is not, however, to present a sketch of the personal incidents of the reign of Alexander II, interesting and characteristic though they are. I want rather to set before you an estimate of impersonal achievement, of what was accomplished by the people as a whole, by Herr Omnes, as Luther used sarcastically to say. But, before starting on our inquiry, I should like to point out that, in his own department of command Tzar Alexander was in reality a leader, and never came to follow passively any one of his advisers, though he listened to many and went part of the way sometimes with one and sometimes with the other. His relations with the liberal statesmen of his time were very curious. He found in the talented, ambitious and restless Grand Duke Constantine the only powerful helper among his relatives, and gave him a prominent share in the great work of emancipation, but as a Viceroy in Poland in the time of the rebellion, the Grand Duke lost his way and marred his career. Nicholas Milutine, the greatest of the Tzar's satellites by his profound and thorough grasp of the situation, his open and inventive mind, his energy and power of work, presented the real connecting link between the reforming government and reforming public opinion, but he was always distrusted by the Emperor, as a "radical," accepted more than chosen by him on critical occasions, and kept in more or less secondary positions. Count Loris Melikoff, who came in at the close of the reign, exerted perhaps the greatest personal influence of all on the Tzar in the weakened and nervous state to which the latter had come; but then Loris Melikoff himself represented the same undecided combination of heterogeneous elements which was characteristic of Alexander II., he was a kind of repetition of his master, with more craftiness and less nobility of disposition. The reactionaries even more than the liberals played the part of tools and occasional helpers. Such was the terrible Mouravieff, the dictator of Vilna: he was let loose on occasions of special danger, but remained outside the circle of real political leaders. Demetrius

Tolstoy, the reactionary Minister of Public Instruction of the seventies, showed his real mettle in the reign of Alexander III, while in Alexander II's time he acted chiefly as the mouthpiece of a more influential person, of the journalist who had the greatest share in drawing up the programme of reaction and converting public opinion to it—of Katkoff. In his last years the Tzar lent his ear a good deal to his advice, and the wavering manner in which he stood between the bilious tribune of reaction and the conciliating Loris Melikoff shows more than anything else to what extent singleness of purpose and clearness of political thought were missing in this sad close of the reign. Of one more figure of this time I will say a couple of words, of Valouyeff, Minister of the Interior in the sixties, not because he was in any way a remarkable man, but because he represents one of the greatest failings of the Russian bureaucracy of these times—and of other times too. He was not a remarkable man, but he seemed one, and talked like one ; he had no ideas, but as many projects and counter-projects as were wanted to meet the emergencies of legislation, and all through the troublous times he steered most successfully his own personal career. In this way Alexander II had no Bismarck by his side, and even if he might have found a Stein in Milutine, he did not wish him to be one, but tried to gather helpers from opposite quarters. These observations are not entirely foreign to the main object of this lecture ; they ought to show that the great work of the sixties was accomplished by a multitude of agencies which were led in a definite direction by the spirit of the time, more than by the plans and efforts of any single person.

In what respect was the country prepared for the great work of social revival ? Its condition at the close of Nicholas' reign seemed desperate. The huge mass was sorely deficient in the production and circulation both of material goods and of ideas. The majority of the people were riveted to the soil by serfdom and ignorance ; the means of communication were in such a state that it took occasionally a year to send convoys and relays from the North to Sebastopol, and social intercourse was so sluggish that when the price of corn stood at 1.50 roubles in the province of Kursk, it fetched 15 roubles in the province of Pskov. The ruling class was mainly represented by the landowners described in Gogol's *Dead Souls*, vegetating in sloth on the back of their "christened property," as the peasants were called, and by the *tchinovniks*, of whom Gogol's *Revisor* gives a graphic description, carrying the same easy-going, thoughtless, corrupt practices into the routine of their official callings. But in this state of society there were redeeming features which come like rays of light into the darkness. The same class of landowners which showed to so little advantage in its daily life of ignorance and private interest, disclosed elements of sound strength when it came into contact with ideals of intellectual and moral greatness. From this class came not only the military men which have served Russia faithfully on many fields of battle; but, what is more, it expanded gradually in the direction of literature and civilization. The brilliant generation of the forties had witnessed the rise of a kind of intellectual freemasonry which laid the foundations of public opinion and conscious thought right in the snow of the Nicholas *régime*. Hertzen, one of the most remarkable representatives of this time, a man who had to leave Russia on account of his advanced opinions, tells us that he nowhere came across such a centre of humanitarian and philosophical thought as the one which had formed itself in Moscow in connection with its University. The influence of this small but high-spirited minority made itself felt more and more by the help of literature and of the press. The force which came to be represented by such men as Pushkin, Gogol and Lermontoff, Bielinsky and Hertzen, Granovsky, Chomiakoff, Samarine, Tourgeneff, Gontcharoff, Stchedrine and many others could not be disregarded. It may be even said that never was the voice of a highly educated minority heard more clearly and followed with more enthusiasm by society than in these days, when the Government did not admit of any direct interference in its affairs and the country had so few channels to form and express its opinions.

The collapse of Nicholas' *régime* gave to this wonderful intellectual movement a practical direction. There could be no mistake about the moral of the Crimean war : just because the rule of Nicholas had been thorough and attended with outward success, its bankruptcy was more striking. The capacity of the country for a better development stood the most difficult of the tests which can be applied to nations by history : evil and defeat called forth a moral revival and a salutary reform.

The era of reforms was brought about by the joint action of a Government which had suffered signal defeat but had to appeal to a long past of successful national leadership, a country poor in material resources and reviled by social abuses, but patriotic in all great emergencies of historical life, and an enlightened minority instinct with ideals of justice and independent thought. The result was amazing. No people has experienced a more thorough regeneration of its institutions than Russia in the sixties : the abolition of serfdom, the creation of self-government, the reform of judicial organization, the introduction of general conscription and shorter service in the army, the improvement of the finances of the Empire, the construction of railways, the modification of the Press law, educational reforms—all these momentous changes came about in the course of a few years. It remains for us to see what was really achieved by the most important of them.

The social reform had to proceed from the abolition of serfdom. Serfdom was by no means an ancient and time-honoured institution in Russia : in South Russia it was less than a hundred years old, having been chiefly transplanted there by the enlightened despotism of Catherine. In Great Russia, the mainstay of the Empire, it was some two hundred years older in its origins. But even there it sprang up gradually and in a way which rendered its existence precarious. It was the result of the consolidation of duties towards the state. The peasants were enlisted to serve their lords as tillers of the soil, because the lords were enlisted to serve the Tzar as warriors. These historical facts had more than an antiquarian significance: they kept up among the subjected people the consciousness of their dignity and the hope that what had been done under the hard pressure of political necessity might be undone in better days. When Peter III freed the landed gentry from the obligation of serving the state (1762), the peasants were convinced that this act would be followed by a corresponding emancipation of the agricultural class. They were right in their guess, although they had to wait almost exactly a hundred years for the completion by history of what was necessary in logic.

And these last hundred years of bondage were in many respects the worst of all. The political idea underlying serfdom had evaporated, but its consequence—the surrender by the state of its most important rights into the hands of the landed proprietors—remained. The squires according to Emperor Paul's expression were considered as the best and cheapest "masters of the police." At the same time these very squires had private rights over the land and the persons of their "subjects." The result was a most odious tyranny—the arbitrary rule of innumerable petty tyrants, backed up by the arbitrary rule of a powerful Empire. Though some faint restrictions on the power of injuring the wretched peasants existed in law, in practice men, women and children were ill-used, sometimes even to death, and retaliation was exceptional even in such extreme cases, as the peasants were denied all direct access to the authorities, even in the way of complaint, not to speak of an action against the lords. I will not dwell on the many memories of caprice, lust and cruelty which have come down to us from these good old times. Just to give you an impression as to this state of things, I may mention one case in which the paternal care of a landowner in regard to his "christened property" is exemplified. In a well-ordered estate the proprietor had solved the problem of ensuring family happiness : once a year the youth of both sexes which had reached a given age were called up to the office : at the bidding of the stewards couples were formed and instantly marched off to church, where the holy rites of marriage were performed for them by the village priest.

There were mainly two restraints on the wanton use of power—the existence of the village community and the self-interest of the owners. As for the first, it drew the agricultural people tightly together : this afforded some check on oppression, and it kept up among the people a sense of fellowship and fair arrangement that was entirely missing in the case of domestic servants, the most wretched class among the serfs. The motive of self-interest kept the masters from injuring their men in the same way as it kept them from injuring their beasts. By the help of such agencies general arrangements were worked out almost by instinct to meet economic requirements : where the soil was too poor or there were openings for industrial or commercial development, labour services were commuted for rents. In the use of servile labour for agricultural purposes customary systems as to the allotment of land and the amount of services arose : cases varied a good deal, but there may be noticed a general tendency towards dividing the week by half, the peasant doing three days "brother's" work for his lord.

Though human nature provides for some working arrangement even in such desperate situations, the difficulties of serfdom were increasing on all sides and every day. The allotment of land grew more and more insufficient with each new generation. In order to find the necessary supplementary means of existence the peasants had to look out for outside work, but this channel was very much blocked by the necessity of obtaining leave from the lord and the tendency of all customary arrangements towards immobility. There were too many mouths in the North and too few hands in the South, but the mouths could not be moved freely to the region where the hands were needed. As a matter of fact the whole distribution of society proved to be wrong: it had originated at a time when the requirements of defence drew the population artificially towards Moscow. In the altered condition of things, at a time of rising husbandry on the black soil of the South, the workmen remained chained to the sand and clay of the North. On the other hand, the state began to perceive that it lost more than it gained by its policy of surrender to the born "masters of the police." It wanted national industry and commerce, and came to understand that they could not be got without a supply of free labour; it wanted Russia to follow Western countries in the ways of material progress, and came to see that the arbitrary power of the lord was not conducive towards that end. Even more directly, it wanted to strengthen its financial resources, and found that it could not put on the screw with proper effect, because the squires had the lion's share in the proceeds of national labour and squandered a good deal of the national capital by their thriftless management.

Under these circumstances the moral forces arrayed against serfdom obtained a firm footing in more than one quarter. The protests of the peasants themselves took the shape of occasional deeds of murder and revolt, which were ruthlessly repressed, but left after them an uneasy feeling that a storm was brewing somewhere. Tzar Nicholas himself could not help admitting that the abolition of serfdom was necessary. "I do not understand," he said once, speaking as "the first nobleman of Russia," "how man came to be a thing, and I can explain the fact only by deception on one side and ignorance on the other. We must make an end to this. It is better that we should give up of our own account that which might otherwise be wrested from us." One secret committee after the other was appointed to inquire into the condition of the peasantry and devise measures to improve their lot, and six times the good intentions of the Government were eluded by the resistance of the nobility and of officials of high standing. The will and energy of the Emperor were kept in check in this case by his fear of shaking the foundations of the state and his hatred of democratic ideas. Only when the charm of Nicholas' *régime* had been broken by the Crimean war, the forces making for emancipation got the upper hand.

Curiously enough the immediate impulse towards agrarian reform was given by the policy of the Government in the Western provinces, where the landed gentry is Polish while the peasant class is Russian or Lithuanian. Already in Nicholas' reign so-called inventories were introduced in the South-West, that is binding agreements between lords and tenants as to allotments and services, and on the 20th of November, 1857, an Imperial rescript to the Governor-General of the North-West was published, which proclaimed the necessity of agrarian reform, and provided the local machinery for carrying this resolve into practice. The effect of this manifestation was tremendous, because it moved the question from the region of secret committees into the demesne of national publicity. Emancipation in the whole of Russia had clearly become a necessity, but a good deal depended on the manner in which it was carried out.

The original intentions of the Government were not very promising. The Ministry of the Interior had taken its cue from the emancipation of the serfs by the German nobility of the Baltic provinces of the Empire : it had been effected under Alexander I, and had resulted in freeing the person of the peasant and leaving him at the mercy of the proprietor as a farmer or an agricultural labourer. The common people in Russia were in dread of such lawless freedom, which they termed the freedom of the wolf. The leaders of progressive opinion, and foremost among them the Petersburg Professor Kavelin, took accordingly a firm stand against this idea; and, fortunately for the Russian peasantry, the most influential of the men to whom the actual shaping of the reform law was intrusted, recognized the national tradition of peasant right to the land under the protection of a village community.

The necessary investigations as to facts and the drawing up of schemes for Russian progress were confided to two sets of boards : provincial commissions, consisting of representatives of the landed gentry and of some members of the administration, and a central commission, the so-called Redaction-commission in St Petersburg, in which N. Milutine was the leading spirit, and which through his influence was composed not only of the usual elements of high bureaucracy, but also of some representatives of the landed interest from different parts of Russia. These last, though drawn from the class whose interest it was to oppose or to restrict emancipation, were in reality the spokesmen of enlightened public opinion, Youri Samarine and Prince Tcherkarssky being the most prominent among them, men of high culture and of a proud spirit of disinterested patriotism. What followed is a striking illustration of the might of well-conceived ideas on a soil adapted to their development, even against the most rancorous weeds of self-interest and prejudice. The action of the provincial bodies led to the elaboration of contradictory schemes : the great majority of the landed gentry was still too much fettered by selfish considerations to entertain plans of a generous and comprehensive reform. But at the same time everywhere there came forward a determined minority which renounced petty considerations of profit and tried to rise to the greatness of the occasion. In the Central Commission a similar minority was making way against the ill-will and the indifference of the rest. It succeeded in drawing over to its side the first chairman, Rostovtzeff, a general with a doubtful past, but with a feeling for the importance and responsibility of his task, and, after the death of Rostovtzeff, who succumbed to work and worry, it checkmated his successor, Count Panin, a most unsympathetic representative of the spirit of subservient bureaucracy engrafted on aristocratic pretensions.

In this way the reform was elaborated and carried out by an enlightened and energetic minority which had won the support of the Government and used the feelings and situation of the absent mass of the peasantry as a kind of dead-weight determinating the centre of gravity of the problem.

Let us turn to the chief provisions which were elaborated in this way, and carried through a High Commission presided over by the Grand Duke Constantine, and through the Council of State in which the Emperor himself used his personal influence to further the scheme. They are embodied in the memorable statute of February 19, 1861. Personal freedom was granted without distinction to all serfs, the agricultural peasants as well as the domestic servants. The first obtained at once a protected tenure of their holdings, but had to pay and perform work for them as long as these holdings were not redeemed by agreement with the owners. Most agreements were effected in the course of twenty years, and only a comparatively insignificant remnant of tenures were subjected in 1881 to enforced redemption. The money for redemption was lent to the peasants by the state, and they had to repay it gradually in the course of 49 years.

The conditions of the settlement were by no means easy: the peasants got everywhere rather less than what they had possessed before emancipation, the minimum and maximum being fixed by statute. We may judge of the burden laid on the peasantry from the fact that at the close of the seventies a peasant's dessiatine (about $2\frac{1}{2}$ acres) had to pay 95 copeks in land taxes, whereas a dessiatine belonging to a squire was taxed merely at 17 copeks. The holdings resulting from this operation were as a rule too small. The statistics of the distribution of land show allotments which stand in marked contrast with the endowment of that part of the peasantry which depended directly on the Crown. About 50 per cent. of the former serf families (*dvor*) live on tenures of 5 to 10 dessiatines, say from 12 to 25 acres. In the fertile South the figures are generally lower, and at the last stages of legislation on the subject a great landowner, Prince Gagarine, succeeded in introducing the provision, that the proprietors could by renouncing all payments from their peasants cut them off with one-fourth of the maximum holding. Thanks to this clever move a large number of farmers in the South live on so-called beggar holdings of a couple of dessiatines, and are economically at the mercy of the neighbouring squires. This goes a long way to explain the agrarian disturbances in the Kharkoff and Pultava provinces which occurred in the course of last spring.

The emancipation left in force and confirmed the customary organization of the peasantry as it existed in 1861. The greater part of Great Russia remained in the hands of village communities, which have a right of re-dividing the land between their component families according to requirements and working strength, and altogether exert a very wide power for regulating village life. As against the state the community is responsible as a whole for the payment of taxes by its members. In the South and West the land is held in severalty by the households. For administrative and police purposes the lowest unit is formed by the village community with its assemblies and elective reeve, while the next instance is formed by a kind of union hundred, the volost, to which several villages are ascribed. The volost has jurisdiction over the peasants of its territory, and delivers judgment in their suits according to customary law, but people not belonging to the peasant class have nothing to do with it. Altogether, nearly 23 millions were emancipated on the ground of the statute of February 19, 1861, and in 1863 and 1866 the peasants directly depending on the Crown received similar allotments and organization.

Another complement of the great reform was the agrarian measure carried out in 1864 by Milutine and his friends in Poland, where the personal emancipation brought by the French in the beginning of the century had left the peasant class in a most precarious condition : this was supplemented after the Polish rebellion of 1863 by a more thorough policy of land allotment than the one which was effected in Russia proper. It may be noticed in passing that the township, *gmina* (from the German *Gemeinde*), is not exclusively a peasant institution here, but embraces all the inhabitants of its territory.

All these tremendous changes were on the whole carried out with great fairness at the hands of the umpires of the peace selected from the landed gentry, and received with dignity and orderly behaviour by the peasants, and this side of their history certainly deserves careful attention, as showing to what extent (notwithstanding the bustle and agitation of the first moment) the measures adopted seemed satisfactory, and met the requirements at least of the immediate future.

The emancipation was more than a reform, it was a peaceful revolution : it changed the economic structure of society by supplying it suddenly with free labour, and it made necessary other reforms—political, administrative and judicial—by altering the social basis on which all arrangements of the former age had been resting. To begin with, the administration could not be left in its former state. It presented a curious mixture of bureaucracy and aristocratic privilege. The absolute power of the Tzar had done away with all restraints in higher and central administration, but had not the means of carrying out its orders all through the Empire. In the same spirit, in which it had surrendered the welfare of the majority of the people to the guidance and self-interest of landlords, it made over to the landed gentry of every province the selection of administrative and police officers, as well as of judges, although the actual appointment was effected by the Government and they had to look to the Government for orders and control. The members of the class who filled the provincial posts, of the *noblesse*, as one might call it, according to the ancient French term, and in distinction to the English nobility, made use of their administrative and judicial offices in the same spirit of private interest, in which every single squire arranged his estate and his "christened property." Bribery, dishonest employment of public money, abuse of power were direct consequences of the system : there were numbers of the people who never came to understand that they were doing anything amiss because they were rather sharp in their administrative practice. To make the picture complete, the presence of absolutism was affirmed everywhere by the governor, a high official directly appointed by the Crown, a kind of Pasha, who was termed officially the Manager of the province and supposed to look to everything, in fact to act as the political providence of the district. It is not difficult to guess the result of this side of administrative organization : a meddlesome tutelage crippling free enterprize, a series of pompous, self-confident, self-indulgent and ignorant proconsuls of whom the best were those who did not take their power too seriously, a conspiracy of official adulation and deceit as to the real state of the country and the influence of pettifogging clerks substituting paper correspondence for real business.

The impulse given by the emancipation shook this rotten fabric in its very foundations. The framing of a new plan was entrusted to a commission presided over by a very doubtful person, Valouyeff. The prevalent public opinion of the time gave it an impulse towards self-government, but it had to encounter a powerful opposition from Petersburg bureaucrats, who were afraid of calling forth an independent action entirely foreign to their habits and rule. One has to keep all these circumstances in mind in order to understand the half-hearted manner in which the necessary legislation was devised and carried out. Anyhow the rights of self-government were proclaimed in the provinces and their subdivisions, the districts, whereas in local affairs only the towns received it. Villages are self-governing only as communes of peasants, the members of other classes being left without common bond. The scope of the *Zemstvo* or *land*-organization, as provincial self-government is called, in contrast with the state bureaucracy, was deemed to be the management of those interests which concern the economic requirements of local society and not the political requirements of the state. It was impossible in practice to give effect to this slippery distinction, which was prompted by the characteristic jealousy of the Government towards its own offspring. In point of fact the Zemstvo was called upon to take into its hands the care of medical and veterinary arrangements within the limits of the province, of primary education, of the relief of the poor, of economic assistance, especially in cases of distress, of ways of communication, of insurance against fire and other calamities, of the collection of statistics and the organization of natural services required by the Government from the population of the province. To meet all these needs it had the right of imposing rates on the landed property of the inhabitants and of making certain bye-laws.

The machinery by which these duties were to be carried out comprised assemblies meeting for short periods in the districts and in the province, and boards to which executive business was entrusted. The franchise was managed according to certain property distinctions, not excluding the peasantry. The functions of the deputies were left without remuneration, while the members of the executive boards were to receive salaries. The chairmen of the boards were not to preside in the assemblies, the chair being taken in those by the officers of the *noblesse*, the so-called Marshals.

The powers of the new bodies were substantially curtailed in many ways. On the one hand, the power of coercive execution of their decisions was denied to them. If anybody did not want to conform to them, if anybody was remiss in paying his rates, and the like, the Zemstvo had to apply for execution to the general police, which had now become quite bureaucratic in its composition. The power of the governor and of different boards presided over or appointed by him had by no means ceased in those very departments to which the

Zemstvo had been introduced, and he had to supervise its action and to confirm its decisions. Everywhere, in fact, the "land" and the "government" were posted with concurrent powers, and a jealous mistrust of each other. It was clear from the first that the reform of provincial administration, though it did away with many evils and afforded some prospects of good, rather opened the lists for a struggle between different sections of society than provided them with a basis on which they could work peacefully together.

It remains for us to point out the change which was effected in yet another department, namely in the organization of justice. Notwithstanding the great efforts which had been made in the reigns of Alexander I and Nicholas I to improve and to codify the law, the modes of administering it were defective in the extreme. We have already seen to what extent the lower courts were permeated by the oligarchical principles of the epoch of serfdom : the landed *noblesse* had to elect the members of these tribunals, and they conducted the business of the courts with the same disregard for human dignity and the purity of justice with which they managed the affairs of their estates : their arbitrary, corrupt practices had become a household word in Russia and abroad. At the same time the police, wielded by other squires, presented an inextricable confusion of administrative and judicial functions. It held amongst other things in its hands the very origin of criminal jurisdiction, the preliminary investigation as to crimes. It was an object of disdain for high people, of corruption for the middle class, and of terror for lower orders.

Apart from their defective composition and corrupt practices the courts of justice did not inspire confidence on account of their procedure. It was based on the inquisitorial system, carried on with closed doors, by the help of innumerable written documents, on the principle of formal proof, without any regard for common sense and equity. No wonder that the era of reforms had to reconstruct this edifice also. In the beginning of the sixties the comprehensive work of remodelling the judicature was carried out in an admirable manner by a commission of lawyers and statesmen, of which Zarudniy and Stoyanovsky were the most talented and meritorious, and on the 20th of November, 1864, the new statute as to the organization of justice became law. It presented a remarkable adaptation to Russian life of principles of law and of judicial institutions, worked out and tried by the history of England, France and Germany. There can be no talk in this case of a mere copying of foreign standards: no single system was followed in an exclusive manner, but the best conceptions of the West were made to serve the requirements of Russian life.

I cannot dwell long on the purely legal side of this great reform, and must content myself with pointing out its chief aspects. It proclaimed the publicity of procedure, and made an end thereby to the crooked ways and hidden abuses of the old tribunals. Instead of the inquisitorial procedure in which the parties in court are reduced to mere nonentities, the way was cleared for a conflict of argument between the parties, and their efforts to maintain their contentions were relied upon to produce a more searching inquiry for truth than the one-sided examination of the court. The preliminary inquest as to criminal acts was confided to magistrates who had more in common with the French *juges d'instruction* than with English coroners. The duty of sustaining the accusation in court was entrusted to public prosecutors, while for the defence of the accused and the representation of civil interests the order of barristers was organized. For the settlement of minor suits and the punishment of minor misdemeanours and crimes justices of the peace were created, and, as a guarantee of their independence, they were to be chosen by the Zemstvo and the towns. The same regard for the independence of the Bench was shown in the original statute by the provision that the judges of the higher courts were not to be removed unless by the decision of a court of law. In criminal cases the trial by jury was introduced with the view of providing the courts of law with an element of common sense and independent judgment, not adulterated by professional narrowness. At the summit of the whole edifice the Senate was placed, as a court for formal revision, a *Cour de Cassation*, as the French say, keeping guard over the uniform and unflinching application of the law all through the Empire. It was altogether a grand reform, even more grand in the spirit to which it bore witness than in the details of its provisions. It proclaimed the rule of law, equality before the law, and the independence of judges, three principles which were all but new in Russian life, and which, if carried thoroughly into effect, would have involved a real progress of the country from a half-barbarous state to the benefits of political civilization.

But such transformations are not possible in so short a time and by so plain a course. The dark past was strong even in its defeat. It had dangerous weapons in its hands—the fear of political reform and the craze of revolution. By the help of these weapons the development of principles avowed and proclaimed by the Government itself was arrested. We have seen already how emancipation was minimized and local self-government crippled. By the side of reformed justice the most glaring contradictions to it were left standing. The citizen remained rightless as against the political police: a man could be subjected to search, imprisonment, administrative expulsion with no law to protect him or to punish the harmful use of discretionary power. Corporal punishment was abolished for the higher classes, but remained in force in regard to common people. A Press law was issued in 1865, but its provisions were made ineffectual one by one, and censorship reinstated in all its glory. Liberty of conscience was guaranteed to foreigners, with some restrictions, but denied to Russians. In political and legislative matters the nation remained a passive mass which had merely to follow orders, although free institutions were revived by Alexander II in Finland.

All these fatal contradictions account for the disappointment and bitterness which followed the exultation of the age of reform and culminated in the desperate war of the terrorists against the Government. Still, as it would be unfair to pronounce a condemnation on the Government that had done so much, because it did not do all, it would be equally unfair to judge of the nation by the outbreak of unruly spirit which carried the most hotheaded of its youth into terrorism. The real trial both for the Government and for the nation turned on their capacity to appropriate and develop in quieter times the memorable reforms of Alexander II.

THE MEANING OF THE PRESENT DEVELOP-
MENT IN RUSSIA.

By Professor Paul Vinogradoff, D.C.L.

People differ a good deal as to the meaning of the present stage of development in Russia itself, and to foreigners it appears as a complete puzzle. They have not the means of following closely the manifestations of the every-day life of the people, because the usual sources to which it is customary to apply—parliamentary debates and the utterances of an unfettered press—are wanting. In this way the current news about Russia is not of a high order, and what generally reaches the eye of Western observers are official announcements (which are commonly disbelieved) and "dreadfuls" of various kinds. The best way to form a judgment is to turn to the great lines traced by history: and what has been said in my former lecture about the era of reforms may, I hope, have left at least this impression that the Russia of our time is most directly connected with the Russia of the sixties. The changes at that time were so great that more than one generation had to work at assimilating their results and meeting their consequences.

To begin with, the social transformation of the country has been, no doubt, very striking. The population has been nearly doubled in the course of some 40 years,—rising from 74 millions in 1858 to about 140 millions at the present moment. Whereas at the beginning of Alexander II's reign there existed only some 1,000 versts of railway in the huge empire, in 1899 there were 48,000 versts in action and nearly 8,000 building, and by this enterprise the drawback of enormous distances is being gradually overcome. Agricultural resources have been developed, chiefly by the spread of cultivation and partly, especially in the West, by the adoption of better methods, and the country counts as one of the great producers of grain for the world market. Industry has sprung up under high-pitched protection and by the influx of foreign capital, so that in the course of ten years (1887—1897) the production of textiles has been doubled, rising from 463 million r. to 946 millions, while the commercial balance of 1898 shows 732 r. for exported goods and 617 for imported, as against a medium export of 227 and a medium import of 205 at the close of the fifties.

The Government is taking more than its share from this great increase of national resources. In 1857 its income was 260 million r. and its expenditure about 350 millions. In 1890 expenditure and income were balanced at just 1,000 million roubles, and in 1900 the expenditure already reached 1,889 millions, being nearly 90 per cent. in excess of the budget of 1890.

Has the increase in national wealth stood in real correspondence to this exceptional rise of expenditure and taxation? There are many facts to show that it has not been the case. It has to be noticed, to begin with, that the greater part of the income is swallowed by the interest of the Debt and the needs of the military establishment in army and navy, and this is certainly a great drag on productive outlay. The construction of railways comes next, and its growth is not dictated merely by commercial, but also, as in the case of the Transsiberian, by strategic considerations. No wonder that such wants as that of National education, for instance, are reduced to ridiculous insignificance. The budget of the Ministry of Public Instruction has never risen to more than $2\frac{1}{2}$ per cent. of the expenditure, and there has been a decrease in a number of years.

On the other hand there can be no doubt that the constant

increase of a taxation which falls mainly on the poor is draining
the resources of the most important class of the Empire, the
peasantry, to such an extent that its members are pushed to
the brink of destitution and in case of any mishap actually
lapse into beggary. The frequent miscarriages of crops and
the famines consequent on them are more than the casual
results of bad weather. They show that the people have no reserve to fall back upon. The reports of the so-called campaigns
of relief testify to appalling conditions. In most cases the
number of cattle and horses owned by the peasantry is de-
creasing. In some districts of the province of Samara, which
counts among the granaries of Russia, there have been years
when one-third and even one-half of the population have been
turned into mendicants. When the tax-gatherer turns away in
despair from such wretched people he fastens the more on
those who have still something left. It may be said without
exaggeration that for the majority of the Russian peasantry the
primary object in life is to earn enough to pay the taxes :
everything else is an accident. The wonder is not at the lack
of enterprise and thrift, but at the endurance which enables
men to toil along at all in the face of such conditions.

This state of affairs is assuming so grave an aspect, that
even in the realm of bureaucracy some apprehensions are
entertained, and projects for improvement are hatched. Even
now a " Consultation " is discussing these questions under the
high chairmanship of the Minister of Finance. It is evident
to everybody concerned, that the difficulty is not merely a
technical one : it is not merely a question of rotation of crops
or of manure. Behind the necessary technical improvements
are looming problems of political economy and of law, and
so much has been avowed by this very Minister who has to
superintend the fleecing of the sheep and is called up now to
look to their health. In one of his reports to the Emperor he
insists on the necessity of a solid basis of law and of right for
the life of the peasantry.

17—2

And truly enough such a basis of right and law does not exist for the great majority of the Russian people. The emancipation from serfdom left it a class with peculiar and inferior institutions. The existence of the village community in itself does not imply the necessity of keeping the peasants outside the general law. The working of the community could be easily adjusted to general rules as to juridical persons. But a peculiar demesne of custom was formed for them nevertheless : everything was to be decided on the ground of indefinite and varying custom within the village or in the court of the volost, by judges elected from among the peasantry itself. This would have been excellent if by the side of these experts in rural custom representatives of trained legal knowledge appeared, to mediate, as it were, between the legal conceptions of the lower and higher orders. But nothing of the sort exists : the volost judges, sometimes quite illiterate, are left to grapple with problems of hereditary succession, family and marriage law, criminal jurisdiction for minor offences, and there is nothing to help them but the advice of pettifogging clerks and the supervision of administrative officers. It must be added that in the few cases when the lawgivers did concern themselves with this demesne of peasant custom the result has not been a happy one—mostly a strengthening of antiquated institutions which seemed to savour of the principle of authority. In such a way, for example, divisions between members of the family and the freedom of moving from place to place have been hampered in a very mischievous manner.

The main idea underlying all these facts amounts undoubtedly to the conception that peasants are not like other people, that they have to be treated as beings of a lower order. The theory which flourished in the Southern States in regard to the negro has a kind of counterpart in the notions of the Russian Government and gentry about the Russian peasant, although this same peasant is being sentimentally extolled when no practical consequence has to be drawn from such declamations. In view of his animal nature, flogging is deemed an appropriate punishment for him and carefully preserved in the practice of administrative officials and of volost-courts, although other classes are exempted from it, at least by law.

From an economic point of view we notice in the life of the single peasant a falling off for the worse, although the aggregate production of agriculture has increased. To understand how matters came to such a pass we have to look back at the settlement which followed emancipation. The peasantry received less than it had held before the emancipation and sometimes it was put off with entirely incommensurate plots; the land they got was, as a rule, of inferior quality; they were often left without suitable pasture and they had to pay a heavy indemnity for what they did get. Some improvements were introduced later on. The indemnity was somewhat reduced and facilities granted for paying it off, a bank was instituted in 1883 to help the peasantry with credit for the purchase of land, emigration was regulated to some extent, but all these measures were not thorough enough, and the country is still facing a state of things which is more than an agricultural crisis, which threatens to become a question of existence for its most important class.

Unhappily the policy of the Government has not only been insufficient in this case, it has been distinctly harmful in two respects: deliberate efforts have been made to reinstate the landed gentry into the privileged position it held before the emancipating acts, and the agricultural population of the Empire, instead of advancing towards the same level as other classes, has been placed under a degrading and arbitrary tutelage. These two features of the present time deserve careful examination.

When the statute of 1861 was passed and put into practice, it became apparent that in the New Russia of free labour and free contract, the gentry was fast losing the position it had possessed in the age of settled establishment and immoveable custom. Not that the members of the class were deprived of means to make good their interests: on the contrary, the immediate effect of the breaking of the old system was to throw such enormous sums of money into their hands as they had never had before, and they retained more than a fair share of the land to which this capital could be applied. But it was evident that most did not know and did not care to enter into the new conditions of life: the money was squandered, the estates mortgaged, and the families of the squires dispersed into all sorts of professions instead of concentrating their efforts on the cultivation of their estates. No wonder that from the ruins of the class different currents arose—its members broke up into three main groups: some definitely joined the middle class which was beginning to form itself in towns, some while remaining in the country sought to lead in a different sense from old, to use their means and their superior political training to obtain influence apart from any privilege, but most of those who remained on the land raised a cry for assistance and restitution. Past services were recalled, past deficiencies slurred over, the state was to make amends for all the uncomfortable consequences of emancipation. One of these gentlemen proposed, for instance, that every parish should be administered by a meeting of the resident *noblesse*, while the chairman of this board should be remunerated by an exemption from paying the debts he had incurred towards the Government. Another preached the advisability of cutting out new estates of the substantial worth of £25000 each for the sake of making comfortable provision for 4000 families of the *noblesse*. The wish that the squires should be granted powers of police over the labourers on their estates and over the adjoining peasantry is constantly recurring with the obvious object to revert to a state of things similar to former serfdom.

The Government let itself be carried away to great lengths by this unblushing agitation. In 1886 it started the bank of the *noblesse* with the aim of providing the squires with credit on the most advantageous conditions: the result has been unlooked for, inasmuch as the money obtained so cheaply was mostly squandered and the thirst for more seems nevertheless unquenchable. In 1886 also it was enacted that a breach of contract by hired labourers was to be considered a criminal offence, and the police were to coerce the labourers to perform their work. In 1897 a special consultation was formed to consider the wants of the *noblesse* and it has formulated some wishes as to the conditions of admission to the privileged order and as to the education of its children. But the greatest boon conferred on the privileged gentry to the prejudice of society and public order has been the institution in 1889 of the so-called Zemskinatchalnik (land-captains or land-administrators).

In the heat of the reaction which characterized Alexander III's reign it was found expedient to strengthen the government in the open country by submitting the villagers to the jurisdiction of civil officers endowed with judicial as well as with administrative functions. The principle of the division between these two powers, a fundamental principle from the point of view of the reforms of 1864, was given up, the justices of the peace elected by provincial councils thrown over, and a very stringent and arbitrary rule put in their place—the rule of the land-captain, appointed by the governor from the gentry at the advice of the marshal of the *noblesse*. The new officer was on the one hand made the centre of all the administrative affairs of his district—sanitary measures, relief of the poor, relief in cases of agricultural distress, supervision as to all material and moral interests of the population. On the other, he was to be judge in the first instance in minor civil and criminal cases. Thirdly he was to act more especially as a guardian and controller in all cases which concerned the peasantry. As one of these land-captains pointedly expressed it: they were to act as nurses to the peasantry. The punishing power of these nurses is very extensive. They have the right of sentencing village elders and judges to prison and are even provided with discretionary power to set a peasant into prison for three days without any form of trial and without any possibility of appeal, simply for supposed disobedience. Coming after the orderly process of law administered by the justices of the peace, a process which the villagers had already learned to respect, the power of the land-captains is considered as a negation of justice. "We have no more judges," a peasant was heard to say, "we have commanding officers."

What guarantees are there, that this exceptional position will not be misused? Some guarantee might have been provided by a careful selection for the posts of these local dictators. As a matter of fact only a small minority of them has received an administrative or judicial training or any higher education at all: most are chosen from the neighbouring squires who have served in the army or not served anywhere and have not been taught anything carefully. Another guarantee seems provided by the right of the inhabitants to appeal from the decisions of the land-captain to sessions, composed of the same magistrates under the chairmanship of the marshal of the district and with the adjunct of a few trained lawyers. It has to be said that even this minority of jurists is exerting some beneficial influence on the lawless practices of the land-captains, but then the decisions of this district board are themselves subject to be overruled by the board of the province in which the legal element is all but absent, and there the procedure stops. The department of this peculiar arbitrary justice is not in direct communication with the Senate which towers over all other courts of law.

All these features show conclusively that the object of the law of July 12, 1889, is neither the improvement of justice nor the furthering of the commonweal, but the establishment of a dictatorship in every locality as an agency of central bureaucracy on the one hand, of the local gentry on the other. In what spirit justice and police are wielded by the land-captains may be gathered from a few facts. During the terrible famine of 1892 the land-captains of some districts of the province of Nijniy opposed systematically the policy of relief and restricted the delivery of bread although the population was literally starving, because they wanted to keep the people at low wages. The Toula land-captain who expressed himself so graphically about acting as a nurse to the peasants made it his special object to enforce by punishments the performance of agricultural work. In another case the peace of peasant households was safeguarded by putting into prison objectionable wives. The celebrated article 61 which provides for discretionary punishment is well in view in the preservation of order. A land-captain had forbidden one of his peasant-fold to pass by his house: one night the villager was nevertheless caught trespassing in the street before the land-captain's house and instantly locked up. One of these magistrates has summed up his observations as to the way justice and police is being administered all over Russia in the ominous words: "there is no indignity which in the beginning of the twentieth century may not be inflicted on a Russian peasant."

We have already noticed that the introduction of land-captains entailed the fall of the justices of the peace. These last remain only in some of the large towns. This reversal of the statutes of 1864 is the greatest and the most wanton breach with the legal spirit and institutions of the era of reforms. The justices of the peace as well as the members of the higher courts had indeed deserved a better treatment. The change achieved by the new *personnel* of the courts and the new methods of administering justice has been simply wonderful and will always remain an example of the might of public spirit and ideal aspirations in human affairs. Where intrigue, casuistry, and bribery had reigned supreme, a system of justice arose which presented all the necessary guarantees of competence and purity, and this in spite of the miserable remuneration of members of the Bench. The justices of the peace were at work in minute cases and for the settlement of minor interests, but their work in the aggregate represented the everyday litigation of society, was conducted in a cheap and expeditious manner, with the greatest fairness and common sense and had earned for the judges the respect of all—but the Government. The Government of reaction estimated everything by its standard of arbitrary rule, and in regard to this the justices of the peace were found wanting.

Trial by jury was even more a thorn in the eye of the leaders of reaction : juries are formed without distinction of classes, their verdict is independent of the command of crown-lawyers, originally it had to pronounce even in cases when officers appeared in the dock, when press-offences were tried. The outcry against this institution which has also speedily taken root in Russian soil has not achieved its destruction, though it has called forth a series of measures for curtailing it.

But in this case as in others the intentions of the reactionary party are even more worth notice than its particular achievements. The real enemy is always the same—law, a law independent of caprice and protection, proudly holding up its head in the face of the powers that be, appealing to the sense of dignity in man and proclaiming the equality of citizens. Such a law is not in favour of late, and reaction has been striving all along to substitute something quite different instead —a spurious administration of sentences, bowing low before might, bending to influence and protection, frowning on those who are not in favour with the authorities, relentless to the weak. A Government which has created the land-captains, and deprived millions of its Jewish subjects of the most common rights of citizens, even of the right of educating their children, such a Government is not a fitting patron of law and justice. What it enforces is obedience to order, not to law, and its contempt of law is exemplified in every way. Even the feeble guarantees of the principle that law is a general enactment obligatory for everybody as long as it has not been repealed, are set at nought by the constant practice of personal orders of the Sovereign, of ministerial circulars and of so-called temporary rules. What has been most carefully elaborated of late years is the discretionary power of governors and general governors under the state of siege. Measures taken in 1881 during the panic created by the murder of the Tzar have been spreading and developing ever since. Nobody is secure against search, arrest, imprisonment and relegation to remote parts of the Empire. From political supervision the solicitude of the authorities has spread to interference with all kinds of private affairs. To-day somebody is sent out by command of a governor because he is suspected of immoral conduct, to-morrow somebody else because he is practising hypnotism, and then again young people guilty of a disturbance in the streets are sentenced to months of imprisonment without the formality of a trial by order of a master of the police. Such is the legal protection we are enjoying in Russia. Nowhere are the benefits of such a rule more conspicuous than in dealing with the youth of the schools. It has been truly said, that all students are placed under special police supervision. And when the police finds that it is not enough to spy on them, it puts them out of the way of doing harm. I will not speak of such proscriptions as attend university riots, like that of 1899 for instance, when in Moscow every fifth man disappeared from the scene. There are more ludicrous and hardly less characteristic cases, as, for instance, when students in quiet times are forced to leave the university town and to interrupt their studies because the Emperor is expected to honour a particular city by his visit, or when the university authorities remain entirely in the dark as to the whereabouts of their pupils and dare not ask for explanations, because the political police does not admit of any inquiries.

It remains for us to consider the historical development of the institutions of self-government created by the reform of January 1, 1864. In the words of one, who has been himself a pioneer of self-government in Russia, the best representatives of society, who had for a long time been dreaming of a free expansion of its forces, threw themselves with all faith, hope and devotion into the work of provincial self-government, in which they saw the dawn of a new era of light. Undoubtedly, both in the eyes of the Government and in those of the public, the opening up of this new sphere of social action was not considered as a self-sufficient end—the Zemstvo was started as a kind of school for greater liberty. Tzar Alexander himself pointed out several times that he did not intend to stop at this grant, and asked his people to wait in confidence for further development in the same direction. But, although political aspirations of a comprehensive kind were present in the minds of the workers, it would be wrong to suppose that they were careless of the work immediately in hand. On the contrary, notwithstanding all natural shortcomings by reason of inexperience and intrigue, the Russian Zemstvo and the new municipal corporations have achieved on the whole most creditable work. They have grappled problems which the aristocratic bureaucracy of former times had hardly entertained, and for the solution of which it had proved entirely powerless. One main idea goes through the whole range of their activity—the striving towards material and intellectual progress of the lower classes, and surely no more noble idea could have inspired these thousands of humble workers.

The most striking results were achieved in the domain of education. Primary schools were all but non-existent in the sixties when the state gave over to the Zemstvo a share in their organization and management; and at the present day, less than 40 years after this period of darkness, in some parts of the country the stage is already being reached of making primary education accessible to all, and everywhere the self-governing bodies are advancing steadily and energetically towards their aim. All the work of building the schools, providing them with teachers and teaching material, supporting the most needy among the pupils and ministering to some extent to their intellectual requirements after school, is carried out by the Zemstvo and the towns, and it is in the most democratic of the provinces, in the far east districts of Viatka and Perm, where there is no landed gentry to speak of, that these intellectual needs are best recognized and most devotedly cared for.

Another department for which the Zemstvo has done great things is the medical and sanitary arrangements for the people. It is hard to conceive the difficulties which have to be overcome in this respect. Enormous distances, bad roads, the rough climate, the scarcity of population and the greater scarcity of available medical men—all these are tremendous obstacles to anything like a rational system of medical attendance. Nevertheless the pioneers of this cause did not lose heart; 30 per cent. of the budget of the Zemstvo has been devoted to it, and the net of hospitals, ambulances, medical centres is spreading gradually over the country.

The material condition of the people has not been absent from the mind of the Zemstvo workers. Their democratic tendencies made them inclined to look at the root of economic distress : extensive inquiries have been rightly deemed necessary to guide the steps in the direction of improvement, and the Zemstvos have carried out most extensive and instructive statistical work which might do honour to any country. On the strength of their intimate knowledge of the wants and resources of the people, the Zemstvo and the educated classes which are seeking a support and an opening in self-government have been able to do great things in the many cases when agricultural distress and famine set in. The funds assigned by the Government and subscribed by benefactors find their way towards the suffering in the innumerable dark corners of the vast country chiefly by the help of the Zemstvo and its assistants, who throw into this work all the unassuming, untiring self-devotion characteristic of the Russians in time of need. In more favoured moments the economic activity of the Zemstvo is mostly taking the shape of furthering agricultural progress by starting model farms, providing instructors, forming stores for the sale of improved implements and machines. The Zemstvo again is trying to check the destructive effect of fires, and though it cannot do much for altering the modes of building in this "country of wood," a great deal is being done for the spread of a system of insurance. Less has been achieved for the relief of the poor and the improvement of means of communication, and one of the reasons for deficiency in these respects may be, that in these questions the competence of the councils of the Zemstvo and of the ordinary police are in a state of hopeless entanglement.

I may be excused in the course of a short lecture from giving more details on these important subjects. Time is pressing, and I have still the other side of the medal to set before you—the sad history of constant restrictions in regard to the Zemstvo on the part of central government. The hope for an extension of the Zemstvo, for a rise from provincial self-government to political freedom was doomed to fail. Already in 1867 the working of the St Petersburg Zemstvo was suspended because it had dared to petition for calling together representatives from all provinces to consult on economic matters of general interest. The only chance which ever occurred in this direction was afforded by the policy of Count Loris Melikoff, who, in the brunt of the fight against terroristic conspiracies, listened to addresses from various provinces and devised a plan of central legislative commissions on a representative basis, a plan approved by the Emperor, but crushed by the untoward success of the conspiracy on the 1st of March. After that event the well-known reaction set in, and when the Zemstvos raised their voices for liberal reforms they were harshly rebuked for their " senseless dreams[1]." Not to speak of parliamentary institutions, even the wish for a local unit of self-government, a self-governing parish or volost, was met with constant rebuffs ; attempts at arranging meetings between the representatives of different provinces for the discussion of common affairs were considered unlawful and forbidden. The Committee of Ministers can boast of a long list of petitions from the Zemstvo, which have been negatived simply on the ground that they applied for measures of general interest ; although it was recognized that in many cases the grievances and the information presented by the petitioners were quite to the point.

Not satisfied with this the Government has been carrying on a kind of systematic persecution against the self-governing bodies, both through its provincial agents and its legislative machinery. Provincial bureaucracy is everywhere at loggerheads with the Zemstvo, and this is the more serious, as this last has no other means of carrying out its decisions than the help of this very bureaucracy, and is bound to seek the confirmation of the governor for all its decrees. The ill-will of provincial administration is the more keen and constant, as the acts of the St Petersburg powers testify clearly to their antipathy towards the Zemstvo. Already in 1866 a most extensive right of coercion was given to the presidents of the provincial councils. In the same year the power to tax industrial and commercial undertakings was taken from the Zemstvo—it had to restrict itself to imposing rates on land. In 1874 the educational management of the primary schools was made directly dependent on Government directors and inspectors on the one hand, the marshals of the *noblesse* on the other, while the self-governing bodies had to restrict themselves to material arrangements. In 1889 all nominations of agents were subjected to the confirmation of the governors. In the eighties a general reform was

[1] The historical words of Tzar Nicholas II to the Marshals of the *noblesse* (January 17, 1895).

attempted, first in a liberal direction, but the labours of Kakhanoff's Commission, which took up that line, came to an untimely end, and a reform began in exactly the opposite sense under Count Dem. Tolstoy. He aimed at nothing less than at making the Zemstvo entirely a tool in the hands of bureaucracy, because in his view self-governing institutions were at variance with the spirit of autocratical government, and produce a cleavage in the system of administration. He did not succeed in carrying out his entire programme, but in 1890 a new statute replaced the one of 1864, and it weakened the self-governing bodies considerably by altering the franchise and giving to them a distinctly aristocratic stamp. In practice this measure led especially to nonplussing the peasant delegates who are treated in the most high-handed manner by the land-captains.

And still, though vitiated in many respects, the spirit of the provincial self-government has not been extinguished; a continuity of development has been kept up, and such bodies, for example, as the Zemstvo of the Moscow province are showing an amazing capacity of doing useful work in the most difficult circumstances. Of late the existence of self-government has been in the balance again, and especially under the late Minister of the Interior and the present Minister of Finance measures have been enacted which strike at the very root of provincial government. The 12th of June, 1900, has been an especially evil day for Russian provincial liberties : the power of the councils to impose rates has been suddenly cut short in an entirely arbitrary manner : no province is to increase rates by more than three per cent. of the imposition of the previous year. It has been pointed out that this method of holding expenditure and self-imposition chained to the budget of previous years is entirely lacking in a rational basis. It just falls as a block on schemes of development, and the greatest sufferers are those who for one reason or the other had held back with their imposition and requirements.

On the same day the organization of relief was placed entirely in the hands of provincial governors, guardians appointed by them, marshals of the *noblesse* and land-captains. In this way provincial bureaucracy, which has shown many times how remiss it is in acknowledging the most pressing needs in this respect and how clumsy in administering to them, has been entrusted with the conduct of all this difficult and responsible business, while the Zemstvo, which presents the most suitable machinery for mobilizing the forces of society for relief, is kept altogether out of the concern. This measure is so clearly misconceived and mischievous that there are signs that the Government will not be able to uphold it.

What I have said may be sufficient to show, I think, that in the course of forty years we have been living in Russia in a kind of civil war—war between an uncertain or reactionary Government and all sorts of claimants of bankrupt interests on the one hand and the rising forces of national consciousness and self-government on the other. What is to be the result of this strife which has marred the life of generations and strikes the whole Empire with weakness? Let us first listen to the views in this respect of the spokesmen of the powers that be. Here is one of them, the well-known procurator of the Holy Synod, Pobedonostzeff. He has taken care to embody his political ideas not only in the form of enactments and measures, but also of literary productions. In the collection of Moscow essays written or edited by him, we may find his appreciations of the chief problems of State and Church. The guiding principle of these appreciations is an unbounded scorn for all Western institutions. Constitutional government is declared to be the great fraud of our time. Majorities are formed by wire-pullers who understand how to mislead and to bribe the electors. The ignorant mass is called upon to perform the most difficult and delicate duty of politics: the duty of selecting the men that have to take charge of government. The mass is not only incompetent to do so, but the better people simply shrink from seeking favour with it. Parliament is not better than a machine for bringing out ill-conceived incoherent laws. The press, which has the greatest share in forming so-called public opinion, has grown to be an irresponsible power, wielded by people singled out by shameless arrogance. These evils may be somewhat tempered in Anglo-Saxon communities by individual independence and personal energy, though even there the United States present striking illustrations of the gross abuses of democracy. As for the rest of the Western world, it is preparing for socialism and social strife. What is one to think of the rule of law, which is extolled by the advocates of Western and especially English institutions? "Those who are called upon to act, to command, are constrained at every moment to look about them for fear of infringing this or the other rule, this or that formality. As laws increase in number, the energy of power necessary for good administration gets weakened, and the law, which ought to help the official, hampers him at every step." What is the outcome of all these negative remarks? A plea for "plain, living, personal institutions," for absolute power, the sanctity of superstition, the wholesomeness of darkness and resignation for the mass of the people, the craving towards an aristocracy which at the same time is recognized as hardly possible in our time. From these barren pseudo-Platonic exaggerations let us turn to another representative of modern bureaucracy, the energetic Minister of Finance, Witte. He has also given expression to his political philosophy in a memoir drawn up against the Minister of the Interior for the use of the Emperor and of some high officials. It was intended to be kept secret from the rest of mortals, but somehow a copy of it got into the hands of political refugees and was published by them. It is undoubtedly a document of the greatest importance, of which historians will certainly avail themselves to depict the turn of mind of Russian statesmen in the beginning of the twentieth century.

The drift of argument amounts to this, that self-government,

even local or provincial, is in its essence a political arrangement and as such opposed to absolute monarchy. If self-
government is to live and to act rationally it has to develop
into a constitution. If it cannot be allowed to do so, it has to
be replaced by a centralized bureaucracy. After granting that
such a bureaucracy leads to arbitrary power and dead formalism,
and quoting the contemptuous remarks of Stein as to official
writing machines, Mons. Witte nevertheless assumes that Russian
bureaucracy is to produce a new political type, unknown to
history, will in fact turn out to be an aristocracy of work and
enlightenment. He applauds the foreign observers who recognize similarities between the condition of Russia and that of
British India or China, and takes his stand on the principle
that the Russian people is lacking in individuality and pre-
destined by its history to be ruled by *tchinovniks* under the
directing force of autocracy. This government will somehow
abstain from arbitrary measures, arrests, exceptional tribunals
and other kinds of oppression, it will guarantee freedom of
labour, thought and conscience. As for society, it must be
left to follow private interests and in them seek an outlet for its
energies. We shall be rather astonished to find that the Zemstvo
is also left a place in this ideal bureaucracy: it ought not and
cannot be destroyed. The Minister of Finance is convinced
that the system sketched in his essay will not only preserve
Russia from falling a prey to the great fraud of our time—constitutional government, but will heal it from its present woes.
His closing words are significant: "Nothing is more apt to ruin
the prestige of authority than a frequent and extensive employment of repression. Measures of repression are dangerous, and
when they get to be continuous, they either lead to an explosion
or else turn the people into a casual throng, into human dust."

These are strong words, and the whole essay is full of
telling epigrams and keen criticism. But it would be difficult
to find in it the sincerity and thoroughness which it preaches
to everybody concerned. Its argument seems based on un-

warrantable assumptions; is not, for example, the optimistic prospect of the future of bureaucracy in Russia such an assumption? In fact, one may almost express the hope that next time the Minister of Finance wants to turn out his colleague of the Interior, he may show as brilliantly that autocracy and bureaucracy are irreconcilable with individual liberty as he has shown in 1899 that they cannot live in peace with local self-government. There seems also a certain confusion of thought in another assumption, namely in the belief that Russia is doomed to remain perpetually in that state of dependence upon paternal government which has been passed as a stage of development long ago in England, more recently in France and Germany. It is altogether curious that Ministers of a powerful Empire should be instinct with such a contempt for the people they rule, that they are unable to devise a better lot for them than the position of the Chinese plebs under the rule of mandarins, or that of the natives in conquered British India. The one thing which strikes one most in these speculations of our present rulers is the absence of positive ideals, the barren scepticism and the hopelessness of their views and plans. They are doomed, even more by their own confessions than by the accusations of their adversaries.

And therein lies the hope for a better future for Russia. The country is evidently on the eve of a new stage of development, and no efforts will avail against the historical forces which drive it towards a new course. The common rights of civilized man which have come to be a self-understood element of European life, cannot be longer denied to the Russians, and it is only to be hoped that the Government in power will not protract much longer its blind resistance to progress. The sooner it gets to be recognized that the dignity and welfare of Russia crave freedom as well as authority, and that the only basis to unite both is law, the easier it will be to solve the problems set before a nation which has a great stake in the destinies of the world.

THE PROBLEM OF THE NEAR EAST.

By G. P. Gooch, M.A.

In the first part of this lecture I propose to discuss the power of the Sultan, and to explain and contrast the theory and practice of Turkish government. In the second part, I shall attack the most pressing problems of the Near East, the Armenian question, the Macedonian question, and the Albanian question. In the third, I shall briefly consider the relation of the Great Powers to the Ottoman Empire.

I.

In order to form a correct idea of the position of the Sultan, we should clearly understand that his power is two-fold, —partly political and partly spiritual.

Taking the political aspect first, we must divide the Empire into two parts, the territory over which the Sultan really rules, and the territory over which he possesses a merely nominal over-lordship. In Europe the Sultan possesses in direct rule the whole of the centre of the Balkan peninsula, that is to say, the country bounded on the west by the Adriatic, on the south by Greece, on the north by Servia and Bulgaria, and on the east tapering away to the tongue of land where the city of Constantine looks forth over Asia. In Asia Abdul-Hamid's direct possessions consist of Asia Minor up to the Russian frontier in the north-east corner, the whole of the great plain of the Euphrates and Tigris as far as the Persian boundary, and almost the whole of the great Arabian peninsula. In Africa he directly rules over the strip of coast between Egypt and Tunis, or, to be more precise, over Barka and Tripoli. The list of his immediate possessions would have to be completed by a long list of islands of the Archipelago.

A century ago the Sultan was undisputed lord in his own house. To-day he is locked out of many of the rooms. In Europe he retains the barren over-lordship of Bulgaria and governs Novi-Bazar under the eyes of its Austrian garrison. In Asia, the little province of the Lebanon has been snatched from his hands, and the Wahabi communities of Arabia defy his authority. In Africa, his rule is shackled by the presence of England in Egypt, of which he retains nothing beyond the over-lordship. The list also includes the large islands of Crete and Cyprus and the little island of Samos.

We must now attempt to measure his spiritual influence. You will perhaps think it strange to speak of spiritual power in connection with the Sultan; but the justification of the phrase lies in the fact that he is the spiritual head of the Mohammedans throughout the world. From the moment that Mohammedanism became an organized movement, that is from the early part of the seventh century, there has been a Khaliph or Head of the Faithful. Theoretically he should be descended from the tribe to which the Prophet himself belonged. But circumstances have been too strong for theory, and, as a matter of fact, the greater number of Mohammedans are content to recognize as their Khaliph the strongest temporal ruler, who of course at the present time is the Sultan. But we must bear in mind the limitations of the Khaliphate. The number of Mohammedans in different parts of the world who do not recognize it is very considerable. In the infancy of the new religion there was a terrible crisis. For some years after the death of the Prophet, Ali, the husband of Mohammed's beloved daughter Fatima, a man of winning personality but weak will, remained in the background. His friends were determined

that he should rise to the Khaliphate, and, on the death of
Othman, he was chosen his successor. After a rule of only
six years Ali was murdered, and rival Khaliphs appeared in
Syria and Arabia. His sons Hassan and Hosein were hunted
down, and their fate is commemorated in the moving tragedy
of the Persian passion-play. The party which had looked to
Ali was called Shiah, while those who rejected his claims took
the name of Sunnis. The gulf has gone on widening ever
since, and differences of race and history now reinforce the
fundamental difference of religious origin. The Shiahs number
about 15,000,000, the great majority of whom are Persians.
But the Shiahs are by no means the only critics of the Turkish
Sultan's spiritual claims. The Sultan of Mecca is regarded as
the true Khaliph by many of the inhabitants of the shore of
the Red Sea, and the Wahabi communities recognize neither
the Ottoman Sultan nor any other potentate. In Africa
he meets with no recognition among the inhabitants of the
Soudan, the followers of the Senussi and other warlike tribes
between Tripoli and Lake Chad, nor among the inhabitants
of Morocco, who find in their own Sultan the true Khaliph,
believing him to be descended from the Prophet himself.

It is easy enough to define the Khaliphate in language,
but it is very difficult to form an idea as to the possible range
of its operation. It has been one of the chief items of the
policy of Abdul-Hamid to develop what may be called the
Pan-Islamic aspect of his power,—witness his embassy to the
Mussulmans of China; and the issue of the Greek war gave
an enormous impetus to the conception. There seems little
doubt that the Sultan is recognized by Mohammedans all over
the world, with the exceptions above mentioned, as having
the power to proclaim a Jehad, or Holy War, against the
infidel. He has not done so; but if he were fighting with
his back against the wall, he probably would do it. What the
effect would be we cannot know; but it is well to remember
what a powerful weapon he holds in reserve.

We must, then, think of the Sultan not merely as the direct lord of about 25,000,000 human beings, living in three continents, but also as the spiritual representative of something like 150,000,000 Mohammedans throughout the world.

I turn to a brief examination of the theory and practice of Ottoman government. On the topmost rung of the ladder stand two great officers, the Grand Vizier and the Sheik-el-Islam, the former the Sultan's right-hand man for temporal matters, the latter the head of what we may call—though the expression is not strictly accurate—the Mohammedan Church. On the second step stand the Ministers,—the Minister of Foreign Affairs, the Minister of Public Works, of War, Finance, and so on, just like any other country in Europe. Next we come to the bureaucracy proper, the Council of State, which consists of the Ministers and of a number of high officials with administrative experience chosen by the Sultan. The Council is divided into a number of departments, by whom the administrative work of government is carried on. The provincial government is entrusted to Valis or Governors of the Vilayets, the unit of Turkish administration.

The work of the departments calls for no special mention, with the exception of that of finance. The first attempt to grapple with a most difficult problem was made 40 years ago in the foundation of the Dette Publique and the Ottoman Bank. But the evil went too deep to be eradicated by these measures, and the debt and confusion were increased by the Balkan and the Russian wars. By 1881 matters had reached such a critical state that an international commission was created to look after the interests of the bondholders. The debt of £200,000,000 was cut down by half, and the greater part of it consolidated; while the Sultan handed over a portion of the excise duties to the commission wherewith to pay 4 per cent. on the reduced loan. Straitened though he is by the payment of interest on the enormous loans contracted by himself and his predecessors, the Sultan finds money for a well-equipped army of 750,000 men. His navy, on the other hand, exists only on paper.

At the head of the spiritual department, as we have already seen, is the Sheik-el-Islam, whom we may call a sort of ecclesiastical Lord Chancellor, since Mohammedan law has never been secularized. Under the Sheik stand the Ulema, a body of men learned in Mohammedan law, endowed with the power of issuing pronouncements on matters affecting the moral and social life of the Faithful.

To complete the sketch of the theory of Turkish government, I must say a word as to the legal position of the Christians. The Ottoman has grouped his Christian subjects into Churches or Millets, each under a head who is recognized by the Sultan as the representative and spokesman of the community. There are, for instance, Millets of Greeks, Roman Catholics, Protestants, Armenians, Jews, Maronites, and so on. The position of the entire body is defined by the ordinances of 1839, the fruit of the reforming zeal of Mahmud, and of 1856, issued by command of the Sultan's allies in the Crimean War. These ordinances guarantee the civil, political, and religious equality of every subject of the Sultan, of whatever creed or race.

Such is Turkish government in theory. What about its practice? It can be summed up in a single word—autocracy. The Sultan is the most autocratic ruler in the world. The Tsar is in theory more autocratic than his neighbour,—for Russia knows no Capitulations and is free from even the shadow of European control; but in practice, as all the world knows, he is hedged round by one of the strongest bureaucracies in Europe. The common type of oriental despot, again, is a very different man from the Sultan. For while he does not, as a rule, work very hard, the Sultan probably works harder than any other potentate in the world. Moreover, his power has been indefinitely increased by the introduction of the telegraph, which brings the most distant provinces as near as the capital.

He is head of the government not one whit less in practice than in theory; he can say "L'état c'est moi" with a measure of truth to which the Grand Monarque with his Colbert and his Louvois could lay no claim. Let us see how successfully he gets rid of every possible clog on his power. The Grand Vizier, to begin with, is usually a man of straw, who can be dismissed at any moment; and, as a matter of fact, he is frequently changed. In the next place, the Sultan has two Ministers for the same work. A Minister of War figures in the official list; but there is also a chief of the military commission which sits in the Palace, and these two functionaries are neatly played off against one another. In a similar way the Minister of Police and the Minister of Justice are delicately balanced. In this contest of wills and division of responsibilities, there is only one point of unity, the Sultan himself. In the spiritual department it is the same. The Sheik-el-Islam theoretically possesses the power to issue a Fetwa deposing the Sultan; and Abdul-Hamid's own brother was so deposed. You may think this is a sword of Damocles hanging over his head; but the Sultan takes good care that the string shall not break, and keeps the Sheik a close prisoner. Abdul-Hamid, I repeat, is the most autocratic person in the world. His policy is *Divide et Impera*. He divides and he rules.

The theory and practice of Turkish laws differ no less than the theory and practice of Turkish government. Finance is everywhere the tell-tale of administration. Take the question of the payment of salaries. When a man is appointed Governor of a certain Vilayet, he is told he will receive, say, £1,000 a year. He may be certain he will never receive the whole of the sum, and if he gets half he will be lucky. It is not long before he receives a telegram:—"Imperial treasury in great straits, £1,000 must be sent without delay." The rule is that instead of the Governor being paid, he has to provide for his pay-master. The province is squeezed and the Governor himself may be trusted not to starve. The taxes, again, are in

theory exceedingly moderate, lower indeed than in the west of
Europe, the total revenue of the Empire amounting to only
about £20,000,000. But they are farmed out; and the farmer
has not only to make his percentage, but to pay back the sum
which he spent to procure the office. Take again the question
of public works. Nothing delights the provincial Governor
so much as the order to make a road. In parenthesis let me
say that there are few roads in the Turkish Empire, except
those which were in existence before the Turks arrived. He
promptly levies a sum from the Vilayet—and the road is not
made. Possibly they have built a bridge halfway across a river
when a new order comes to make another road. And this has
been going on for the five centuries during which the Turk
has been in Europe. The Turkish peasant is as honest as
the Christian; but the Turkish official is corrupt beyond belief.
There are exceptions, of course; but they are few.

Next there is the question of public order. The police are
naturally supposed to maintain security of life and property in
Turkey as elsewhere. As a matter of fact, it is not too much
to say that they are often little more than licensed brigands.
I might give you a dozen quotations from Consular reports
and the works of travellers; but two will suffice. The judgment
uttered by that gallant soldier, General Williams, the defender
of Kars, after long experience, was that no words could portray
the infamy of the Turkish police. That was strong enough;
but it is not stronger than that of Professor Ramsay, who
knows Asia Minor as well as any living Englishman, and who
declares the police to be the greatest scourge of the country.

As security of property and person is endangered by the
police, so is security of mind destroyed by spies. The Sultan
has organized an elaborate system of *espionage*, and employs
spies to spy on his spies. The *agent-provocateur* is one of
the pillars of Turkish rule. One authority estimates that he
receives over 100 reports every day; and those who know him
believe that he leaves few of them unread. That no length

of service, no unbroken record of loyalty, serves as a defence against the poisoned darts of suspicion has been shown once again only a few months ago in the disgrace and banishment of Fuad Pasha, the details of which are fresh in our minds.

What I have said as to the evils of Turkish government applies to the Mussulman no less than to the Christian peasant. He suffers as much as the Christian from the absence of a proper financial system and public order, and perhaps even more from spies.   There are, however, four ways in which the Christian is exposed to suffering from which the Mussulman is free.   The first is religious bigotry, which, though less common than a sort of contemptuous toleration, may yet at any moment burst into a flame.   The second is inequality before the law, or, rather, before the judge, the word of a Christian weighing nothing beside the word of a Mussulman. The third is physical outrage, not only by the police and the soldiery but by officials and private citizens.   Less grievous but often bitterly felt is the obscurantism which hangs over Turkey like a dark cloud, and stunts and starves the intellectual life.   I am not forgetting Robert College ; but that noble institution would disappear to-morrow if the Sultan had his way.

The Ottoman *régime* has been compared to that of an army of occupation, and I do not know a more concise or accurate description.   The saying " The grass never grows where the Turk has planted his foot " is as true to-day as ever it was.   If the most remarkable feature of Ottoman rule is its badness, the next is its unchanging character, and the third its vitality.   In words which remind us of Macchiavelli's famous sentence about the papacy, Fuad Pasha, the reformer, gave forcible expression to the thoughts of every observer.   " Turkey is a most wonderful country, for it survives though every official strives its utmost to ruin it."   If the Empire is to perish from internal decay, its death will take a long time.   The following passage from the most instructive book ever written about Turkey should be borne constantly in mind :—

"When one reads European reports on the condition of
"the Turkish provinces, or reflects on the wonderful things
"one has seen with one's own eyes, one is inclined to think
"the system cannot go on. It is annually proved that the
"machinery of government is collapsing, that there is no
"money and no food, that no one can pay any taxes, and that
"everybody must starve. Yet it all goes on. They that had
"been skinned are skinned again; and they that were starving
"are starving still—but not dead. This year, as last year,
"when the inevitable pay-day comes round, it is found that
"the Porte has performed some mysterious operation and has
"plenty of money again. It may safely be affirmed that if any
"European Power were to undertake to finance Turkey, the
"whole place would be bankrupt in a week, and need years
"of recuperation. Political economy seems to be one of those
"things which must be accepted or rejected as a whole[1]."

I said that the Ottoman *régime* is no worse and no better
than it ever was. The countless efforts that have been made
by the Powers to reform Turkey have taught us that reform
begins when the government of the Turk disappears. Equally
futile have been the attempts to reform Turkey from inside.
The first was undertaken by Sultan Mahmud, the Peter the
Great of Turkey, the friend of Stratford Canning and the
patron of Reschid. It was an heroic effort, as unexpected
as the liberalism of Pio Nono; but it left no more traces on
Turkish rule than a ripple on the surface of a river. The
Edict of 1856 cannot fairly claim a place in a sketch of the
reform movement, issued as it was, as every Turk and every
Christian knew, at the command of the Powers. The second
genuine movement for reform owed its origin to the group of
able and earnest statesmen of whom the most prominent was
Midhat Pasha. When a successor to Abdul-Aziz had to be
chosen, Midhat secured the election of Murad, after obtaining

[1] *Turkey in Europe*, by Odysseus.

from him a promise to issue a Constitution. The Constitution was issued, and a Parliament met. Representatives from Bagdad greeted spokesmen of the Balkans, and members from Asia Minor rubbed shoulders with delegates from distant Arabia. It was the hey-day of the Young Turks. Nationalists no less than reformers, their aim was the application of European ideas by Turkish brains and Turkish hands. What they might have accomplished is a matter of speculation, for the Sultan went mad and was deposed, and his brother, the present Sultan, immediately dissolved the Parliament, which has never re-assembled. The Young Turk party of to-day possesses no leader and no real policy; and it is by no means certain that the Christian subjects of the Porte would obtain from it, were it in power, the treatment to which they have a right.

The greatest obstacle to reform is the character of Abdul-Hamid. The author of the incomparable sonnets on the Purple East describes him as "immortally, beyond all mortals, damned"; and Earl Percy tells us that he is a most painstaking and conscientious ruler. Men will continue to differ about his character; but the main features of his policy are not a matter of dispute. He has centralized the government, and he has enormously increased the claims and the power of the Khaliphate. On the other hand, despite his extraordinary skill in playing off the Powers against one another, he has lost more provinces and more subjects than any of his predecessors. His reign is a record of striking successes and striking failures, both military and diplomatic. For a fuller comprehension of the Sultan's character and policy we must turn to those parts of his Empire where the inherent antagonism between Turkish and Christian ideals gives rise to problems that clamorously demand solution.

II.

The Armenian problem is in one respect more complicated than either the Albanian or the Macedonian question, for there is no such place as Armenia on the Turkish map. It is not bigotry on the part of Turkish cartographers, and it is not ignorance. The province that we loosely describe as Armenia is a district in which only one in three of the population is an Armenian, and contains only half the Armenians. To put it in another way, the Armenians are a race but not a nation. Seventeen hundred years ago Gregory Thaumaturgus, a disciple of Origen, brought them the Christian faith, and they have built their lives and their history round the Gregorian Church. They have never formed a state, and they have never become a nation.

During the nineteenth century, when excitement reigned in almost every part of the Turkish Empire, the history of the Armenians remained singularly uneventful. It was not until the emancipation of Bulgaria, Servia, Roumania, and Montenegro, that thoughts and hopes of reform and even of nationality began to stir. For the next ten years nevertheless they remained high in the favour of the Sultan. As the best military posts fell to Albanians, so the best civil appointments were occupied by Armenians. But about 1890 the influence of the English and American missionaries in Armenia and of such bodies as the Anglo-Armenian Association, began to revive and reinforce the thoughts implanted by the events of the later seventies. Secret societies—they had to be secret—sprung up in the cities of the Levant. The Sultan, who had till then regarded the loyalty of the Armenians as unimpeachable, began to entertain suspicions. It would help us to enter into his feelings if we were to believe that Russian missionaries were secretly inciting the natives of India to another Mutiny. By one of those revulsions of feeling commoner in the East than in the West, the Sultan passed from unqualified confidence to the most credulous suspicion. He knew perfectly well that the Armenians of the country were an unwarlike and unambitious people, and that the active spirits and the secret societies were confined almost entirely to the towns; but he had persuaded himself of the existence of a wide-spread conspiracy, and he began to take steps to combat it. The Kurdish horsemen were armed, and in 1894 the first blood was shed. The inhabitants of the district of Sasun refused to pay their taxes on the ground that the Kurds had left them nothing wherewith to pay. The answer was a massacre. Nearly a thousand fell at Sasun, and during the remainder of 1894 and throughout 1895 perhaps 100,000 more. It was no unpremeditated outburst of popular fury. The massacre was carried out with almost military precision, often by Turkish troops and Turkish officials, and in many cases was begun and concluded to the sound of the trumpet. Moreover, Catholic and Protestant Armenians were unharmed. Apart from the direct evidence of the Sultan's complicity, no one who realizes the nature of the Turkish system will believe that a step of such magnitude was taken without his approval. In 1896 the Armenians in Constantinople, crazed by the terrible events of the last two years and by a daily and hourly fear of massacre, made a frantic attempt on the Ottoman Bank. The blow was clumsily conceived and clumsily executed. Every step was known to the authorities, and when the attack was made the clubs that had been specially manufactured for the occasion had been distributed. The massacre of some 6,000 Armenians was effected in a couple of days under the eyes of the ambassadors of the signatories of the Treaty of Berlin. The two years' tragedy was at an end, leaving memories and problems behind it.

The problem of Armenia is of unusual complexity, owing to the fact already pointed out that the Armenians are nowhere in a majority, and because English policy in 1878 makes it difficult to win Russia to any plan that we may propose. Though Russian troops at Kars were almost within ear-shot

of the massacres, not a man was moved. Till the diplomacy
of the period is known, we cannot finally pronounce on the
conduct of the Powers throughout these terrible years. We
only know that for various reasons,—the recollections of
Russia, the ambitions of Germany, the isolation of England,
the indifference of France, the timidity of Austria, the weakness of Italy,—the piteous appeals of the defenceless victims
fell on deaf ears. The massacres have ended for the time;
but the problem is still with us. The late Duke of Argyll,
a life-long champion of the Armenians, was strongly in favour
of inviting and even imploring Russia to occupy the province.
Russia alone was in the position to terminate Turkish misrule;
and the duty of rescuing the remnant of an afflicted Christian
race was so imperative that the only instrument by which it
could be effected must be employed. One obvious objection
to the Duke's plan is that Germany would hardly consent to
such increase of Russian power in Asia Minor, and, at least as
long as the *entente* with Turkey lasts, would refuse to allow the
spoliation of her *protégé*. Besides, it is by no means certain
that Russian rule would be welcomed by the Armenians, who
fear that their Church might suffer as much from the Muscovite
as from the Turk. Another massacre may bring with it Russian
occupation; but it is not the most probable nor perhaps the most
desirable solution of the problem. The proposal urged at the
recent Pan-Armenian Congress at Brussels and by most friends
of Armenia is the occupation of the country by international
troops and the appointment of a Christian Governor. Such a
plan needs time for its accomplishment; but there is no reason
to delay the appointment of a largely increased number of
Christian Consuls, who must be well backed up by their
respective Foreign Offices. The work of rescue and defence
will also receive assistance from the gradual opening up of
Asia Minor by railways and trade.

Since the termination of the Armenian massacres, no part
of the Turkish Empire has commanded so much attention as

Macedonia. A century ago the inhabitants of the Balkans would have been classified as Mussulmans and Christians. Such a classification affords us little help to-day. The relation of Christian subjects to Mussulman rulers is only one of the factors of the problem before us. The history of the Balkans in the nineteenth century may be summed up in a single phrase. It is the story of the disentanglement of the Slavs from the Greeks and of the disentanglement of the Slavs from one another. It would take too long to relate even in outline the fortunes of the various races. We can only remind ourselves that Greece was freed in the early part of the century by the aid of England, France, and Russia; that Roumania, Servia, Montenegro, and Bulgaria threw off the yoke with the aid of Russia a generation ago; and that almost the whole of the centre would have followed suit if Russia's treaty with the Porte had been allowed to stand. But the settlement of San Stefano was revised at Berlin, and Macedonia was thrust back under the Ottoman yoke.

Before we discuss the various proposals for the solution of the Macedonian problem we must form some general notion of its features. Macedonia is a mosaic of races and we must perforce spell out the pattern. Let us begin with the Bulgarians. The Balkan peninsula is the land of the Slavs; but the most forceful race in it is not Slavonic at all, nor even Aryan. The Bulgars, who entered Europe in the seventh century, are ethnically related to the Magyars, the Finns, and the Turks themselves; but the intercourse of centuries has broken down many a barrier. The Bulgarian language has utterly disappeared; and though travellers profess to distinguish certain Bulgarian characteristics, the fusion with the Slav in blood and habit is almost complete. After playing no inconsiderable part in medieval history, they were lost in the general mass of Balkan Christians till a generation ago. In 1870, the Bulgarians throughout the peninsula were removed from the jurisdiction of the Greek Patriarch, and placed under an Exarch of their own. Pan-Slavism was in the ascendant at St Petersburg, and the development of Russian power in the Balkans was kept constantly in mind. The Sultan was willing enough to throw another apple of discord among his subjects, and was delighted when, two years later, the new Church was excommunicated by the Patriarch. Thus, aided by Russian sympathy and Greek rivalry, the idea of a Bulgarian nation grew up round the institution of the Exarchate. The massacres of a few years later formed one of the causes of the war of 1877, which in its turn led to the establishment of a Bulgarian State. Seven years later the new State was augmented by the union with Eastern Roumelia. There are many Bulgarians outside Bulgaria, especially in the districts adjoining Eastern Roumelia and in Monastir and other large towns, and it is among these that the Macedonian Committee and the clergy of the Exarchate are working for the extension of Bulgarian influence. Though Sarafof and his successor in the presidentship of the Committee have been arrested, it is unsafe to say that Prince Ferdinand looks with real displeasure on a propaganda that may bring him an increase of influence or even of territory.

After the Bulgarians, the Servians—the only pure Slavonic race of Macedonia. Though Servia is a smaller and poorer state than Bulgaria, her traditions are as imposing, her ambitions as great, and her interest no less direct. The Servians are the only nation of Europe except the Swiss who have no access to the sea. When the door of the Adriatic was locked by the Austrian occupation of Bosnia and the Herzegovina, many eyes were turned to the south-east. But the idea of an outlet at Salonika or some other point on the Aegean is recognized to be a dream. On the other hand, there is a Servian no less than a Bulgarian irredentism; for the Vilayet of Kossovo, often called Old Servia, abutting on the southern frontier, is predominantly Servian. In this district the propaganda is carried on through the usual medium of Church and schools, and since the quarrel with Bulgaria has received the countenance and support of Russia, evidenced only this year by the consecration of Firmilian as Servian Bishop of Uskub.

The third race is the Greeks. Till the middle of the last century the belief that Greece was the residuary legatee of the Balkans was widely held. There were many reasons why this should be the case. Greece was the only part of the peninsula which had won its freedom. The Balkan Christians were one and all subject to the Greek Patriarch at Constantinople. Numbers of Bulgarians and Servians and Vlachs spoke Greek. Greek schools alone kept alight the lamp of learning in the peninsula. The greater part of the trade in every town was in Greek hands. In a word, the importance of the Greek lies not only in their numbers in the south of Macedonia and in the coast towns but in prescription and the uncontested superiority of their culture.

The fourth of our ethnic factors is the Vlach, a race Slavonic neither in blood nor language, but a branch of the Roumanian stock speaking a Latin language. While the Bulgarian, the Servian, and the Greek are chiefly to be found in the towns, the Vlachs live in villages scattered about the country, and usually perched high up on the top or in the hollows of the hills. They are most numerous in the spurs of the Pindus range; but from their scattered abodes, their unambitious character, and the distance by which they are separated from Roumania, no extensive propaganda is possible. The life-work of Apostolo Margariti has not been wholly wasted, for he has at least induced many Roumanians to interest themselves in their distant relatives; but politically it has been without effect. The Vlachs stand apart from the other Christians of the Balkans, and believe that they have more to fear from the predominance of Bulgaria or Servia or Greece than from the continued rule of the Turk.

The fifth factor is the Turk himself. We must carefully avoid the common error which confounds the Turk and the Mussulman. All Turks are Mussulmans; but there are tens of thousands of Mussulmans in Macedonia who are not Turks. The Turks proper are most numerous in the district east of a line drawn from Sofia to Salonika. In the west and centre they consist for the most part of soldiers and officials. We have no exact figures for Macedonia; but it is certain that the ruling race is by no means the largest.

The sixth factor is the non-Turkish Mussulman, the descendant of the converts of the time of the Turkish irruption. Though no Christian race deserted its religion in such a wholesale manner as the Albanian, such Mohammedans are to be found in every part of the country and among all the peoples I have mentioned, some of them distinguished by a special name like the Pomaks of Bulgaria. It is needless to say that these converts are often very lax in their adherence to Islam.

To make our catalogue complete we must not omit the Jews, who are found in greatest number at Salonika. The expulsion of the Jews from Spain led to a large influx into the Turkish Empire, and many of them write their language in Turkish characters. With such an example of Christian government before their eyes as Roumania the Jews must be counted on the side of the Turk, who has usually treated them as well as he is capable of treating anybody.

In the utter absence of reliable statistics and in the confusion that inevitably arises when language is no sure test of race, it is impossible to form an exact conception of the ethnic factors of the Macedonian problem; and the above sketch must suffice as an introduction to the question that will now occupy us, namely, the proposals for unravelling this tangled skein.

The first proposal is to leave things as they are, and to let the races fight out their quarrels by themselves, so long as the *status quo* is not disturbed. This is the plan consecrated by the Russo-Austrian *entente* of 1897 and blessed by resourceless politicians in every land. No one who knows Turkish rule can wish or believe that this policy will continue to hold the field. The second plan, fortified by the great authority of M. Bérard, equally contemplates the permanence of Turkish rule, but hopes for and is willing to make efforts to secure its improvement. This proposal is of course merely a *pis aller*, resting on the assumptions that European jealousies render a protectorate impossible and that racial divisions stand in the way of autonomy.

A third proposal contemplates the cession of Macedonia to one or other of the existing Balkan states. The most powerful and indeed the only real candidate is Bulgaria; but Bulgaria nearly doubled her bulk by the lucky windfall of Eastern Roumelia, and there is a general feeling that she has had enough. Besides, though Stambuloff and his policy are long since dead, and Prince Ferdinand welcomes Ignatieff to the Shipka celebrations, the favour of Russia has never been completely regained. If the task is beyond the power of Bulgaria, still less is Servia in a position to undertake it. She has an unpopular king, a weak dynasty, and an army which lost every fragment of *prestige* in her wanton war against Bulgaria in 1885. Besides, the majority of Servians dream of a Greater Servia, to which Macedonia would contribute nothing but Old Servia. Equally impossible is it that Greece should assume control. She is on excellent terms with Roumania, but she is not beloved in the Balkans. When Tricoupi sounded Bulgaria in 1891 with a view to common action against the Turk, Stambuloff immediately informed the Sultan. The rise of the Slavonic states, the intrusion of Russia into Balkan politics, the crushing defeat of 1897, when she learned that the Bulgarians and the Servians would not lift a finger to help her throw off Turkish rule, have totally changed the position that she once held. You will sometimes hear of pushing back the frontier of Thessaly, and the Ethnike Hetaeria has not surrendered the Great Idea. But the dream of a revived Greek Empire, which from time to time floated before the vision of such men as the Prince Consort, Stratford Canning, and Tricoupi, no longer counts any adherents of weight. It has been truly said that Hellenism penetrates no further than the sea-breeze. The work of Greece in the regeneration of Macedonia is educational, not political. In a word, much as the races of Macedonia hate the Turk, they hate one another still more. No one will kill Charles to make James king.

The proposal that Macedonia should pass under the control of a single Balkan state is of course never made outside the limits of the nations concerned; but a compromise by which these vaulting ambitions might be harmonized if not satisfied is often put forward in other quarters. Why, it is asked, should not each state receive a portion of the territory, since the whole inheritance is not for any man? If the plan could be carried out, it would deserve our warmest approval. The difficulty lies in the extraordinary intermixture of races. As we have already seen, the Bulgarians cluster thickest in the north-east, the Servians in the north-west, the Greeks in the south and along the shores of the Aegean. A division on these lines would be at least conceivable, if it did not leave the whole of central Macedonia without a master. Who, for instance, is to have Monastir, the centre and key of Macedonia? Attractive as the proposal at first sight appears, its difficulties become the more formidable the more carefully it is studied.

Another solution is that Austria should step into the place of Turkey. She is already a great Balkan Power. She has possessed Dalmatia for two centuries, she has done excellent work in Bosnia and the Herzegovina, and she is in military occupation of Novi-Bazar. She is already the sentinel of the Balkans; why could she not be their ruler? She is so strong, and so near, and so experienced, that some people say, "Let her take the Macedonian question and settle it." Unfortunately it is very doubtful if she would consent. If she consented, it is most improbable that Russia would give her permission. And in the third place it is doubtful whether the Macedonians themselves would accept her or any other Power without a struggle.

The last and in my judgment the best solution is to make Macedonia an autonomous province. "Why not Macedonia for the Macedonians?" asked Gladstone. Why not Macedonia for the Macedonians, policed by European troops, including regiments from the Balkan States, paying the Sultan tribute, like Egypt and Crete and Bulgaria, and with a Prince chosen by the Christian Powers? A wave of Slavonic feeling may force the hand of the Tsar as it forced the hand of his grandfather. The Turkish tide has been receding from Christian Europe for two centuries, and is receding still. The maintenance of a *status quo* which involves the rule of the Turk over the Christian is by its very nature provisional; and the anarchy of this summer proclaims that never was the rescue of Macedonia so urgent a duty as it is to-day.

I have left to the last Albania, because the Albanian question can be discussed and could be settled independently of Macedonia. If you take a map you will see that Albania is the strip of coast which runs south from Montenegro to the Greek frontier, and is bounded on the east by Macedonia. Though visible from the Italian coast no part of Europe is so utterly unknown. The people, who appear to be the descendants of the ancient Illyrians, are almost entirely untouched by civilization. You will find flattering mention of them in Byron; but in reality many of them are little better than savages. Though the story of the English consul who always drove about with his wife for a protection is perhaps *ben trovato*, it is certain enough that life is less secure in Albania than in any part of Europe. The Albanians are the Kurds of European Turkey. There is no homogeneity, religious or political. Nearly half the population are Mussulman, that is, they are descended from those who embraced Islam to escape from the disabilities of Christians. There are also a considerable number of Catholics, a few Protestants, and a few members of the Greek Church. The Ghegs of the north differ in some ways from the Tosks of the south; but they all live under a rule of clans, like the

Highlanders of old, the Sultan's authority being hardly more than nominal. The Albanians are born soldiers, and improve their natural gift by sanguinary struggles among themselves.

The future of Albania has exercised almost as many minds as the future of Macedonia. The propinquity to Italy, the fact that so many Albanians—among them the ancestors of Crispi—have made their home in the peninsula, the marriage of Victor Emmanuel to a Montenegrin princess, and other causes, have turned the eyes of many Italians in that direction. Yet those who recommend the occupation are no friends of Italy; to conquer and to hold that mountainous and barren country, in which, as it has been said, a large army starves and a small one is defeated, would almost certainly prove beyond her strength, and might involve a recurrence of the disasters of Abyssinia. For a similar reason we must reject the idea entertained in certain circles at Athens by which Albania should be joined to Greece in the same relation as Norway stands to Sweden. The Vilayet of Jannina is largely Greek; but the Vilayet of Scutari would never consent to such a plan, and could easily defeat any attempt to enforce its realization. A third suggestion, that of Albanian autonomy under one or other of the Pretenders who trace their descent from Scanderbeg, is impracticable owing to the fundamental divergence between north and south, the clan system, and the powerlessness of such a *régime* to keep order on the eastern frontier. My own view is that when the time comes for dealing with the Macedonian question an effort should be made to induce Austria to take over Albania. With the memory of the stubborn conflict in Bosnia and the Herzegovina, it is doubtful if she would undertake the task. If she were to consent she would confer a great boon on Albania, and by putting a stop to the raids on the eastern frontier would greatly facilitate the establishment of Macedonian autonomy.

I do not propose to deal with the question of the future of Constantinople, for it cannot in any sense be called an urgent problem.   In the first place, the Christians who live there have little to complain of; and in the second, the emancipation of Macedonia, defined as the Treaty of San Stefano defined it, would leave Eastern Thrace in Turkish hands.   The best hope for the Macedonians lies in their power to persuade Europe that their emancipation necessitates no such change in the balance of power as the expulsion of the Turk from his capital would involve.

III.

Adequately to describe the relation of Europe to the Ottoman Empire would be to recount a large part of modern history.   All that we can do is to recall such events as are indispensable to an understanding of the situation as it exists to-day.

In speaking of the Great Powers we may briefly dismiss Italy.   Cavour sent troops to the Crimea not because the House of Savoy was interested in the questions at issue, but in order to bring Italy into notice and to secure a standing at the Congress that would assemble at the close of the war.   Italy's interest in the Eastern question is confined to Albania,—an interest for which it is improbable that she would be willing to make any real sacrifice, and which indeed, as her wisest statesmen know, is hardly worth them.

Scarcely greater is the interest of France, though her relations with Turkey since the time of Francis I. have been frequent.   The last forty years have witnessed a notable decline of her *prestige* in the Near East.   The influence at Constantinople which Louis Napoleon gained by the Crimean war he lost by his decided action in the Lebanon only five years later, and never regained.   The interest of France in the East is based on her claim to protect the Latin Christians.   But the Protectorate grows more shadowy and ineffectual every year, partly owing to the absorption of French statesmen in other problems, partly to the strained relations between the Pope and the Republic, and partly to the growth of German influence. When M. Delcassé gave orders to seize Mitylene some months ago, it was whispered that his object was not merely to obtain the payment of debts but to revive the waning influence of France in the Levant. If this was his intention it has not been realized. No Power can gain or retain influence either with the Sultan or with his subjects without a definite policy, and France has none. The Armenian crisis showed the world that she is no longer to be reckoned among the forces that shape the destinies of south-eastern Europe. During that anxious time the words were the words of M. Hanotaux, but the voice was the voice of Prince Lobanoff. Whatever else the Franco-Russian alliance involves, it means that France gives Russia a free hand in the Near East, withdraws any ambitions that she entertained, and lends her support to those of her ally.

The policy of Austria, as revealed in the *entente* of 1897 with Russia and in her periodical admonitions to the Balkan States, is to put off as long as possible the day when the future of European Turkey has to be decided. What her policy will be when that time arrives must depend in great measure on her internal condition at the moment and on the personality of her ruler. It is sometimes said that Austria will never rest until she reaches the Aegean; but it seems to me much more probable that she considers that her Empire is already heterogeneous enough, and that she would be contented with the transference of Bosnia, the Herzegovina, and Novi-Bazar to her in full sovereignty, perhaps with Albania thrown in. It was the wish of Sir William White that she might become the official protector of an autonomous Macedonia; but it is doubtful whether she would feel disposed to accept any position in which responsibility was unaccompanied by power. In a word, it does not seem probable that Austria would wish to stake her fortunes on a struggle for the whole or part of Turkey in

Europe. The possibility of a break-up of the Austro-Hungarian Empire is a question too large and too remote to be discussed in this lecture.

It is little more than a century ago that English statesmen began to seriously occupy themselves with the Eastern question, and during the whole period two schools of opinion have existed in relation to it. In 1791 the power and ambitions of Catherine the Second so alarmed Pitt that he proposed an alliance with the Porte. The plan was warmly attacked by Burke and Fox with the argument that applies to-day. Turkey, said they, was the enemy of civilization, and no European Power ought to ally with her. Such an impression was made by their opposition that no more was heard of the proposal. Thirty years later Canning determined to aid Greece to throw off the Turkish yoke, but died too soon to witness the success of his plans. After his death the policy of Pitt was revived by Wellington and Palmerston, and dominated English statesmanship until the death of Beaconsfield. Their idea, put in the simplest language, was that the Eastern question concerned Europe as a whole and ought not to be settled by Russia alone. Since Russia refused to take this view of the question she must be watched and, if necessary, resisted. Such was the opinion held by almost every English statesman and diplomatist. But we must again distinguish two schools of thought. The first, represented by Palmerston, and, at least during the greater part of his life, by Stratford Canning, sincerely believed that the Turk was not very different from other people, and that with time and peace the Sultan would be able and willing to set his house in order. This conception was officially proclaimed when Turkey was admitted into the comity of nations by the Treaty of Paris. The second, represented by such men as Aberdeen and Gladstone, thought no better of the Turk than Bright or Cobden or Freeman, but felt that Russian aggression ought to be resisted. There was much to be said for this line of thought; but the Crimean war ought not to have been undertaken unless the Allies were able and willing to take effective measures for the protection of the Christian subjects of the Porte. But this is precisely what they refused to do. The late Duke of Argyll, a member of the Government that waged the war, used to say that the war was justifiable, and that it was the peace that was at fault. The Powers on that occasion expressly disclaimed the right of interfering in the domestic concerns of the Turkish Empire; and though the Sultan had to listen to plenty of plain speaking, the rescue of the Lebanon was the only occasion on which we intervened to protect the Eastern Christians. The Turk knew well enough that Europe was paralyzed by the feud between Russia and England. When Russia invited England in 1876 to co-operate in the solution of the Balkan crisis, she refused, and suggested a conference at Constantinople. The conference met; but when the Ambassadors handed in their plan the Sultan merely laughed in their face. We did not intervene in the Balkan war; but we were within an ace of doing so, and we challenged the legitimacy of the Treaty of San Stefano. The Treaty of Berlin effected valuable work; but two terrible mistakes were committed. Christian provinces that had been emancipated at San Stefano were handed back to the Sultan; and the machinery of European supervision, which had utterly broken down, was once again set up. The Sultan knew that he would be no more hampered by the new treaty than by the old; and the secret Convention of Cyprus emphasized the intention of England to continue to champion the Turk against the Muscovite. But the long lane had now reached a turning. The defeat and death of Beaconsfield gave the premiership to the man who had declared for the expulsion of the Turkish government, bag and baggage. The advent of Lord Salisbury did not involve a return to the policy of Palmerston and of Beaconsfield, which indeed he characterized at a subsequent period as that of "putting our money on the wrong horse." But the Armenian crisis revealed the impotence of England either to arrest the Sultan in his career of crime or to fulfil the moral obligation incurred by her policy and solemnly recorded in two international treaties. Owing to our preoccupations in other parts of the world, to our loss of faith in our traditional policy, and to the emergence of new influences in the diplomatic arena, we have lost our commanding position in Constantinople. The outcry of English merchants in Turkey is only another evidence of the loss of our influence and the relaxation of our grip.

In the enumeration of the Great Powers, I have kept to the last the two which, in my judgment, are destined to play the principal part in determining the future of the Near East. From the time that Peter the Great made Russia a Great Power, the Muscovites have turned longing eyes towards the south; and since the accession of Catherine II the exploitation of Turkey has been one of the cardinal tenets of every Russian statesman. The most formidable foe of the Ottoman Empire during the 19th century was the Tsar Nicholas, whose lifelong aim was to secure part of the inheritance of the Turk. Commencing his reign by aiding Greece to throw off the yoke of her oppressor, he changed his tactics and proceeded to pose as the Sultan's only friend. The revolt of Mehemet Ali forced Mahmud to look round for a helping hand, and as no other was held out to him he was forced to accept the aid of Russia on her own terms. The Treaty of 1833 registers the high-water-mark of Russian influence. Nicholas had made Turkey a Russian province; but he had overreached himself. The danger of Turkey and the indifference of the other Powers passed away, and a strong feeling grew up against Muscovite domination, which was changed to intense indignation when it became known that the Tsar had discussed the partition of Turkey with the English ambassador. Nothing was wanting to precipitate a conflict but a *casus belli*, which presented itself when Russia claimed a Protectorate over the Christian subjects of the Porte. The Crimean war which followed was not allowed by Russia to turn her thoughts from the goal, and when the Balkan crisis occurred 20 years later she returned to the struggle. The Powers which had supported Turkey on the previous occasion now left her to fight her battles alone. She was defeated, and signed the Treaty of San Stefano when the Russian troops were in sight of Constantinople. Russian diplomacy once again overreached itself; and the Great Powers stepped in to modify the settlement. But their interference was only momentary, and the idea of responsibility for the Eastern Christians that had reigned since the Crimean war faded away, in large measure owing to the influence of Bismarck. During the years that followed the Balkan war Russian influence at Constantinople was supreme and practically uncontested.

The international aspect of the Eastern question has been completely transformed during the last few years by the intrusion of Germany into a domain from which she had hitherto held aloof. Though publicists such as Roscher and Rodbertus had prophesied and recommended the developments of later days, the corner-stone of Bismarck's foreign policy was to stand on good terms with Russia, and not to thwart her in the attainment of her highest ambitions. With this end he kept Prussia from joining the Allies in the Crimean war. To this end he dedicated his whole strength during his ambassadorship at St Petersburg. With this object he secretly urged Alexander to denounce the Black Sea clauses of the Treaty of Paris during the Franco-German war. Throughout the discussions at Berlin in 1878 he kept the same object steadily in view, though it pleased Prince Gortchakoff to represent him as counter-working his policy. Even when he made the Dual Alliance he guarded himself by a secret understanding with the Tsar. His views never changed. The Eastern question, he said, was not worth the bones of a Pomeranian grenadier.

With the accession of the present Emperor and the fall of Bismarck all this was changed. The ground had already been prepared for a new policy. The pioneer of German influence was General Von der Goltz, who in the early eighties began the task of reforming the Turkish army and obtaining orders for material for German firms. In 1888 a German company was formed to construct railways in Anatolia. The Armenian crisis afforded the new ruler an excellent opportunity of consolidating his influence at Constantinople. All expressions of sympathy with the Armenians were sternly repressed, and while the massacres were still in progress the Kaiser sent the Sultan a photograph of himself and his family with a flattering message. The Cretan crisis and the Greek war were utilized in the same way, and in the following year the Emperor paid his memorable visit to Constantinople on his way to the Holy Land. In 1899 the greatest triumph which any European Power has gained in connection with the Eastern question in the recollection of living man was achieved by Germany. Through the instrumentality of Dr Siemens, the indefatigable Director of the German Bank and Chairman of the Anatolian Railways, permission was obtained for a company formed under German auspices to continue the railway from the Konia to the Persian Gulf. How much further Germany will go and whether she is willing to risk a conflict with Russia is a question that depends for its answer on the general position of European politics.

When I say that Germany or Russia is supreme at Constantinople, you must not think that the Sultan is at heart more friendly to those Powers than to the others. Like other men, he desires to be left alone, and his dislike to those who interfere with him is as strong as ever. He regards the Christian Powers with the same contempt and suspicion that he has always felt. He resents their officiousness, and is ever scheming to rid himself of their control. He would like to abolish every trace of bondage, and he actually attempted to deprive the Greeks of their rights under the Capitulations after the war.

My object in this lecture has been to explain the nature and difficulties of the most pressing problems of the Near East, and to describe the chief forces which are at work. It is no part of my duty to anticipate history. Who will reduce Albania to order; whether Macedonia will be partitioned or receive autonomy; whether the German or the Russian will be supreme in Asia Minor; what power will succeed the Ottoman on the Golden Horn, are questions on which it is interesting to speculate but which it is impossible to answer. All that we know is that the Turk will never change, and that the ultimate solution of the Eastern Question, foreshadowed by history and demanded by justice, is the termination of his rule over the Christian.

PAN-ISLAMISM.

By Professor E. G. Browne, M.A., M.B.

It is a prevalent and on the whole a good custom that, in speaking on any obscure or unfamiliar subject, one should begin with a definition of its meaning. Now unfortunately I was not permitted to choose the subject of this lecture, which, as you see from your programmes, is described as "Pan-Islamism." I certainly should not have chosen this subject for myself, because in the first place (and this you will admit is a serious objection), I am not quite sure what it means; and, in the second place, I am still less certain whether any such thing really exists. If it exists at all, it is presumably to be sought in the Muhammadan East; and if it exists there, some equivalent expression ought to be forthcoming in Arabic, Turkish, or Persian. To the best of my knowledge no such expression can be found: the term could only be translated by some periphrasis, such as *Ittiḥádu 'l-Muslimín* ("Alliance" or "Union of the Muslims"), and this fact appears to me to indicate that the idea connoted by the term is a Western, not an Eastern, conception, since every people, so far as I know, possess words to express ideas with which they are familiar, or at any rate ideas native to the race.

This being so, it was by no means easy to frame a definition of "Pan-Islamism" which should conform to the Arabian standard indicated by the aphorism, *Khayru 'l-kalámi má qalla wa dalla*—"the best expression is that which is briefest and most significant." In despair I finally consulted one of my Muhammadan friends, who without hesitation supplied me with a definition in some dozen words, which, in default of a better, I give you for what it is worth. "Pan-Islamism," he said, "is a mare's-nest discovered by the *Times'* correspondent at Vienna."

Still, the word connotes a certain idea, which, whether true or false, it is our present business to examine. "Pan-Hellenism" is the most ancient of this class of words; but on referring to the source whence, according to my Muhammadan friend, the term "Pan-Islamism" originated, I found a whole series of parallels, such as "Pan-Americanism" and "Pan-Germanism," "Pan-Celtic," and "Pan-Slavonic" movements, and so forth. "Pan-Anglicanism" is, of course, used in a different sense: our English aspirations after racial union and expansion we now denote by the word "Imperialism," which, almost unknown in this sense twenty years ago, now occurs in a dozen places in almost any English newspaper you buy at a bookstall.

Now first of all you will notice a very essential difference (and, I would add, a very significant difference) between the term "Pan-Islamic" and its congeners, "Pan-Hellenic," "Pan-Germanic," "Pan-Slavonic," "Pan-American" and "Pan-Celtic," for all these denote the aspirations of a *race*, whilst Pan-Islamic refers to the aspirations of a *religion*. Now there are at least three great religions at present existing in the world which lay claim to universality: Christianity, Buddhism, and Islám, the religion of Muḥammad. Why is it that for the last alone we find a word intended to connote an alleged determination or aspiration on the part of its professors to unite more closely together for defensive or offensive purposes, and to sink all minor differences in order to secure the triumph of their faith, or at least to protect it from the attacks of hostile creeds? Or, to omit Buddhism (which, in most countries where it is professed, has undergone admixture with other doctrines, and ceased, for this and other reasons, from active proselytizing), why are the aspirations of Europe mainly racial, while the aspirations of Western Asia—or, to speak more accurately, of the Muhammadan peoples—are mainly religious?

The answer is that (whatever the explanation may be) religious feeling is, as a rule, much stronger, and racial feeling much weaker in the East than in the West. I do not mean to imply that racial pride does not exist in Asia, for it does in some cases exist strongly; but it is rather the pride of family, tribe or clan than of the nation as a whole. Before the advent of Muḥammad the Arab tribes devoted much of their rhetorical ability to aspersing the characters, pedigrees and conduct of the neighbouring clans: they were good haters, and such derive no satisfaction from wasting their hatred upon a distant alien race. The Persian of the present day is never tired of glorifying his native town and decrying all others; dilating, if he be of Shíráz, for example, on the avarice of the Isfahání and the rascality of the Tabrízí, and dismissing Qum and Káshán with the epigram :—

سگ كاشی به از اكابر قمِ، با وجودی كه سگ به ز كاشيست،

"*A dog of Káshán is better than the nobles of Qum,
Notwithstanding that a dog is better than a man of Káshán.*"

Amongst the Ottoman Turks alone, of all Muslim nations, so far as my observation goes, does patriotic feeling, as we understand it, exist; and even in this case I am inclined to think that the idea was imported in the first instance from France, within the last forty or fifty years, at the time of that Renaissance which is associated chiefly with the names of Kemál Bey, Shinásí Efendi and Ziyá Páshá, and which in a brief space of time transformed Turkey from an entirely mediæval and Oriental into a comparatively modern and semi-European empire.

Again, I do not wish to imply that religious fervour is

lacking in Europe, or that the East is more religious than the West, so far as the practical or ethical side of religion is concerned. But the Eastern conception of religion differs from the Western in several important respects: notably in this, that Dogma and Metaphysic arouse far more general interest and excite far more eager controversy in Asia than in Europe. One of the burning questions of Islám in the ninth century of our era was whether or no the Qur'án—the Word of God—had, or had not, existed from all eternity; and we find the Caliph of that period, who strongly held the latter view, refusing, on the occasion of an exchange of prisoners with his Byzantine enemies, to receive back such of his captive subjects as preferred the opposite opinion; deeming the recruiting of his army a small matter compared with the prevalence of distasteful dogmas within his realms.

Now if this preponderance of religious over racial feeling has been in some way a source of weakness to the Muhammadan nations, it has undoubtedly, on the other hand, largely conduced to the spread of Islám, which, as you are well aware, continues even at the present day to make steady progress both in Asia and Africa. It is often asked why, considering the vast amount of labour and wealth expended in Christian missionary enterprise, and the complete or almost complete absence of any such organized propaganda on behalf of Islám, Muhammadanism continues to make more progress in Asia and Africa than Christianity. There are, no doubt, several reasons; but the chief one, in my opinion, is that the convert to Islám, no matter to what race he may belong, is on the whole admitted freely and ungrudgingly to the social privileges, as well as the obligations, of the community with which he has cast in his lot. Whatever he may have lost by severing himself from his former co-religionists, he at least gains something in compensation. Can we say frankly that the same holds good of the convert to Christianity? How many Christian missionaries even (not to speak of officials, civilians, colonists and soldiers professedly Christian) are prepared to accept a "native convert" (to use the expression sanctioned by custom) on terms of even approximate equality? I would even venture to say that, at any rate in the more civilized Muhammadan countries, such as Turkey and Persia, the lot of the Muhammadan negro slave is on the whole preferable to that of his free Christian brother in the West.

Another reason which has no doubt conduced to the spread of the Muhammadan religion is the extreme simplicity of the formula which embodies the essentials of its creed—"*Ashhadu al-lá Iláha illa 'lláh, wa ashhadu anna Muhammad^{an} 'abduhu wa rasúluhu*" ("I bear witness that there is no god but God, and I bear witness that Muḥammad is His servant and His apostle"). No one has the right to go behind this formula, or to enquire how the confessor understands the word "God," or what he understands by the prophetic mission of Muḥammad; points on which, in fact, the most diverse views have been and are entertained by the different sects of Islám. Yet in another way the very elasticity of this formula militates against any close community of feeling or strong sympathy between these sects, whose attitude towards one another is well expressed in the traditional saying ascribed to Muḥammad[1]:

$$ \text{سَتَتَفَرَّقُ أُمَّتِى عَلَى ثَلْثٍ وَ سَبْعِينَ فِرْقَةً ٱلنَّاجِيَةُ مِنْهَا} $$
$$ \text{وَاحِدَةٌ وَ ٱلْبَاقُونَ هَلْكَى،} $$

"*My Church shall become divided into seventy-three sects, whereof one only shall be saved, while the rest shall be lost.*"

In considering the possibility of a Pan-Islamic movement, that is to say of an offensive and defensive alliance of all the Muhammadan nations, it is necessary in the first place to take due account of the diversities of beliefs and aspirations implied in the above tradition. Whether it be genuine or not (and

[1] Shahristání, ed. Cureton, p. 3.

there is little doubt that it is spurious) makes no difference
to its importance as indicating the consciousness of the Muhammadans of the extent to which their religion is rent by
schism, and schism, moreover, which hinges on vital questions
of doctrine. And in the second place we must briefly glance
at the history of Islám since its first foundation, and consider
to what extent its votaries ever have been politically united to
such a degree as to enable them to present a united front
against the unbelievers. In this brief historical retrospect,
which is essential for the understanding of the present state of
Islám, I shall touch on the following points :—

1. The Achievement of the Prophet Muḥammad, and in
particular the change which he effected in the condition of his
people, the Arabs.

2. The brief period of the Orthodox Caliphs (A.D. 632—
661) who immediately succeeded him, which period in the
eyes of orthodox Muslims constitutes, as it were, the Ideal
Theocracy of the Apostolic Age.

3. The Umayyad Caliphate (A.D. 661—750), and the causes
of its fall, which involved the loss by the Arabs of the dominant
position which they had hitherto held in Islám.

4. The 'Abbásid Caliphate (A.D. 750—1258), its character,
as estimated by Muslim historians, its disruption, decay and
final destruction by the Mongols.

5. The claim of the Sultans of Turkey to the position of
Caliph, and the extent to which this claim has been, is, or is
likely to be recognized by the Muslim world. This brings us
directly to the question of Pan-Islamism, which presents itself
as two separate problems, viz.:—

1. Is it likely or possible that the Sultan of Turkey should
be recognized as Caliph, or spiritual and temporal head of
Islám, by the bulk of the Muhammadan peoples?

2. Is it likely or possible that any other claimant should succeed in obtaining such recognition?

We begin, then, with—

1. *The Achievement of the Prophet Muḥammad.*

To form a just estimate of Muḥammad's work it is essential to have some idea of the condition in which he found the Arabs, and the condition in which he left them. It is not fair to judge an Arab reformer (if objection be held to the title "Prophet," as applied to him) of the seventh century of our era by the standards which prevail in Europe or America in the twentieth. The question here is not so much whether his teaching would raise or lower the ethical, social and religious tone of London, Paris, Berlin or New York, as whether as a matter of fact it did raise these things in Arabia. And here, I think, the answer must unhesitatingly be given in the affirmative: the condition of the Arabs generally was enormously improved, alike in its social, political, and ethical aspects, by the victory of Islám over the heathenism which had hitherto prevailed in the Arabian Peninsula. And, remarkable as was the rapid diffusion of Islám under the Prophet's immediate successors, so that by the end of the seventh century it extended "from the Atlantic to the Indus, and from the Caspian to the cataracts of the Nile[1]," Muḥammad's triumph over his own stubborn and stiff-necked people was, as it seems to me, a yet greater victory. It is true that the pagan Arabs were by no means deeply attached to their gods, which they would revile and even pelt with stones when things went contrary to their wishes; but at least these old gods were more intimate and familiar than the remote and awful Alláh Ta'álá, or Supreme God, for whom Muḥammad claimed their exclusive homage. Still more distasteful to them were the obligations—prayer, fasting, and, above all, alms-giving—which the religion of

[1] Stanley Lane Poole's *Mohammadan Dynasties*, p. 6.

Islám sought to impose upon them. All their strong clan-feeling and exaggerated sense of family obligations (which included in particular the duty of avenging to the utmost any insult or injury inflicted on any kinsman or member of their tribe) revolted, moreover, from the idea of a fraternity based solely on a common religious belief, and a justice which would deal out equal measure to every Muslim, irrespective of family, tribe or race. Yet such equality of all believers was clearly the Prophet's ideal, even if at times some resurgence of the old feeling of kinship obscured or marred it. Thus in the Qur'án we read (xlix, 10): "the believers are only brethren, therefore make peace between your two brothers"; and again (xlix, 13): "the noblest of you in God's sight is he who most feareth God"; while the following tradition is even more explicitly directed against racial pride and the arrogance of noble birth : " O man ! God hath taken away from you the arrogance of heathen days and the ancient pride in ancestry; an Arab hath no other precedence over a non-Arab than by virtue of the fear of God; ye are all the progeny of Adam, and Adam himself is of the earth."

We may therefore take it that Islám was from the first opposed to racial pride and exclusiveness, and though, as I have said, there was before Muḥammad's time but little sentiment of national unity amongst the Arabs, the sentiment of racial pride was strongly developed. The following verses, for example, taken from the *Muʻallaqa* of ʻAmr b. Kulthúm of the tribe of Taghlib —one of the most celebrated pre-Muhammadan poems— breathes sentiments which would not be out of place in the mouth of a modern " Jingo "[1]:—

وَ قَدْ عَلِمَ الْقَبَائِلُ مِنْ مَعَدٍّ، إِذَا قُبَبٌ بِأَبْطَحِهَا بُنِينَا،

بِأَنَّا الْمُطْعِمُونَ إِذَا قَدَرْنَا، وَ أَنَّا الْمُهْلِكُونَ اِذَا ٱبْتُلِينَا،

[1] See Ludwig Abel's edition of the *Muʻallaqát* (Berlin, 1891), pp. 25— 26, ll. 94—103.

وَ أَنَّا ٱلْمَانِعُونَ لِمَا أَرَدْنَا، وَ أَنَّا ٱلنَّازِلُونَ بِحَيْثُ شِئْنَا،

وَ أَنَّا ٱلتَّارِكُونَ إِذَا سَخِطْنَا، وَ أَنَّا ٱلآخِذُونَ إِذَا رَضِينَا،

وَ أَنَّا ٱلْعَاصِمُونَ إِذَا أُطِعْنَا، وَ أَنَّا ٱلْعَازِمُونَ إِذَا عُصِينَا،

وَ نَشْرِبُ إِنْ وَرَدْنَا ٱلْمَاءَ صَفْوًا، وَ يَشْرِبُ غَيْرُنَا كَدِرًا وَ طِينَا،

لَنَا ٱلدُّنْيَا وَ مَنْ أَضْحَى عَلَيْهَا، وَ نَبْطِشُ حِينَ نَبْطِشُ قَادِرِينَا،

نُسَمَّى ٱلظَّالِمِينَ وَ مَا ظَلَمْنَا، وَ لَكِنَّا نُبِيدُ ٱلظَّالِمِينَا،

مَلْأَنَا ٱلأَرْضَ حَتَّى ضَاقَ عَنَّا، وَ نَحْنُ ٱلْبَحْرَ نَمْلَأُهُ سَفِينَا،

" *The clans of Ma'add learned, when tents were [first] erected in their pebble-strewn ravines,*

That we are the food-givers when we prevail, and that we are the destroyers when we are tried in battle;

And that we defend what we will, and that we alight where we please;

And that we reject when we are angry, and that we accept when we are contented;

And that we protect when we are obeyed, and that we go forth to war when we are rebelled against;

And if we reach the well, we drink the clear water, while others drink the turbid and muddy remnant.

Ours is the world and whosoever dwells therein, and when we attack, we attack as men who prevail.

We are called oppressors, yet we have not oppressed, but have [rather] destroyed the tyrants.

We have filled the earth until it is become too narrow for us, and the sea also we have filled with ships."

The pride of race displayed in these lines, which are merely one sample out of many, is very evident; but it is in the tribe, not the nation, that the poet exults. The Prophet Muḥammad

not only succeeded in subordinating this clannish feeling to the
sense of national unity, but by his behaviour towards non-Arab
converts to his doctrine, such as the Persian Salmán and the
negro Bilál, strove by practice as well as by precept to secure
to all believers a footing of approximate equality. As for what
Islám effected in ameliorating the social and moral condition
of the Arabs, I know of no better statement of the benefits it
conferred than that given to the Christian ruler of Abyssinia
by the spokesman of the Muslims who, in the dark days of
persecution which preceded the Flight of the Prophet from
Mecca to Medina (an event which marks the beginning of
Islám's triumph, and which is therefore appropriately adopted
by the Muhammadans as the beginning of their era), sought
refuge at his court from the enmity of their heathen countrymen.

"O King!" said the spokesman of these fugitives[1], "we
were a barbarous folk, worshipping idols, eating carrion, committing shameful deeds, violating the ties of consanguinity,
and evilly entreating our neighbours, the strong amongst us
consuming the weak; and thus we continued until God sent
unto us an Apostle from our midst, whose pedigree and integrity
and purity of life we knew, to summon us to God, that we
should declare His Unity and worship Him, and put away the
stones and idols which we and our fathers used to worship in
His stead; and he bade us be truthful in speech, and faithful
in the fulfilment of our trusts, and mindful of the ties of consanguinity and the duties of neighbours, and to refrain from
forbidden things and from blood; and he forbade us from immoral acts and deceitful words, and from consuming the property
of orphans, and from slandering the virtuous; and he commanded us to worship God, and to associate naught else with
Him, and to pray, and give alms, and fast."

These men realized, then, very clearly what Islám had done
for them, and how much it had raised them from their former
condition; while as regards polygamy and slavery—two of the

[1] Ibn Hishám's *Life of the Prophet*, ed. Wüstenfeld, p. 219.

things most often charged against Islám—they were neither introduced by Muḥammad nor confined to the Muslim lands : rather they were tolerated, under vastly ameliorated conditions, because·no reformer nor prophet can carry the people to whom he is sent, either in knowledge or practice, further than the majority of the well-disposed are prepared to go. It is question-able, in short, whether any single reformer ever so materially raised so great a number of his people so much in so short a time as Muḥammad raised the Arabs (material far from promising for his enterprise, as we have already seen), to whom primarily his teaching was addressed. Indeed it is doubtful whether, in his moments of greatest optimism, he ever dreamed that his religion would so rapidly spread so far beyond the confines of the Arabian Peninsula. Living to see that Penin-sula practically—at least in name—obedient to the Law which he had brought, he was able to say ere his departure, "To-day have I perfected unto you your religion."

We now pass to—

2. *The Period of the Orthodox Caliphs.*

This period in the history of the Caliphate is very short, but very important. It is short; for in all it lasted less than thirty years (A.D. 632—661), and ere much more than half of that time had elapsed those seeds of discord were sown which culminated in the battle of Ṣiffín (A.D. 657), when, for the first time, the sword of Muslim was turned against Muslim. It is important, because it saw alike the great conquests and the first schisms of Islám, and because the conversion of vast numbers of non-Arabs and the acquisition of immense riches derived from the conquered lands—chiefly Persia and Syria—introduced new conditions, tendencies and temptations which did not fail soon to make apparent their results.

For a time, however, the unity of Islám—"Pan-Islamism" in the true sense—and the ideals of the Prophet continued to prevail, though he himself had passed away. Princes and nobles, foreign or Arabian, converts or captives, were amazed when they sought out the "Commander of the Faithful" at Medina, to behold one who in nowise differed externally from his fellow-citizens; who, as the Muhammadan historians tell us, slept on a mat on the ground, wore the roughest raiment and ate the coarsest food, so that one of them, speaking of the luxury he voluntarily abjured, said that, if he wished it, "the finest honey and the softest barley-bread" would be within his means.

"Know further," says the historian al-Fakhrí[1], "that their austerity in respect of food and raiment was not due to poverty, or inability to procure the most sumptuous apparel or the sweetest meats, but they used to act thus in order to put themselves on an equality with the poorest of their subjects, and to wean the flesh from its lusts, and to discipline it till it should accustom itself to its highest potentialities; else was each one of them endowed with ample wealth, and palm-groves, and gardens, and other like possessions. But most of their expenditure was in charitable uses and offerings...... As for their victories and their battles, verily their cavalry reached Africa and the uttermost parts of Khurásán, and crossed the Oxus."

This, then, is the ideal to which the pious and orthodox Muslim has in all subsequent times looked back with admiration and affection, and for the return of which he ardently hopes when he dreams of a Mahdí who shall come in the fulness of time to restore the true faith, vanquish the unbelievers, and "fill the earth with justice after it has been filled with iniquity."

Now let us pass to—

3. *The Umayyad Caliphate* (A.D. 661—750),

which offers the most complete contrast to the period which we have just been considering. The great conquests, indeed, continue, but the old simplicity and piety are gone, and the

---

[1] Ed. Ahlwardt, pp. 89—90.

still older aristocratic arrogance and racial pride are back once more in full force. These Umayyads, Muslims in name, but, with one exception, pagans in feeling, had no idea of allowing the foreign believer whom they despised, or the rival clansman whom they hated with the old traditional fervour, to enjoy like privileges with themselves. Feeling themselves to be an imperial race, they fell back on—

> "the simple, wise old plan,
> That those shall take who get the chance,
> And those shall keep who can."

And the result of this was that they fell to quarrelling with one another, thus affording opportunity to the subject-races (to whom, contrary to the principles of Islám, they refused the rights and privileges which all true believers were entitled to claim) to rise against them and overthrow them. With this overthrow the power of the Arabs as a dominant nation really came to an end, and their place was actually, if not nominally, taken first by the Persians and then by the Turks. The Arabs became a great people, and for a little time played a great part in the world's history because they were actuated by a great Idea; they lost the great Idea, and desired dominion for its own sake; and then the very Idea whence they had derived their power became its destroyer. They set Race above Religion, the accidental kinship of Blood above the essential affinity of a common Aim and Idea; and in a short while it was as one of their last great generals and prefects said—

عَلَى ٱلْإِسْلَامِ وَ ٱلْعَرَبِ ٱلسَّلَامُ

" *Goodbye to Islám and the Arabs.*"

And it is significant that in those successive rebellions which first shook and finally shattered the Umayyad power, the religious classes, even when Arabs,—the old Companions and Followers of the Prophet, the Qur'án readers, zealots and pietists—were commonly to be found in large numbers on the side of the subject races, whose rights as Muslims they as Muslims felt bound to assert.

4. *The 'Abbásid Caliphate* (A.D. 750—1258).

The 'Abbásid Caliphs were raised to power by the revolt of the Persian Muslims against the Arab secular power of the Umayyads. There were other causes at work, which have been carefully studied by Van Vloten in his admirable essay, *Sur la Domination arabe, le Chiítisme et les Croyances messianiques sous le Khalifat des Omayades* (Amsterdam, 1894), but this was the chief one; and the 'Abbásids seldom forgot, in their choice of ministers, advisers and generals, that it was to non-Arabs that they owed their victory. For a time (and especially in what Tennyson calls "the Golden Prime of good Haroun Alraschid") the dominant influence was Persian; later it was Turkish. For the rest, the 'Abbásid dynasty was, as the Muhammadan historian al-Fakhrí says[1], "a treacherous, wily, and faithless dynasty, wherein intrigue and guile played a greater part than strength and energy, particularly in its latter days. ...Yet withal it was a dynasty abounding in good qualities, richly endowed with generous attributes, wherein the wares of Science found a ready sale, the merchandize of Culture was in great demand, the observances of Religion were respected, charitable bequests flowed freely, the world was prosperous, the holy shrines were well cared for, and the frontiers were bravely kept; nor did this state of things cease until its last days were at hand, violence became general, government was disturbed, and dominion passed from them." This was the time when civilization, science and culture were in the hands of the Muslims, whilst mediæval Europe was wrapped in darkness and barbarism, glad to borrow a little light on Philosophy, Medicine, or Mathematics from Avicenna the Persian or Averroes the Moor. So far as "filling the earth with justice"

[1] Ed. Ahlwardt, pp. 176—177.

was concerned, however, the 'Abbásid Caliphs did not materially excel their Umayyad predecessors, so that we find a disillusioned poet exclaiming[1]:

" *O would that the tyranny of the sons of Merwán* (i.e. *the Umayyads*) *could return to us,*
And would that the 'justice' of the sons of 'Abbás were in Hell-fire !"

يَا لَيْتَ جَوْرُ بَنِى مَرْوَانَ عَادَ لَنَا،

وَ لَيْتَ عَدْلُ بَنِى مَرْوَانَ فِى النَّارِ،

Even during the days of their greatest power and splendour the 'Abbásids never had even the nominal allegiance of the whole Muhammadan world. Spain was lost to them from the first; North Africa soon followed; and both that and Egypt passed a little later into the hands of the heterodox anti-Caliphs of the "Sect of the Seven." Gradually the more distant provinces, even when still acknowledging the suzerainty of Baghdad and remaining nominally loyal, became practically independent, until at last, in the middle of the thirteenth century, the flood of Mongol devastation swept down on Western Asia, destroying even the semblance of unity in the Muhammadan Empire, and extinguishing finally the historical Caliphate. This Mongol invasion was one of the most frightful calamities which ever befel so considerable a portion of the human race; Islám never recovered, either politically or socially, from its effects; and as for its methods, they were thus summed up by one of the few survivors who escaped from the sack of Bukhárá :—"They came, destroyed, burned, slew, spoiled and departed[2]."

آمدند و کندند و سوختند و کُشتند و بُردند و رفتند

[1] Van Vloten, *La Domination arabe*, p. 69.

[2] The *Ta'ríkh-i-Jahán-Kushá* of Juwayní, one of the most important sources for the history of the Mongol invasion, but unfortunately un-published, and rare even in manuscript.

The historical Caliphate, then, came to an end when al-Musta'ṣim, the last 'Abbásid Caliph, was starved to death by order of Hulágú the Mongol, in A.D. 1258.

We come now to

5. *The claim of the Ottoman Sultans to the dignity of Caliph.*

This claim dates from the Conquest of Egypt by Sultan Selím I, in A.D. 1517. When he had overthrown the Mamelukes and occupied Cairo, he, by threats or promises, induced the titular Caliph—the descendant of one of the 'Abbásid princes who had fled thither after the sack of Baghdad by the Mongols—to transfer to himself the title and visible insignia of the Caliphate—the sacred standard, sword and mantle of the Prophet, which are now preserved at Constantinople.

Now I have done with the historical retrospect which, brief and inadequate though it be, must, I fear, have proved somewhat wearisome to you. And the two main points I wish you to grasp before discussing the possibility of a Pan-Islamic movement at the present day are :—

(1) That the political unity of the Muslims only survived the Prophet's death some twelve years, and that never since that time have all his followers agreed as to who was his lawful representative.

(2) That though it cannot be asserted that all, or even the majority, of the " 73 sects " spoken of by Muhammadan writers were of any great importance, while many which were once important have long ceased to be so, even when they have not altogether disappeared, there nevertheless do remain certain differences so fundamental and so antagonistic that I cannot imagine any permanent, or even protracted, reconciliation being effected between them. The great division in Islám is, of course, that between the Sunnís (or " orthodox ") and the Shí'a

(or "heterodox") Muhammadans. If you read about the origin of this schism, which goes back to the period immediately succeeding the Prophet's death, you may be tempted to think that it is a mere quarrel about the claims of individuals; and that since the individuals concerned have been dead for nearly thirteen centuries the quarrel might now be buried in oblivion. But this is not so; for, firstly, the Persian Muslim, who chiefly represents the Shí'a party, is, as a rule, more interested in all which was said or done—or which is alleged to have been said and done—by 'Alí, whose cause Persia from the first espoused, than in the accession of a new king or the disgrace of an old minister at the present day; and is more concerned with the politics of Medina in the seventh century than with the politics of England or France or Germany—or even Russia—in the twentieth. And secondly it is not a mere question of persons and names, but of radically antagonistic theories personified as men. To the Persian, 'Alí stands as a hero, half deified and wholly Persianized, who is at once the champion and the incarnation of the Theory of Divine Right: the whole religious history of Persia might be described as the search for Avatars —for Divine Incarnations—a search which is prosecuted just as eagerly to-day as it was in the days of the early Caliphs. To the Persian the democratic ideal is hateful to the last degree; and the Arab theory that a Caliph, or supreme head of both Church and State, can be chosen by popular suffrage (a theory most strongly enunciated by the Khárijites, another of the oldest sects of Islám, but more or less accepted by all Sunní Muhammadans) is the Abomination of Desolation. Granted, then, that all the Sunní Muhammadans could be induced to recognize either the Sultan of Turkey or anyone else as their supreme over-lord, spiritual and temporal, it is to me inconceivable that Persia, which is practically entirely Shí'ite, should ever consent to join them. And if it be urged that, though Persia has played a great part in the world's history, she is actually, in spite of her considerable size (roughly equal to France and Spain together), so thinly populated by so unwarlike a people that she may be regarded as a negligible quantity, I would remind you that she is at least autonomous, and able to afford a *pied-à-terre* to this nation or that, as she pleases; while geographically she forms a solid wedge driven through the centre of Muhammadan Asia, entirely separating the Sunnís of Turkey from the Sunnís of Central Asia, Afghánistán and Balúchistán, and loving them little, if at all, more than her non-Muslim neighbours. The antipathy between Turk and Persian is profound, and, in my opinion, indestructible, and is both national and religious. A dervish at Khúy, in North-West Persia, boasted to me that he and some of his fellow-dervishes had accompanied the Russian army during the Russo-Turkish War, and aided the Russian arms by their prayers. I need not say that I do not ascribe the victory of the Russians entirely to this cause; and I daresay that the whole story was a figment of the dervish's fertile imagination, and that he was never near the seat of war at all; but that is neither here nor there: I merely refer to the incident as indicating how little sympathy exists between the Persians and Turks on the ground of religion. There can be no doubt that the geographical and religious position of Persia is a source of very great weakness to Islám in Asia, and would fatally embarrass any scheme which an Ottoman Sultan might form for uniting Muhammadan Asia under his sway. Nor does it appear that the Arabs are much more attached to the Turks than are the Persians.

But it was not so much of Asia as of Africa that the *Times'* correspondent was thinking in the letter of March 22, 1900, wherein he announced his discovery, or rather the discovery of the Austrian Catholic organ, the *Vaterland*, whence he derived his idea. The latter journal seems to have given a sensational account of African Muhammadans (instigated, as is implied, by the Turkish Government) recruiting corps for the Boer army, in order to shatter the British power, and of Turkish flags hoisted by Muhammadan states bordering on Lake Chad;—stories just about as credible as that the Sultan had seriously intended (as was also reported in the press) to send an army-corps to assist "his old allies the English" in the late war. But neither of the alliances above-mentioned, even had they been conceivable, would have had the remotest connection with Pan-Islamism.

But Muhammadanism is undoubtedly, for reasons which I have already indicated, making great progress in Africa; and Africa, as we have abundantly seen, is a land of vast potentialities. There was the great movement originated by the Mahdi of the Soudan, which might have ended very differently if it had happened before the days of steam and gunpowder; and there is still the mysterious Shaykh Senúsí to be reckoned with. But whatever movements of this kind may take place—and I am far from denying their possibility—I do not think that they will be engineered by Turkey, to whose leading-strings neither the Wahhábís of Arabia, nor the dervishes of the Soudan, showed the slightest inclination to entrust themselves. From such upheavals Turkey, as it seems to me, has more to fear than to hope; for they can only be produced by religious teachers of a type which does not readily submit itself to established governments. Theocracy, not Empire, is the ideal of such enthusiasts as are alone capable of evoking a militant Muhammadan revival, and the movement in every case will inevitably remain, so long as it endures, under the direction of those who generated it, who are not likely to present it, with all its potentialities, to any Sultan or Shah, as though it were a tame tiger effectively muzzled.

Now Islám is an immense subject, whether it be studied from the historical, the geographical, the political, or the literary and scientific point of view; and it is most difficult—nay, almost impossible, for anyone, especially any European—to obtain a true and comprehensive view of it in all these aspects. My friend Dr Reich, to whose lectures most of you no doubt had the pleasure of listening, says that no one can write or speak intelligently on history or politics unless he has lived in at least three or four different countries long enough to be practically familiar with the institutions, ideas and mode of life of their inhabitants. If this be true of Europe, it is true in still greater degree of Asia, where the difficulty of obtaining full admittance into the society and ideas of the people is very much greater. Difference not so much of language—for that can be more easily overcome—as of tradition, custom, social conditions, above all, religion, make it very difficult for a European to enter into full sympathy with the spirit of the East. And without sympathy there can be no comprehension; for to understand how a given person or people is likely to behave under given circumstances, we must feel with them, understand their motives, their hopes, their fears, and their prejudices. Some of you, perhaps, regard the Asiatic as an essentially inferior being to the European, and think that he ought to feel honoured by your interest and attention. But that is not the Asiatic point of view. Under the most favourable circumstances it takes some time to arrive at that point of view, and when you have arrived at it you will probably experience a surprise not perhaps wholly agreeable. The European is to him not merely an unsympathetic but an uncleanly person—one who eats disgusting things, pork, crabs, and the like—and whose habits, gestures, attitudes, gait and garments are distasteful and undignified. All this is quite distinct from the religious point of view, from which he is in addition an unbeliever. Courtesy, fear, or that control of expression which is regarded as the mark of good breeding, generally prevents the Asiatic (and I am here speaking of the genuine non-Europeanized Asiatic) from revealing his sentiments; but they are none the less both strong and real. At best, the European is to him an ingenious artificer, wholly absorbed in material aims; very useful as a dentist, a clockmaker, or other supplier of material needs, but full of a tiresome and useless activity, and a stranger to higher spiritual interests.

The Western nations, in whatever else they may differ, nearly all agree in believing in what is called " Progress," and this belief lies at the root of that unceasing activity which is to the East at once so irksome and so incomprehensible. Movement may be forwards, backwards, or backwards and forwards in no definite direction ; and mere alteration of position is not necessarily advance. Such change is, it is on all hands admitted, the characteristic of this material world, " the world of genesis and disintegration," as the Muhammadans call it ; but it is associated in their minds rather with the idea of corruption than of evolution. The deep-rooted Pessimism of Asia, and her exaltation of the Subjective over the Objective aspects of life, are two of her most constant and characteristic habits of mind. These ancient countries, which have lived so long, seen so much, and suffered so much, have lost that cheerful optimism which is the precious possession of the young ; they have seen so many empires succeed one another, so many governments—some better, some worse, mostly worse—pass away, that they have come to regard empire as a transient dream and government as a necessary evil.

When the head of the rebel Musʻab b. az-Zubayr was placed before the Umayyad Caliph ʻAbduʼl-Malik, one who was present said, " O Commander of the Faithful, I have seen a wonderful thing in this place." "And what is that ?" asked the Caliph. " I have seen," replied the man, "the head of al-Ḥusayn, the son of ʻAlí, laid before ʻUbayduʼlláh b. Ziyád, and then the head of ʻUbayduʼlláh b. Ziyád laid before al-Mukhtár, and then the head of al-Mukhtár laid before Musʻab b. az-Zubayr, and now I see the head of Musʻab b. az-Zubayr laid before thee[1]." Similarly Persia has seen the Assyrians displaced by the Medes, the Medes overthrown by the Achæmenians, the Achæmenians

---

[1] See al-Yaʻqúbíʼs history (ed. Houtsma, Leyden, 1883), vol. ii, p. 317.

by the Greeks, the Greeks by the Romans, the Romans by the Parthians, the Parthians by the Sásánians, and the Sásánians by the Arabs, not to mention the vicissitudes of later times. Is it wonderful that the sense, not of progress, but of mere "change and decay" should be deeply borne in upon them, and should find expression in such verses as :—

إِنَّمَا ٱلدُّنْيَا فَنَآءٌ لَيْسَ لِلدُّنْيَا ثُبُوتٌ،

إِنَّمَا ٱلدُّنْيَا كَبَيْتٍ نَسَجَتْهُ ٱلْعَنْكَبُوتُ،

*" Naught in the world shall endure ; naught shall abide 'neath
     the sun ;*
*Earth is a mansion as frail as the web which the spider hath
     spun."*

In our rare moments of humility and introspection, we Europeans sometimes reproach ourselves with our habit of scribbling on ancient monuments—a bad habit which we suppose to be peculiar to ourselves. Well, we may console ourselves with the knowledge that the Persians at any rate have the same habit, though the reflections they record are generally very different in tone from those which would occur to a European. We all know the sort of things which are to be found recorded in a visitor's book in any European hotel or place of interest, and on an ancient monument, which lends itself less readily to this sort of literary enterprise, I suppose the typical inscription of a European, if it exceeded the mere name, would run something like this : " Arrived here at 3.30 p.m. on such-and-such a date ; sun very hot, but a refreshing breeze. Food and accommodation on the way bad. [Signed] X. Y. Z." Contrast this with the following specimens written by Persian travellers on the ruins of Persepolis. The first runs :

  *" Where are the proud monarchs of yore ?   They multiplied
treasures which endured not, even as they endured not."*

The second is :—

*" Where are the kings who exercised dominion
Until the cup-bearer of Death gave them to drink of his cup ?
How many cities which have been built between the horizons
Lay ruined in the evening, while their dwellers were in the
    Abode of Death ?"*

Can you wonder if the spirit which expresses itself in these
and a thousand similar ways refuses to interest itself in Western
projects for the making of railways, the "opening up," as it is
called, of countries which only desire to remain closed, and the
creation of needs which are in many cases at least as much of
a curse as a blessing ? Persia has, I believe, the unique distinction of having introduced both the railway and the printing-
press, and of having, after fair trial, cast them out again, finding
the manuscript or lithograph as good as the printed book, and
the horse, ass and camel as suitable for her purposes as the
locomotive. Of course if you want to save time, the railway,
the telegraph, the book of reference and the index save it ; but
if you do not—if to-morrow and the day after are but the waves
on an ocean which, willing or not, you must needs cross, however little you like the passage—then they are useless. Yet it
is so hard for the West to understand this ; as hard, perhaps, as
it is for the East to understand why the West does not save,
but rather creates, labour, even unnecessary labour. Perhaps
by the time that Europe and America understand why Asia
does not want railways, Asia will understand why Europe and
America care about such things as cricket, football and golf.

On the whole, if one reflects a little, one cannot help being
sorry for Asia. She wants chiefly to be let alone, and that is
just what we will not do. Our press is always inventing what
are called "Questions" of the Near East, the Far East, and the
like, some of which, I see, are being treated of in these lectures.
These questions generally in essence amount to this : "So-and-
so has something which I want : how can I get it, and how can

I prevent other people from getting more than I do?" The point of view of So-and-so—the intended victim—must necessarily be somewhat different, and if he is weak, his only hope lies in creating such discord between those who propose to plunder him (or "open him up"—for it comes to the same thing) that they shall fall on one another instead of on him. This, in essence, is the policy, the natural, logical and only possible policy, of nations circumstanced like Turkey or China, both of which have pursued that policy with equal skill and tenacity of purpose. We talk in the West of the "Yellow Danger," the "Black Danger," and the like; but what are these compared with the "White Peril" which threatens Asia? To resist this Peril, a Peril ever more imminent and insistent, Asia will naturally use all the resources at her disposal, invoking such assistance as she can, from whatever quarter, and casting amongst her foes such apples of discord as may lie ready to her hand. The religious sentiment may, and doubtless will (since it is in Asia, as we have seen, one of the strongest sentiments) be called into play, as will the conservative or reactionary spirit, the prejudice against alien habits and ways of life, and all other forces which may avail to check the plunderers; but this is not Pan-Islamism, and I should regard an alliance between Turkey and China as at least as possible as an alliance between Turkey and Persia, though Persia is Muhammadan and China is not. Whatever Asia may do will be prompted by fear rather than religious fanaticism.

As regards Africa, the case, as I have said, is different; but concerning Africa I have not the necessary "*Anschauungen*" (again to borrow from my friend Dr Reich) to speak with any assurance. But a great militant Muhammadan movement, originating in Africa, would not, in my opinion, involve Asia to any great degree.

The question which I am supposed to answer in this lecture is, "Is Pan-Islamism a possibility?" I have tried to answer it, according to my knowledge and judgment; and the gist of the answer is this: It is less possible than Pan-Americanism, Pan-Germanism, and all the other " Pans " which I enumerated at the beginning of my lecture; and only a shade more possible than what I may perhaps be allowed to call Pan-Christianism; a thing of which, for all our " Progress," we are not yet within measurable distance[1].

[1] Only since I delivered this lecture have I been able to obtain and read the interesting paper entitled *La Mecque et le Panislamisme* contributed to the *Revue de l'Histoire des Religions* (Paris, Leroux, 1901 : tirage-à-part of 20 pages) by Snouck-Hurgronge, who is probably the greatest living authority in Europe on the Islám of to-day. While admitting that " there is no solidly organized Pan-Islamic propaganda," he adds : " there is certainly a very pronounced Pan-islamic tendency in all classes of Muhammadan society, of which tendency Constantinople is the political centre "; while " the religious centre of the movement is at Mecca." In face of such an authority I cannot feel the same certainty as to the correctness of the views expressed in this Lecture, which, nevertheless, I continue to hold.

ENGLAND AND THE UNITED STATES.

By T. J. Lawrence, LL.D.

LECTURE I.

We have recently rejoiced over the good feeling which manifested itself between British and Boers in South Africa as soon as hostilities between them ceased. We trust that the mutual respect which produced this feeling will continue, and enable the two races to work together side by side at the task of building up a realm which will be their common country.

No such feeling graced the end of the struggle between Great Britain and her revolted North American Colonies. In this case the parties to the war were not required to live under one government, and that the government of the victors. All they had to do was to go their separate ways without annoying or injuring one another. In this they failed conspicuously. It was not so much the war as the events which followed the war that permanently embittered feeling on both sides, and gave for generations afterwards to the relations between the two countries that character of distrust and acerbity which they have but lately lost, let us hope for ever. The rough common-sense of nations teaches them to overlook and forget unjustifiable deeds done in the heat of conflict, except perhaps in the cases, happily rare in modern warfare, where foul deceit or deliberate cruelty has been added to other elements of evil. But injury done by one state to another in cold blood, calculated breaches of good faith, insolence, attempts to stir up internal or external strife, constant suspicion in official quarters, and violent popular abuse—these things leave behind a heritage of hatred which the wisest of statesmen and the best of peace-makers find it difficult to dispel.   Unfortunately none of them were absent from the relations between Great Britain and the United States during the thirty years which followed the recognition of American Independence by the Treaty of 1783. Instead of wondering how it was that the two kindred peoples came to wage with one another the war of 1812, we should be filled with thankfulness because that was the only occasion on which they have come to blows since they existed together in the world as separate and independent states.

This seems a hard saying; but a short account of the events which followed the peace will justify it.   The Americans, full of exultation over their victory, and preoccupied with their domestic concerns, were supremely indifferent to the fact that, under the loose confederation into which they had entered, Congress lacked the power to perform many of the obligations it contracted with foreign powers.   England felt herself humiliated by the success of the colonists.   It was a terrible blow to her pride to find her armies foiled and her garrisons captured by raw militiamen fresh from the ploughtail, and ragged Continental soldiers, who did indeed know how to shoot, but whose drill would have driven into frenzy the barrack-square martinets of Europe.   Moreover some of the wisest thinkers of the time shared the conviction of King George III that "if any one branch of the Empire is allowed to throw off its dependency, the others will inevitably follow the example."   Nothing short of national ruin was anticipated by many; and added bitterness was caused by the reflection that the American triumph was largely due to France, the ancient enemy who had been utterly beaten and driven from the North of the American Continent in the war which ended only twenty years before.   To a nation in this temper, sick and sore at heart and full of gloomy apprehension for the future, any opportunity of retaliating upon those whom it regarded as the prime cause of its misery would be welcome; and it would certainly be in no mood to find excuses for failure on their part to fulfil obligations they had under-taken. That there were such failures is now generally ad-mitted. Professor Hart, of Harvard, in his *Formation of the Union*, says : "The Treaty of 1783 had provided that Congress would recommend to the States just treatment of the loyalists; the recommendation was made. Most of the States declined to comply : men who had been eminent before the Revolution returned to find themselves distrusted, and sometimes were mobbed; their estates, which in most cases had been con-fiscated, were withheld, and they could obtain no considera-tion." Undoubtedly the letter of the Treaty was kept when Congress made the earnest recommendations stipulated for in the fifth article. But such fulfilment was merely technical. The British Government imagined that it had obtained some measure of protection for the Royalists. It found itself put off instead with a useless formula. A more direct breach of faith occurred in another matter. The fourth article provided that creditors on either side should "meet with no lawful impedi-ment to the recovery" of their debts. What followed shall be told in the words of the distinguished American historian I have quoted before : "The action of the States in placing obstacles in the way of collecting debts due to British merchants before the Revolution was a vexatious infraction of the Treaty. Five States had passed laws for the partial or complete confiscation of such debts, and even after the Treaty Pennsylvania and Massachusetts passed similar Acts." These violations of international agreement were open and defiant; but the same may be said of acts done by the other side. When the British forces evacuated New York in November, 1783, they took away with them into freedom 3,000 slaves; whereas the seventh article of the Treaty declared that the soldiers of the King should be withdrawn "without causing any destruction, or carrying away any negroes or other property of the American inhabitants." If too much was removed from New York, too little was taken away from certain other places. The Treaty provided in the most emphatic terms for the evacuation of every "port, place and harbour" within the territory of the United States; but for more than ten years British troops remained in occupation of Detroit, Mackinaw, Niagara, and other posts along the Great Lakes. In April, 1794, the Canadian authorities took a still stronger step. Lieutenant-Governor Simcoe built a fort at the foot of the rapids of the Miami river, in the southern portion of what is now the State of Ohio, and was then territory in dispute between the Western borderers and the Indian tribes, but far within the boundary assigned to the United States by the Treaty of 1783. This fort was garrisoned by three companies of regular troops, and played for some time an important part in that policy of aiding the Indians with arms, and secretly inciting them to hostility, which was carried on for years with varying degrees of unfriendliness along the North-western border. The existence of such a policy has often been denied; but no candid person can read the fourth volume of that book of entrancing interest, President Roosevelt's *Winning of the West*, without coming to the conclusion that over-zealous under-lings constantly practised it, and in 1793 and 1794 it was carried out by high officials with much energy and little con-cealment. The statesmen of Great Britain, absorbed in a life and death struggle with Revolutionary France, never dreamed that the rough backwoodsmen, who were slowly driving the Indian tribes from their hunting-grounds, were laying in the wilderness the foundations of political communities which within a generation would become great and powerful States in the American Union. Nor is their ignorance a proof of folly. It was shared by most of the American statesmen of the time. The circumstances of the young Republic almost forced them to keep their eyes fixed on Europe. But the determining factors in the destiny of the American people were being worked out along the shores of the Great Lakes, in the valley of the Ohio, and down the long reaches of the far-stretching Mississippi. Even Jefferson, whose purchase of the Louisiana territory from France in 1803 opened the way to the Pacific and made the United States a great world-power, had no such objects in view. What he wanted was free access for his people to the Gulf of Mexico. He would have been content with New Orleans and a little strip of territory extending to the sea. Napoleon thrust upon him in addition the vast tracts to the West of the Mississippi.

But our object is, not to point out how the American Republic became great almost in spite of itself, but to shew why it commenced its career as a member of the family of nations on very bad terms with the State from which the great majority of its people had sprung. We have seen how the Treaty which recognised its Independence and fixed its boundaries was violated by both sides. Each exclaimed against the other; and each had fluent excuses for its own conduct. To the curious in such matters I recommend a study of the diplomatic correspondence of 1791—1793, between Jefferson, then the American Secretary of State, and Hammond, the newly-appointed British Minister to the United States. But when matters were discussed with a view to business, and not merely for effect, the fact that the Treaty had not been properly observed was taken for granted. Pitt told Gouverneur Morris that he wanted a new Treaty. Morris replied that " he did not see what better could be done than to perform the old one." Nothing is further from my purpose in this lecture than an attempt to apportion praise or blame. It is possible to make out some sort of a case for this, that, or the other breach of the stipulations. The surrender by the British of the interests of the negro slaves who had assisted them was disgraceful; and General Carleton's contention that the words of the Treaty could apply only to captured negroes, and not to those who had joined his forces of their own free will, if it was a quibble at all, was a quibble that furthered the cause of freedom, since it enabled him to carry away from New York in 1783 many black men who must otherwise have been left behind to slavery. A Congress which could not pay its soldiers or its judges spoke but the bare truth when it declared its inability to do more than recommend good treatment of the loyalists to States which habitually flouted its demands. Great Britain's retention of her hold on the Lake forts had the *lex talionis* in its favour. Still, when the process of justification has been carried as far as possible, the fact remains that important stipulations were habitually disregarded on both sides. Hence flowed constant irritation. Each nation firmly believed the other to be a deliberate wrong-doer, and hated it accordingly.

Soon fresh causes of dissension arose. In colonial times the Americans enjoyed the right to trade with other British colonies, and a profitable commerce sprung up between New England and the West Indies. Soon after the peace this was prohibited by the British Government, to the great loss and chagrin of the merchants of Massachusetts and New York. The war which broke out in 1793 between England and France was fraught with disastrous consequences to that prospect of improved relations between the United States and the mother-country, which rejoiced the hearts of men of good will for a little time when Jay's Treaty of 1794 warded off imminent hostilities. It provided for the withdrawal of the British garrisons from the frontier posts, and settled most of the other questions which had arisen out of the Treaty of 1783. But unfortunately it dealt either inadequately or not at all with the new difficulties to which I have just referred. Great Britain claimed the right to prevent American vessels from engaging in trade between the home ports of its enemies and their colonies, when such trade was thrown open as a war measure after having been rigorously prohibited in time of peace. This was called *The Rule of War of* 1756, and an arguable, if not a conclusive, case can be made for it in International Law. But the further claim of England to take out of American merchant vessels on the high seas sailors of British nationality, and impress them for her fighting navy was utterly untenable. Even in cases where there was no doubt about the national character of the seamen thus treated, it amounted to a forcible application of British law within the jurisdiction of the United States. When the nationality was doubtful or disputed, as was constantly the case, the injury was greater. And in the considerable number of instances where in wantonness or ignorance undoubted American citizens were taken, a most unwarrantable outrage was committed. It is true there was sometimes great provocation. Asylum was occasionally given to deserters by American captains; and the American flag was used not so much to protect the rights of Americans as to cover wrongs done to the British. American sympathy went out to France rather than to England in the Revolutionary wars. This was not to be wondered at, seeing that French blood and French treasure had been freely poured out in the cause of American independence a few years before. But it helped to keep alive feelings of anger among the English people, and stiffened them in their resolve to grant no concessions to a nation which disliked them and wished them ill. The tone of British diplomacy grew arrogant. The claims of Great Britain on the ocean increased. Napoleon, defeated at sea, started his "Continental System" with the design of ruining England by closing the Continent of Europe against British goods. Great Britain retaliated by her Orders in Council. The Berlin and Milan Decrees followed. The belligerents struck at one another through the sides of neutrals. America was the great neutral, and her trade suffered accordingly. When the warfare of retaliation was at its height France endeavoured to capture any vessel which traded with Great Britain or her colonies, or submitted to British search; while Great Britain forbade neutral vessels, with certain exceptions, to trade with any French port or any port under French influence. Nor were these threats idle.   In 1807 nearly 200 American vessels were captured by British cruisers.   The French rules were even more oppressive than the English ; and the conduct of Napoleon in his negotiations with the United States was marked by a duplicity which was absent from British diplomacy.   But Great Britain's power at sea rendered her better able than France to carry out her threats ; and she was in consequence denounced with more vigour and hated with more bitterness than her foe. Indeed the fate of the mother-country in her dealings with her greatest daughter has been to act as a sort of lightning-conductor, and draw off to herself the indignation which might with equal or greater justice have struck elsewhere.   It was so at the end of the eighteenth century, when Spain was far more deeply involved than England in intrigues to prevent the Western expansion of the new Republic.   It was so in the commercial difficulties of the early years of the nineteenth century, when France, the greater sinner, was popular, and England, the lesser, regarded as an unscrupulous tyrant.   And it was so in the middle of the century, when England's recognition of the belligerency of the Southern Confederacy was resented as an unwarrantable and unfriendly act, while little or nothing was said of similar recognition by other powers.   The unhappy beginning of the international relations between the two countries will account for this, but does not make it any the less unfortunate and deplorable.

The treatment we have just recounted stung the United States to the quick.   Even Jefferson, the most pacific of Presidents, was forced into retaliation when in 1807 the *Leopard*, a British cruiser, carried out by force a search of the *Chesapeake*, an American frigate, and took out of her several deserters from the royal navy.   This was done in defiance of the law of nations, which confines the exercise of the belligerent right of search to merchant vessels of neutrals ; and the exclusion of British men-of-war from American ports which followed cannot be regarded as too severe a retort.   Other measures were taken,

mostly of a feeble and tentative character. The most famous
of them, the embargo which forbade merchant vessels, whether
American or foreign, to leave the ports of the United States,
worked more harm to American than British commerce. It
was intensely unpopular among the commercial classes in
whose interests it was resorted to. They were furious when
they saw their export trade reduced by four-fifths in one year ;
and when the price of wheat fell more than half the agriculturists supported them in their demand for repeal. A
substitute was found in a measure excluding British and French
vessels from American ports ; and the hated embargo went the
way of unpopular laws in a democratic country. Negotiations
with Great Britain followed ; and it was thought at one time
that an agreement had been reached on the basis of the withdrawal of the Orders in Council. But the British Minister had
exceeded his instructions. He was ordered home and another
sent. Then followed such a series of incidents as are happily
rare in the intercourse of civilised States. The etiquette of the
Presidential dinner-table gave rise to undignified squabbles, in
which the names of ladies were freely used. These, together
with accusations on the one side of trickery and insult, and on
the other of gross insolence and discourtesy, led up to a refusal
to do business with the new envoy and a demand for his
immediate recall. The failure of Mr Erskine's negotiations and
the practical dismissal of Mr Jackson were the forerunners of
the war of 1812. In 1811 reparation was at last made for the
attack on the *Chesapeake*, but the tardiness of the concession
deprived it of all grace. Like the withdrawal of the Orders in
Council two days before the outbreak of hostilities, it was too
late. The American Government was slow in resolving upon
war, but when once it had made up its mind, it was not to be
turned from its purpose by a belated surrender of some of the
points at issue. Few acts of greater unwisdom have been perpetrated in the course of history. Great Britain brought upon
her back a new foe in the crisis of her life-and-death struggle

with Napoleon. The United States, in the supposed interests of its sea-borne commerce, but in the face of the fierce opposition of its commercial classes, made a powerful diversion in favour of France at a time when the success of the Imperial armies in their invasion of Russia meant the closure of the whole continent of Europe to American trade. Had the Americans prevailed, their last state would indeed have been worse than their first. Had England conquered, the North American continent would have been covered by weak confederations, hostile to each other and a prey to the intrigues which were filling the Old World with misery and bloodshed.

The war itself was by no means the procession of triumphs it is represented in some American histories. Neither, on the other hand, was it the easy success for Great Britain that her Government and people anticipated. They learned in it the time-honoured lesson, which comes home to them with the force of a new revelation about once in each half-century, that, since wars are fought with firearms, those who can shoot best and possess the best weapons to shoot with, are exceedingly likely to prevail, even though they are wofully deficient in the matter of uniform and their supplies of pipe-clay are lamentably small.

The Peace of 1814 is best described as a disappointment for both sides. The Americans gained by it literally nothing, unless the reference of several frontier disputes to arbitration be accounted a national gain. Not a word was said about impressment. The question of the Fisheries was not touched. No commercial facilities were granted. The practice of blockade was not regulated. There was no promise of indemnity for illegal captures. The British were in much the same position. They had demanded a rectification of the North-West frontier in their own interests, and the carving out of a territory for their Indian allies from the dominions of the United States. They obtained neither. The basis of the

Treaty was the *status quo ante bellum*. It might have been reduced to one Article :

"Whereas Great Britain and the United States of America are tired of fighting, it is agreed that they shall leave off and be at peace from the date of the ratification of this Treaty."

But though the Treaty did little directly, the war did much indirectly. It convinced the statesmen of Europe that the United States was a factor to be reckoned with in international complications. Great Britain felt a new respect for the brave and skilful seamen who had captured her frigates on the Atlantic, beaten her flotilla on Lake Erie, and preyed upon her commerce even in Dublin Bay. There was no denying the warlike prowess of the rough militiamen of Kentucky and the backwoodsmen from Tennessee, whose deadly fire drove back the Peninsular veterans of Pakenham from the cotton-bale entrenchments of New Orleans. On the other hand the Americans learned by sad experience that the conquest of Canada was a task beyond their power, and found that the strength of England at sea, when once it was fairly brought into action, was far more than a match for their infant navy. The successes and failures of the struggle were fairly equal on both sides ; and each thought far better of the other than it did at the commencement of the war. The capture of Washington by the British in August, 1814, was a brilliant feat of arms, marred by the burning of the Government buildings and the White House, an utterly unwarrantable act, even though the Americans had set the example by destroying a few Canadian villages. The memory of it has done something since to keep up the old feelings of irritation ; but the wound it caused has been almost healed under the influence of sober thoughts and friendly feeling. The best remark concerning it I have ever read is to be found in a note at the foot of a page in Montgomery's *American History*, "The truth is that both sides perpetrated many acts which time should make both forget and forgive."

We have seen how the Treaty of 1814 settled nothing. Yet it was the beginning of a long era of settlement. Its fate in this respect was happily just the opposite of the Treaty of 1783, which, purporting to settle all things, was the beginning of a long era of unsettlement. Unforeseen events created trouble then. Unforeseen events put an end to trouble thirty-two years later. Napoleon fell, and with his disappearance his Continental System disappeared also. Peace put an end to oppressive Decrees and Orders in Council. American trade sprang forward by leaps and bounds. In two years the revenue of the central government increased more than fourfold. With the cessation of maritime warfare the wrongs connected with impressment vanished. Great Britain never formally surrendered her claim to take her seamen out of American vessels; but she had no further occasion to enforce it; and by-and-by the disuse of the barbarous practice of impressment as a means of recruiting for the royal navy caused the cessation of all its unhappy consequences.

But in the new epoch of appeasement man did not play a merely passive part. Jay's Treaty of 1794 had provided for the appointment of Boards of Commissioners to settle by a process akin to arbitration certain territorial and commercial questions. This excellent example was followed in 1814, when no less than four boundary disputes were referred to Commissions. The first was concerned with several islands in the Bay of Passamaquoddy and one in the Bay of Fundy, which were claimed by both the United States and Nova Scotia. In 1817 three of them were adjudged to the Republic and the rest to Great Britain. The second referred to the boundary from the source of the river Saint Croix to the St Lawrence. The Commissioners disagreed, and in 1821 made separate reports. The matter was then referred according to the terms of the Treaty to a friendly sovereign. The King of the Netherlands was chosen in 1827, and in 1831 he made an award which went in some respects outside the terms of the reference. On this ground it was rejected by the Senate of the United States, and fresh negotiations with Great Britain were initiated. After several failures the matter was at last settled by the Ashburton Treaty of 1842. The line then agreed upon was fiercely denounced on both sides; but was at any rate better than the war which would in all probability have resulted had the question of the North-Eastern boundary been left open much longer. The third and fourth matters were connected with the details of the water-boundaries along the line of the St Lawrence and the Great Lakes, and these the Commissioners were able to settle in a satisfactory manner in 1822.

Nothing is more remarkable in the history of the relations between Great Britain and the United States than the frequent resort to arbitral or quasi-arbitral processes to settle differences great and small, unless it be the light-hearted way in which differences have been created by sheer ignorance or utter carelessness. It will hardly be believed, but it is nevertheless quite true, that the plenipotentiaries who negotiated the Treaty of 1783, in determining the boundaries of the United States used a map of 1755 called Mitchell's Map, but, as Professor J. Bassett Moore tells us in his monumental work on the *International Arbitrations of the United States*, "Though the same map was used by both sides in the negotiations, on no copy of it were the lines intended by the negotiators jointly and formally entered, and no map was officially attached to the Treaty." Hence arose endless trouble, especially in 1842 and 1843, during and after the negotiation of the Ashburton Treaty, when discoveries of conflicting maps, marked with irreconcilable boundaries on the frontier then in dispute between Nova Scotia and Maine, caused great dissatisfaction with the line agreed to in the Treaty, and led to charges of sharp practice, which produced much irritation.

The first and the last of the now settled boundary questions will provide us with further illustrations. In 1783 the frontier of the United States was to commence at the "north-west angle of Nova Scotia," which was defined as "that angle which is formed by a line drawn due north from the source of the Saint Croix River to the Highlands." Hardly was the Treaty ratified than it appeared there was no Saint Croix River. The name had been given to some stream, it was difficult to say which, by the early French explorers. Map-makers had used it indiscriminately. As the country was settled and surveyed it turned out that no map was accurate, the famous map of Mitchell being no exception. Great Britain claimed the Schoodiac as the true Saint Croix, the United States the Magaguadavic. Jay's Treaty referred the question to three Commissioners, who were to settle what river was "truly intended" by the Treaty of 1783. In two years they pursued their investigations, and came at length to the conclusion that the Schoodiac was "the river truly intended under the name of the river Saint Croix in the said Treaty." The decision itself was a happy settlement of a difficult question, but the phraseology in which the Commissioners were obliged to clothe it was absurd; for the evidence before them clearly shewed that the intentions of the negotiators of 1783, two of whom they examined, went no further than the non-existent Saint Croix on the inaccurate map of Mitchell. Our final example of the light-hearted inaccuracy of which I spoke, and its unfortunate effects on the subsequent relations between the two countries, shall be taken from the agreement as to the Oregon question in the Treaty of 1846. By its first article the frontier line was to be drawn along the "forty-ninth parallel of north latitude to the middle of the channel which separates the continent from Vancouver's Island, and thence southerly through the middle of the said channel, and of Fuca's Straits, to the Pacific Ocean." It turned out that, instead of there being but one channel separating the continent from Vancouver's Island, there were several. The United States, of course, immediately claimed that the line should pass through that which was nearest to Vancouver's Island, while, equally of course, Great Britain contended that the passage closest to American territory was the true one. Thus the national ownership of a number of the small islands which dotted the intervening space was placed in dispute; and, as citizens of both countries were settling upon them, awkward complications sometimes arose. In 1859 a pig came very near to bulking as big in history as the geese which saved the Roman Capitol from the barbarians. He lived a blameless life on San Juan Island, as a cherished possession of the Hudson's Bay Company. One day he was found dead. An American squatter on the island was accused of having shot him; and the real or supposed culprit was threatened with arrest and trial under British law. To prevent this the island was occupied by American troops, and the Commander-in-chief of the forces of the United States was hurried to the spot. When there he arranged with the British authorities for a joint military occupation of the island by the armed forces of the two powers; and the danger of a collision was for the time averted. Playing with fire is proverbially dangerous. Playing with pigs seems equally so in some parts of the world. The dispute about the channel lingered on for years, till the famous Alabama Treaty of 1871 referred it to the arbitration of the Emperor of Germany, who decided in favour of the claim of the United States to the Haro Channel. Partitioning the unknown with a light heart and a bad map is a process which causes in the long run much more trouble than it saves at the time. If the two Governments could manage to acquire the habit of consulting experts before they make their agreements, their negotiations might perhaps take a little longer time to complete; but when completed they would not be found useless, and require to be gone through over again several times to the accompaniment of violent popular agitations.

We have already seen that the marvellous westward expansion of the United States was the greatest factor in the development of the internal political life of the nation. It was also a fertile source of international complications. At the end of the war of independence, France and Spain desired to bound the new Republic by the Alleghanies. But in this matter Great Britain, the enemy, proved more friendly than the two allies, and the frontier line was drawn at the Mississippi by the Treaty of 1783. But it did not reach to the sea ; and as the advancing wave of settlement rolled over Kentucky and covered Ohio and Tennessee, it was felt that New Orleans could not long remain in the hands of a foreign power which refused to give a right of free navigation of the great river down to the Gulf of Mexico. When the Creole city and the whole vast territory of Louisiana passed in 1800 from weak Spain to all-conquering France, the rough and ready Westerners came rapidly to the conviction that the strong government of Napoleon would interpose a formidable barrier, not only to their trade, but to their further advance into the wilderness. Spain they might tolerate, because they knew they could disregard its threats and treat its sleepy officials with contempt. But France, entrenched on the banks of the lower Mississippi, and holding the rich lands beyond in its iron grip, would throttle the young and vigorous communities which were already sending their advance-guard of hardy pioneers across the great stream. Even Jefferson saw the seriousness of the situation, in spite of his French proclivities, though he was far from grasping its full significance. In 1802 he wrote that from the moment France took possession of New Orleans "we must marry ourselves to the British fleet and nation." To avoid this to him most undesirable consummation, and to satisfy his Western supporters, he opened the negotiations which ended, as we have already seen, in the purchase of all French Louisiana for fifteen million dollars in 1803. Hardly knowing what he did, and caring only for free access to the southern sea, he doubled the area of the United States, opened the way to the Pacific for her Lewises and her Fremonts, and rendered it possible for an English poet to sing of her as

> "Girt with two oceans, crowned with Arctic snow,
>   Sandalled with shining seas of Mexico."

It has been given to but few men to change the history of the world without suspecting that anything wonderful had been achieved; and conspicuous among those few stands the great American democrat.

One consequence of the cession was a vigorous crop of boundary questions. Spain then possessed the Floridas; and no man knew where Louisiana ended and West Florida began. Texas, too, was hers; and its limits were vague and disputable. In the far West the untrodden wilderness was somewhere and in some way divisible between the heirs of France and the owners of Mexico. And in the extreme North the Hudson Bay Company kept jealous watch at all its posts, lest enterprising Yankee traders should spoil its markets and claim for the United States the territory on which they settled. The disputes with Spain were terminated by a series of agreements which culminated in the Treaty of 1819. It was a triumph of American diplomacy; for not only did the young Republic acquire Florida by purchase and secure a favourable boundary-line from the Gulf of Mexico to the 42nd parallel of north latitude, and from thence to the Pacific, but John Quincy Adams, the American negotiator, induced the Spanish Government to cede to the United States all its claims to the territory north of the line agreed upon, and thus obtained for his country fresh grounds on which to base its arguments in the controversy which had already broken out with Great Britain. The vast district in dispute was called Oregon, and the controversy is known in history as the Oregon Boundary Question. A full account of it would occupy more than all the time at our disposal, and lead us through complicated differences with regard to such matters of fact as the nature of Drake's discoveries, and the existence of certain Spanish navigators who are alleged to have seen and done marvellous things along the coast of what is now British Columbia. We must therefore be content with a brief outline.

The Mississippi having ceased to be a boundary river in 1803, it became necessary to define the frontier between the new possessions of the United States in the North-West and the

British dominions which formed the territory of the Hudson's Bay Company. This was done in 1818, but only in part. From the most north-westerly point of the Lake of the Woods to the Rocky Mountains the boundary was to run along the forty-ninth parallel of north latitude. But with regard to the country west of the Rockies, the Plenipotentiaries were unable to come to an agreement, and under the name of Oregon it remained in dispute for a long time. All they could do was to throw the district open for a period of ten years to the joint occupancy of the citizens of both States. Other attempts at a settlement were made at frequent intervals; but all failed. In 1827 the outcome of long negotiations at London was simply the extension of the joint occupation for an indefinite period, each party having the right to terminate it on giving a year's notice to the other. The claim of the United States varied for a time, but after the Treaty of 1824 with Russia it settled down to the line of 54° 40′ north latitude. On several occasions, however, it was intimated that a frontier drawn along the 49th parallel would be accepted as a compromise. The chief anxiety of Great Britain was to obtain the Columbia river; but she offered to consent to the line of the 49th parallel up to the point where it strikes that stream, if the boundary were continued along the middle channel to the Pacific Ocean. The records of travel were ransacked by both sides for proofs of first discovery and first settlement, and learned arguments were exchanged on moot points of the international law of occupation and the title gained thereby. Meanwhile the white-tilted emigrant-waggons were crowding in long procession along the Oregon trail. Fierce fights with the Indian tribes were common incidents of the march; and when at last the land of promise was reached the agents of the Hudson's Bay Company often took care to place all possible difficulties in the way of the new-comers. The Company was violently denounced in Congress. The constant cry throughout the land was, " Why are foreigners permitted to domineer over American citizens ? " And at last the programme of the successful party in a Presidential election was crystallised into the famous formula " Fifty-four-forty or fight." But the responsibilities of office sobered the fire-eaters ; and in 1846 President Polk agreed to a treaty which ran the boundary along the 49th parallel, not to the sea, but "to the middle of the channel which separates the continent from Vancouver's Island," and from thence around the southern shore of the island to the Pacific. Thus Great Britain gave up the mouth and lower waters of the Columbia river, though she gained for her subjects by the Treaty the right to navigate it freely. On the other hand she obtained the whole of Vancouver's Island, while the United States gave up the line of 54° 40′ for which a large portion of the nation had professed itself ready to go to war not long before. The settlement was so eminently reasonable that we may well wonder why it was not arrived at sooner. The only point connected with it which caused subsequent trouble arose from the vagueness of the description of the channel through which the boundary line was to be carried to the open ocean. We have already seen how this was settled by the Emperor of Germany in 1872.

By this last transaction the final touch was put to the task of delimiting the northern frontier of the United States. A long series of controversies with Great Britain was ended, and a fresh sanction given to the principle of arbitration. More than once in the course of the ninety years which had elapsed since the great American Republic commenced its independent existence had the two countries come near to blows over questions of disputed territory. Earth-hunger had been a fertile source of quarrels ; but the influences that made for peace had been more potent. The purchase of Alaska by the United States has added yet another boundary controversy to the long list of those which have already arisen. The peaceable settlement of these difficulties of the past gives confidence to the hope that the near future will see the north-western frontier of British Columbia determined without the horror and crime of a war between two free and kindred peoples.

LECTURE II.

LEAVING behind the boundary disputes dealt with in the previous lecture, we will now turn our attention to another set of differences. When the political separation came in 1783 the most valuable of the fishing grounds which had been the common heritage of all the American subjects of the British crown were situated in the waters of those provinces which still remained faithful to their old allegiance. The Americans naturally desired access to them as before. The British as naturally wished to keep them for themselves. The matter principally concerned the New England States; and John Adams, as their special representative among the Plenipotentiaries, fought hard for the "right of fishing." He gained by the third article of the Treaty "the liberty to take fish of every kind on such part of the coast of Newfoundland as British fishermen shall use......and also on the coasts, bays and creeks of all other of his Britannic Majesty's dominions in America." During the war of 1812 the hardy seamen of Maine and Massachusetts made no peaceful visits to British territorial waters, and in the Treaty which ended it the fisheries were not mentioned. A controversy soon arose upon the subject. The United States claimed that the rights they possessed before the Revolution continued in existence after they had become independent. Treaties might define them and provide for their exercise, but did not create them. War might put an end to them for the time; but they revived with the conclusion of peace. England, on the other hand, held fast to the contention that privileges reserved to British subjects could not be claimed by Americans as of right after they had cut themselves adrift from Great Britain and ceased to owe allegiance to its king. But what the mother-country would not concede as a right, she was willing to grant as a favour, but with certain limitations and subject to various conditions. The Treaty of 1818 embodied these views. It granted a "liberty," not a right, and it carefully restricted the exercise of that "liberty" to definite portions of the coast of Newfoundland and Labrador. Moreover in giving permission to American fishermen to land and cure fish on any unsettled part of these coasts, it provided that when the parts in question became settled they should not continue to be used without previous agreement with the settlers. It is easy to see that this provision would be fruitful of trouble as the country peopled up. Moreover the constant use of the phrase "bays, harbours and creeks," or some variant of it, gave rise before long to the question, What is a bay? To this day that question has never been satisfactorily answered. When liberty of fishing is granted in a bay it tends to become very large, at the expense of the territorial waters. When fishermen are excluded from a bay, those who are shut out are apt to claim that what the excluders deem a bay is really a portion of the open sea. Thus it was that difficulties innumerable arose; and they were soon complicated by other matters, such as the purchase of bait and the binding force of local laws. Twice they were dealt with by stipulations based upon reciprocal concession of privileges. But the Reciprocity Treaty of 1854 came to an end in 1866; and the fishery clauses in the Treaty of 1871 were "denounced" by the United States Government in 1883, and ceased to exist in 1885. Since then we have muddled on as best we could. The failure of subsequent agreements has revived the Treaty of 1818, which is largely obsolete and inapplicable. In 1887 Mr Chamberlain, the present Colonial Secretary, went to

America as an agent of the British Government, and succeeded in negotiating a Treaty which would have settled all disputes. But it failed to satisfy the Senate of the United States, and was refused ratification. Since then the fisheries have been carried on under a less formal agreement, called a *modus vivendi*, which rests on executive sanction only, and could at any moment be terminated by either side. There is a good deal of loose gunpowder strewn about Canadian shores; and it is much to be hoped that some just international agreement will soon render it innocuous.

The best security for peace is a strong desire on both sides to be peaceful; and this cannot exist without friendly feeling and mutual respect. At the beginning of the nineteenth century there was little of either between Great Britain and the United States. We have seen how relations grew less strained as the century advanced, and after the war of 1812 had cleared the air. The Clayton-Bulwer Treaty of 1850 is a proof of better feeling. The two countries had so far drawn together that they felt themselves able to co-operate for an important international purpose. The construction of a railway across the Isthmus of Panama had been begun, and plans were afoot for the building of a ship-canal from ocean to ocean. At that time the route through the territory of the Republic of Nicaragua was most in favour, and it seemed likely that a serious attempt would soon be made to cut a canal along it. Great Britain and the United States therefore entered into an agreement by treaty to co-operate in furthering the construction of the canal, to guarantee its neutrality when made, and to invite other powers to join them in bringing about this neutral-isation. Neither party was to exercise any exclusive control over the canal, or erect or maintain any fortifications com-manding it. Each was bound not to make use of any protectorate or alliance for the purpose of erecting or main-taining such fortifications, " or of occupying, fortifying or colonising Nicaragua, Costa Rica, the Mosquito Coast, or any part of Central America, or of assuming or exercising dominion over the same." The eighth article of the Treaty applies the principles set forth in the preceding seven to any other canal that might be cut, whether by the Panama route or elsewhere. Subsequent events gave this article a preponderating importance. The Nicaraguan plan dropped, was revived, and has now dropped again. There is little doubt that the canal, when made, will follow the line of the abandoned works of M. de Lesseps, and be cut through the narrowest part of the Isthmus.

Soon after the agreement of 1850 was made, a dispute arose as to the proper interpretation of the clause which forbade the exercise of dominion over any part of Central America. Great Britain possessed a group of islands off the coast of Honduras called the Bay Islands. She also exercised a Protectorate over the Indians of the Mosquito Coast. The United States contended that she was bound to give up these possessions, while the British Government maintained that the Treaty applied only to future acquisitions. At last, however, she ceded the Bay Islands to the Republic of Honduras. This was in 1859, and early in 1860 she surrendered her Protectorate over the Mosquito Indians. President Buchanan, in his annual Message to Congress, spoke of these arrangements as constituting "a final settlement entirely satisfactory to this Government." There can, I think, be no doubt that the Treaty was deemed, at the time it was made and for many years afterwards, a wise and statesmanlike document. The reason for the great change of feeling with regard to it which afterwards came over the American people will be stated later in this lecture.

We now come to a period in the relations between Great Britain and the United States which no person sincerely desirous of amity between them can look back upon without regret. In 1861 the great Civil War broke out, and for four years the men of the North and the men of the South were engaged in mutual destruction. When the struggle was at its height a million soldiers wore the blue uniform of the North, and the Southern "Boys in Grey" reached to more than half that number. They fought out their fight with a courage and tenacity worthy of the greatness of the issues at stake, and the virility of that strenuous race which in little more than two generations had subdued a continent, and carried its homes and its institutions from the Ohio to the Golden Gate, from Portland in Maine to Portland in Oregon. It was my lot some years ago to talk with many of the heroes and heroines of that awful time. I saw the victorious banners of the Massachusetts volunteers hanging, honoured and revered, in the State House at Boston. I saw the Southern veterans bear their tattered battle-flags through the streets of Richmond when they laid the remains of their President to rest in the capital they had so well defended. The long green mounds raised in Oakwood Cemetery over the remains of the "Unknown" dead of Antietam, and Chancellorsville, and Gettysburg, impressed me more than anything else with the truth of the sad, proud Southern poem, which tells how

> "All over our loved Virginia
>   From the mountains to the sea,
> In nameless graves by men forgot
>   Sleep the soldiers who followed Lee—
> Our Southern dead who made for Lee
>   His imperishable name,
> And wrote it in their own hearts' blood
>   High on the arch of fame."

And, as I heard in the North, from the lips of actors in the scenes they described, stories of life and liberty risked to help the escape of fugitive slaves into free Canada, of months of long-drawn agony in Libby prison or exultant marching with Sherman through Georgia to the sea, I began to realise something of that burning enthusiasm that sent to the front such unemotional beings as the woodmen of Maine and the trappers of Wisconsin, chanting Julia Ward Howe's magnificent *Battle Hymn of the Republic*:

> "In the beauty of the lilies Christ was born across the sea,
> With a glory in His bosom that transfigures you and me;
> As He died to make men holy, let us die to make men free,
> And work till Jesus calls.
> > Glory, glory, halleluia!
> > Glory, glory, halleluia!
> > We'll work till Jesus calls."

For the best men and women of the North it was indeed a holy war. Loyalty to the flag, and all the flag symbolised, was with them almost a religion. And the flag had been flouted and fired upon; the Union had been broken; the Constitution, as they understood it, violated. Next to love of the Union came with them hatred of slavery, and the whole South was in arms to preserve it, making it part and parcel of the constitution of the Confederacy in the words, "No law...... denying or impairing the right of property in negro slaves shall be passed." To preserve the Union, to free the slaves, men offered up their lives and women their broken hearts. I would not for one moment be taken to imply that enthusiasm and self-sacrifice were peculiar to the North. I have talked with sweet, low-voiced Southern women, who bore uncomplainingly cold and privation, while they made their own dresses into clothing for their sick and famished soldiery. And I know full well how Pemberton's men held Vicksburg till only rats were left for meat, and how the shoeless veterans who surrendered at Appomattox had marched and fought for days on nothing but parched corn. It is all over now; and those who faced each other so bravely on a hundred battlefields are loyal fellow-citizens of the greatest Republic the world has ever seen. But it was very different then; and the men who stood for national unity and human freedom were filled with bitter anger against England when they found that her sympathies were mainly given to the South. The press of Great Britain had much to answer for. It gave itself airs of vast superiority. It magnified all that was little, and sordid, and mean in the great tragedy, and steadily closed its eyes to the nobler elements which abounded. To earnest Northern abolitionists it seemed as if we, here in the old home of freedom, could find nothing better to do in the agony of a kindred nation than look on and jeer. How strong that feeling was, how long it endured, one little bit of my own experience will illustrate. At Cincinnati a dear old lady entertained me most hospitably, not because I had any claim upon her, but simply because I was a wandering Britisher whom chance had thrown among the circle of her friends. With true American kindness she not only welcomed me to her table and made me free of her house, but planned excursions for me and drove me in her carriage across the Ohio into beautiful Kentucky. She loved the old country; but for all that she could not forgive it what she deemed its partisanship for the South in the Civil War, and still carefully kept a scrapbook full of extracts from the *Times* and other English papers, sneering at the North and predicting the triumph of the Confederacy. I tried to explain that this attitude of mind had been by no means universal in England, that, though the governing class were largely Southern in their sympathies, the predominant opinion among the artisans had been in favour of the North; but my friend would not be comforted. There was the book and the testimony, and I could not gainsay it.

Multiply my hospitable lady by many millions, and throw into her tenacious feminine regrets a strong dash of masculine indignation, and you get the feeling towards Great Britain which dominated the mind of the North during the Civil War and for many years afterwards. Our Government strove honestly to be neutral; but it was constantly accused of studied partiality towards the South. We recognised the belligerency of the Confederates, as did most other powers. It was impossible to do otherwise, for that indeed a most notable war was being waged by both land and sea was a fact as evident as the sun at noon. But though we took official cognisance of what was patent to all the world, we steadfastly resisted the blandishments of Louis Napoleon, Emperor of the French, who desired us to join with him in a recognition of the Confederacy as an independent State. Such a recognition would have been a terrible blow to the cause of the North; and that it did not take place is due to the British Government. Yet we were held up to execration, and France was but mildly rebuked. But I do not for one moment attempt to maintain the untenable proposition that the Government of Washington had no good cause of complaint against Great Britain. Southern cruisers were built in our ports, escaped from them by eluding the vigilance of authorities who were sometimes not unwilling to be hoodwinked, received at some appointed rendezvous their armament and fighting crew, and then proceeded to depredate upon American commerce under the authority of commissions signed by Jefferson Davis, the President of the Southern Confederacy. No wonder the North complained bitterly, and accused the English ministry of a lack of " due diligence " in their efforts to prevent " the fitting out, arming, or equipping " of the *Alabama* and her sister cruisers. It is impossible to enter now into the details of the controversy that followed. Part of it was very technical, and involved difficult and doubtful points of International Law. The two powers took different views of the nature and extent of the duties of a neutral state. Great Britain held that she was not bound to prevent the departure from her waters of a vessel built in them for a belligerent, unless it attempted to leave them a finished instrument of warfare, ready at once to commence hostilities against its foe. She also held that when such a vessel had escaped, and received its commission as a ship of war, it was entitled to all the immunities granted by the law of nations to public vessels, and could not be arrested on any subsequent visit to the ports of the State where it had been originally equipped. The United States maintained that, if the intent to make war was clearly shewn, the neutral was bound to prevent the escape of the vessel, whether its equipment was complete or rudimentary, and that the receipt of the commission, which was really the completion of the offence, could not operate to protect the ship from the punishment of its guilt. Over and above these two great questions of International Law there were others also, some legal, some practical, and some mixed questions of law and fact, such, for instance, as these :—What is the measure of due diligence ? Did the British authorities at Liverpool exert themselves as they ought to prevent the escape of the *Alabama* ? Should the *Shenandoah* have been prevented from leaving Melbourne on her cruise to the whale-fisheries off Cape Horn ? There were two sides to all these questions, except perhaps the last but one ; but at the time no Northerner would believe it. To him the British Government wilfully sinned against light in order to bolster up the cause of the slave-holding Confederacy. To the British public, on the other hand, he and his Department of State appeared as strident voices perpetually raised in unreasonable complaint. An examination of the literature of the controversy would be the work of a life-time. To attempt it in a lecture would provoke either groans or laughter. But I may perhaps be allowed to quote from my own book on International Law the few sentences in which I attempted to give a summary view of the general dispute. " On one side we find a tendency to rely upon technical subtleties and substitute legal quibbles for substantial justice, and on the other a disposition to magnify grounds of offence and seek causes of quarrel in acts hitherto deemed perfectly innocent. It cannot be doubted that in the matter of arming and equipping belligerent ships in neutral waters, the older authorities, including several who belonged to the United States, supported the British view. It is equally true that many modern writers hold the stricter doctrine put forward in the controversy by the American advocates...... The explanation of the puzzle is that no certainty existed, or could exist at the time in question. Both doctrine and practice were in a transition state. The older rule no longer satisfied the awakened conscience of civilised nations ; but no clear and definite usage had grown up to provide a substitute for it."

For years the relations between the two powers were in a most critical condition. In 1861 Queen Victoria and the late Prince Consort earned the blessing of the peace-makers by toning down a warlike despatch on the *Trent* affair, and thus rendering it possible for the United States to recede from an untenable position without loss of self-respect. In 1863 occurred the case of the ironclad rams, built by Laird and Co., of Birkenhead, ostensibly for a French firm, but really for the Confederate Government. Mr Adams, the American Minister, supplied proofs of this to the British Foreign Office, and sent in remonstrance after remonstrance. In the last of these, written to Earl Russell, then our Secretary of State for Foreign Affairs, when one of the rams was on the point of departure, he says in all seriousness and after having received special instructions from his Government, "It would be superfluous for me to point out to your lordship that this is war." Fortunately the law officers of the Crown found the evidence sufficient. The rams were seized, and then bought by the British Government for the royal navy. In 1869 Mr Charles Sumner made a great speech before the American Senate, in which he maintained that Great Britain was responsible for doubling the duration of the war, and for all the national losses caused to the United States by the diminution of sea-borne commerce, the destruction of the carrying trade, and the decreased tonnage of the merchant navy. Having thus added some scores of millions to the bill England was expected to pay, he proceeded on a subsequent occasion, when asked by Mr Fish, the Secretary of State, for his opinion on certain unofficial proposals for a settlement, to suggest that Great Britain should abandon Canada as a preliminary, after which other matters might, he thought, be disposed of amicably and thoroughly! We have to remember that Mr Sumner was no irresponsible politician, eager for notoriety, and careless of consequences as long as he obtained it. He was a great Abolitionist leader, a senator, and the chairman of the Senate Committee on Foreign Relations. He represented a force which had to be reckoned with; and it is mainly due to him that, as we shall soon see, the Geneva Arbitration was nearly wrecked on the rock of the consequential or indirect damages. Fortunately he did not succeed in blocking the way to renewed harmony. At that time wise men controlled the destiny of the nations on either side of the Atlantic. After the failure of several attempts to negotiate a settlement, five British Commissioners were sent to Washington, where they met a similar body appointed to act for the United States. The High Joint Commissioners, as they were called, held thirty-seven sittings, in the course of which they succeeded in drawing up a Treaty for the settlement of all outstanding disputes between the two countries. The demands upon Great Britain on account of the depredations of the Southern cruisers had become known generically as the Alabama claims. These were the principal subjects of discussion, and it was proposed to refer them to arbitration. The difficulty as to the divergent views of neutral obligations held by the two Governments was got over by the sixth article of the Treaty, which laid down three rules for the guidance of the arbitrators. Great Britain placed on record her opinion that these rules were not in force as part of International Law at the time when the claims arose, but consented to be judged by them in order to bring the controversy to an amicable conclusion. Both parties agreed to observe them in future, and to bring them to the notice of other powers with a view to their general adoption. This last undertaking has never been carried out, on account of disputes as to the meaning of some parts of the rules, and the difficulty of reaching an agreement upon them.

The arbitrators appointed under the Treaty met at Geneva

in 1872. The British and American Governments presented cases and counter cases, and both were represented by counsel. The proceedings were nearly wrecked at the beginning, when it was discovered that claims for the prolongation of the war and other national losses were included in the American case. Great Britain at once objected; and her Government asserted that such claims were excluded by the words of the Treaty. It seems clear that the British Commissioners imagined that they were so excluded, while the American Commissioners, in equal good faith, imagined they were not. A fresh controversy was thus engrafted upon the original dispute, and, as neither side would give way, it looked as if the arbitration would lapse. Fortunately the arbitrators found a solution of the difficulty. They met and came to the conclusion that the indirect claims did not constitute "good foundation for an award of compensation or computation of damages between nations." The great obstacle being thus removed, the arbitration proceeded, and on September 14, 1872, the arbitrators gave their award. It decided in favour of the United States on most of the points at issue, and gave damages against Great Britain to the amount of three million pounds. The money was promptly paid; but a large section of the British public was profoundly dissatisfied with the award, and Sir Alexander Cockburn, the British arbitrator, drew up an elaborate dissentient judgment. Yet the real triumph belonged, not to the United States, still less to Great Britain, but to the principles of justice and brotherhood. It was far more important to settle by arbitration an irritating controversy, which had more than once driven the two nations to the verge of war, than to secure an absolutely flawless judgment. There are some propositions in the award to which most international jurists would refuse their assent; but the fact that it was made and submitted to testifies to real progress along the difficult pathway that leads to the far-off ideal of universal peace. From the Geneva Arbitration dates not only the improved relations between the two great English-

speaking peoples, but also the modern eagerness to refer international controversies, whenever possible, to the decision of an
impartial tribunal.

Time presses and we must hurry on. It will be necessary
to leave out some questions entirely, and to deal but briefly
with the more important ones that remain. We have already
seen how the Treaty of 1871 provided for the settlement of
fishery disputes and the determination of the San Juan
Boundary. These presented no great difficulty at the time,
though the former have been a source of much trouble since.
But the probability that the long-delayed canal through the
Isthmus of Panama would at length be constructed brought the
Clayton-Bulwer Treaty into prominence as a source of controversy. It has shared the fate of so many of the diplomatic
instruments negotiated between the two countries. Drawn up
to end a difficulty, it has itself produced many more disputes
than it settled. In 1881, when it seemed likely that M. de
Lesseps would succeed in piercing the Isthmus, Mr Blaine, the
Secretary of State in the Cabinet of President Garfield, issued
a despatch in which he stated that the United States could not
allow European Powers to guarantee the neutrality of the
Panama Canal. On receipt of this document, Earl Granville,
then Foreign Minister of Great Britain, reminded Mr Blaine of
the Treaty of 1850, which pledged the United States to that
policy of common action he now desired to repudiate. Then
followed a long diplomatic controversy, in which the representatives of America endeavoured to shew that the conduct of
Great Britain had either destroyed the Treaty or rendered it
voidable at the pleasure of the United States. In this they
were singularly unsuccessful ; but the argument that the conditions under which the Treaty was made had entirely changed
since 1850 was much more cogent. The marvellous development of the Pacific States, the vast dimensions of American
commerce, the preponderating nature of American interests in
the districts concerned, undoubtedly gave the United States

a moral claim to demand a revision of the settlement entered into by Mr Clayton and Sir Henry Bulwer. And this was the solution finally reached after twenty years of intermittent bickering. The Government of Washington quietly dropped the untenable contention that the Treaty of 1850 was already void, and Great Britain agreed to substitute for it another Treaty, which allows the United States to construct and manage the canal, and applies the principle of neutralisation in such a way that the protection of the waterway, when made, is confided to the forces of the great Republic.

The Behring Sea question was another difficulty, which, while it lasted, placed a somewhat severe strain on the increasing friendship of the two countries. By the purchase of 1867 the United States acquired all the rights connected with Alaska which were possessed by Russia, its former owner. They construed these to include jurisdiction over British sealing vessels in the vast area of open ocean known as Behring's Sea. Great Britain remonstrated against the seizure and confiscation of the property of her subjects engaged in plying their lawful avocations in waters which she contended were outside territorial jurisdiction. She admitted that the seal-herd required protection against indiscriminate slaughter, but held strongly to the view that such protection must be afforded by international regulations, and not by the municipal laws of the United States. The controversy lasted from 1886 to 1893, in which latter year the award of an arbitral tribunal, to which it had been referred by mutual consent, was passed upon it. The judgment was in favour of the British contention. Behring Sea was declared open to the fishing vessels of all nations, but in the matter of the capture of seals they were placed under an elaborate code of regulations, drawn up by the arbitrators. There has been much controversy since as to the efficacy and sufficiency of these rules ; but the principle of regulation by international agreement is not likely to be challenged in future.

We now come to the most serious of recent troubles between the two countries—a difficulty most unhappy in its inception, but most happy in its termination and its consequences. It arose out of a long-standing territorial dispute between Great Britain and Venezuela. Both sides claimed vast districts in the almost unknown country between the Republic and the territory of British Guiana. Many attempts had been made to agree upon a boundary line, but they had all ended in failure. England was willing to arbitrate, with but certain reservations to which Venezuela would not consent. In this state of affairs President Cleveland intervened on the plea that the famous Monroe Doctrine brought the matter within the cognisance of the United States. He pressed for an immediate settlement by direct negotiation between the two parties, or for unrestricted arbitration. Lord Salisbury desired to except certain districts already occupied by British settlers from the reference to an arbitral tribunal; and moreover he contested the applicability of the Monroe Doctrine to the question in dispute. That famous enunciation of American policy appeared first in the Message of President Monroe to Congress on Dec. 2, 1823. Hence it bears the name by which it is known, though it was really drawn up by John Quincy Adams, Monroe's Secretary of State. The Monroe Doctrine is not one doctrine, but two. The first sets forth that the American continents "are henceforth not to be considered as subjects for future colonisation by any European powers." This was denied at the time by Great Britain and other States; but it has since been rendered applicable by events. There is now no part of North or South America which has not been brought under the dominion of some civilised power, whatever might have been the case in 1823. The other branch of the Monroe Doctrine referred to the contemplated attempt of the Holy Alliance to recover for Spain her revolted American Colonies. With this in view the President, speaking as head of the nation, warned the powers of Europe that "we should consider any attempt on their part to extend their system to any portion of this hemisphere as dangerous to our peace and safety." Great Britain received this declaration with almost as much enthusiasm as did the people of the United States. It had indeed been suggested by Canning, and was an important part of his plan to defeat the designs of the Holy Alliance. From the beginning, then, England stood by her trans-Atlantic kinsmen in proclaiming the closure of the American Continent against the State-system of Europe. But President Cleveland went far beyond this wholesome principle when he enunciated the proposition that " it would be the duty of the United States to resist by every means in its power, as a wilful aggression upon its rights and interests, the appropriation by Great Britain of any lands which after investigation may be determined of right to belong to Venezuela." These words were part of the Special Message of December 17, 1895, which electrified two hemispheres and seemed likely for a few days to lead to war. It proposed the appointment of a Commission of American jurists and states-men to investigate and report upon the question at issue, and the enforcement of their decision upon Great Britain. Fortu-nately public opinion in this country kept cool, and we contented ourselves with pointing out that no self-respecting nation could accept at the sword's point a boundary prescribed for it by a foreign power. The intervention of the merchant princes and religious leaders of America soon cooled down the popular ferment, and warded off the risk of war. Mr Cleveland's Commission was appointed, but it never presented a report. Lord Salisbury arranged with Mr Olney, then Secretary of State, for an arbitral tribunal to decide the boundary contro-versy. In 1899 the arbitrators made their award, which gave Venezuela less territory than Great Britain had offered her more than once in the course of the controversy, but confirmed her claim to a post at the mouth of the Orinoco, which we had confidently affirmed to belong to us.

This Venezuelan boundary question shewed with what ease

the two great English-speaking nations could be brought within measurable distance of war. Thinking men stood aghast at the danger they had escaped so narrowly; and in casting about for means to prevent its recurrence they hit upon the expedient of creating a tribunal to which all disputes between Great Britain and the United States should be referred, if they could not be settled by diplomatic means. Some such plan as this had long been the dream of philanthropists and philanthropic statesmen. The legislatures of the two countries had passed resolutions in its favour, and now the opportunity of carrying them into effect seemed to have arrived. Hopes ran high when that distinguished and devoted worker in the cause of peace, the late Lord Pauncefote, succeeded in negotiating with Mr Olney a General Arbitration Treaty. It was signed in Jan. 1897; but the bright prospect it opened out was over-cast when, in the following May, the Senate refused to ratify it. The disappointment was bitter; but some compensation for it has been found in the Hague Arbitral Convention of 1899. That great international instrument provided for the creation of a "permanent Court of Arbitration, accessible at all times"; and among the signatory Powers are Great Britain and the United States of America.

And now, ladies and gentlemen, I am tempted in dropping the pen of the historian to don the mantle of the prophet. But it would be madness to commence to prophesy in the fifty-sixth minute of an hour's lecture. I know I am speaking to many Americans; and it may be that in a far-off age the severed branches of the Anglo-Saxon race will again unite as members of some great federation of mankind. Meanwhile our best hopes for the immediate future lie in generous cultivation of that new sympathy that grew up when the old country saw with pride the liberation of Cuba and the dash of Dewey's sea-dogs into the harbour of Manila. Out in the far Pacific the westward advance of the United States has met the eastern vanguard of England, and, thank God, we have come together as friends and brothers! Surely there is not one among us now who can read unmoved those noble words of Whittier's in his appeal " To Englishmen ":

> "'Thicker than water,' in one rill
>   Through centuries of story
>   Our Saxon blood has flowed, and still
>   We share with you its good and ill,
>   The shadow and the glory."

Standing here in ancient Cambridge, almost beneath the walls of Emmanuel College, from whence John Harvard went forth to found in new Cambridge the College which still bears his name, myself a member of that other College, our youngest and our smallest, which was founded here by the grandson of that Sir George Downing who was among the first graduates of Harvard, I venture to answer Whittier in his own words but very slightly altered:

> " Joint heirs and kinsfolk, leagues of wave
>   Nor length of years can part us ;
>   Our right is yours to shrine and grave,
>   The common freehold of the brave,
>   The gift of saints and martyrs."

And we, who share this glorious heritage, assuredly hold it in trust for the benefit of humanity. Be it ours so to labour and to pray that England and America may through the coming centuries

> " Sit side by side, full summ'd in all their powers,
>   Dispensing harvest, sowing the To-be,
>   Self-reverent each, and reverencing each,
>   Distinct in individualities,
>   But like each other even as those who love."

POLITICAL PROBLEMS OF THE FAR EAST
WITH SPECIAL REFERENCE TO JAPAN.

By IAN C. HANNAH, M.A.

I SUPPOSE it is already a platitude to point out that the political and commercial centre of gravity for this planet is passing away from Europe. No doubt the earth is ruled by races who proudly trace their descent from the early inhabitants of these storm-swept northern shores, but European homes—homes in the noblest sense of the word—now exist in every clime, from New Zealand to Quebec, from Florida to New South Wales. Thousands upon thousands of our race, bred under far distant skies, come here, no longer as to the centre of the world, but merely as pilgrims to the cradle of the people whose civilisation now dominates the earth. The more vigorous of the nations of Europe are thoroughly alive by now to the *necessity* of establishing their influence in other continents than their own, it is *our* peculiar good fortune (as Professor Seeley has pointed out in his lectures on the Expansion of England) that *we* really *belong* to the New World rather than to the Old, or at least we can take our choice as to which we will devote our attention, much as the Japanese during the past half-century have had the opportunity of choosing whether they will form the most distant bulwark of the unchanging East or the furthest outpost of the restless West. The events of the century that has just passed away have—in my own opinion at any rate—demonstrated more clearly than ever before that the ceaseless struggles of Europe concern *us* comparatively little ; our nearest neighbours are our own colonies, our fastest friends the United States and Japan.

In 1520 the illustrious navigator Magellan, having threaded the beautiful channel of the Straits that now bear his name, burst into the vast expanse of ocean which he himself named the Pacific, because no storm happened to be raging at the time. Four centuries ago it seemed, perhaps, the most solitary region of the earth,—it was very far distant from Europe, its limits were altogether unknown, few sails dotted its unexploited waters, such commerce as it possessed was purely coastal, the very dwellers on its shores themselves knew absolutely nothing about any other part of it than their own. The present state of affairs is different indeed, for to-day the Pacific is become one of the most important districts on the globe,—lines of great mail-steamers traverse its once solitary waters in every direction, some of the chief shipping ports of the world are found on its shores, new and powerful European states have been born on the continents that bound it, every one of the six great Powers of the earth has territory washed by its waves. Eastward and southward it touches the youngest of all the nations, to the west it still laves the coasts of the most ancient of existing empires. Here indeed the Far East with its glorious past,—placid, self-complacent China and Corea, is confronted by the Far West, with its glorious future,—bustling California, aspiring British Columbia. The cutting of the Panama Canal,—placing the United States in a very real sense indeed at the very centre of the world,—must also enormously increase the accessibility and the importance of the Pacific.

But it is merely with a corner of the vastest of the oceans that we are at present concerned, a corner which I will venture to say is a most interesting part of the earth to the student of contemporary politics. For beyond question, except in the case of developments at present altogether unexpected, the future of the gigantic but shiftless empire of China will be the most momentous question to be solved in the international relations of the century that has just begun. The fate of India was settled by a few intrepid individuals about whose actions the rest of the world knew little and cared nothing, but the unification of the earth by electricity and steam, the eager competition of commerce, the desire—laudable no doubt on the whole—for distant dependencies on the part of the nations of Europe make it certain that not a civilised community on earth will be indifferent as to the fate of China.

And new developments are coming almost every year. The maritime expansion of our great sister-nation and her occupation of the Philippines, her new ideals, undreamt of a few brief months ago,—the rapidly increasing importance of our own colonies of Canada and Australasia,—the eager scramble for the once little thought of islands of the Southern Seas, with other matters of the same kind that affect the Pacific are giving questions that have their centre in the Far East a circumference that is ever expanding.

I need not recall to any of you—even in outline—how the latest phase of the eternal Eastern Question was ushered in, when, owing to the influence of the glorious Renaissance, Prince Henry the Navigator and his helpers laid down the keel of a new European navy, and the Portuguese—even then a second-rate power—prepared the way not only for new and unheard of triumphs for Christianity and the West over Islam and the East, but for the Europeanisation of the whole earth. In preceding centuries the East had encroached much upon the West, the Cross was driven by the Crescent from its last foot-hold—politically—on the mainland of Asia, the Crusades had ended in disgraceful rout, an Oriental power was firmly seated in one of the fairest cities of Europe. The first town ever founded by the Christians, the seat of the Eastern Cæsars, had become the very headquarters of the Moslems, the capital of the Ottoman Sultans. But since that time the mysterious and once glorious East has been crushed with a rapidity unknown in the West; one proud empire after another—from the Mediterranean to the Pacific—has gone to fragments at a touch from the rude hand of Europe.

But, up to the present, one Empire, the most wonderful in many respects that the earth has ever seen, has still survived. The Chinese, though a laughing-stock among the nations, a byword for corruption and folly, miserable in the extreme as to their social condition, are still ostensibly an independent people; their Empire on the map of Asia looks almost as imposing as it did in its palmiest days. I cannot deal, however cursorily, with the history or the old-time greatness of China; I wish merely to have you bear with me while I try and consider the Chinese in three of the most notable characteristics that for centuries have marked them as a people. We will speak of them (1) as Empire-builders, (2) as Diplomatists, and (3) as traders and artisans.

And first, as Empire-builders. It may perhaps seem strange at the present day to recollect that only a little more than a century ago the Chinese Dragon dominated the Far East,— from the rugged cliffs of Formosa to the rocky plateau of the Pamirs, from the frozen plains of the Amur to the torrid swamps of Siam. The inhabitants of half a continent looked with awe and reverence to the Imperial City of Peking. And while the Roman legions of Titus were camped round the Holy City, seventy years after the birth of Christ, the Chinese dominions had stretched to the West at any rate more widely still: the victorious banners of the illustrious dynasty of Han were carried to the very shores of the Caspian Sea.

Here then is an empire that existed when Egypt and Mesopotamia were the dominant powers of the Eastern Mediterranean, an Empire that was venerable before Rome was founded, that was a centre of light and learning in the East during the darkest ages of the West, an Empire that exists to-day, and almost at its greatest extent. What is the cause that has given the Chinese their so notable success, how have a people that loathe war, that possess not a shred of patriotism, maintained their dominion till now,—when the companions of their youth have long passed away and the very name of some of them is forgotten? And the fact that their Empire has often been partitioned, sometimes for centuries together, surely makes its power of recuperation and its abiding strength more remarkable still. The long endurance of the dominion of everlasting China is absolutely without parallel in the East, and in the West it is but feebly rivalled by the Empire of eternal Rome. I cannot pretend to explain it, but I may point out two things that might help you to appreciate it.

1. While others have usually founded their power on military prowess and their own strong arm the Chinese have ever relied on sanctions that are purely moral. Their Emperor's claim to be the Vicar of Heaven, sole mediator between God and man, ever maintained in victory or defeat for forty or fifty centuries, has exercised an enormous influence on the minds of the people of the Far East. A sort of vague mysterious reverence for the ancient Empire of China is met with among populations of all sorts of races from the Indian frontier to Corea. Is it altogether fanciful to suggest an analogy with the marvellous vitality of the Papacy?

2. While proclaiming the Emperor to be God's viceroy for the whole world, to whom all other sovereigns and rulers whatever must needs be tributary, it was not in this capacity that the first founders of the Empire appealed to their own people for obedience to their sovereign. They based this claim upon a surer footing still. They bade the people regard the Emperor as the common father of the nation, they told them that they must revere him as children must honour their parents. In other words they deliberately based the sanction for their government on what is perhaps the one principle in nature that can never be called in question. A marvellous knowledge of human nature, foresight of no ordinary kind! I do not for one moment believe in the political future of China :

the Chinese are not a military race, and, except during the earliest times, their Empire has been at its greatest extent only when some foreigner sat on the throne. China's neighbours at the present day are no longer semi-civilised, superstitious communities, but powerful, well-organised states with a contempt for the traditions of Asia. Neither China nor any other distinctively Oriental state can ever again hope to be counted among the "powers" of the world. Yet I do believe that in speaking of this everlasting endurance of the Chinese Empire from the mists of prehistoric antiquity to the twentieth century we are dealing with a subject that we do not and that we cannot fully understand, there may be some element that is capable of acting in a way that no man can foresee. The Chinese may be forced to bow to European domination, but their unchanging race-feeling (for patriotism it is not) can never be permanently crushed.

Let us secondly consider the Chinese as Diplomatists. They certainly have many of the qualities that are useful in Asiatic diplomacy. A friend of my own, shortly before I left Tien-Tsin, overheard two Chinese, concluding a bargain, engage in a violent discussion. And when they had finished one of them said to the other, "You certainly are a most accomplished liar." Instead of knocking him down he merely bowed in all apparent humility and said, "You really must not pay me such extravagant compliments as that." Only two years ago the Empress-Dowager, in language that was in no way ambiguous, commanded the massacre of all the foreign residents in China, nor was it her own fault if the order was not carried out. To-day the old lady is autocrat of China still, she is fawned upon and flattered by the representatives of all the great Powers of the world. Here is a triumph of diplomacy that, to say the least, is remarkable. What manner of woman is the person who has achieved it?

She is illiterate, she is so superstitious that she cannot take a step without consulting an astrologer, her edicts and her actions prove more eloquently than anything else what the state of her knowledge must be. As to her morals, the reformer Kang-yü-Wei himself assured me that in the most corrupt court of Asia she was notorious for the profligacy of her life. By strength of will and by marvellous cunning an ignorant and unscrupulous concubine, whom fortune made mother of a puppet Emperor, has with complete impunity to herself duped the diplomacy and defied the might of Europe and of Japan; to-day she is to all appearance more firmly seated than ever in a power that she wields to the woe of almost everyone concerned[1]. One might search the whole annals of the world in vain for any record of a more notable diplomatic victory than this.

Even among Asiatic peoples the Chinese have ever been remarkable for the extraordinary shrewdness of their diplomacy. In early days they contrived to induce almost all their mainland neighbours to acknowledge their Emperor's claims even while they were in difficulties at home and in no position to assert them by force of arms. To-day they understand the art of playing off one western Power against another fully as well as do the Turks.

Thirdly, we are concerned with the Chinese as merchants and as artisans. While most of the peoples of the East—and notably the Japanese—have always agreed with mediæval Europe that fighting was the "only fit profession for a gentleman," the Chinese have ever held merchants in the highest honour, and they have a proverb that good men do not enter the army. I do not believe that any political future can, in the present state of the world's progress, be in store for a people that has no patriotism and that is unwilling to fight, but the Jews have given us a convincing example of what part on the earth a people may play after their political independence has

[1] *Strictly of course the Empress is by race a Manchu and not a Chinese, but two centuries and a half of intercourse have rendered the present imperial house entirely Chinese for every practical purpose.*

passed away. And as traders, bankers, and artisans the Chinese are in no way inferior to the Jews. If ten million Jews, lords of not a square inch of land or of a single ship, are to-day so great a power in the world, what may not be accomplished by forty times that number of Chinese? The untiring industry, the sober habits, the indifference to comfort, and many other characteristics of the Chinese constitute a danger to the toilers of Europe and America that may one day become acute. The legislation on the subject of Asiatic immigration in every white country that is exposed to it is the clearest confession that it is so. The Chinese, even if they do not retain one foot of territory of their own, without a soldier or a sailor marching under the standard of the Dragon, may yet dominate the commerce of the world as the Jews, despite the cruellest persecution, have dominated before now the whole traffic of Europe and the Mediterranean. Europe may laugh at the idea of new invasions of locust Mongol hordes, but the yellow peril for all that may not be the less dangerous. China, defenceless yet defiant, self-complaisant yet helpless, is, and it is to be feared must long remain, a danger to the peace of Europe, to the civilisation of the world. Never was reform more needed than it is at the present day, seldom indeed were the prospects of it more gloomy. It may well be doubted whether even now there exists a single Chinese who would not prefer in his inmost heart to chase the hated foreign devils from his sacred soil and to return to the venerable methods of his ancient kings. Her huge unexploited mineral wealth, the strategic importance of her territories, the unwarlike character of her people, make China even more a bone of contention among her more vigorous neighbours than Persia, Turkey, or Corea.

And now let us leave a country that *breathes* ruin and squalor and decay, that herself is ashamed of her present and for ever points to the past. Separated by a narrow strait, easily in sight of the mainland of Asia, lies a very different land, an empire that has traditions little less venerable than those of

China, that is still ruled by a dynasty which has endured two millenniums and six hundred years, and which yet is a new country as truly as the United States itself.

Half a century ago the Japanese were still in the middle ages, their country was absolutely closed to all intercourse with the outside world, their barons ruled their little principalities exactly like independent sovereigns and were for ever waging war with one another, their Emperor was practically a prisoner in his own palace, the national administration was in the feeble hands of the later Shoguns of the Tokugawa line. The deepest sleep rested on Japan, her quiet valleys and lovely towns were almost as unaffected by the spirit of the age as are the fastnesses of Tibet to-day. In 1852 a fleet of modern ships of war, flying the flag of the United States and commanded by Commodore Perry, dropped anchor in Yedo Bay, and let in the full light of the nineteenth century on the feudal dust of Japan. The astonished and at first unwilling inhabitants were forced to open their country to the commerce and intercourse of the world. Another Asiatic power was compelled to come out of her shell. There seemed to be nothing specially remarkable about the event, for much the same thing had been brought about before from one end of Asia to the other—by the Portuguese, the Spaniards, the Dutch, the English, the French, and the Danes, and the result had been ever the same. The placid old empires of Asia had gone down, one after another, at the first contact with the fiery adventurers from Europe. For a year or two it was imagined that Japan would be no exception to the rule; even the Russians (with all their knowledge of the East) realised so little of her spirit that they tried to help themselves to some Japanese islands[1] that command the strait between Japan and Corea.

Soon however it became apparent to the most careless that an animal of a *very* different kind had this time been aroused. The Japanese saw the necessity for learning what the Euro-

[1] Tsushima, now an important Japanese naval station.

peans had to teach them. Feudalism was abolished, the authority of the Emperor was restored, the administration of the country was reorganised: steamers and railways, a postal service, telegraphs, representative institutions, newspapers, a new army and a new navy with the other ordinary institutions of a western state transformed Japan into a European country with a thoroughness that would have startled most people had it taken four or five times as long as it did.

In a brief half-century a despised Oriental state, which at first no one imagined was in any special particular different from any other Oriental state, awoke from the long slumber of centuries, asserted her right to be treated as an equal by the proudest empires of the West, and then quietly took her place, unchallenged, as by no means the least influential of the six great Powers of the world. It is well worth our while to enquire what were the causes that made possible this marvellous transformation, absolutely without any kind of analogy in all the annals of the world. And when studying the past of the Japanese we can find that in two particulars at any rate throughout their long history this people have ever been closely in sympathy with some of the noblest of Europe's ideals, and utterly opposed to the whole spirit of Asia. This is a matter that I want specially to emphasise, for I believe that the essentially non-Asiatic traditions of the Japanese constitute a key that more than anything else will help us to understand the politics of the Far East to-day. It is no mere accident or temporary coincidence that so clearly marks off the Japanese from all their geographical neighbours. The characteristics of our allies to which I would particularly direct your attention are, in the first place, their fervent patriotism, and, in the second, that receptive spirit and total absence of self-complacency which so emphatically distinguish them from all other Asiatics.

(1) I make no apology to Europeans or Americans when I claim for the Japanese an extraordinary and unique

patriotism. Among them love of country as the very highest duty of man to which all else must invariably be subordinated is, I believe, as nowhere else, deeply implanted in every section of the community from the highest noble to the meanest coolie.

After the troublous times of the civil war of the Restoration when the Shogunate was abolished for ever and the Emperor was restored to the prerogatives of his fathers, it was found that the new arrangements were absolutely farcical while feudalism survived; but the Restoration itself had been brought about by some of the feudal barons, and practically every soldier that Japan contained was under their direct command. The difficulty was got over by a notable act of patriotic self-denial. Following the lead of the most influential of their number, who saw that it was now for the best interests of the state, the barons (or daimios, to give them their common Japanese name) consented to lay down their local jurisdiction and to surrender their revenues and lands into the hands of their sovereign—to end, in fact, the ancient privileges of their order entirely, though no one could have compelled them, at any rate at the time, to do anything of the kind. The pensions that they received in compensation were altogether insignificant compared with their former possessions, but there were no complaints, for the whole nobility of a country preferred their empire's prosperity to their own.

I heard once from an Englishman employed to carry out some public works in Japan that his workmen were not very anxious to obey a foreigner, and gave him a good deal of trouble. At length he overcame their mutiny, not by any threats or promises, but simply by representing to them that when the account of the affair got to Europe it would create a bad impression and bring disrepute upon Japan. What effect would such an argument as that have had on the working classes of any other country in the world? Many other stories of the same kind might be told to illustrate the patriot-

ism of the Japanese, and to show how universal it is. I need
not insist on the fact that it is a virtue altogether indigenous ;
patriotism in any sense that we should understand the word
has no existence on the mainland of Asia,—least of all in
China or Corea. During our own wars with the Chinese we
have never had the faintest difficulty in getting as many coolies
as we liked to pay for to assist in the operations of our army,
and they have always worked with every bit as much zeal as if
they had been helping to support their own government instead
of to attack it. It is notorious that the Chinese officials sold
shells manufactured in the Tien-Tsin arsenal to the Japanese
after war was declared, and substituted clay models, carefully
painted to resemble the real articles, for their own armaments.

(2) The second characteristic that so clearly and so emphatically differentiates the Japanese from all other Asiatics is a total
absence of the dogged, hide-bound conservatism of Asia. The
founders of Japan, like the founders of Rome, had little enough
civilisation of their own, but when the gentle missionaries of
Buddha and others brought to them the refinement of the mainland they keenly and unhesitatingly made use of it. Nor did
they blindly adopt it. They carefully examined it, they assimi-
lated it, they made it thoroughly Japanese and rejected whatever seemed unsuited to their needs. This spirit of receptiveness
has ever been with them. When the Portuguese navigators—
pioneers of Europe—gave them some knowledge of the civilisation of the West, they showed themselves most eager to make
use of it. An old flint-lock gun presented to a daimio in
Kiusiu served as a model in the construction of many more
till every part of Japan was provided with European fire-arms.
Francis Xavier, the Jesuit, who laboured for some years in
their midst, frequently insists in his letters on the prevalence
of this spirit of inquiry among them. Never had he visited a race
so anxious to acquire information. And travelling through
Japan at the present day the truth is ever impressed on one
more and more that in adopting and adapting the complicated

civilisation and the newest thought of Europe, the present generation are but carrying on the policy of their ancestors, who long ages ago adopted and adapted the civilisation of China, and with it the religion of India. Breach with their past there is none, they are no mere copyists, no idle borrowers, they never can leave the civilisation of the West as they find it. Already they have shown themselves capable of developing it,—the rifle carried by their soldiers, an excellent weapon, was designed by one of their own officers, while of the twenty or thirty leading medical men of the world two or three are Japanese. The organisation of their army and navy, as was conclusively demonstrated during the recent troubles in China, is at least equal to anything that their teachers can show. Nothing *could* be more false than the old (but, I trust, now long exploded) theory, that the Japanese are merely apeing the fashions of Europe, like children playing with some new toy. I am convinced that a student of Japanese history and of Japanese character might have prophesied the westernisation of the country, that has so taken the world by surprise, at the time when Commodore Perry's fleet first sailed into Yedo Bay.

It seems that we have here an extreme instance of the influence that geography exercises on national character : there can be no doubt that the race nurtured among the lovely valleys of Japan is of the same stock as the race that has been developed on the dreary, featureless plains of China, but the two peoples differ from one another in their spirit and ideals, as far as it is possible for two civilised nations to differ. This will be less surprising when we recollect that the very sharp division between the East and the West does not correspond to any ethnological cleavage. And it is not too much to say that the further geographical boundary between the East and the West is in truth not the broad expanse of the Pacific, but the narrow strait that separates Japan from Asia. In the spirit and aspirations of her people Japan is as western as any country in the world, her institutions are more thoroughly European than those of half the countries of Europe. I mean that Japanese methods really differ from the methods of the Teutonic and Scandinavian peoples far less than our own differ from those of some peoples of southern and eastern Europe.

Before passing on to consider the subject of Japan's strategic position I cannot refrain from saying one word on a subject that I am sure must be of special interest, to some at any rate in this audience—Japanese Art. The unification of the world has made our own art so cosmopolitan that national schools have now been well-nigh obliterated among ourselves, but Japan still has a school of her own that will repay the most careful study. And in their own peculiar province, such as depicting the beauties of nature in her gentler and smaller moods—in painting flowers and birds and beasts,—in landscape gardening, and in adapting their timber buildings to their situations among rocks and trees, the artists of Japan are surely unrivalled. Art has most sadly declined since the opening up of the land; in the elder Japan the barons and Shoguns were its munificent patrons, quality was preferred to quantity, artists were often content to devote the whole of their lives to a single piece of work. The stern necessities of present-day conditions have given the best intellects of the Empire other things to think about than painting pictures of Fuji-Yama or carving peacocks out of camphor wood, while for the European market real masterpieces are very unprofitable compared with what is cheap and nasty; thus works of art are sent to this country that no self-respecting Japanese would allow to remain in his scullery. It is very much to be hoped that this sad state of affairs may be but temporary. Americans at any rate are already realising that there is something worth studying in the best art of Japan, and every traveller in the country must have been struck by the way in which a genuine love of art there affects the whole nation to an extent unknown perhaps even in France. The inhabitants of the remotest villages are proud of the scenery of their district, take a personal pleasure in the carvings and ornamental grounds of their temple, and as a rule keep their own delightful little gardens extremely tidy.

As in the case of so very many other things, the art that Japan once borrowed from her mainland neighbours she has made thoroughly Japanese. It would be rash to say she has surpassed the finest work of her teachers, but a real love of the beautiful has become the common property of the Japanese people in a way that is utterly undreamt of among the stolid, unimaginative Chinese.

Some appreciation of the strategic position of Japan is of extreme importance to an understanding of the part she is likely to play in the future history of the world. An unbroken chain of islands (the Kuriles, Japan proper, the Loo Choo Archipelago, Formosa, and the Pescadores), extending from Kamchatka to the Tropics, completely dominates the maritime approaches to the northern provinces of China, to Corea, and to Asiatic Russia. The naval station of Tsushima commands the passage between Kiusiu and Corea, and cuts the communications between Port Arthur and Vladivostock. The Pescadores, which contain some very good harbours, control the Formosa Channel and the routes to Shanghai from Europe. The harbours and naval stations of Japan herself are among the finest in the world ; her important seaside cities are situated on bays or fjords whose entrances can be fortified and mined ; they are so well defended by nature and design that in time of war almost the whole of the Japanese navy could be available for offensive operations abroad without serious anxiety for the safety of the home-land. In the long course of her history Japan has been invaded but once, that was by the forces of Kublai Khan, and it ended most disastrously for the aggressors. The rocky and mountainous nature of the country, with the fiercely patriotic and very warlike nature of the inhabitants, seem to give an almost absolute guarantee for the future against any similar disturbance, even supposing the fleet to have been decisively worsted at sea.

The present population of Japan is more than forty-four millions, its area is smaller than that of the British Isles, and its surface is much more occupied by mountains. Nevertheless from the people subsisting chiefly on rice, it is still almost, if not quite, self-supporting for food-stuffs. This, however, cannot possibly be permanent; foreign markets are absolutely indispensable to Japan as to ourselves, while her overflowing population and numerous emigrants naturally make her anxious for colonial possessions, and it is inevitable that she should look to her thinly-peopled neighbour, Corea, as a legitimate field for her own expansion. Thus, apart from any sentimental feeling she may cherish for her first teacher and for the only empire that is older than her own, Japan is even more vitally interested than other commercial powers in the maintenance of the integrity of China and the preservation of the open door. While Europe and America have plenty of other markets for their goods, Japan has at present very little trade beyond the limits of Asia, her merchants are dependent very largely indeed on their customers ·in the Chinese Empire.

Of the wisdom of our traditional policy of permanent neutrality in Europe, with just a pardonable leaning to our own kinsmen, the German and Scandinavian races, there can, I imagine, be not the shadow of a doubt, but we can hardly expect to be permanently neutral all over the world. The alliance that after long years of consideration we have at last entered into with the Japanese seems to be a peculiarly happy one. It is a compact based on common interests in trade, a common policy to the tottering Empire of China, common methods of government, common aspirations, common ideals. With America amicably neutral—and she could not possibly be hostile—the Allies may confidently count on being able to command the sea, and therefore, as it seems to me, it constitutes the strongest possible guarantee that in present circumstances could exist of permanent peace in the East.

I must apologise for having felt quite unable in the brief

course of a single lecture to attempt to deal with the politics of the Far East in any systematic manner. I have confined myself to the ocean; I have not even mentioned Russia, the dominant factor on the land. I have merely attempted to draw your particular attention to a few leading features of a great and an extremely interesting problem. Let me exhort you most earnestly to study the whole question for yourselves. I do not for one moment disparage the advantages of a knowledge of ancient history, but I do affirm that an appreciation of present day conditions in every great division of the world is of even greater importance to enable us to realise our great responsibilities as to what is often called the "white man's burden," and to fulfil our duties as citizens of the different nations of the West.

In conclusion let me humbly ask pardon if anywhere I have obtruded my personal views or aired any prejudices of my own. Patriotism, the moment it leads to anything like national bias, is absolutely out of place in a Lecture Room; and if I have said one single word from any other point of view than that of an impassive observer of events in the Far East, I desire wholly and unhesitatingly to retract it.

For EU product safety concerns, contact us at Calle de José Abascal, 56–1°, 28003 Madrid, Spain or eugpsr@cambridge.org.

www.ingramcontent.com/pod-product-compliance
Ingram Content Group UK Ltd.
Pitfield, Milton Keynes, MK11 3LW, UK
UKHW020806190625
459647UK00032B/1954